IRANIANS & GREEKS IN SOUTH RUSSIA

BY

M. ROSTOVTZEFF

Published by Left of Brain Books

Copyright © 2021 Left of Brain Books

ISBN 978-1-396-32234-1

First Edition

All rights reserved. No part of this publication may be reproduced, distributed, or transmitted in any form or by any means, including photocopying, recording, or other electronic or mechanical methods, without the prior written permission of the publisher, except in the case of brief quotations embodied in critical reviews and certain other noncommercial uses permitted by copyright law. Left of Brain Books is a division of Left of Brain Onboarding Pty Ltd.

Table of Contents

Preface	1
I. Introductory	5
II. The Prehistoric Civilizations	22
III. The Cimmerians and the Scythians in South Russia (VIII-Vth Centuries B.C.)	46
IV. The Greeks on the Shores of the Black Sea, Down to the Roman Period	82
V. The Scythians at the End of the Fourth and in the Third Century B.C.	113
VI. The Sarmatians	149
VII. The Greek Cities of South Russia in the Roman Period	190
VIII. The Polychrome Style and the Animal Style	230
IX. The Origin of the Russian State on the Dnieper	262
Bibliography	277

Preface

THIS book is not intended to compete with the valuable and learned book of Ellis H. Minns on the same subject. Our aims are different. Minns endeavoured to give a complete survey of the material illustrating the early history of South Russia and of the views expressed by both Russian and non-Russian scholars on the many and various questions suggested by the study of that material. I do not mean that Minns' book is a mere compendium. In dealing with the various problems of the history and archaeology of South Russia Minns went his own way; his criticism is acute, his views independent. Nevertheless his main object was to give a survey as full and as complete as possible. And his attempt was successful. Minns' book will remain for decades the chief source of information about South Russia both for Russian and for non-Russian scholars.

My own aim is different. In my short exposition I have tried to give *a history of the South Russian lands* in the prehistoric, the proto-historic, and the classic periods down to the epoch of the migrations. By history I mean not a repetition of the scanty evidence preserved by the classical writers and illustrated by the archaeological material but an attempt to define the part played by South Russia in the history of the world in general, and to emphasize the contributions of South Russia to the civilization of mankind.

In doing so I was obliged to use every kind of material, especially the rich archaeological evidence furnished by the South Russian excavations. Notwithstanding this dominant use of archaeological material, my book is not a handbook of South Russian archaeology, nor is it an investigation of one section in the history of Oriental and classical art. I have tried to write history, using the archaeological evidence in the same way as I should use, and have used, in this book written documents or literary sources. Such an attempt is not new. Many eminent scholars have employed this method in attempting to write the history of the ancient Orient in general and of its different parts. The same method should be used more widely in historical surveys of the Roman provinces, as of course it has been used for the history of Gaul by Camille

Jullian, for the history of Africa by Stéphane Gsell, for the history of Britain by the late Francis Haverfield, for the history of Belgium by Franz Cumont, and for the history of Germany by many writers, and especially by H. Dragendorff. But I should like to call for a more rational use of archaeological material than has been usual hitherto. For me archaeology is not a source of illustrations for written texts, but an independent source of historical information, no less valuable and important, sometimes more important, than the written sources. We must learn and we are gradually learning how to write history with the help of archaeology.

South Russia, with its enormous wealth of archaeological material, presents a favourable opportunity for such an experiment. The results of my historical investigations are of course far from final or complete. We know but little of the history and archaeology of Central Asia and of the Iranian world. The scientific exploration of the Caucasian lands and of the upper course of the Euphrates is still in its infancy. The mystery of the early history of Asia Minor, and especially of its north-eastern part, has just begun to dispel. And it is precisely these lands which provide the key to the leading phenomena of the early history of South Russia. If I have succeeded in showing the importance of these connexions for the development of South Russia, and the importance of South Russia for understanding the main features of the civilization of these lands both in the early and in the later period, during the rule of the Scythians and that of the Sarmatians in the South Russian steppes, I shall consider the main part of my task accomplished. I do not deny the importance of the Greek influences in South Russia, but at the same time I do not regard South Russia as one of the provinces of the Greek world. South Russia has always been, and remained even in the Greek period, an Oriental land. Greek influence in South Russia was strong, it is true, but the current of Hellenism met another current there, an Oriental one, and it was this which finally carried the day, and in the period of the migrations spread all over Western Europe. The attempt to hellenize the South Russian steppes was not a complete success; much more successful was the attempt to orientalize the semi-Greek world of the northern shores of the Black Sea. In the civilization which the Sarmatians, the Goths, the Huns brought with them to Western Europe it is the Orient which plays the leading part; the Greek, the Western, and the Northern elements are of but secondary importance. Such is the leading idea of my book.

My book was written not in Russia but in England and in France. The proofs were corrected in America. In writing it I was unable to recur constantly to the original sources preserved in the Russian museums, as I should if I had been in Russia. Nor was I able to consult friends and colleagues, still in Russia, on many questions which they would have helped me to elucidate. Unfortunately Russia is closed to me for a long time to come. This explains why I have been obliged to quote from memory many books and articles which formed part of my private library in Petrograd. It also explains the choice of illustrations. Most of them are reproduced from photographs which I brought with me from Russia. But some of them I was obliged to take from photographs and drawings already published in printed books. I am very much obliged to the Cambridge University Press and to Dr. Ellis H. Minns for permission to use some of the drawings, and one of the maps, from the work of Minns. But, generally speaking, in the choice of my illustrations I have tried to avoid reproducing well-known objects, especially if they have been published by Minns, and to figure, for the most part, such monuments as are either unpublished or published in an unsatisfactory way. For permission to reproduce unpublished objects my warmest thanks are due to Dr. D. G. Hogarth, Keeper of the Ashmolean Museum, to Sir Hercules Read and Mr. G. F. Hill, Keepers of the British Museum, to Mr. Edmond Pottier, Keeper of the Louvre, to Mr. Ernest Babelon, Director of the Cabinet des Médailles at Paris, to Mr. Edward Robinson, Director of the Metropolitan Museum, and to Mrs. E. Meyer, of New York.

The text of my book was written partly in French, partly in English. For the translation of the French part and for a thorough revision of the English I am indebted to the self-sacrificing kindness of Mr. J. D. Beazley. I cannot find adequate words to express my warm thanks to that accomplished scholar for his help. He assisted me also in reading the proofs and in arranging and composing the illustrations. I also owe a great debt of gratitude to Dr. Ellis H. Minns, who read the proofs of my book.

But for the scientific spirit of the staff of the Clarendon Press my book could never have been published in such beautiful form and with so many illustrations.

The index was compiled by my wife, Mrs. S. Rostovtzeff.

I dedicate my book to some living and many dead friends. To these men I am indebted for what I know about the history of South Russia.

MADISON (WIS.), U.S.A.
November 1921.

I.
INTRODUCTORY

THE early history of South Russia has never been treated in a purely historical way. South Russia has never been studied as an integral portion of the ancient world, and as one which took a share, sometimes a very important share, in the general development of Oriental and Greco-Roman civilization. Archaeologists, attracted by the astonishing wealth of the Greek, Scythian, and Sarmatian finds in South Russia, have been content to classify and to date the objects without utilizing them for the purpose of history: historians and epigraphists have applied themselves to tracing the history of the Greek colonies in Russia, and have not attempted to understand it as part of a more general history—that of South Russia as a whole, and that of the entire Oriental and classical world. Proof of this will be furnished by a short survey of archaeological discovery in Russia, and of the literature which it has called forth.

The first persons to interest themselves in the national antiquities of Russia, and the first who tried to comprehend their historical and artistic value, were for the most art French emigrants who found a welcome and a home in Russia after the French Revolution. These emigrants exercised considerable influence on Russian intellectual life at the beginning of the nineteenth century, and in particular, they did much to awaken in official and intellectual circles a lively interest in the numerous relics of classical antiquity, which were being unearthed in South Russia, and especially at Kerch, the ancient Panticapaeum. It would take too long to enumerate all the Frenchmen who worked side by side with the Russians at this task: a few names must suffice. I shall mention the Duc de Richelieu, whose stay at Odessa was of great importance for the intellectual life of South Russia in general, and whose enlightened influence strengthened the interest in national antiquities which was growing up in the great commercial city; the Comte de Langeron, governor of New Russia at the beginning of the nineteenth century;

Cousinéry, French consul at Odessa, who formed the first large collection of the coins of the Greek colonies in South Russia. These were official personages; still more was accomplished by educated and devoted workers who consecrated their lives to the discovery and study of classical antiquities in South Russia. I shall cite only two names. Paul Dubrux, a French emigrant, Chevalier of St. Louis, found refuge at Kerch from the storm of the Revolution. He did not enjoy the brilliant official career which was vouchsafed to some of his compatriots: a modest chinovnik, quiet and honest, he lived and died poor. His classical knowledge—slender enough—his energy, and his material resources, he devoted to the study of classic soil in the peninsula of Kerch, and to archaeological investigation in that still unexplored country. Every scholar knows what part he played in the discovery, accidental it is true, of the splendid tumulus of Kul-Oba. His report of the excavation is far superior, both in truthfulness and in precision, to all the others, and the value of it can hardly be exaggerated, since the find still remains one of the richest and most important of its class. It is less generally known that it was Dubrux, more than any one else, who laid the foundation of the historical topography of Kerch and the Kerch peninsula: it was his minute researches and his sometimes heroic excavations, carried on without money in a waterless and foodless desert, which formed a basis for the subsequent endeavours of Blaramberg, Dubois de Montpéreux, and Ashik to identify extant ruins with the localities mentioned by ancient geographers. It is a regrettable fact that in historical topography we have made little advance since Dubrux. The work of Blaramberg, another emigrant, was less valuable than that of Dubrux. But Blaramberg was a man of great energy and wide vision: we are indebted to him for some interesting publications, and above all for the foundation of the two most important museums in South Russia—those of Odessa and Kerch.

I must also mention the great services rendered to classical archaeology in Russia by other French scholars. Dubois de Montpéreux, by his great work *Voyage autour du Caucase*, Sabatier, and Raoul Rochette, helped to draw the attention of the learned world to the discoveries in South Russia. Dubois de Montpéreux, an eminent geologist, has left us a lively and faithful picture, from the archaeological point of view, of the Crimea and the Caucasus in the middle of the last century.

Thanks to the constant interest of the imperial family, and of aristocratic and official circles, archaeological research in South Russia soon became regular if not systematic. From the beginning of the nineteenth century there was always an official agent at Kerch to collect antiquities and to make scientific excavations. With the foundation of an Imperial Archaeological Commission in 1859, the organization was considerably enlarged: year by year the members of the commission excavated the numerous barrows and cemeteries scattered over the vast steppes on the shores of the Black Sea, and on the banks of the great Russian rivers. The results obtained were of the highest importance. Those who were able to visit the Museum of the Hermitage before the Russian Revolution will remember the deep impression produced upon all visitors, whether specialists or not, by the two great rooms on the first floor—the Kerch Room and the Nikopol Room. The ordinary sightseer was struck by the accumulation of gold objects in these rooms, by the enormous quantity of jewels, of gold and silver plate, of engraved gems. The less unsophisticated were astonished to find so many masterpieces of Hellenic art, sometimes of types unknown in other museums. But the scholar, above all, carried away quite novel impressions: realizing that in these rooms he was in the presence of a new world, in which Greek art appeared in an altered, sometimes almost unrecognizable form, and in which side by side with this art, another art was revealed, new and strange.

The thousands of objects which filled the Hermitage came almost entirely from excavations conducted by the Archaeological Commission. Year after year the treasures poured in. Each excavation, prosecuted with knowledge and perseverance, afforded new series of objects, no less artistically interesting and no less scientifically valuable than the old. The cemeteries of the great Greek colonies, Panticapaeum, Phanagoria, Chersonesus, Olbia, and the ruins of these towns—two of which were excavated systematically, Olbia by Farmakóvski, Chersonesus by Kosciuszko-Waluzinicz and Loeper— furnished immense numbers of pure Greek products, imported from Asia Minor, from Athens, and from other Hellenic centres. The finest groups of Ionian vases came from Olbia and Berezán, which were methodically excavated by Ernst von Stern, from Panticapaeum, and from the Tamán peninsula: black-figured and red-figured ware, the Panathenaic vases, Hellenistic and Roman pottery, are represented in the Hermitage by superb series. The Greek jewellery, as we shall see, is unequalled: most of it came from those great stone chambers, surmounted by stately tumuli, at Kerch, at Theodosia, at Anápa, and in the peninsula of Taman, which were the tombs of the kings who ruled the Bosphorus and the tribes dwelling in the Taman peninsula. The fineness of this jewellery enables us to appreciate the creative genius of the Greek goldsmith in the fifth and fourth centuries B.C. The wooden coffins, sometimes painted, are frequently masterpieces. The gold and silver vases are various and beautiful. It would be a long task to enumerate all the classes of Greek objects yielded by the ruins and cemeteries of the Greek cities.

Simultaneously, another group of discoveries was being made in the great barrows on the Russian steppes, in the basins of the Kuban, the Don, the Dnieper, and the Dniester. I cannot mention them all. In the first period of exploration, up to 1880, the following were the most important, the order being geographical: the barrows of Chertomlýk and Alexandrópol on the lower Dnieper, excavated by Zabêlin in 1859-63, monumental tombs of Scythian kings, belonging to the fourth or third century B.C.; the series of kurgans called the Seven Brothers, on the Kuban, excavated by Tiesenhausen in 1875 and subsequent years, royal tombs of the fifth and fourth centuries B.C.; several barrows of native princes near the Greek colony of Nymphaeum in the Crimea, belonging to the fifth and fourth centuries B.C., excavated by different persons from 1867 onwards (a part of the finds is now in the Ashmolean Museum at Oxford); some enormous kurgans in the Taman peninsula, especially the so-called Bolsháya and Málaya Bliznítsa (Big and Little Twins) and those on the Vasyúrinskaya Gorá, explored by Tiesenhausen, Zabêlin, and Lutsénko in 1864-8, and belonging to the fourth and third centuries B.C.; the group of graves near Phanagoria (Artyukhóv's farm), of the third or second century B.C., excavated in 1879 and 1880; the Greco-indigenous cemetery of the ancient Gorgippia, now Anápa, explored at various times, especially in 1879-80, by different persons; finally, the great treasure of Novocherkássk on the Don, which yielded a rich series of gold objects belonging, as I believe, to the first century B.C. or A.D.

Nicolas Veselóvski began his systematic excavations about 1880. He was a man of boundless vigour and of singular tenacity, and his good fortune never deserted him. The discoveries which we owe to him have not yet been properly appreciated: it is to be hoped that their scientific importance will soon be realized. We are not concerned here with his researches in Turkestan: his other discoveries concern us very nearly. His methodical exploration of the Kuban valley brought to light a number of tumulary graves which belong to the copper age and may be dated in the third millennium B.C.; of these I shall speak in my next chapter: also a series of barrows belonging to a widely different period, from the first century B.C. to the third century A.D., which enable us for the first time to form an idea of the Sarmatians and their civilization. At the same time, and in the same region, he discovered groups of graves dating from the sixth to the fourth centuries B.C., which furnish an almost exact parallel to Herodotus' description of Scythian funeral customs: unfortunately, the richest of these finds, that of Kelermés, was not made by Veselóvski but by an amateur. Side by side with his exploration of the Kuban valley, he continued the work of Zabêlin in the region of the lower Dnieper and of the Don, as well as in the Crimea, and here also he achieved remarkable success. Most of the barrows which he excavated contained burials of the same period as Chertomlýk and Kul-Oba, that is to say, the fourth and third centuries B.C. The greatest prize was reserved for the end of his life: in 1911 and 1912 he presented us with the treasures of the Solókha tumulus, which surpass everything found hitherto on the lower Dnieper or in the Crimea.

I lack space to mention the work done by other explorers, but I should like to speak for a moment about the scientific exploration of the middle Dnieper. Kiev was always a centre of intellectual life; and here, especially in university circles, it was not long before a keen interest came to be taken in the national antiquities of the country. Systematic excavation began in the middle of the nineteenth century and has continued without interruption. Certain names should never be forgotten—Fundukléy, Antonóvich, Tarnóvski, Vólkov, Bêlashévski, and above all, Chvojka and Count Bóbrinskoy. Chvojka's momentous discoveries revealed, on the one hand, a palaeolithic settlement at Kiev, and, on the other, a great centre of neolithic and chalcolithic culture on the middle Dnieper, connected with the civilization of the Danube, and characterized by painted pottery decorated with spirals and maeanders. Count Bóbrinskoy gradually explored, in the region of Smêla, the so-called Scythian culture, which begins in the eighth century B.C. and ends towards the Roman period. Both Chvojka and Bóbrinskoy have also made us better acquainted with the civilizations of the 'urn fields' in the first and second centuries A.D.: these belong, in my opinion, probably to Germanic, possibly to Slavonic peoples.

The discoveries of which I have spoken were accompanied by publications, often very handsome ones, of the monuments collected in the course of the excavations. The first great comprehensive publication, *Les Antiquités du Bosphore Cimmérien*, was principally devoted to the products of Greek art: it was planned by a French scholar, Gille, who was keeper of one of the departments in the Hermitage at the middle of the nineteenth century. This work was followed, after a short interval, by another equally handsome publication, that of the Scythian antiquities discovered by Zabêlin, *Antiquités de la Scythie d'Hérodote*. Both books were remodelled, and combined with the Russian and Oriental antiquities of the Middle Ages, in the great work of Count Tolstóy and Professor Kondakóv, *Russian Antiquities*. The three works are still classics; moreover, they are well known outside Russia, thanks to the republication of the first and the translation of the third by that distinguished scholar Mr. Salomon Reinach, who, by these publications, and by a number of articles in the *Revue archéologique*, has helped to maintain the interest of Western scholars in the South Russian finds of the classical period.

These works were concerned with the figurative monuments: the task of publishing the written monuments, the inscriptions, was undertaken and brilliantly accomplished by Vasili Látȳshev in his well-known repertory, *Inscriptiones antiquae orae septentrionalis Ponti Euxini* (vols. i, ii, and iv; a second edition of the first in 1912), which is a complete collection of the Greek and Latin inscriptions found in South Russia. The same author has compiled a repertory, almost exhaustive, of the passages in Greek and Latin writers which refer to South Russia (*Scythica et Caucasica*, vol.i, *Auctores Graeci*, vol. ii, *Auctores Latini*). In addition to these publications the results of current excavation were given year by year in the periodical organs of the Archaeological Commission—its Reports (Otchëty), its Materials (Materiálȳ), and its Bulletin (Izvêstiya)—and these were supplemented by the publication of the archaeological societies, especially the societies of St. Petersburg, Moscow, and Odessa, and of enlightened persons who were interested in Russian archaeology, for example, Khanénko's *Antiquities of the Dnieper Region* and Count Bóbrinskoy's *Smêla*.

It would be difficult to say of other countries what can now be said of Russia, that almost all the treasures found in the country have been published, and most of them reproduced as well, and are at present accessible to any one who will consult the works of native scholars.

A vast quantity of material has been collected and published. But that it has been studied and understood, that it has been utilized to reconstruct the story of South Russia at the dawn of history, I should hardly care to affirm. Apart from the French archaeologists whom I have already mentioned, the Germans were the first who paid attention to the antiquities of South Russia. Koehler, Koehne, Boeckh, Neumann, and Stephani made the earliest attempts to explain them scientifically: Stephani above all. He was Keeper of the Hermitage, a regular contributor to the Reports of the Archaeological Commission, and the author of the great *Antiquités du Bosphore Cimmérien*: year after year he compiled for the reports long and learned articles, in Russian and in German, on the antiquities of South Russia. Stephani's works are well known: his vast erudition, founded on the most extensive reading, makes them a perfect storehouse of information; his judgement is sound when he is dealing with Greek objects; and his interpretations of religious representations are sometimes very happy. But he was never able to understand monuments that were not purely Greek. Just as he refused to recognize Mycenaean culture, so his learning, limited to the Greek world, was incapable of detecting the Oriental and prehistoric elements in the antiquities of South Russia, and of appreciating the significance of those elements.

Unfortunately he exercised a very powerful influence on succeeding generations. Vladimir Stásov and Nikodim Kondakóv had divined the necessity of understanding the native civilization as such, but they did not succeed in putting their idea into practice, and the book of Tolstóy and Kondakóv, which I have already mentioned, is a mere repertory, though a very useful one, of archaeological material. But Kondakóv and Stasóv stood almost alone. Much has been written about South Russia, but the writings are always dissertations on the Greek towns, commentaries on the fourth book of Herodotus, or studies of one or two isolated objects. Even the great work of Minns, an extremely useful and an extremely learned book, is but a repertory, although as a repertory almost faultless: what he gives us is a juxtaposition of Scythians and Greeks, two separate parts, copiously illustrated, and no more. The same is true of Latȳshev's erudite works, and of the recent articles by Ernst von Stern. The point of view is everywhere the same: that of the Hellenist in whose eyes the native world has only a relative value, by virtue of its influence upon Greek life in the Greek cities.

My own point of view in all these questions of South Russian history is a different one. I take as my starting-point the unity of the region which we call South Russia; the intersection of influences in that vast tract of country—Oriental and southern influences arriving by way of the Caucasus and the Black Sea, Greek influences spreading along the sea routes, and Western influences passing down the great Danubian route; and the consequent formation, from time to time, of mixed civilizations, very curious and very interesting, influencing in their turn Central Russia on the one hand, by way of the great Russian rivers, and on the other Central Europe, especially the region of the Danube.

I shall treat these matters with greater detail in succeeding chapters: for the resent I should like to state in general terms, what the classical world gave to South Russia, and what it received from South Russia in return.

South Russia is a great region of steppes, which merge into the steppes of Central Asia on the east and those of Hungary on the west. But nomadic life is not the only type of life which can flourish on the South Russian steppes. They provide excellent pasturage, but at the same time, if employed for agriculture, they yield admirable results, thanks to the richness of the black soil, to the comparatively favourable rainfall, and to the great rivers which cross them from north to south. Consequently the Russian steppes, open on all sides, attracted not only the Eastern nomads, but also the hunting and agricultural peoples of Central Russia and the Danubian region: these settlers became closely attached to their new home, and remained there for century after century. There is ample archaeological evidence to prove it. In the period of the earliest burials with contracted skeletons, the use of cereals was already known, and there is nothing to show that the makers of these graves were not the same people from the neolithic period as far down as the arrival of Cimmerians and Scythians in the Iron Age. No doubt this population was affected by influences from various quarters, particularly from the Caucasus, the Black Sea, and the region of the Danube. There was probably migration and partial infiltration of tribes from east, north, and west. But the mass of the population remained unchanged, and retained for centuries its old customs, its old observances, and probably its old beliefs.

Much has been written about the corridor of the steppes—the great migrational route along which the Oriental hordes poured into Central Europe. It cannot be denied that the corridor existed, and was used by the nomads of Central Asia. But the instability of life in this corridor has been greatly exaggerated.

In speaking of life on the South Russian steppes there is one fact of the deepest significance which is usually ignored and which completely changes the aspect of the problem. The nomads from the East were invariably conquering tribes, not numerous, but well organized, which imposed themselves on a sedentary agricultural population. This is true of the first conquerors, the Cimmerians; of the Scythians who followed them; and of the Sarmatians who took the place of the Scythians. The new-comers found admirable pasturage for their beasts in the steppes. The subject population was a comparatively wealthy one, so that tribute was easy to exact. Finally, the invaders inherited the commercial relations of the conquered. In consequence they had every inducement to settle down in that fine country for as long a period as political conditions allowed. As long as their military forces were sufficient to defend the conquered territory against attacks from east and west, they stayed in South Russia and did not dream of leaving it. Hence the conquerors were never mere passengers in the Russian steppes: they founded more or less stable kingdoms. So the Cimmerians, who settled round the straits of Kerch (the Cimmerian Bosphorus): so also the Scythians, whose political centre, as we shall presently see, was originally the valley of the Kuban and later the steppes between Don and Dnieper.

These protracted sojourns of conquering peoples in South Russia, and the establishment of settled states, resulted in the formation of material cultures combining elements of an indigenous culture which was already, as we shall see, considerably developed, with the elements of Oriental civilization brought by the conquerors. These mixed civilizations also absorbed cultural elements coming from the south by way of the Caucasus and the Black Sea.

This significant fact lends additional interest to the history of the Cimmerian power, of the Scythian state, and of the Sarmatian and Gothic states. Little is known of the Cimmerian civilization submerged by the Scythians. Yet there is an important consideration which leads one to hope that future discoveries will dispel the mystery. A glance at the map will show that the corridor of the steppes forms two securely protected pockets. One is the Kuban delta, the peninsula of Taman: the other is the Crimea, especially the region of Ketch and the mountainous part of the peninsula. It was here that the Cimmerians, hard pressed by the Scythians, finally resorted, and united with the Greeks to form the kingdom of Bosphorus: here that the Scythians, vanquished by the Sarmatians on the east, and by the Thracians on the west, took refuge in the second century B.C.: here, lastly, that the Goths, beaten back by Turkish and Mongolian invaders, founded the kingdoms of the Tetraxite Goths and the kingdom of Mangup. We are therefore fully justified in hoping that in this part of the world we shall find sure traces of the Cimmerians, not only from the period of Cimmerian supremacy on the northern shores of the Black Sea, but from other periods as well.

The permanence of certain political formations in the steppes of Russia is a fact of extreme importance. It enables us, above all, to realize the nature of the Scythian kingdom—a formation almost completely Iranian, a northern counterpart of the kingdom of Darius and Xerxes. We are but ill acquainted with the Iranian world, although its influence on classical civilization was enormous. We are fortunate in being able to study another portion of it, different from that which create the Persian kingdom. The Iranians of the Black Sea were not confined to the northern shore. It has been demonstrated by recent discoveries, that a considerable section of the Scythian tribes established itself on the other side of the Black Sea, in the country which afterwards became Armenia and Pontus. The question has often been asked, how Pontic civilization acquired its Iranian character, and what was the origin of the Iranian traditions of Mithridates. It has been suggested that the country was conquered and colonized by Persia. But we must bear in mind that the Persians were not a colonizing people, and that their long supremacy in Asia Minor and in Egypt left but faint traces behind it. I am therefore inclined to believe that part of the population of Pontus,

Cappadocia, and Armenia consisted of Scythians who settled there at the time of the great Scythian invasion in the seventh century. I shall discuss this question later; for the present I merely remind the reader that there existed in Armenia, during the classical period, two districts called Sakasene and Skythene, that is to say, districts inhabited by Sacians and Scythians. Further, there was in Pontus a religious festival called Sakaia: many attempts have been made to explain the name; it can easily be accounted for by the presence in Pontus of persons calling themselves Sakai and forming an important section of the population. I should like to mention here, for I shall not return to the subject, certain archaeological data which point to striking resemblances between the two shores of the Euxine, the northern and the southern. First of all, the general physiognomy of the town of Panticapaeum is remarkably similar to that of several cities on the southern shore, particularly Amisos and Sinope. The relation between acropolis and town, and the general situation, are the same: in both places important alterations were made in the physical structure of the acropolis rock; the character of the cemetery is the same in both, consisting almost exclusively of two types of monuments—rock-cut chambers, and massive barrows surmounting tombs of dressed stone. The same features recur in Paphlagonia, as described in the masterly work of Leonhardt. We must notice in particular the great tomb of Kalekapu, where the sculptural decoration, consisting of Babylono-Persian griffins with heads of horned lions, lions, and so forth, though later, as Hugo Prinz has pointed out, than the architectural decoration, is still of the archaic period, the seventh century B.C.: the sculptured figures seem to me to present a remarkable resemblance to the figures on coins of Panticapaeum and to works of Panticapaean toreutic art. Compare the treatment of the arms of Panticapaeum, the griffin and the lion, on the gold staters of the Bosphorus in the fourth century B.C., with the corresponding figures on the Kalekapu tomb. Compare with the same figures the lions and griffins on the silver vases from Solokha. I am inclined to see in the Paphlagonian sculptures, or in their Assyro-Persian prototypes, the immediate sources from which the Panticapaean metal-workers derived their inspiration.

PLATE I

CLAY FIGURINES OF SCYTHIANS FROM CAPPADOCIA
IV-III Cent. B.C.
1, 2, 4. Ashmolean Museum. 3. Louvre.

We observe also remarkable analogies between certain products of Cappadocian art and objects found in Scythian graves of the period between the sixth and the third centuries B.C. I would draw the reader's attention to a number of cast bronze pole-heads which have been discovered in Cappadocia (pl. II and pl. V, 3): sometimes representing an animal perched on a rattle, sometimes a figure or a pair of figures, geometrically stylized, of the Great Goddess of Asia. The only parallels to these curious objects, of which there are several examples in the Louvre and in the British Museum, are furnished by pole-tops found in Scythian barrows of the period between the sixth and third centuries B.C., and in Western Siberia. Let me also mention the terra-cotta statuettes from Pontus and Cappadocia in the Ashmolean Museum and in the Louvre, which undoubtedly represent Scythian horsemen (pl. I). These horsemen are treated in the same manner and in the same style as the Scythian horsemen on works of Panticapaean toreutic dating from the fourth or third centuries B.C.

In conclusion, I would draw attention to a curious coincidence: terra-cotta wagons have been found in Pontus and in Cappadocia which reproduce, beyond all doubt, the wheeled abodes of the nomads: a well-preserved example may be seen in the Ashmolean Museum. Now, as far as I know, the only analogous objects come from South Russia. We have two series of them, one belonging to the Bronze Age, the other to the first and second centuries A.D. A chariot which closely resembles the Ashmolean specimen was found in a Kuban grave of the Bronze Age: a whole group, of much finer execution, in Panticapaean graves of the first and second centuries A.D.

These resemblances between the two shores of the Euxine cannot be explained by commercial intercourse, but only by community of race; by the existence of similar layers of population in both regions: a layer which may be called autochthonous; a Thraco-Cimmerian; and a Scytho-Iranian layer.

Let us now return to the Scythians of South Russia. We find in South Russia, as I have already said, a whole of products partly manufactured by the Iranians themselves for the Iranians by the Greeks. This Iranian world is the pre-Zoroastrian one which disseminated the cults of Mithra and of Anaitis, the two Iranian divinities who exerted a potent influence of the classical civilization of Hellenistic and Roman times. Unfortunately these Iranians, the Scythians, have left us no written monuments. But their figurative monuments, which have come down to us in great numbers, enable us to approach the difficult task of reconstructing their political, social, economic, and religious life.

This Iranian society was not isolated. Through the Greek colonies it had constant intercourse with the inhabitants of the Mediterranean seaboard. The development of the Greek colonies, and the character which Greek civilization assumed on the shores of the Black Sea, is a subject of the greatest importance. More of this later: for the present I will only observe that the Greek colonies on the Black Sea owed their very existence to the formation of stable kingdoms on the Russian steppes: the Cimmerian, and later the Scythian kingdom. The Black Sea colonies, exposed as they were to attack from the north, could only survive and prosper if the surrounding country was in a more or less settled condition. Just as the prosperity of the Greek colonies in Asia Minor depended on the existence of the kingdoms of Lydia and of Persia, of which they were the maritime outlets, so Olbia, Panticapaeum, and Chersonesus only throve because a united kingdom in the Russian steppes guaranteed them free intercourse with the peoples on the banks of the great Russian rivers. Scythians and Greeks constituted an economic unit, and their mutual influence was necessarily the dominant factor in their lives.

This close relation led to very interesting results, above all to the foundation of the kingdom of the Bosphorus in the very home of Cimmerian power. A Milesian colony with a barbarian name, gradually transforming itself into a territorial power supreme on both banks of the Cimmerian Bosphorus, governed by a dynasty of archons, and later by kings with partly Greek and partly Thracian names: this unique phenomenon is surely worthy of the closest attention. It must not be forgotten that the existence of this kingdom was of capital importance for the Athenian state before, during, and after the Peloponnesian War. The Bosphorus was sometimes the principal or the only centre of supply providing the Greek world with cereals and with fish.

What is the explanation of the complex aspect of the Bosphoran state and the peculiar features of Greek civilization in the Bosphorus? I shall treat the question in my fourth chapter. I will confine myself here to stating a few outstanding points. The archons of Panticapaeum styled themselves archons of Panticapaeum and of Theodosia, and kings of the native peoples, Sindians, Maeotians, and the like. This twofold authority gives the key to the explanation. The state of the Bosphorus was a coalition of the population of the Greek cities and of the natives inhabiting part of the Crimea and of the Taman peninsula. The Thracian names of the Bosphoran dynasts show that the native population, or at least the dominant part of it, was of Thracian stock: it possessed a high and ancient civilization, and was promptly hellenized. It must be borne in mind that the straits of Kerch—the Cimmerian Bosphorus, an old and significant name—were the centre of the Cimmerian kingdom, and that the Cimmerians were probably of Thracian origin. Is it not natural to suppose that the Bosphoran state was a Greco-Cimmerian state, and that this alliance gave the new body strength to resist the attacks of the Scythians and to preserve its independence even against the imperialism of Periclean Athens?

We shall follow the political and social fortunes of the Bosphoran state in our fourth chapter. But before I go farther, I would draw the reader's attention to one or two important considerations. How curious, this semi-Greek tyranny which lasted for centuries and gradually changed into a Hellenistic monarch with the same characteristics as Bithynia, Pontus, Armenia, Parthia, and Commagene—hellenized states resting on Thracian, Iranian, Thraco-Iranian, and Syrian foundations! How interesting, the mixed religion which slowly developed in the Cimmerian Bosphorus! How singular this prolific art, working mainly for export to Scythian dynasts and the Scythian aristocracy! How remarkable, the social and economic organization, based on great domains methodically exploited, on a complex system of exploration, and on active and regular commercial intercourse with the neighbouring kingdoms!

The Scythian kingdom, on which the material prosperity of the Greek colonies and of the Cimmerian Bosphorus depended, was succeeded in the Russian steppes by an ascendancy of various Sarmatian tribes—Iranians, like the Scythians themselves. The Sarmatians, as every one knows, played a prominent part of the history of the Roman Empire. It was they, with the Germanic and Thracian tribes, who dealt the first formidable blows at the young Roman power on the Danube. It was they who mingled with the Goths and spread with them over Central Europe as far as Italy and Spain. What did we know about the Sarmatians before the recent discoveries in the Russian steppes? A few lines of Tacitus, of Valerius Flaccus, of Arrian, a few phrases in Ammianus Marcellinus, the reliefs of Trajan's column and of the arch of Galerius at Salonica: altogether very little.

The excavations in the Kuban barrows, the great find of Novocherkássk, the gold plaques from Siberia, the discoveries in the Ural steppes, showed for the first time that the Sarmatians were by no means barbarians. Iranians like the Scythians, they brought a high culture along with them, and adopted elements from Greek and Greco-Scythian civilization. As soon as they reached the banks of the Don and of the Kuban, they entered into close relations with the inhabitants of the Bosphorus and mingled with the population, transforming the kingdom of the Bosphorus, both politically and in religious matters, into a semi-Iranian state.

What is extremely important, is that out of all these elements, the Sarmatians created a peculiar culture and in particular an original and characteristic style of art. I refer to the renaissance of the Scythian animal style, which combined with the use of precious stones and enamel, led to the formation, at Panticapaeum and in the Russian steppes, of the polychrome style of jewellery which was adopted by the Goths and is wrongly called Gothic. The style is not Gothic at all: it is Iranian—if you like, Sarmatian. And it was not the Goths but the Sarmatians who introduced it into Central and Southern Europe.

These then are the links uniting South Russia with the classical world. There are others which unite it with Central Russia and with the Slavonic Russia which was to be. From the remotest period, progress in South Russia has invariably been echoed by progress in Central and Eastern Russia. The Copper Age, the Bronze Age, and, most of all, the Iron Age in Russia were deeply influenced by the south. The Iron Age on the Volga, and even more on the Kama, peculiar as it is, is bound by a thousand ties to the Scythian world of South Russia. And it was the Sarmatian epoch which impressed its character on the Middle Iron Age and on the earliest Slavonic antiquities, which were influenced, on the other hand, by uninterrupted contact with the Greek culture of Byzantium and with the Oriental world of the Turkish and Mongolian nomads who inherited the Greco-Iranian civilizations of South Russia.

PLATE II

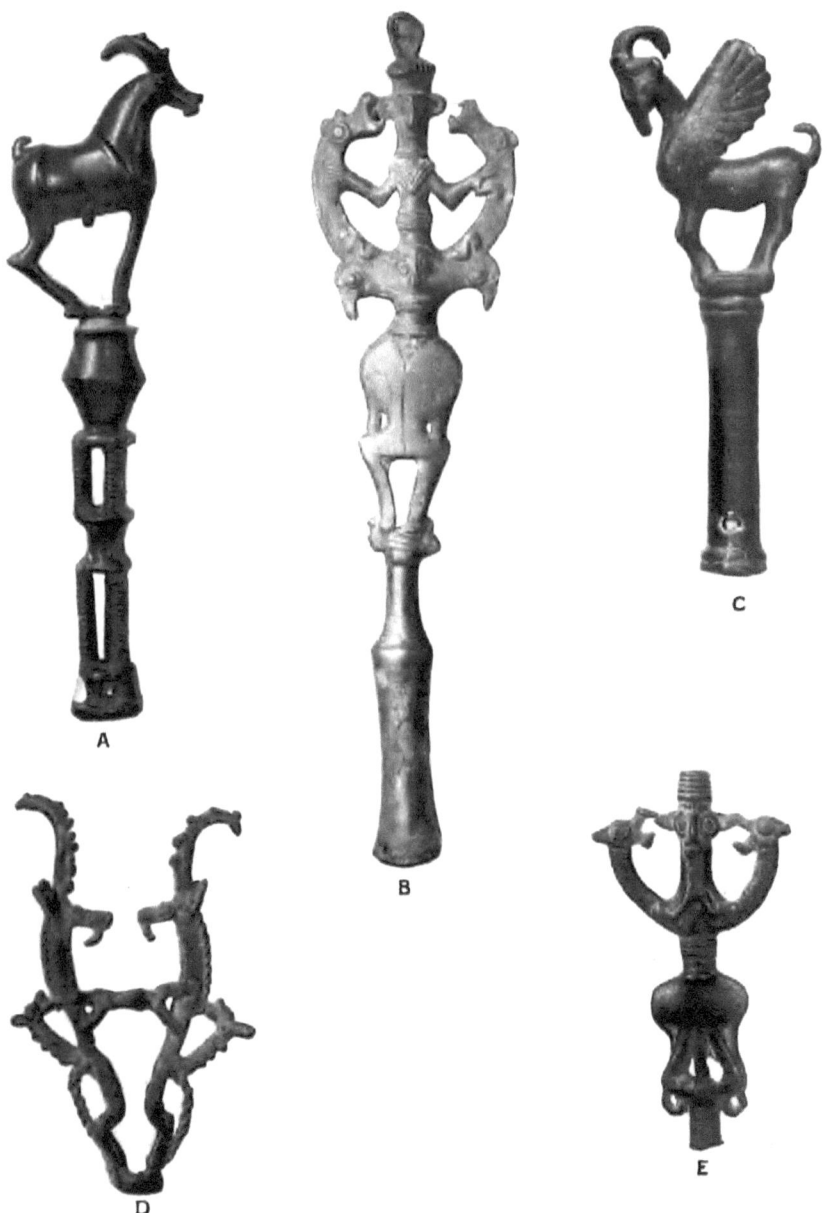

BRONZE POLE-TOPS FROM CAPPADOCIA
British Museum and Louvre

II.
THE PREHISTORIC CIVILIZATIONS

THROUGHOUT the classic East—in Mesopotamia, in Elam, in Turkestan, and in Egypt—the dawn of civilized life is marked by two phenomena, one characteristic of the neolithic age, the other of the earliest metal periods. I refer to the splendid development of pottery in the neolithic period, especially painted pottery with naturalistic and geometric decoration; and to the wonderful impetus which civilization received, in all these places, at the metal epoch. The painted pottery of Central Asia, of Susa, of Turkestan, of Mesopotamia, of Asia Minor, of Egypt, still belongs to the prehistoric period; but in several of these regions the age of metals inaugurates a historic period which is accompanied not only by artistic development but also by written documents. The proto-historic epoch is marked by rich civilizations which make copious use of metals, especially copper and, later, bronze—never iron—and which we are accustomed to call copper and bronze civilizations, on the analogy of the prehistoric epochs in Central Europe, although the names are singularly inappropriate to the abundant and varied life of the East in the third millennium B.C.

Southern Europe passed through the same stages. No need to speak of the brilliant Cretan or Aegean civilization, in which a period of neolithic painted pottery, and a chalcolithic period, were succeeded by a rich historic life, with which we are ill acquainted it is true, but only because we are unable to decipher Aegean texts. We must examine, however, the corresponding phenomena in the civilized life of Central and Eastern Europe, seeing that the region of the Russian steppes was one of prime importance, as the home not only of a neolithic painted pottery but of a metal civilization of particular splendour.

The two areas do not coincide. The painted pottery is characteristic of the neolithic and chalcolithic epoch on the banks of the great western rivers, the Dniester, the Bug, and the Dnieper, whereas the metal culture principally flourished on the banks of the Kuban at the other extremity of the steppes.

The neolithic painted pottery of the Ukrainian or Tripólye type, so called from a hamlet near Kiev where Chvojka found the first examples, belongs to a group of Central and South European pottery which we call spiral and maeander pottery. Wherever it is found, it is partly painted and partly incised. Its presence has been observed in several districts, from the shores of the Adriatic to the shores of the Black Sea. Its expansion coincides approximately with the basins of the Danube and its tributaries, of the Dniester, the Bug, and the Dnieper. I cannot deal with all the difficult and delicate questions which have been raised by the various types of this ware: which came first, incised or painted decoration; what was the principal centre, the shores of the Adriatic, or the shores of the Black Sea; and what is the relation between this pottery and the different racial groups which subsequently formed the population of Western Europe.

What concerns us chiefly is the generally accepted fact that the Tripolye type of painted pottery—the pottery of South Russia, Galicia, and Rumania—is the richest and most highly developed branch of the family, and the most original as well. The shapes show great wealth and variety compared with those on the Danube and its tributaries. The ornamentation is by no means restricted to spiral and maeander. As in the contemporary pottery of Susa, the geometric decoration is combined with geometrizing animal and vegetable decoration which uses as ornaments figures of men, animals, and plants. Even the arrangement of the ornament in parallel zones, and the so-called metopic style of decoration, is not unknown in the painted pottery of South Russia. In South Russia, as everywhere else, the spiral and maeander pottery is accompanied by numerous clay figures of very various primitive types, representing human beings—especially women—animals, pieces of furniture, and sacred implements.

The systematic excavations of Chvojka and of Volkov on the Dnieper, of Ernst von Stern in Bessarabia, of Hubert Schmidt in Rumania, and of Hadaczek in Galicia, have shown that the men who produced the painted pottery were by no means wholly primitive: they were no longer hunters or nomads: they dwelt in villages, sometimes fortified; owned houses of a common neolithic form, half cave, half hut; lived on agriculture; and had a great number of domestic animals at their disposal. We have no decisive evidence as to their mode of burial. The best-preserved pots and figurines were found neither in houses nor in tombs, but in curious structures suggesting, on the one hand, a Roman columbarium, on the other, a temple for religious ceremonies connected with funerals. These structures are sometimes of considerable size; they were roofed, and had walls of clay and wattle; the floor, of rammed earth, was littered with all kinds of funeral offerings, especially vases, some of them perhaps funerary urns containing the bones and ashes of the dead. The structures are always found in groups, arranged in concentric circles with two or three larger ones in the middle: they were built on flat elevations beside a river or a ravine.

These buildings all date from the neolithic or the chalcolithic age: none is later. To the same period belong the thousands of graves which are found, often in fairly large groups, all over South Russia, not only in the steppes but in the woodland as well—graves covered with a barrow, and containing contracted skeletons more or less thickly daubed with red paint. The oldest graves of this kind are very poor ones and undoubtedly belong to nomads. It has often been asked, how these graves are related to the neolithic and chalcolithic villages and funerary structures described above, those which are characterized by the pottery with spirals and maeanders. I cannot linger over this question; but I believe that the neolithic population which produced the spiral and maeander pottery superposed itself on a portion of the population with contracted skeletons, influenced it profoundly, and was absorbed in its turn by new-comers of the same origin as itself. This process of influence and absorption introduced noticeable alterations into the life of the nomads who buried their dead in the contracted position and covered them with red paint. We find evidence of the change in a good many different places. In the district of Khárkov, as Gorodtsóv has observed, the nomads gradually became a sedentary agricultural people, modified their type of sepulchral structure, and developed their primitive pottery by introducing new shapes and by decorating their vases with incised, and sometimes painted, ornaments, borrowed from their neighbours in the region of the Dnieper. This new civilization, which was also affected, in its weapons and metal implements, by the chalcolithic culture of the Kuban, exercised, in its turn, a very powerful influence on Central Russia, where it gave rise to the so-called Fatianovo civilization. Again, in the region of the Dnieper, the Bug, and the Dniester, the superposition of nomads upon the agricultural population produced a mixed culture which lasted right through the bronze epoch, and which is represented by a number of barrows recently excavated near Sevastopol, near Odessa, and in Podolia.

The most important point to observe is that civilized life never ceased in the western part of South Russia, and that during the Bronze Age the inhabitants remained sedentary and agricultural. They had no rich metallic culture until the arrival of conquerors bringing iron. This is easy to understand. There is no copper in the Russian steppes, and none in Central Russia. The only good copper mines are far away—in the Ural, in Transcaucasia, and in Hungary. Objects produced in these regions found their way to the Russian steppes. But we cannot expect to find such objects in great numbers. The steppes had nothing to offer in exchange for precious articles. The time had not yet come when the corn, the fish, and the leather of South Russia found a certain and permanent market in countries which abounded in gold, silver, copper, and iron.

The conditions in the valley of the Kuban were very different. The Kuban valley, rich in natural produce, always served as a granary for the mountainous and alpine regions of Central Caucasus, which had plenty of fruit but were poor in cereals. Now Central Caucasus and Transcaucasia abound in metals, especially copper and iron. It is well known that the most ancient Greek writers always affirmed that iron and even copper—as to copper there was a difference of opinion—were 'invented' by the peoples of Transcaucasia. A recently published papyrus from Oxyrhynchus, containing fragments of Hellanicus, gives a new version of the current story: according to this version, the use of iron weapons was introduced by one Saneunos, a Scythian king. I have not the least doubt that the mines of Transcaucasia furnished much of the copper which was fashioned into weapons, implements, and objects of art in Mesopotamia; as to the precious metals, especially gold, I need only recall the legend of the Argonauts and the Golden Fleece: I shall return to the question later. Silver was extracted in great quantities from the mines in the country of the Chalybians. Is it not natural that the copper and precious metals of the Caucasus should have easily found their way, probably by sea, to the fertile valley of the Kuban? We know that the inhabitants of the Black Sea littoral, and, particularly of the Crimea and the Caucasian coast, were always intrepid sailors, and that in historic times they practised a piracy which was difficult to repress, even with the regular fleet of the Bosphoran kingdom. I am convinced that it was they who from the earliest times transported the metals of Transcaucasia to the seaports in the Straits of Kerch. These seaports were probably active hundreds of years before the Greeks settled there. One of them was certainly Panticapaeum. The barbarian name of the town, and the legend, preserved by Stephanus of Byzantium, that it was founded by a son of Aietes, king of those Colchians who appear in the story of the Argonauts, testify to the great antiquity of the town, to its ancient intercourse with the Caucasus, and to its existence as a seaport long before the arrival of the Milesians. I take it that two other seaports had the same history, Phanagoria and, in particular, Hermonassa, which are situated on the other side of the straits, at the mouth of the Kuban. With regard to Hermonassa, Hecataeus informs us that there was another place of the same name, near Trebizond, the chief port of the Transcaucasian mining district. Perhaps Trebizond, a very ancient Greek colony, took part in the foundation of the Caucasian Hermonassa, at the period when the Greeks were planting colonies in the principal centres of civilized life on the Black Sea. I have no doubt that the Carians, and after them the Ionians, inherited their commercial relations from their prehistoric predecessors. We need not be surprised, therefore, that the oldest cemeteries in the Kuban valley, which belong to the copper age, are exceptionally rich, especially in weapons, implements, and artistic objects, of copper, silver, and gold, which can only be compared with the objects of the same copper period from the ruins and cemeteries of Elam, Mesopotamia, and Egypt.

The most interesting of these Kuban graves is that discovered by Veselóvski in the town of Maikop, under a monumental kurgan 10.65 metres high (fig. 1). At the level of the soil a circular enclosure had been made of undressed stone, and in the centre a great sepulchral trench dug, 1.42 metres deep. The walls of the trench were lined with wood, and the floor was of pebbles. At the corners, wooden posts supported the wooden roof of the tomb. A thin layer of earth was placed on this roof, and above it another much broader roof. Inside, the grave was divided into three by partitions, one partition dividing the grave into two halves, the other dividing one of the halves into two others. The chief part of the tomb, the southern, was reserved for the corpse, which lay in a contracted position with the hands raised to the head. The whole skeleton was covered with red paint. The funeral furniture of the principal grave was extremely sumptuous: the skeleton was strewn all over with gold ornaments, originally, no doubt, sewn on to the clothing figures of lions, in two sizes (pl. IV, 5 and 7); figures of oxen (pl. IV, 6); rings; rosettes; gold, turquoise, and carnelian beads. Under the skull were found two narrow strips of gold, pierced with eyelets, probably for sewing ornaments on to them (pl. IV, 1); earrings; and other gold jewels. Beside the skeleton were six gold and silver rods, four of which passed through figures of oxen, of solid gold and silver, attached near their lower ends (pl. IV, 2-4). The upper ends of the rods were pierced for laces or ribbons. Alongside the rods were seventeen vases of gold, silver, and stone, two of them with engraved designs (pl. III, 1-4): of these I shall speak later. The tomb also contained several weapons and implements of polished stone and of copper, and several copper and clay vases. In each of the two other compartments there was another skeleton covered with red paint, one female and one male: the furniture was similar, but less rich. Farmakovski has inferred, from a minute study of the objects in the tomb, that the principal personage was buried with a tiara, of cloth or felt, on his head, and that this tiara was ornamented in front by two golden diadems studded with golden rosettes; that the gold and silver rods probably belonged to a funeral canopy, the edges of which were decorated with gold plaques; that at the interment the rods of the canopy were placed beside the body, and the body covered with the curtain of the canopy. The dead man was evidently no ordinary person, but the chief or king of a tribe.

The Maikop grave is no exception. Although the explorers of the Caucasus paid little attention to graves with contracted and painted skeletons, and directed most of their efforts to discovering richer Scythian tombs, they were nevertheless so fortunate as to find four graves contemporary with the Maikop grave and rivalling it in the splendour of their furniture. As to graves with similar though poorer furniture, they can be counted by dozens if not by hundreds. It is quite certain that in the copper age the Northern Caucasus, especially the valley of the Kuban, was thickly populated, and that the inhabitants were wealthy enough to build monumental tombs and to surround the dead not merely with rough clay vessels but with precious objects of copper, gold, and silver. I shall give a short account of the four finds mentioned above.

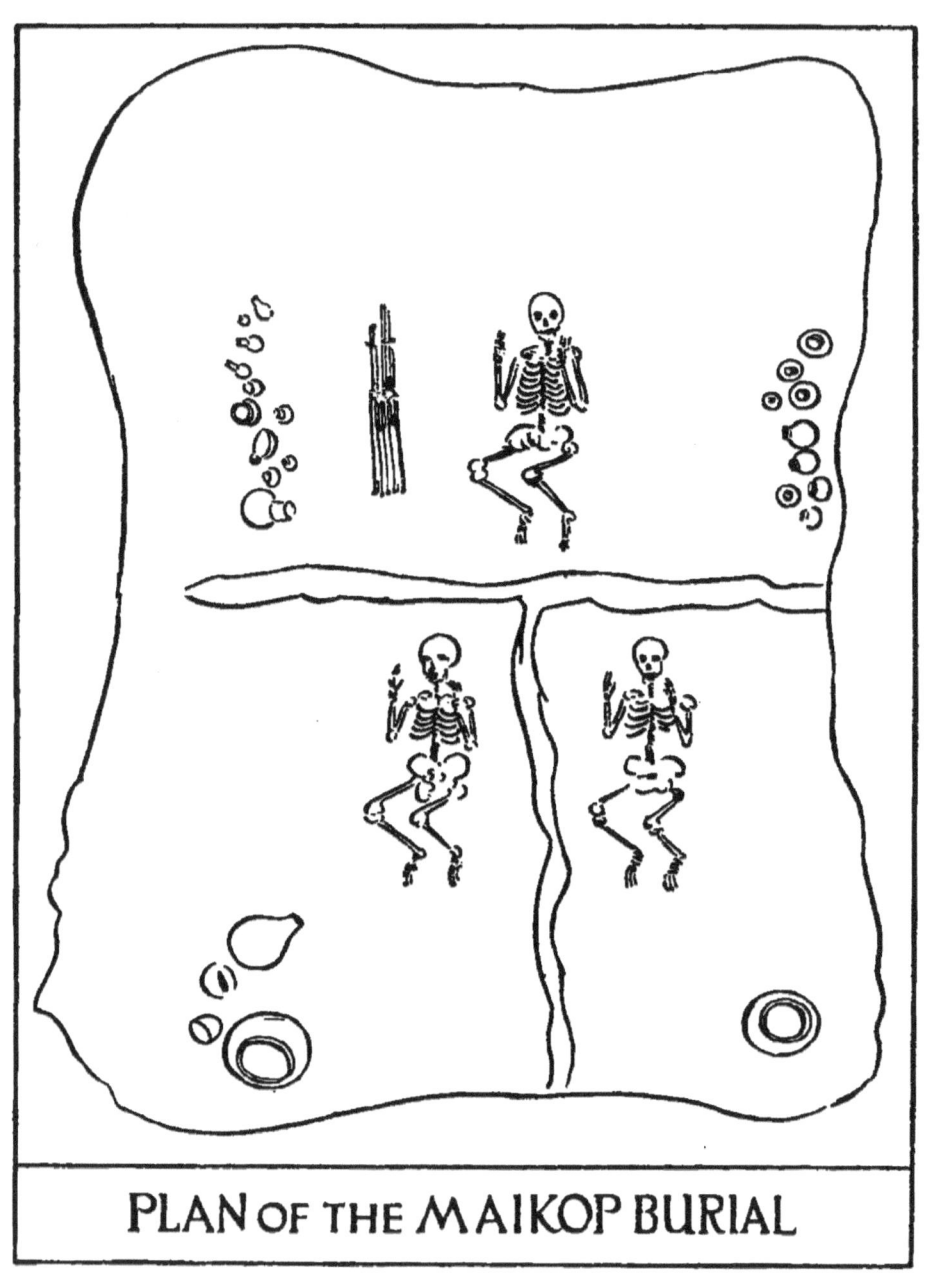

Fig. 1.

PLATE III

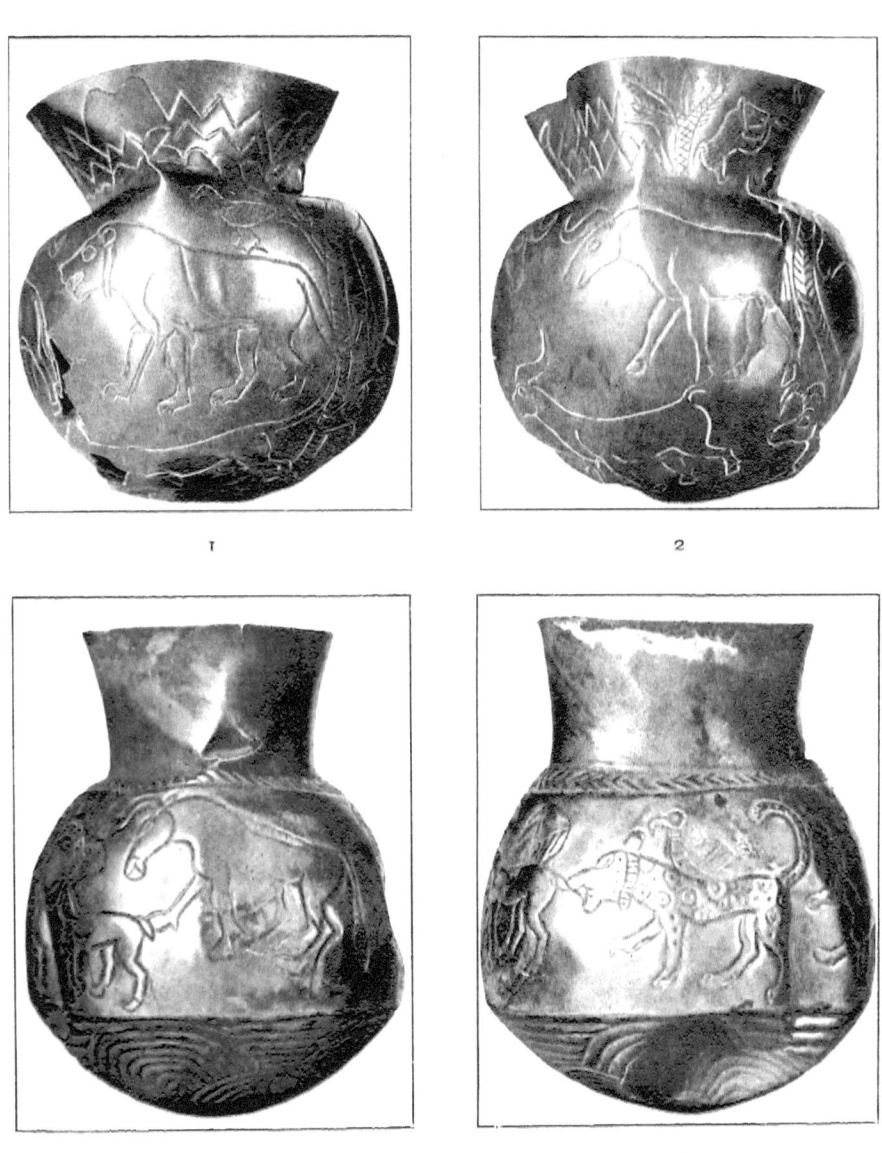

TWO ENGRAVED SILVER VASES FROM MAIKOP
Third Millennium B.C. Hermitage, Petrograd

PLATE IV

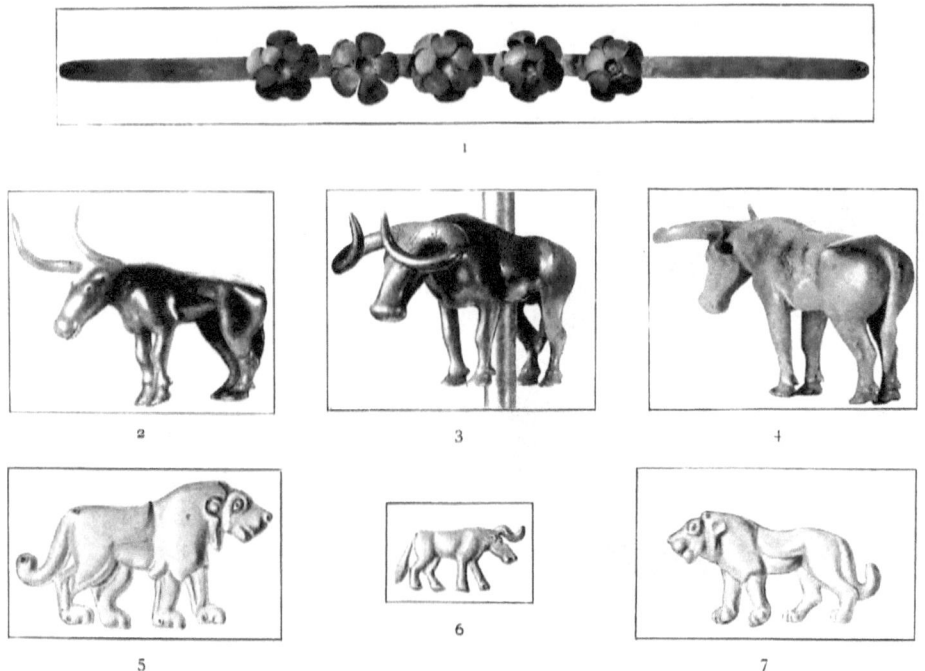

1. GOLD DIADEM. 2-4. MASSIVE GOLD AND SILVER FIGURES OF BULLS.
5-7. GOLD PLAQUES SEWN ON CLOTH.
From Maikop. Third Millenium B.C. Hermitage, Petrograd.

In 1898, while digging for clay in the Cossack village (*stanitsa*) of Staromyshástovskaya, workmen found a silver vessel of the same ovoid shape as the Maikop vases; it contained a number of precious objects resembling those at Maikop: a golden diadem with rosettes, a silver figure of an ox with a hole in its back for suspension or for the insertion of a rod, hundreds of gold and carnelian beads which originally formed to one or more necklaces and bracelets, a lion's head in gold, belonging to one of the necklaces, and several earrings each composed of gold rings of various sizes interlinked.

Even more extraordinary are the two graves discovered in kurgans near the village of Tsárskaya. The wooden framework of the Maikop grave is replaced by stone structures which recall, with singular insistence, the well-known dolmens of the same period in Northern Caucasus. These structures were composed of big slabs forming stone-boxes or tomb chambers each divided into two by a cross-slab. Both chambers had stone roofs, one roof being gabled, the other flat. One corpse was buried in each stone-box; the corpse occupied one compartment, the other was filled with tomb furniture. In both graves the bodies were contracted and covered with a thick coat of red paint: the same paint was used on the walls of the second stone-box and on certain objects in the grave. The furniture of both graves was extremely rich and copious: it is of the same character as at Maikop, but the objects are clumsier and less distinguished. There is no doubt, however, that Maikop and Tsárskaya Stanitsa are contemporary. The Tsárskaya kurgans show the same combination of stone and copper implements, without any bronze, the same wealth of gold and silver, the same shapes of earring, and the same abundance of stone and metal beads. It is impossible for me to enumerate the scores of objects found in these graves: I shall indicate only the most characteristic. Among the weapons, the forks or spikes are particularly curious: one of them is decorated with little human figures. Curious also, the remains of a fur coat and of other garments in the second stone-box. The dead man was covered by a black fur coat, the fur turned outwards, with a silver collar; under the fur was a tissue of yellow down, and under this, on the body itself, remains of a linen garment with a painted border of purplish red.

The last grave which I wish to mention was found in 1909 at Úlski, a village of the Mountain Tatars. The most interesting finds were a model of a wagon and fragments of five or six female statuettes in clay and of two others in alabaster. This grave is undoubtedly later than the preceding: for, first, the grave is in the loose earth and not in the virgin soil; secondly, the skeleton lies in an extended position; and, thirdly, the type of pin is more advanced. Nevertheless, it still belongs to the copper age or to the early part of the bronze age.

All these graves of which I have spoken bear witness to a high development of cultural life in the Northern Caucasus during the early copper age. But the copper age is of course a relative conception: it does not provide an absolute chronology. Yet absolute chronology is of the utmost importance to us. Is the copper age in Northern Caucasus contemporary with the copper age in Mesopotamia, in Turkestan, or in Egypt? I believe it is, although most investigators deny this and attribute our finds not to the third but to the second millennium B.C.

The reasons for my conclusion are derived from a stylistic comparison of the artistic objects, especially the engraved silver vases, with similar objects found in Mesopotamia and in Egypt.

ENGRAVINGS ON THE MAIKOP VASE

Fig. 2.

I will begin with the engraved vessels from Maikop (pl. III), as they are the most artistic objects among the Kuban finds. The first (pl. III, 1-2) has the usual shape of the Maikop vases—ovoid body, wide neck, no foot, two handles nailed to the neck for suspension. The engraved decoration (fig. 2) is disposed as follows: on the neck is represented a chain of mountains, interrupted by two spreading trees. Between the trees, a bear is standing on his hind legs to reach the fruit: the fruit is not indicated. On the body of the vase are two rivers flowing from the mountains and meeting in a sea or lake which occupies the bottom of the vase. At the mouth of one river a bird—duck or goose—is sitting on the water: at the mouth of the second, a water-plant, probably a reed, grows on the bank. On the body of the vase are two rows of animals, four in each row: in the first row, a bull, a wild ass—or rather Przhevalski's horse—, a lion with a bird on his back, all facing left, and a second bull facing right: in the second row, a wild boar, a panther, and two antelopes, all facing left. The streams of the rivers are partly concealed by the bodies of the animals.

The second vase (pl. III, 3-4) is of nearly the same shape, but the neck is narrower and longer. The bottom is occupied by a large rosette, which consists of three rows, one above the other, of round leaves placed crosswise, the same type of rosette as those which were sewn to the diadems of Maikop and Staromyshastovskaya. The whole body of the vase above the bottom is filled with a row of five animals and of three birds, all facing left: an antelope, a bull, a panther, a bird, and an antelope and a panther with birds on their backs. Below the neck of the vase is a narrow hatched strip.

The shape of both vases, in its main lines, recalls the celebrated Entemena vase found at Tello. The technique is the same, each vase being hammered out of a single piece of metal. The engraving is not so delicate in the Maikop vases as in the Entemena vase, and reminds one rather of the engraving on the famous Kish spear-head, the form of which, I may remark, is very like that of the spear-heads from Tsárskaya Stanitsa. The primitiveness of the Maikop engravings, compared with the Entemena vase, is shown by the treatment of details: for water, leaves and branches, fur, horns, manes and plumage, the Maikop engraver uses simple straight lines set in parallel rows. In this respect the engraver of the Entemena vase works more freely than the artists of the Maikop vases, of the mother-of-pearl plaques from Tello, of the bone objects from proto-dynastic Egypt, or of the asphalt and ivory plaques from Elam. Look at the stylization of the lions' manes, and the plumage of the eagles, on the Entemena vase: there is no parallel to them on the Maikop vases, but only on the more developed palettes and the bone mountings of stone knives in proto-dynastic Egypt.

The general arrangement of the figures on the Maikop vases and on the Maikop canopy is identical. It is the most archaic type of decoration: the elements which it uses are figures of animals, a most exclusively naturalistic, disposed either in parallel rows, or in complete disorder. There is hardly any attempt to combine the figures into groups, and such attempts as are made are of the most primitive description; in the second row of the first vase the paw of the panther is placed on the back of the antelope; and in both vases some of the animals have birds on their backs. We may notice in the two bulls on the first vase a timid suggestion of the later heraldic scheme of confronted animals. At the same time, some of the animals show a powerful realism, a striking faculty of keen observation. Such a combination of primitive methods in composition with strong naturalism in the rendering of individual animals is entirely foreign to later periods in the evolution of art. We come across survivals of it both early in early Ionian art and in the Scythian animal style, but it is sufficient to put these classes of monuments beside our vases, to be convinced that in all essentials they are totally different.

The only analogy to this mixture of realism and of primitive schematization is presented by the oldest monuments of Elam and Egypt: the archaic Elamite seals with rows of animals, and the various products of pre- and proto-dynastic Egypt, especially the bone mountings of stone knives and articles of toilet and furniture in bone and ivory. Less typical are the Egyptian stone palettes, where we already meet with attempts to unite the animals into groups, or to combine them with human figures, and so to produce a more elaborate arrangement. Some of these monuments, however, even later examples such as the well-known palette with three rows of animals and one of trees, preserve the primitive features of earlier productions; worth noticing, the resemblance in the treatment of trees on this palette and on the Maikop vases. But the primitive scheme on the Maikop vase is made more complex by the introduction of two rivers and a lake, of trees and mountains. In early Babylonian and Egyptian art, the introduction of landscape elements into the increasingly complicated representations comes comparatively late: in Babylonia not earlier than the reign of Naramsin, on his celebrated stele and on contemporaneous seal-cylinders: in Egypt, during the earliest dynastic period, for instance, on the mace-head of 'King Scorpion'. A glance at the monuments will show that the treatment of the landscape is entirely different from that on the Maikop vase. It must be noticed, however, that in the stylization of water the Maikop vase is akin to the mace-head of King Scorpion, while both differ greatly in this particular from the Babylonian monuments with their system of transverse, instead of longitudinal, lines although the system is more advanced on the mace-head, where the lines are undulated, than on the Maikop vase, where straight lines are disposed in triangles. In the above-mentioned Babylonian and Egyptian monuments, the landscape is subordinated to the figures, and an effort is made to combine both elements into a whole, whereas on the Maikop vase landscape and animals are merely juxtaposed, the only exception being the bear climbing the tree. This very primitive treatment of landscape is by no means unknown in the earliest artistic monuments of Egypt. It is particularly interesting to compare the landscape on the vase with painted scenes of the same type on the ovoid clay pots of pre-dynastic Egypt. On the neck of such pots we often find a representation of a chain of mountains, and on the body rows of animals in the desert or by the Nile, sometimes in combination with trees, and beneath the animals what are probably ships floating on the river, thou some scholars prefer to recognize fortified villages. The most detailed representation of the kind, comprising a great number of human figures, was found painted on the walls of a prehistoric tomb at Hierakonpolis. The transition to the later system of landscape treatment is seen in bone objects, on which an elephant is sometimes portrayed standing on a mountain. The Maikop vase shows the same transitional character: here we find a survival of prehistoric motives, a juxtaposition of two entirely distinct schemes of ornamentation, and a first timid attempt to subordinate landscape to figures.

The arrangement of the decoration on the second Maikop vase is no less typical. The nearest analogy to this arrangement is furnished by the well-known ivory mounting of a stone knife in the collection of Lord Carnarvon. Here as there—if the representation on the Maikop vase is unrolled—the centre is formed by a rosette. Round this rosette, with feet towards it, is a row of animals all moving in one direction. In both objects the purpose of the artist was plainly to represent wild beasts chasing tame animals—a goat and a bull. The likeness between the two designs is remarkable.

I now pass to the rendering of the separate animals. The lions on the Maikop vase, and the lions sewn to the canopy, are of one and the same type. This proves that all the objects of the find were made in one workshop. The lions are characterized by a vivid naturalism, by a heavy, clumsy build, and by the primitive rendering of such details as eyes, ears, tails, and paws. The mane, for example, is either not rendered at all, or only summarily indicated, so that it assumes the form of a collar. In this respect the lions of Maikop differ widely from the lions of the Entemena vase and of the Egyptian palettes. I should like to draw particular attention to the form of the eyes, which is invariable in all the Maikop animals: the eye is either a circle with a dot in the middle, or it has a more oval shape and lacks the dot. Bénédite, who has collected all the material as regards primitive renderings of the eye in pre-dynastic and proto-dynastic Egypt, considers these two forms the most ancient of all. The eyes are sometimes exceedingly large.

An almost perfect analogy to the lions of Maikop is to be found in the lions on ivory mountings of stone knives, especially those from Gebel-el-Araq and in the Carnarvon Collection. These have all the peculiarities of the Maikop lions: the same heavy and swollen body, the same absence of mane, the same round eyes, semicircular ears, and upturned tail. Of the same type are the lions on other knife mountings, for instance, those at Brooklyn and in the Pitt-Rivers Collection, and on numerous articles of toilet and furniture from Hierakonpolis. This similarity is the more important as it testifies still further to the close relation, often pointed out by scholars, between these monuments and corresponding articles in Mesopotamia. On the other hand, the lions of the stone palettes are much more fully developed, freer in their movements, and more elaborate in detail, for instance in the mane. An intermediate position is occupied by the gold mounting of a mace-handle from Nubia. The whole structure of the lions on this handle is still of the early Asiatic type, the only difference being that the artist is already trying to represent the mane, significantly enough by means of geometric patterns as in the second Maikop vase.

Before proceeding I must point out the close resemblance, in general ornamentation and in the treatment of animals, between the Nubian handle and, on the one hand, the Maikop objects, on the other the Egyptian ivories. The embossed work of the Maikop gold plaques and of the Nubian handle finds a parallel outside Egypt in the Sumerian objects from Astarabad recently published by myself.

We may also notice the great similarity between the panthers on the second Maikop vase and on the Nubian handle: in both we find a tendency to render the fur of the animal by means of geometric ornaments. The same peculiarity may be observed in the well-known gold plaques, forming the mounting of a stone knife, in the Cairo Museum.

The bulls of the Maikop find do not differ from each other or from the Staromyshastovskaya figurine. The type is constant: a huge head with an exceedingly long, almost square muzzle, enormous lyre-shaped horns, a massive body with drooping hind-quarters, short heavy legs, big round eyes with a dot in the middle. This type of bull is entirely foreign to Egypt. The only parallels are furnished by Elamitic and by one or two Sumerian monuments; especially Elamitic seals, and seal-impressions on proto-Elamitic tablets. Very curious, the wild ass or Przhevalski's horse, the oldest representation of a horse on monuments. The animal on the Maikop vase is certainly not an ass: a glance at the rows of asses on Egyptian palettes makes that clear. The only counterpart to our animal is the probably contemporary figure on an ivory plaque from Susa. The likeness is conspicuous: the same muscular body and expressive head, the same treatment of the mane and tail by means of straight lines.

The wild boar and the bear are peculiar to our find. There are no representations of these animals on early monuments of the Near East or of Egypt. The types of bird are almost identical with those on various bone and ivory objects from Egypt. The Maikop birds are of course rougher and less individual than the Egyptian, but the stylistic treatment of the plumage is the same in every detail.

The analysis of the artistic monuments of Maikop has shown throughout a very close affinity with the earliest monuments of the Near East and of Egypt, which belong to a period when the arts of Egypt and Asia were still closely related, and did not present any of the very marked differences observable during the historic period. The monuments of Maikop, though very similar to those of Elam, Sumer, and Egypt, are as original as any of these groups. I have no ground for affirming that the monuments of Elam were imported from Mesopotamia, nor can I suppose that there was regular and systematic importation from Mesopotamia to Egypt, or inversely. The objects of the same period found at Astarabad seem not to have been imported. The same is true of the North Caucasian monuments described above: they are certainly local products. Farmakovski has tried to prove that the chain of mountains on the Maikop vase reproduces the main outlines of the Caucasian mountains viewed from the north: he may be right; the likeness is indeed striking. But the Maikop vases have many other peculiarities. The rendering of the mountains is much more naturalistic than on the Egyptian pots. The group of the bear and the tree presents the first attempt to combine tree and animal into a heraldic scheme, and remains unparalleled. The idea of giving a kind of map, or perhaps a representation of Paradise with its rivers, lakes, mountains, trees, and animals, is novel and indeed unique. The same attempt was made in Egypt with the same elements, but the methods adopted were entirely different. Finally, as Elam, Sumer, and Egypt have each their peculiar fauna, so has Maikop: for the elephants, giraffes, and snakes of Egypt we have the wild boar, the bear, and the proto-horse. We are evidently dealing with a new branch of a great artistic movement, a movement which spread, in the period of transition to metallic culture, wherever it found the conditions favourable: that is to say, to Turkestan, to Elam, to Mesopotamia, to North Caucasus, to Egypt. It is worth observing that in all these regions the rich civilization of the copper age gave birth to a still richer and more highly developed civilization of bronze. So also in North Caucasus. It is well known that the Caucasus and Transcaucasia were homes of one of the richest and most interesting developments of the bronze civilization: witness the wonderful discoveries in the cemeteries of Kuban and in many parts of Transcaucasia. I feel sure that this outburst originated in that high development of civilized life in Northern and perhaps in Southern Caucasus during the copper age, which is certified by the finds above analysed. I cannot deal with this problem at length, but I must draw attention to two cardinal points. In the bronze age the typical form of grave in the Caucasus is a combination of barrow with the so-called stone-box, which is undoubtedly a late imitation of a real dolmen, as in the Kuban raves described above. The same fact may be observed in the Crimea. The influence of the copper age on the bronze age cannot be denied. The second point which shows uninterrupted evolution and close connexion between the copper and the bronze age, is the intimate relation between the animal style which characterizes Caucasian ornamentation in the bronze age, and the primitive animal style of the Maikop grave. The influence of the primitive animal style is visible both in the strange bronze belts of Transcaucasia and Kuban, and in Transcaucasian pottery. The peculiar combination of a fully developed geometric style with a very refined animal style has no analogy either in Mesopotamia and Iran or in Western Europe. The general arrangement of the decoration (rows of animals), and the geometric treatment of the animals and their different parts, both originated during the copper period.

I will now give a brief analysis of the different categories of objects which are typical of the North Caucasian group of burials. I must first of all observe that the general assortment of objects is exactly typical of the copper, not of the bronze age. I have dealt with this subject at length in my article on the Treasure of Astarabad: here I will emphasize only the most important points.

The assortment of weapons in the North Caucasian burials is no less, and perhaps more, archaic than in the Astarabad treasure: there are no swords, whereas swords are numerous in all bronze age burials; and no arrows: the principal weapons are spears with leaf-shaped heads; daggers reproducing the form of the Egyptian stone daggers; axes; and forks or spikes with two or three prongs. Closely related to these peculiar forks are the very primitive hooks, undoubtedly weapons and not agricultural implements. Both forks and hooks seem to have been widespread in South Russia during the cooper age: they have been found, for instance, in many of the graves in the Khárkov district. Outside Northern Caucasus and South Russia the fork as a weapon is peculiar to the Orient. In my article on the Treasure of Astarabad I mentioned similar weapons found in Turkestan, and later, as a religious symbol, in Transcaucasia. I should like to add that this weapon is by no means foreign to Mesopotamia. In Mesopotamia as well as in other countries, almost all primitive weapons became emblems of different deities. The ancient spear and the so-called boomerang became emblems of Marduk (see Ward, *Seal-Cylinders*, pp. 399 ff.); the mace-head, of Shuqamuna, a Cassite deity related to Nergal (*ibid.*, p. 403, 17). The fork, in its turn, was used as the emblem of Ramman-Adad, and came to represent the thunderbolt; the prongs consequently acquired the form of rays (Ward, *ibid.*, p. 399, 9). I am inclined to think that the sceptre of Ninib developed out of a combination of two primitive weapons—a fork with two prongs, and a mace. It is worth noting that these symbols were very frequently represented as standing on sacred animals: the spear and boomerang on a dragon, the sceptre of Ninib on a griffin, the thunderbolt on a bull (see *Collection de Clercq*, Nos. 169, 173, 230, the dynasty of Ur): thus providing an excellent analogy for the bulls fastened to the rods of the Maikop canopy (if a canopy it be: it is equally possible that the rods were sceptres, symbolizing the religious power of the king). Incidentally, I must point out that the best analogy for the ornamental treatment of the upper part of these rods is presented by a Sumerian monument: the copper mounting of the lower part of a mace from Tello, which is decorated with the same hatched ornament as the rods of Maikop (see Cros-Heuzey, *Nouvelles fouilles*, p. 22). Besides these forks there is another weapon which is characteristic of the Northern Caucasus and the adjacent parts of South Russia: I mean the copper points, ὀβελοί, for fastening to spears (see *Comptes Rendus*, 1898, pl. IV, 54 and 55): the same weapon has been found in Elam (*Délégation en Perse, Mémoires*, vol. viii, p. 146, fig. 297).

Toilet articles were very numerous in the Caucasian finds. A remarkable quantity of gold rings and gold beads were found in the graves. This abundance of gold rings, and particularly the string of rings, in different sizes, from Staromyshastovskaya, leads me to think that they were not mere ornaments, but units of exchange, like the 'lake-dwellers' purses' of the pile dwellings in Switzerland, and other finds of the same class and time.

The toilet articles in the Caucasian graves enable us to verify the chronological result which we obtained from a stylistic analysis of the finds at Maikop and Staromyshastovskaya. The profusion of gold and silver objects in the Caucasian burials is, as I said, remarkable. It rivals the wealth of the famous treasure of Priam which belong to the second period of Troy. But at the same time, the shapes of the toilet articles on the Kuban are far more primitive than at Troy, although the general assortment presents the same aspect in both places. In both places we find a limited choice of weapons—no swords or arrows, only spears and axes: in both, costly articles of feminine adornment, in three types—first, golden diadems; secondly, necklaces and bracelets of gold beads; thirdly, earrings: in both, a fine collection of gold and silver vases: in both, sets of large and small copper vessels. The absence of pottery in the treasure of Troy may be due to its being a treasure and not a burial.

But in spite of this similarity, a comparative analysis of separate articles in the two finds shows that the Kuban articles are far more primitive than those of Troy. Take the diadems and the earrings, take the gold and silver vessels. It is evident that the Kuban burials belong to the pure copper age, the Trojan treasure to the early bronze period.

Let me analyse the various categories of objects more carefully. I begin with the vessels. In the two series, only the plainest and most primitive forms coincide—the spherical and the wide-necked ovoid. The more complex forms are represented in the Trojan finds alone. The Kuban vases have no true handles, only riveted suspension tubes. In Troy handles are common enough, though some of the vessels preserve the old fashion. No offset feet at Maikop, many at Troy. The copper vessels of Maikop and Tsárskaya have the same primitive shape; they have no handles: at Troy, handles had already begun to be used.

Now let us turn to the diadems. The foundation is the same at Troy and in the Caucasus—a long narrow strip with rounded ends and holes for sewing the ornaments through. But the ornaments differ greatly. They are much richer and more complex at Troy, although the forms of the individual ornaments remain very primitive.

The same is true of the necklace and bracelet beads. Great quantities of gold beads were found both at Troy and in the Caucasus. There were no stone beads in the Trojan treasure. All the plainest forms of bead, at Troy and in the Caucasus, coincide: pearl-shaped beads; the same with ribs; annular; hemispherical; beads like pairs of truncated cones; others like perforated quadrilateral tubes. But more elaborate forms, rosettes, spirals, leaves, and so forth, are peculiar to Troy. Many of the types, chiefly the simplest, have been found in Sumer as well. The Kuban earrings are very primitive: plain rings, rings with beads appended sets of rings. In Troy the earrings may be reduced to the same prototypes, but they are often very elaborate.

The pins at Troy are various and complex, especially the heads. On the Kuban they are very simple, as in the burials with contracted skeletons generally. The only effort to improve the form consists in bending the upper part of the pin: there is no trace of an attempt to wind this bow into a spiral or to give it the shape of a swan's neck, as was usual in the bronze age. In the Úlski grave, but there alone, the crooked ends of the pins were provided with balls, just as in the burials of the middle Hittite period near Carchemish.

Finally, we must notice that in Troy the ornament is already pure geometric, with no traces of the elaborate animal style which we found in Elam, in Mesopotamia, in Egypt, and in the Caucasus.

The foregoing analysis proves that the finds of Troy and the finds of the Kuban, though akin, are not contemporaneous, the Kuban finds being much older.

I have already pointed out more than once that the Úlski grave is later than the other burials in the Kuban. It is interesting to note, that in this grave, and there only, female statuettes, of a very primitive type, were found. These statuettes, as is well known, are common in Europe as well as in Asia. The typology of them is still unexplained; but we must notice the very striking resemblance between our statuettes and, on the one hand, those of the Aegean Islands, on the other, the clay statuettes of the Laibach moors. The Aegean statuettes are certainly pre-Mycenaean, and the Laibach figures still belong to the copper age.

To conclude this rather dry and tiresome analysis I will endeavour to estimate the significance of my deductions for the earliest periods of the evolution of human civilization. The more we learn of the copper age, the more important it is seen to be. This epoch created brilliant centres of cultured life all over the world, especially in the Orient. To the centres already known, Elam, Mesopotamia, and Egypt, we can now add Turkestan and Northern Caucasus—perhaps the Caucasus as a whole. The bloom of civilization in the Caucasus was by no means a brief one. I have already tried to show that the rich development of the bronze age in the Caucasus owed nothing to foreign centres. I see no trace of the Mycenaean influence suggested by Hoernes; nor do I see any relation to the bronze age of Western Siberia, the Altai, and the Ural Mountains. The Caucasian bronze age is very peculiar and very original. The only possible connexion is with Mesopotamia and the Asia Minor of the Hittite period. But I do not believe that this connexion came about in the usual way, by influence due to conquest, migration, or commercial intercourse; I think that in all these countries the roots of development lay in a great copper age civilization which in each centre arose quite independently and proceeded on different lines, although it presented analogous features in all. How to explain the common traits I cannot tell. Are we to suppose a common origin somewhere in Asia, or a common state of mind which, just as in the palaeolithic and neolithic periods, gave rise to the same productions everywhere, quite independent of one another and only slightly influenced by very insignificant intercourse? In any case, the peculiar evolution of Hittite civilization cannot be explained without assuming a great centre of copper age civilization in Asia Minor as well. As yet we have no monuments testifying to the existence of such a centre, but I feel convinced that further investigation in Asia Minor will add one or more items to the long list of centres of civilization in the copper age.

A most important centre of such civilization existed, as we have seen, on the Kuban, contemporaneous with, and akin to, the other centres of the same epoch in Nearer Asia and in Egypt. Do we know anything of the people which produced this culture? The inhabitants, autochthonous as we have every reason to believe, of the region adjacent to the Sea of Azov are described by the Greeks as forming a single nationality. The Greeks knew them by the generic title of Maeotians, derived from Maeotis, the ancient name of the Sea of Azov. Two Maeotian tribes are often mentioned as the strongest and most numerous: the Sauromatians in the delta of the Don, and the Sindians on both shores of the straits of Kerch, the Cimmerian Bosphorus. These tribes captivated the imagination of the Greeks by one of the peculiarities of their social structure: the part played by women in military and political life. Female sovereigns, female warriors among the Sauromatians were a commonplace in Greek ethnographic literature from the earliest times. The same feature, we learn, characterized the Maeotians and the Sindians: remember the romantic story of Tirgatao reported by Polyaenus. Owing to the gynaecocracy which prevailed among the dwellers by the Sea of Azov, the semi-historical legend of the Amazons came to be localized on the shores of that sea. These female warriors, according to Herodotus, migrated to the steppes near the Sea of Azov after their defeat by the Greeks in their original home, Themiscyra, on the northern shore of the Euxine. Landing close to the Sea of Azov, they came to blows with the Scythians and ended by marrying the youth of Scythia and forming the semi-Scythian Sauromatian State. The legend is undoubtedly aetiological, but it bears witness to historical facts: to constant relations by sea between the straits of Kerch and the southern shore of the Euxine; to a fierce struggle between the Maeotian peoples and the Scythian conquerors, terminating not in a complete Scythian victory but in compromise and intermarriage; to the co-existence of two racial elements on the shore of the Sea of Azov, and to strong Scythian influence on the Sauromatians. Let us remember, before going further, that the Sauromatians, who were Maeotians, are not to be confounded with the Sarmatians, who do not appear on the Don until about the fourth century, and who were an Iranian people, patriarchal and not matriarchal.

The matriarchal life of the dwellers by the Sea of Azov was closely connected with their religious beliefs. Their chief divinity was the Mother

Goddess. In the historic period, the peninsula of Taman was covered with sanctuaries of this deity, whom the Greeks identified with their Artemis, their Aphrodite, their Demeter. The organization of the sanctuaries was the same as in Asia Minor. In the sanctuary near Phanagoria there was a legend attached to the temple: Herakles was said to have come hither in his contest with the Giants: the goddess concealed him in a cave, and delivered the Giants to him one by one. No doubt both Herakles and the Giants had been overcome by the attractions of the goddess, who thus resembles the Supreme Goddess of the banks of the Dnieper, the mother of the mythical Scythian chiefs. She appears, therefore, to have been a Mother Goddess, goddess of the productive forces of Nature, like the Mother of the Gods and the Potnia Theron of Asia Minor.

As far as I know, almost all students of the Amazonian legend, led astray by the semi-historic character of the story, have been induced to explain it by an historical misconception. The beardless Hittites—that is the latest explanation—were taken for women and so gave rise to the legend. Others consider that the Cimmerians were, so to speak, the proto-Amazons. Nothing is less likely. Why not adopt a much simpler explanation? The Amazons are localized wherever there was an ancient cult of the Mother Goddess; wherever that cult was connected, as it regularly was, with a social and political organization of matriarchal type wherever women were not only mothers and nurses, but warriors and chieftains as well. The matriarchal stratum and the cult of the Mother Goddess are very ancient in Asia Minor. They are the mark of the pre-Semitic and pre-Indo-European population—the autochthonous population, if we care to use the word. Semites and Indo-Europeans brought with them patriarchal society and the cult of the supreme God. This cult imposed itself on that of the Mother Goddess, but did not destroy it, least of all in Asia Minor. With the cult of the goddess, the Amazons, her warrior priestesses, likewise survived.

Not only the cult of the Mother Goddess, but also the matriarchal structure, persisted for a very long time in certain places, especially on the shores of the Black Sea—in the immediate neighbourhood of the Greeks—among the Sindians, the Maeotians, the Sauromatians, and, in the Crimea, among the Taurians, who sacrificed travellers to their Parthenos, their virgin goddess. It is quite natural that the Greeks, who created the legend of the

Amazons on their first contact with the matriarchal tribes of Asia Minor, should have made the Amazons of Asia Minor emigrate to South Russia and the Caucasus, where matriarchy, the cult of the Mother Goddess, and the specific ritual of that cult remained in full vigour.

This somewhat lengthy digression was necessary in order to show that the Sauromatians, the Sindians, the Maeotians, and the Taurians were really the oldest inhabitants of the Kuban, and that it was probably they who created the civilization of the copper age, and who were able to infuse it into their conquerors, the Cimmerians, and later the Scythians. To show, also, that civilized life never ceased on the banks of the Kuban, and that the Maeotian tribes were the element in the population which developed that civilization, under the influence of their neighbours, often their masters, the Cimmerians, the Scythians, the Greeks.

III.
THE CIMMERIANS AND THE SCYTHIANS IN SOUTH RUSSIA (VIII-VTH CENTURIES B.C.)

THE oldest historical allusions, Greek and Assyrian, to South Russia belong or refer to the eighth and seventh centuries B.C., and tell us of two peoples who played a prominent part at that period, and not in the history of South Russia alone: the Cimmerians and the Scythian. The Assyrian documents—oracles, letters, and chronicles—belong to the reigns of Sargon II, Sennacherib, Esarhaddon, and Ashurbanipal, that is, to the second half of the eighth and to the seventh century, and reveal to us a somewhat troubled period in the annals of the two great states in the basin of Euphrates—the Chaldian kingdom of Van (Armenia), and Assyria.

Indo-European tribes were advancing from the east and north to the frontiers of these kingdoms. The tribes which are constantly being named are the Gimirrai (Cimmerians) and the Ashguzai (Scythians), the former attacking the Chaldian kingdom from the north, the latter pressing forward, step by step, into the eastern portions of the Vannic and Assyrian kingdoms.

I cannot dwell long upon the history of these movements. We know that the Cimmerians forced their way to the Vannic frontier as early as the end of the eighth century; invaded part of the kingdom, which was enfeebled by contests with Sargon II, in the last years of the century, after 714; and probably succeeded in mingling with the Vannic population. At the beginning of the seventh century, when Rusas II was king of Van (680-645 B.C.), and Esarhaddon and Assurbanipal of Assyria, the Cimmerians, in alliance with Rusas II and with several Indo-European tribes, such as the Medes (Madai), the Mannaeans, the Sakerdians, began a fierce struggle with Assyria. There is good reason to suppose that this struggle was partly caused by the heavy pressure of the Scythians, advancing eastwards in force on the Vannic kingdom and its eastern neighbours. The common interest of the Scytnians and of the Assyrians accounts for the alliance concluded between Esarhaddon and the Scythian king, Bartatua, which was undoubtedly aimed at the allied Chaldians and Cimmerians. The defeats which the enemies of Assyria sustained in this conflict, and the subsequent advance of the Scythians, forced the Cimmerians, about 660, to invade Asia Minor, where they encountered resistance from the kingdom of Lydia, assisted by Assyria. Repulsed the Cimmerians renewed their onslaught in 652, and succeeded in destroying the Lydian kingdom and pillaging the whole of Eastern Asia Minor. A fresh Assyrian attack, and the victorious advance of the Scythians about 637, broke the power of the Cimmerians, and reduced their kingdom to a fraction of Cappadocia, which remained permanently Cimmerian: Cappadocia was always called Gimir by the Armenians. It was now the turn of the Scythians: they carried terror and destruction all over Asia Minor, especially the southern and eastern parts, which they ruled for twenty-eight years. Some parts of the country were occupied by the Scythians permanently: Sakasene and Skythene in Armenia were always peopled by Scythian tribes. It was the Medes, and after them the Persians, who put an end to the anarchy which these two terrible invasions had caused in Asia Minor.

Parallel with this Assyrian tradition, which is confirmed by the archaeological data mentioned in the first chapter, we have another tradition, this time Greek, referring to the same events, not, however, from the point of view of Asiatic history, but from that of the Greeks who dwelt on the northern shore of the Black Sea. We hear in the Odyssey of a people called Cimmerians who lived in a mythical country of fog and darkness on the shore of the Euxine. Greek mythology always connected the Black Sea, the Euxine, with the world of departed spirits. The White Island of Achilles, the land of the Hyperboreans, the Crimea, were at once real countries and regions peopled with the souls of heroes. It is the same in the Odyssey, although the writer of the passage may well have heard of real Cimmerians inhabiting the northern shore of the Black Sea. A little later, Greek historic tradition incorporated in its historical and geographical treatises distant memories of the events which took place in the Asia of the seventh century B.C. I mean the traditions which tell the story of the world empires of Ninus and Sesostris. Many attempts have been made to reconcile these historic legends with the established facts of Mesopotamian and Egyptian history. For my own part, I believe that the legends do reflect historical tendencies in these countries, but that it is very difficult to assign them to a definite period. Had I to choose among more or less probable hypotheses, my choice would fall on the period in which the last Assyrian and Egyptian dynasties, having repulsed the Scythian attacks, were anxious to justify, by means of such legends, their aspirations to that universal dominion which was crumbling under Iranian assaults: at that epoch, I should conjecture, the legends were transmitted from east to west and became part of Greek historical tradition.

More important, and nearer to the truth, is the Greek tradition which tells the story of the conquest of South Russia by the Scythians and of their struggles with the Cimmerians. It may be supposed to have grown up from the sixth century onwards in the Greek colonies on the shores of the Black Sea, and to have been based on ancient local tradition.

Some echoes of this tradition have been preserved by Herodotus and by Strabo, who tell us of a great Cimmerian kingdom by the Black Sea, occupying the northern shore of the Black Sea, with its nucleus on both shores of the straits of Kerch. Aeschylus, Herodotus, and Strabo give the names of several localities, situated in what was later the kingdom of the Bosphorus, which were closely connected with the Cimmerians: the straits of Kerch were invariably known, in Greek tradition, as the Cimmerian Bosphorus; a part of the straits, near Panticapaeum, was called the ferry of the Cimmerians; a number of fortified places on the straits were called the Cimmerian forts; the whole country is described by Herodotus as the Cimmerian land, especially the northern part of the Taman peninsula, which is separated from the rest of the peninsula by an earth wall which was believed to be Cimmerian; finally, there were two towns, on the banks of the straits, which bore the name of Kimmerikon or Kimmerie.

Erwin Rohde wished to explain these reminiscences as due to the archaizing tendency of the kings of the Bosphorus, anxious to connect their kingdom with Homeric legend. It cannot be denied that the tyrants and the peoples of the Bosphorus had a kind of romantic tenderness for the traditions which linked the kingdom with the Amazons, the Arimaspians, and the Cimmerians. One has only to think of the hundreds of vases in the so-called Kerch style, belonging to the decadent period of red-figured vase-painting, with representations of Amazons fighting with Greeks, of Arimaspians fighting with griffins. But this by no means implies that all these traditions were invented by the tyrants of the Bosphorus. The rulers and their subjects merely laid hold of a tradition which already existed and had often been repeated, and perpetuated it in their art and in their literature. Like the legends of Amazons and Arimaspians, the geographical names which recall the Cimmerians unquestionably go back to the sixth or the seventh century, and at that period we have no right to suppose that the earliest Greek colonists were archaistically minded, or that they regarded the Cimmerians with particular warmth. There is no doubt that when the colonists arrived they found strong and actual traces of the Cimmerians in their new home.

Herodotus, who probably used an earlier literary source, very likely Hecataeus of Miletus, was able to tell the story of the last moments of the Cimmerian kingdom. The Scythians expelled them, vanquished them, and pursued them along the shores of the Black Sea and into Asia Minor. Herodotus' account, though mingled with much legendary matter, is possible and probable. We have already spoken of the Scythian advance in the Assyrian East. It may well have been part of a general advance of Scythian tribes mixed with Mongolians, moving simultaneously along both shores of the Caspian Sea: one body passing north of the Caspian and pouring into South Russia, the other coming from the South Caspian littoral and making for the Vannic kingdom and the Assyrian empire.

Was it this advance that drove the Cimmerians to the Caucasus and the kingdom of Van? Not necessarily. The constant intercourse between the Crimea and Northern Caucasus, and between the Crimea and Transcaucasia—the kingdom of Van—an intercourse which is attested by the archaeological data cited in our second chapter, would lead us to suppose that the southward and westward movement of the Cimmerian tribes began long before the Scythian advance. By their distant expeditions and conquests, the Cimmerians probably enfeebled their centre on the shore of the Black Sea, so that the Scythians were able to split the Cimmerian kingdom in two, and to weaken and destroy, one after the other, the detached wings, after cutting off the advanced bodies of Cimmerians, southward and westward, from their head-quarters, the Cimmerian Bosphorus. My reason for preferring this hypothesis to the Herodotean version is the fact, vouched for by the Assyrian sources, that a Cimmerian movement on the Vannic kingdom took place a long time before the advance of the Scythians: the Cimmerians appear in Asia about the second half of the eighth century, whereas the Scythians do not figure in Assyrian monuments until the time of Esarhaddon. This view is corroborated by Strabo, who mentions a Cimmerian invasion of Asia Minor by way of Thrace and the Dardanelles, which presupposes a branch of the Cimmerian people established near the mouths of the Dnieper and expelled from that region by the Scythians: this branch was also known to the authority used by Herodotus: its existence bears witness to the wide expansion of the Cimmerian empire. However this may be, it is certain that the Scythians occupied the entire region which had previously belonged to the Cimmerians in the Russian steppes. But I doubt if they succeeded in dislodging the Cimmerians from the Taman peninsula, any more than in conquering the Crimean highlands, which were peopled by the Taurians. There is a very obscure tradition, often repeated by Greek writers, of a fierce struggle between the Scythians and the Maeotians, especially the Sindians, on both shores of the Cimmerian Bosphorus and on the shores of the Sea of Azov. The legend of the origin of the Sauromatians, mentioned in my second chapter, and another, reported by Herodotus, of a prolonged conflict between the Scythians and opponents who according to Herodotus were the sons of Scythian women by slaves, according to other very ancient authorities, Sindians, suggest that the Scythians were unable to penetrate into the Taman peninsula, which is protected by marshes on one side and by the Cimmerian Bosphorus on the other. They even tried to cross the straits in winter, but probably without success. The Cimmerians and Sindians managed to organize resistance and to preserve their independence.

To judge from the testimony quoted above, the Cimmerians remained sufficiently long on the shores of the Black Sea to leave numerous vestiges behind them when they were expelled. Unhappily we have no evidence, either as to the time of their first appearance in South Russia, or as to the length of their stay. Were they descendants of the autochthonous inhabitants who made the graves with contracted skeletons; or conquerors from the north, the west, or the east? The question is as difficult as that of their nationality. Certain indications would lead us to recognize in the Cimmerians one or more peoples of Indo-European, probably Thracian, origin. Strabo, in a passage which has often been quoted, identifies them with the Trerians, who were certainly Thracians. Others, on the strength of royal names like Teuspa, which seem to be Iranian, have argued in favour of their Iranian extraction. I prefer the former hypothesis, and for the following reasons. In the Assyrian references, and in such passages of Greek writers as go back to good sources, the Cimmerians are never confused with the Scythians. On the other hand, certain facts can only be explained by a Thracian origin: first, the presence of numerous Thracian names, side by side with Iranian ones, among the inhabitants of Tanais in the Roman period; secondly, the existence, hitherto unexplained, of a dynasty of kings with Thracian names ruling in the Cimmerian Bosphorus and in the Taman peninsula from the fifth century B.C. I can only account for these facts if there was a strong Thracian element in the population of the Greek towns in the state of the Bosphorus, and especially among the governing classes. I would say the same of the reigning families among the Sindians in the Taman peninsula.

Unhappily, we have no archaeological data to verify these hypotheses. I have every reason to believe that two seventh-century graves—one discovered in the interior of the Taman peninsula, the other near Kerch on a hill called Temir Gorá—belong to the indigenous population, to the native aristocracy of Cimmerians mixed with Sindians. My supposition is confirmed by the very peculiar weapons found in the former of the two graves, especially the bronze battle-axe, and by the openwork belt-clasp, with two lions in a heraldic attitude, from the same tomb (pl. V, 1, 2, 4): both axe and clasp are quite different from the objects typical of Scythian sixth-century graves, and the clasp recalls the heraldic figures on the pole-heads of Cappadocia—another refuge of the Cimmerians (see pl. II and pl. V, 3). A bronze statuette of a galloping horseman with a quiver, in a style recalling the Cappadocian bronzes, may represent a native horseman, a Maeoto-Cimmerian chief of the region of the Kuban (pl. V, 5). Finally, I am inclined to recognize Cimmerians or Sindians in the opponents of the Scythians on the Solokha gorytus (pl. XXI). There is a strong contrast between the tall, handsome figures of these two warriors, apparently victorious, and the Scythian horseman and foot-soldiers with their half-Mongolian faces, who bear the same weapons as are always found in Scythian graves. The weapons of the victorious foot-soldiers resemble those from the Taman grave: the principal piece is a battle-axe of bronze or iron.

PLATE V

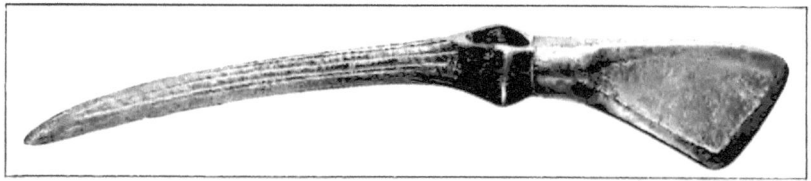

1

2

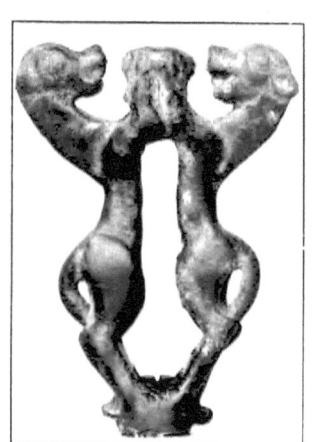

3

4

5

1, 2, 4. AXE, ARROW-HEADS, BELT-CLASP (ALL BRONZE) FROM A
TAMAN GRAVE
VII Cent. B.C. Hermitage, Petrograd
3. BRONZE POLE-TOP FROM CAPPADOCIA. British Museum
5. BRONZE STATUETTE OF A HORSEMAN FROM THE KUBAN
Hermitage, Petrograd

I should also like to draw attention to a curious and interesting find from Bessarabia, published by Ernst von Stern. It belongs to the late bronze age, consists of personal ornaments in diorite, in silver inlaid with gold, and in bronze, and recalls finds of the same class and period from Hungary and from Troy.

I would also mention the famous treasure of Mikhalkovo, and the Daljy fibula which is closely akin to it. Hadaczek, who published a minute study of the Mikhalkovo find, proposed—I think with good reason—to connect it with the Cimmerians. The objects from Mikhalkovo and Daljy are decorated in a mixed style, at once animal and geometric. The Mikhalkovo animal style is very different from the Scythian animal style, and reminds one of the objects found at Kuban in the Caucasus and of Transcaucasian pottery, which are known to belong to the end of the bronze age and to the early iron age, just the period in which we might place the first attempts of the Cimmerians to cross the Caucasian mountains and establish themselves in Transcaucasia. There is a rather strange object in the British Museum which is perhaps connected with the objects from Mikhalkovo: a bronze celt of highly developed form, decorated with geometric ornaments, and with a figure of a goat or deer, engraved in a style which resembles that of Mikhalkovo and of Kuban. It was said by the vendor to have come from Kerch.

All these data, however, are too meagre and too doubtful for convincing conclusions.

It is a curious coincidence that the features of armament and costume—bow, spear, and battle-axe—which distinguish the warriors whom we have supposed to be Cimmerians, are reported as characteristic of the Massagetians, whose name recalls that of the Getians, a Thracian people. May we not hazard the hypothesis—a slight modification of Franke's theory—that the Cimmerians were a Thracian people who formed part of the great Indo-European migration: the migration taking place in two bodies, one composed of Iranian and the other of Thracian peoples; the Thracians occupying, in the course of the migration, the shores of the Black Sea and the region of the Danube? We shall see that the Thracians were always the bitter enemies of the Scythians, and that, though driven back by the Scythians, they made many efforts to reconquer the steppes of South Russia.

We do not know the exact date of the events and conflicts which led to the substitution of Scythians for Cimmerians in the South Russian steppes. Herodotus makes these struggles contemporaneous with the invasion of Asia by Cimmerians and Scythians. There is no objection to this date. If we accept it, we must place the conflict of Scythians and Cimmerians in the seventh century. We must notice, however, that this period of expansion has left no traces in the archaeology of South Russia. We have no Scythian graves of the seventh century: the earliest dateable Scythian graves belong to the sixth. The reason is simple. The seventh century, in South Russia as in Asia Minor, was a period of perpetual struggles, and the Scythian state, as we know it from Russian tombs and from the description in Herodotus, was not consolidated until the sixth century.

In the sixth century, however, the Scythian kingdom is firmly established, and presents all the features of a settled and centralized state, although it rested, as we shall see, on a feudal basis. For its frontiers we have the account in Herodotus, supplemented by archaeological evidence. An important centre, not mentioned by Herodotus, was the valley of the Kuban. The barrows of Kelermes, the barrows in the villages of Úlski, Kostromskáya, Vorónezhskaya, Máryinskaya, Elizavétinskaya, and others, give us a splendid series of raves, several of which belong to the sixth century, others to the fifth and some to the fourth. Only one later tomb can be attributed to the Scythians, that of Karagodeuáshkh, which dates from the second half of the fourth century or the first half of the third: and Karagodeuáshkh is in the immediate neighbourhood of the Taman peninsula.

Scythian graves of the same period as those in the Kuban valley, the sixth and fifth centuries B.C., have been found in the level part of the Crimea (the Golden Tumulus near Simferópol), in the steppes between Don and Dnieper, close to the Dnieper (Tomakóvka), in the district of Poltava (the tumulus of Shumeyko's farm), and near Elisavetgrád, between the Dnieper and the Bug (the Melgunóv tumulus). This suggests that in the sixth and fifth centuries B.C. the centre of the Scythian state was not in the neighbourhood of the Dnieper, as Herodotus asserts, but farther to the east. Unfortunately, the steppes on the western shore of the Sea of Azov, presumably the centre of Scythian dominion at this period, have never been explored.

It is clear, therefore, that the Scythians ruled the whole region of the South Russian steppes; with the probable exception of the mouths of the Kuban and the Don, where the Cimmerians and the Maeotians held out against their assaults, and the Crimean highlands. But their power extended still farther west. We have conclusive evidence that in the sixth century there were compact bodies of Scythians dwelling in Hungary: this is proved by well-established archaeological finds which have often been studied. The date of these finds is certain, the sixth century B.C. They may be compared with the celebrated Vettersfelde find, published by Furtwängler and belonging to the sixth or fifth century B.C. Vettersfelde, as is well known, is in northern Germany, in the old Slavonic country of Lusatia.

The question arises, whether the Hungarian and Prussian finds bear witness to Scythian ascendancy, or only to Scythian expansion, in regions so remote from the centre of their power. It will be possible to decide this question, when we have more information about the tumuli scattered throughout Bulgaria and Rumania. The finds hitherto made, of which I shall speak later, point to Scythian ascendancy in southern Bulgaria and in the Dobrudzha from the fourth century onwards. Future excavation will show, whether it was confined to that period, or already existed in the sixth century.

This vast territory was governed by conquerors who formed but a minority of the population. It has become customary to speak of the whole of South Russia as peopled by Scythian tribes. Nothing is farther from the truth. Even the description in Herodotus, who is responsible for the habit of applying the name of Scythians to all the inhabitants of South Russia, shows us that the Scythians were no more than a group of Iranian tribes, mixed with Mongolians and constituting the ruling aristocracy. As conquerors and as a dominant minority, the Scythians developed a strictly military organization, resembling the military organization of all the nomad peoples who succeeded them, the Khazars, the various Mongolian tribes—the Torki, the Pechenêgi, the Pólovtsy—and the Tatars. The military chief was the king, who dwelt in an armed camp, surrounded by his army, which was always in battle readiness. In time of peace, the king, the princes and the cavalry lived on the revenues provided by the conquered regions and on the produce of their herds—horses, oxen, cows and sheep. The herds were kept by subjects, whose status did not greatly differ from that of slaves. Being nomads—warriors, herdsmen and hunters—and desiring to preserve their nomadic habits and their nomadic military organization, the Scythian tribes chose for their residence the steppes between Don and Dnieper, which did not lend themselves to agricultural development. But other portions of their kingdom had been agricultural and remained so: the valleys of the Dnieper and its tributaries, the valley of the Bug, and part at least of the Kuban valley. These portions, administered by governors, who were supported by troops, paid tribute in kind. For this purpose the Scythian state was divided into four provinces, each province being subdivided into nomes or districts. We do not know what was the relation between these governors or nomarchs and the king, but we have every reason to suppose that they were so many semi-independent princes, bound to the central power by military and financial ties.

The creation of a strong and united state in the South Russian steppes had momentous consequences. The existence of the Cimmerian kingdom or state had already given rise to commercial intercourse between South Russia and the Mediterranean. Apart from the constant communication between the southern coast of the Black Sea and Asia Minor, which found an echo in the myth, probably Carian in origin, of the Argonauts, and which was probably concerned with the export of metals, we know that the Carians founded several stations on the straits of Kerch and on the Black Sea. They were followed by the Teians (Phanagoria), the Clazomenians, and the Milesians (Panticapaeum). The main object of these establishments was to exploit the fisheries of the Sea of Azov and the Cimmerian Bosphorus. The natives, who were in perpetual conflict with the Scythians, welcomed this colonizing activity, which supplied them with fresh, well-armed assistance. From the very first, they were strongly influenced by the Greeks. Nowhere do we find more Greek pottery of the seventh and sixth centuries than in the Taman peninsula. The same causes led to the creation of a fishing colony at the mouth of the Dnieper and the Bug; this colony was Olbia, and it had a branch on the island of Berezan. All these colonies led a struggling existence in the seventh century: in the sixth, they advanced by leaps and bounds. Excavation has shown, that the sixth century was a period of unequalled prosperity for Panticapaeum, Phianagoria, Hermonassa, and all the Greek cities of the Taman peninsula, as well as for Olbia and the cities in the region of the lower Dnieper.

This powerful impetus can only be explained by the consolidation, in the sixth century, of a strong and settled state on the shores of the Black Sea. Just as the Greek colonies of Asia Minor, and of the southern and western shores of the Black Sea, owed their prosperity to the existence of firm governments in their rear, the Lydian and the Persian kingdoms, so the development of the Black Sea colonies into wealthy and populous cities was due to the formation of the Scythian state in the steppes of South Russia.

The Iranians were always frightened of the sea: they never were and never wished to become sailors. But they were always anxious to be in regular touch with the sea, so as to sell their wares and purchase the products, which they prized highly, of Ionian Greece: stuffs, jewels, metal for weapons, wine and oil. They gave in exchange the goods which they received as tribute from their subjects: corn; leather, the product of their stock-rearing; slaves, raided from neighbouring countries; furs and precious metals, toll levied on the trade with north and east. In order to maintain this intercourse, profitable to themselves and especially to the kings and the aristocracy, the Scythians favoured the Greek colonies, left them unmolested, entered into personal relations with them, and probably contented themselves with levying a nominal tribute as a sign of sovereignty. Neither from Herodotus, nor from other sixth or fifth century sources, do we hear of any conflict between the Greek colonies and the Scythians. As a consequence both parties, the Greeks in the towns, and the Scythian aristocracy, grew, as the excavations show, extremely rich. I shall return to the subject of the Greek colonies: I now proceed to give a brief account of the results of excavation in the Scythian barrows of this period.

Our knowledge of Scythian funerary ceremonial in the sixth and fifth centuries B.C., derived from the barrows excavated in the valley of the Kuban, corresponds pretty nearly with Herodotus' account of the obsequies of Scythian kings and princes. Herodotus' description is as follows:

'The kings are buried in the land of the Gerrhoi. When the king dies, they dig a great square pit. The belly of the corpse is slit, cleared, filled with chopped sedge, frankincense, parsley seed and anise, and sewn up again, and the body waxed over, and put on a cart, and brought to another tribe. The tribesmen do as the Royal Scythians: they lop their ears, they shave their hair, they slash their arms, they slit their foreheads and noses, they thrust arrows through their left hands. Then they convey the corpse in the cart to another tribe: the former tribe going with them. When they have gone round all the tribes with the corpse, they are in the land of the Gerrhoi, who are the farthest of the subject tribes, and the burial ground is reached. There they put the body in the grave, on a mattress, and stick spears on either side of the corpse, and poles over it, and a roof of mats. In the empty part of the grave they bury one of the king's concubines, whom they strangle, and his cupbearer, a cook, a groom, a servant, a messenger, horses, and firstlings of all his possessions, and cups of gold: they do not use silver or bronze. After this they all make a great mound, striving with each other in their eagerness to make it as great as they can. A year after, they do something else: they take the best of the king's attendants; the king's attendants are true-born Scythians, commanded by the king to serve him, for they have no bought slaves; well, they strangle fifty of them, and his fifty fairest horses, and they gut them and clean the belly and fill it with chaff and sew it up. Then they set two half-wheels, without the spokes, ends up, each on a pair of posts: and make many such frames, and run a stout stake through each horse lengthwise from rump to neck and hoist it on to the frame, so that the first half-wheel supports the shoulders, and the second the belly by the groin, and the legs all hang free. They bridle them and bit them, and take the reins forward and fasten them to pegs. Then they mount one of the fifty strangled youths on each horse: they run a straight stake through the corpse along the spine as far as the neck, and the piece of the stake which hangs out below they fasten into a socket in the stake which runs through the horse. They set these horsemen in a circle about the tomb, and then retire.'

The excavations have not confirmed every detail of Herodotus' account. But they give the same general picture of the funeral of a nomad chief, the owner of herds of horses and of immense wealth in gold and silver. I will endeavour to give, not a description of a particular tumulus, but a general view of the sepulchral ritual as revealed by excavation in the Kuban valley, illustrating my account by plans of various tumuli (figs. 3-5).

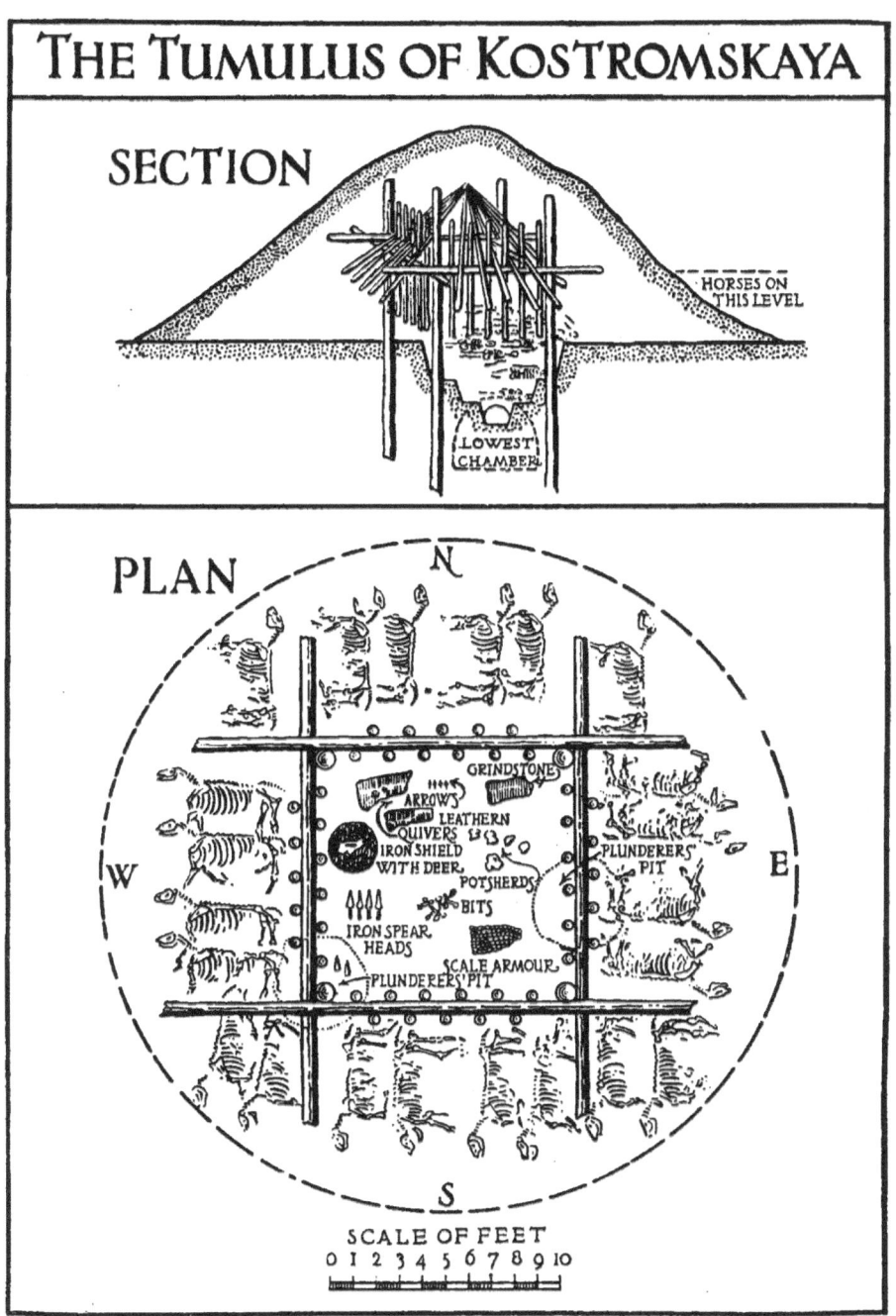

Fig. 3.

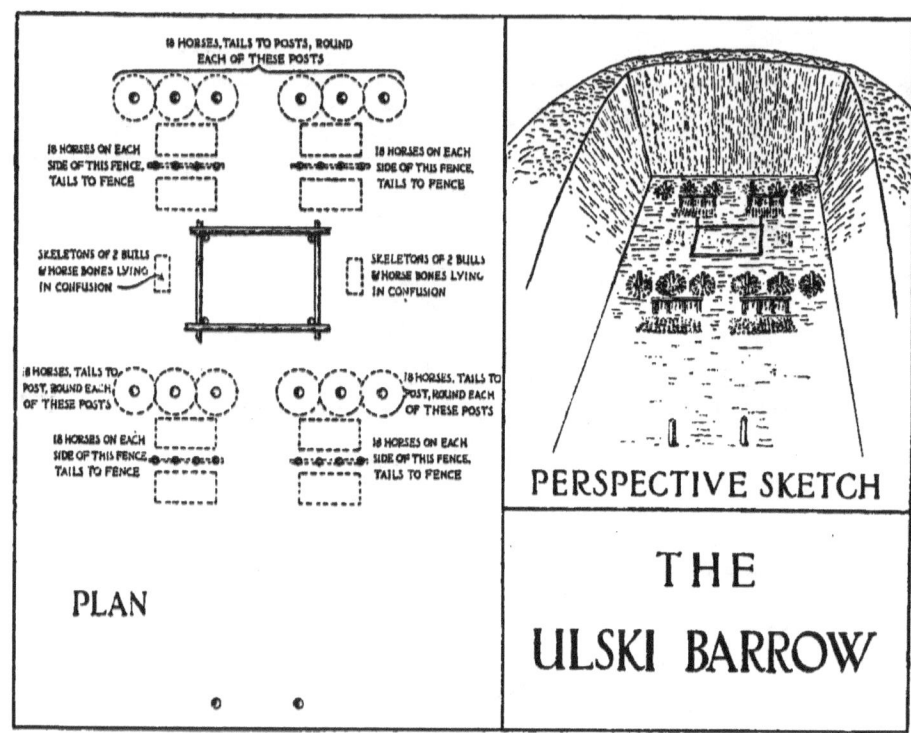

Fig. 4.

Before constructing the grave of a Scythian chieftain, a clearing was made in the steppes. A trench, often of considerable size, was then dug in the virgin soil, with a corridor sloping down to it. Beams were placed along the walls of the trench and of the corridor: the trench was covered with a conical, and the corridor with a gabled roof. The roof of the tomb chamber was also supported by strong beams planted in the middle of the trench. The cubical frame of the tomb was probably lined with mats and rugs, so as to make an almost exact copy of a nomadic tent. Under the tent, another smaller one was sometimes constructed to contain the body of the chief and the treasures which were buried with him. In the fourth century, under Greek influence, this tent was replaced by a chamber of dressed stone with a wooden roof. Round the central tent containing the chief's body, other skeletons are nearly always found, sometimes female, but usually male, the female richly adorned, the male unadorned but furnished with weapons. Round the chamber, on the edge of the trench, bodies of horses sometimes several hundreds, were disposed in regular order. In the Úlski tumulus (fig. 4) the bodies of the horses were grouped round the pillars of the tent, with wooden structures, almost certainly horse-stalls, beside them. In one of the tumuli at Elizavétinskaya (fig. 5), two chariots were found in the corridor leading to the trench and to the sepulchral tent, each drawn by six horses, two abreast.

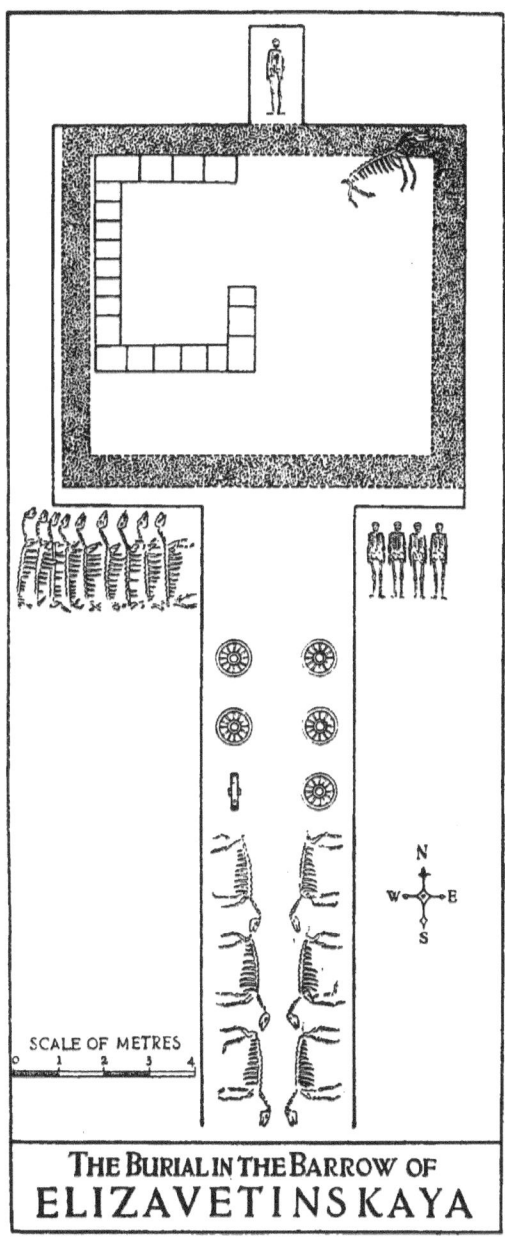

Fig. 5.

The wealth buried with the chieftain was sometimes enormous. The objects were not accumulated haphazard. Even in the sixth century, there was a regular funerary procedure. The chief was buried with his richly decorated panoply; with sacred vases of gold and silver—rhyton, phiale, drinking cups; with a number of copper vessels, of a purely Asiatic shape, containing meat, and with Greek amphorae containing oil and wine; with women, bejewelled, and arrayed in festal costume; with armed retainers; with horses, their bridles bedizened with gold, silver, bone and bronze. Beside the horses, we often find bronze rattles crowned with heads of animals or birds, and a great number of bells. The rattles were undoubtedly fixed on wooden poles: they are very frequently found in sets of four, all alike. There is every reason to suppose that these objects formed part of one or more funerary canopies.

From these data we can reconstruct the Scythian funerary ceremonial: essentially a nomadic ceremonial, cruel, bloody, and luxurious; closely resembling, in its essential features, the Chinese funerary ceremonies of the Han and later dynasties. The grave itself was a reproduction of the sumptuous tent in which the dead man had dwelt. The body was borne to the sepulchral tent in procession. The dead chief, and the persons sacrificed in his honour, clad in festal attire and accompanied by the sepulchral furniture, were placed on funeral chariots, each drawn by six horses, or on biers carried by retainers. Canopies were held above the bodies, attached to poles surmounted by rattles and covered with bells: if the body was conveyed in a chariot, the canopy was set up over the chariot (pl. X, B, D, E). The procession was probably preceded by one or more standard-bearers, the standards being crowned, like the poles of the canopy, by emblematic figures in bronze (pl. X, A, C). As the horses also wore bells (pl. X, E), the procession made a vast din, intended to drive away the evil spirits. When the sepulchral tent was reached, the bodies were laid in the grave, with the objects grouped about them; the horses were slaughtered and their corpses disposed around and within the tent; the canopy and the chariot were broken and placed near the tomb, sometimes in the corridor. The ceremony over, the grave was covered with earth, and a barrow, of imposing height, raised above it. A primitive, materialistic and superstitious rite, thoroughly nomadic. In itself it presents little historical interest.

PLATE VI

ENGRAVED AND GILT SILVER MIRROR
From Kelermes, Kuban. VI Cent. B.C. Hermitage, Petrograd

But the objects interred with the bodies are extremely interesting, and enable us to apprehend the various currents of civilization which met in the South Russian steppes. The richest archaic finds were made in the barrows of Kelermes on the Kuban, in the barrow excavated by Melgunov near Elisavetgrád, and at Vettersfelde in the south of Prussia. The two former finds are contemporary and almost identical, the third presents some essential differences and belongs to a later period, the sixth to the fifth century B.C. I shall begin with Kelermes, a find which has never been entirely published. Among the rich and varied objects from Kelermes, we can clearly distinguish the furniture of one or more male burials and of one or more female. What strikes us particularly in these objects is their mixed character.

Side by side with objects which were undoubtedly imported from Asia Minor, and which offer all the characteristic features of sixth century Ionian and Aeolian art, such as the engraved silver rhyton with Greek mythological subjects, a bronze helmet of pure Greek shape, a gold diadem decorated with rosettes and flying birds, we have objects the origin of which cannot be determined except by an exhaustive analysis of their style and their subjects. I refer particularly to the gilt silver mirror, engraved with figures of animals in a peculiar style, and with a figure of the Great Goddess of Asia, πότνια θηρῶν (pl. VI). To the same category belong several articles of uncertain use, perhaps belt-clasps, decorated with animals' heads and inlaid with amber in a technique which reminds one of cloisonné enamel (pl. IX, 2). It might be supposed that these objects were made in Persia by artists of Asia Minor. Besides these, we have objects of pure Oriental style which were probably made in the Persian kingdom during the sixth century B.C., precious specimens of that archaic Persian art with which we are but ill acquainted. Characteristic examples are two gold vases in a purely Oriental style recalling that of late Assyrian objects (pl. VII), and a gold-plated scabbard ornamented with fantastic figures of quadrupeds, some of them with fish-shaped wings and human foreparts, all drawing bows (pl. VIII, 2). It must be noticed that the side-projection of the scabbard is not decorated in the Assyrian style, but in another quite different style. The figure is that of a deer, lying down or leaping, with heads of eagles forming a border. This style, very primitive, and at the same time highly refined, is what is called the Scythian animal style: it predominates, though mixed with Assyrian motives, in a number of most important objects from the Kelermes find. One of them is a battle-axe of iron plated with gold, the handle of which is decorated with a series of animals, standing or at rest (pl. VIII): another is a golden lion, which probably adorned the breast-piece of a scaled corslet (pl. IX, 1): there are also several gold plaques which were sewn on to garments. The golden lion is particularly interesting because of the curious combination of the Scythian animal style with amber incrustation in the cloisonné manner mentioned above. Another feature of these objects which deserves attention is the simultaneous use of the Scythian animal style and of the Assyro-Persian style. In the scabbard the contrast between the two styles is very strongly marked: yet it cannot be doubted that the different parts of the scabbard were all fashioned by the same artist. In the battle-axe the two elements are similarly juxtaposed, but here it is the Scythian animal style that predominates.

The same mixture is observable in the objects found by General Melgunov, in the eighteenth century, near Elisavetgrád, and recently published by Pridik: they include a scabbard which is almost a replica of the scabbard from Kelermes. Remains of a canopy came to light. Just as at Maikop in the copper age, the lower ends of the poles which supported the canopy were wrought separately in gilt silver: likewise the pole-tops, which closely resemble those from Maikop. The tissue which covered the canopy was decorated with gold eagles, wings displayed. Very characteristic also, the golden torc or diadem, the rosettes of which are inlaid with onyx.

I must also mention another find of this period: the tumulus of Shumeyko's farm, in the district of Poltava: it dates from the sixth century, as is shown beyond question by a fragment of a black-figured vase. The most important object in this find is a dagger, the sheath of which is mounted in gold and decorated with embossed figures in the Scythian animal style (pl. VIII, 3). Here we must notice the combination of embossed work with very delicate granulated work. The pieces of bridle-trappings in bone, found in the same tumulus, are examples of the pure animal style, with its characteristic predominance of birds' heads.

PLATE VII

1

2

TWO GOLD CUPS FROM KELERMES, KUBAN
VI Cent. B.C. Hermitage, Petrograd

PLATE VIII.

1, 2. IRON AXE AND IRON SWORD WITH WOODEN SCABBARD, all covered with gold. From Kelermes, Kuban. Hermitage, Petrograd.
3. IRON DAGGER AND SCABBARD, COVERED WITH GOLD. Shumeyko's Farm, near Romny. Kiev, Archaeological Museum VI Cent. B.C.

I shall often have occasion to speak of that Scythian animal style which we here encounter for the first time: but I shall mention, before going farther, its most characteristic features. I said above that it was at once very primitive and highly refined. The main principle is the purely ornamental treatment of the animal figure. In the archaic specimens which we have before us, there is none of the geometrical tendency noticeable in the pottery of Susa, nor any tendency to transform the figure of the animal into a vegetable ornament. In general, the animals are treated realistically. And the realism is vigorous and powerful. But at the same time the animal figure is used exclusively as ornament. There is no attempt to form groups or scenes: the sole preoccupation of the artist is to decorate the object with a number of figures. The only kind of group is the antithetic or heraldic. For the sake of ornamental effect, the artist does not hesitate to place his animals in attitudes which are sometimes taken from nature, but which are immoderately exaggerated and occasionally quite fantastic. He allows himself to cut the animal into pieces, and to use the head of a bird, for instance, as if it were an ornament. The bird's head is often repeated dozens of times, and is employed to form friezes and borders. A common practice is to shape the extremities of animals as birds' heads or griffins' heads. As a general rule, however, the artist shows no predilection, as yet, for the fantastic creatures of Babylono-Assyrian art: he restricts himself to real animals naturalistically rendered. Note that he already employs a polychromatic inlaid technique, even for the figures of animals: for example, for the ears of the golden lion from Kelermes; also in the belt-clasps from the same place, and in the diadem from Melgunov's find.

In the weapons, then, and in the tomb furniture from Kelermes, we find Greek objects side by side with Assyrian and with specimens of a mixed style which we may call Scytho-Assyrian: on the other hand, in the chariot ornaments, in the canopies, and in the horses' trappings, the Scythian animal style reigns unopposed. Take the pole-tops from the canopies: rattles surmounted by heads of animals and birds, strange standards representing a human eye planted in the middle of the head of a bird of prey, the surface of the head being ornamented with figures of animals and with beaks and eyes of birds (pl. X). There is nothing of the kind in the orientalism of Ionian Greece.

PLATE IX

1. GOLD PECTORAL OF A SCALE-CORSLET. VI CENT. B.C.
From Kelermes, Kuban. Hermitage, Petrograd

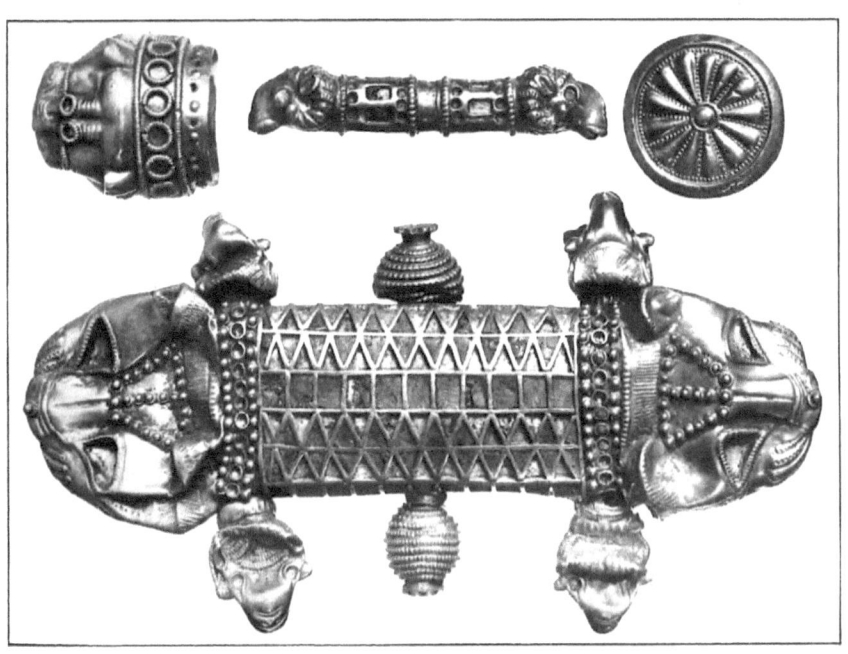

2. GOLD ORNAMENTS INLAID WITH AMBER. VI CENT B.C.
From Kelermes, Kuban. Hermitage, Petrograd

Scythian civilization changes its aspect in the fifth century. Look for a moment at the Vettersfelde find, and the others that go with it, look at the tumuli of the Seven Brothers in the Kuban valley, and the native tumuli in the cemetery of Nymphaeum. The Vettersfelde find consists of a dagger-sheath, a pectoral, a horse's frontlet in the form of a fish covered with figures of animals, plaques from a bridle, and jewels. The shapes of these objects are purely Iranian, the decorative principles also—rows of animals one following another, extremities transformed into animals' heads, and so forth. But the animals themselves are the work of Greek artists, and exhibit all the peculiarities of Ionian animals: the arrangement also betrays the hand of a Greek. Thus we see Ionian craftsmen working for the Scythian market, executing special orders, an adapting themselves to the taste of their customers.

The same tendency is observable in other finds which are closely akin to that of Vettersfelde: the tumulus of Tomakóvka on the lower Dnieper, and the so-called Golden Tumulus near Simferopol in the Crimea. We notice particularly a pronounced taste for polychromy. The polychromy is obtained by means of coloured enamels fastened to the objects in a technique which is the precursor of cloisonné enamel. Good examples are the sword-sheaths, almost identical in both finds and very like the dagger-sheath from Vettersfelde; and the lioness from the Golden Tumulus, which either decorated a quiver or was placed on the corslet as a pectoral badge. The body of the lioness is covered all over with scales of enamel, each scale consisting of a compartment filled with coloured inlay.

I must also mention a very characteristic find from the Kuban, which belongs to the same period: a round openwork clasp or phalara of bronze (see fig. 21 B in chapter VIII). The frame is formed by two lions biting each other's tails, and in the middle there is a lioness with head regardant: the whole design is vigorous and effective. The motive recurs on a number of bronze plaques from the barrows of the Seven Brothers, of which we shall presently speak. It is interesting to know that a find resembling that of Kelermes was made in Southern Caucasus, at the village of Zakim in the district of Kars. The chief piece is a bronze belt in the same style as the objects from Kelermes. We can see one of the routes by which objects of the Kelermes type reached Northern Caucasus.

PLATE X

BRONZE POLE-TOPS AND A BRONZE BELL
From the Kuban. VI, V Cent. B.C., Hermitage, Petrograd

Extremely important finds have been made in the group of kurgans on the Kuban which the inhabitants call the Seven Brothers. Some of the graves certainly go back to the fifth century B.C.; another may be later, of the fourth century B.C. Unhappily the objects have never been thoroughly studied, although Stephani devoted several pages to them in the Reports of the Archaeological Commission. Some of the finds are pure Greek: Attic red-figured and black varnished vases; silver vases engraved and gilded (pl. XV, 3); bronze candelabra; jewels of exquisite finish, for example, a pair of snake bracelets (pl. XV, 1); gold plaques sewn on garments; and so forth. As far as I can judge, some of these articles were made in Athens, and others in Asia Minor. The gold plaques may have been manufactured at Panticapaeum, on partly Greelz, partly Scythian models. But side by side with Greek imports, we have Oriental; such as the silver rhyton terminating in the forepart of a wild goat (pl. XII, A), which recalls Hittite and Cappadocian works of art. It is exactly analogous to the famous handles from Armenia, part of a bronze vase, one of which is in the Louvre and the other in the Berlin Museum; and to certain bronze objects, of the same type and the same provenience, now in the Louvre. We may perhaps assign the same origin to the numerous rhyta of gold and horn, terminating in the foreparts of animals, which were placed in the tumuli of the Seven Brothers: we still possess the golden portions—the lower ends and the plaques which decorated the mouths (pls. XII, B, C, and XIII): the plaques are embossed with figures of beasts and birds of prey, sometimes fantastic, devouring goats, deer, or hares. The same style appears on the famous silver plaque, the pectoral of a corslet, with figures of a deer suckling her young, and, below it, of an eagle with wings displayed. We are so unfamiliar with the art of Eastern Asia Minor, that it is not easy to find convincing analogies: the style, in my opinion, is at any rate not Ionian. It must be noticed that side by side with plaques of exquisite work we find others which are unquestionably imitations, influenced by the Scythian animal style. In a find which has lately been acquired by the Berlin Museum, and has not yet been published, I saw objects which were perfectly analogous to the plaques described above.

The only articles from the tumuli of the Seven Brothers, which show the Scythian animal style in a pure form, belonged to bronze horse-trappings: prodigious numbers of horses were buried with the dead. In these there is a tendency, unknown in the sixth century, to transform the animals into palmettes and other floral ornaments (see fig. 21, C, F, G, and fig. 22, A, B, E, in chapter VIII).

I have already stated, that the native graves in the cemetery of Nymphaeum, the raves of the hellenized Scythians of the Crimea, present the same characteristics as the tumuli of the Seven Brothers, and belong to the same period, the fifth and fourth centuries B.C.

The fourth century brings no change on the Kuban, beyond the continual growth of Greek influence, which even shows itself in the choice of armour: for example, besides the Greek helmets, greaves and Greek corslets come into vogue. A fine specimen of a Greek breastplate was recently found by Veselóvski in a tumulus in the village of Elizavétinskaya (pl. XIV). The head of Medusa which decorates it looks archaic, but is merely archaistic, and belongs to the end of the first half of the fourth century. We must observe, that at the end of the fifth century and the beginning of the fourth strong Athenian influence makes itself felt, not only in the style of the jewellery, but also through steadily increasing importation of Attic pottery. The Scythian chieftains had a special liking for the large Panathenaic vases with their representations of athletic contests and their majestic figures of the warrior goddess Athena. A Specimen was found in the grave which I have just mentioned.

But Greek influence was not able to kill the Scythian style, which always predominates in horse-trappings. The Scythian style is elaborated and developed, but it remains purely Asiatic. It presents us with strange combinations of floral and animal motives, the animals prevailing. I shall treat the subject at greater length in my eighth chapter. The bronze objects in this style were not the work of Greek craftsmen: a Greek might lay hold of the forms and accept the decorative principle, but he could never create such purely Oriental objects as the bridle plaques from the barrows of the Kuban and the Crimea. Two currents can be detected: one from the south, from Mesopotamia; the other from the north, where in the forests and marshes elk and reindeer fought with the famished wolves: all three animals were unknown to Greek decorative art. The artists were natives, and they are just as likely to have worked in the steppes of the Caucasus as in the Greek towns of the Cimmerian Bosphorus.

To conclude. The Scythian civilization of the fifth and fourth centuries B.C. is already completely formed in the sixth century. It is an aristocratic civilization of nomadic chiefs, mixed and composite. Besides the native element, primitive, but elaborate, even refined, there are two streams of importation and of influence in the sixth century: one Oriental, probably coming from Mesopotamia by way of the Caucasus, and from Asia Minor through the Greek colonies on the southern shore of the Black Sea; the other Greek, coming from the Ionian and Aeolian colonies in Asia Minor. The former weakens towards the end of the fifth century and then almost disappears, the other grows and develops. The Greek artists of Asia Minor begin to work for the Scythians, and to consult their taste. But they have only a general notion of Scythian life: they know the forms of Scythian objects, and the Scythian love of the animal style; but the spirit of their work remains Ionian.

The predominance of the Oriental aspect in sixth-century Scythian civilization is a fact of capital importance, and one which is generally acknowledged. What was the costume of the Scythians of South Russia in the sixth century we do not know. But as we are well acquainted with their costume in the fourth and third centuries, from the representations which I shall quote in the fifth chapter, and as this costume is purely Oriental, we may suppose that it had not changed since the sixth century. It is the Iranian costume which we know from the reliefs of Naksh-i-Rustam and Bisutun (Behistun), and from other monuments of Persian art. I shall not discuss it further, as the facts are well known and have been studied over and over again. As to armour, apart from the bronze helmet and greaves, which were borrowed from the Greeks, the panoply of the Kuban barrows is Iranian: Iranian the scaled corslet with pectoral badge—a kind of cunningly wrought bronze shirt: the spear and the javelins; the arrows with bronze heads of the triangular form which spread with the Iranians all over the ancient world, beginning in the early iron age; the bow of the shape known to the ancients as Scythian and frequently described both by ancients and by moderns; the gorytus, quiver and bowcase in one, of wood covered with leather or metal, an Iranian speciality; the short iron sword; the scabbard, with its side-projection for the chains or straps by which the sword was suspended from the warrior's belt, a type of scabbard convenient for cavalrymen and regularly represented in Persian art; finally, the dagger, often attached by straps to the warrior's left leg, again a handy fashion for cavalrymen armed like foot-soldiers. All this is familiar and has often been set forth: recently by Minns.

It is not so generally known, that the horse-trappings, which we can reconstruct with the aid of many hundreds of pieces from tombs, and particularly the bridle, are of pure Iranian type. The frontlet, the ear-guards, the temple-pieces, the pectoral, the plaques which studded the straps especially at the intersections, the pendent bells, in a word the whole bridle, can only be compared with the horse-trappings in Hittite and Assyrian representations. The pieces, and the system of adjustment, are the same: and there is the same profusion of metal on the straps. But there is one important difference: the ornaments of Assyrian and Hittite bridles are almost always geometric, whereas the Scythian ornaments, with few exceptions, show the forms of that peculiar animal style which I have already described. In my account of Scythian funeral customs, I mentioned more than once that the corpse was protected by a canopy, spread over the funeral car or carried by retainers, which was supported by four poles with rattles on the top crowned either by figures of animals or by animals' heads. The poles supported a piece of cloth, on which gold plaques were probably sewn. Several of the rattles are crowned with heads of bulls, mules, or griffins (pl. X, B-D). The use of funeral canopies is purely Oriental: we saw it at Maikop, in the copper age, and it persisted all over the East. Oriental also the use of poles surmounted by heads of animals or other emblems: these poles occur in all parts of the Babylonian world; there they signified sceptres or standards, and nearly every divinity is accompanied by one. A similar emblem was borne in front of the Assyrian king: they were the first military standards. So also in Egypt and in the Hittite empire. The Scythians were undoubtedly influenced by this Oriental custom. The pole-top reproduced on plate X, A probably did not form part of a canopy. Its peculiar shape, and its apotropaic decoration, suggest that it was a standard, or one of a pair—for two were found—which were carried at the head of the funeral procession. The shape of the canopy poles was naturally modelled on the standards of the gods or of the kings. The heads seem to be primarily apotropaic: the bell is certainly so. It is interesting to observe that the same custom appears in Cappadocia: I have already mentioned a number of bronze pole-tops from that country in the Louvre and in the British Museum (pl. II): the poles themselves were of wood or iron. These pole-tops are sometimes in the form of a goat perched on a rattle—a purely Assyrian type, which influenced western Siberia: but most of them present a stylized figure, or two figures one above the other, of the Great

Goddess, the Mistress of Beasts. Curiously enough, we find the same goddess on a pole-top, belonging to a canopy, from the kurgan of Alexandrópol, which we shall study in our fifth chapter. The use of the Cappadocian pole-tops may have been funerary or ritual like the South Russian examples, they are furnished with rings for straps or cords.

Thus costume, armour and funeral outfit of the sixth-century Scythians, are all purely Oriental with hardly any Greek influence. Oriental also, as we have seen, the style and technique of most of the objects found in sixth-century Scythian tombs. I need not dwell upon the imported Oriental articles mentioned above: their neo-Assyrian and Ponto-Cappadocian style can be recognized at a glance. Some of the objects in this style are enriched with amber inlay. They need not perplex us. Oriental art, especially Elamitic and Sumerian, used inlay at all periods to diversify the surface of statues, metal objects and palace walls. It is true that the cloisonné method of inlay was not practised till after this period. But we may believe that cloisonné also was invented somewhere in Babylonia or Assyria. Almost the same process was employed for ivory in the neo-Assyrian objects from Nimrud, lately published by Hogarth and by Poulsen, and similar processes were current in Egypt, from the earliest times, for metal objects decorated with precious stones. That the same technique continued to be used in Iranian art, may be seen from two great finds of Iranian objects, both belonging to the fourth century B.C.; the treasure from Turkestan in the British Museum, published with a commentary by Dalton, and the Susa find published by de Morgan and now in the Louvre. These two finds offer striking analogies with the jewellery from the Kuban, and give undoubted proof of common origin. With the inlaid objects I should connect a group of metal articles, chiefly of bronze and of silver, which belong to Scythian horse-trappings of the archaic period: openwork roundels attached to a metal disk, the hollow parts filled with some black substance (fig. 6). This technique also is purely Oriental: parallels are to be found both in Babylonia and Assyria and in Egypt. It is particularly interesting to note, that the same processes were used for Similar objects in Transcaucasia at the end of the bronze and at the beginning of the iron age: we have many tombs from this period, thanks to the excavations of Belck, Roessler, Ivanovski and others, and some of them are astonishingly rich: in nearly every tomb we find roundels like those of the Kuban, and openwork pendants, often in the form of birds or animals, the cavities filled with black inlay. The same technique was in frequent use for sword-hilts and other articles. We may be sure that in this matter Transcaucasia acted as the intermediary between the Euphrates valley and Northern Caucasus. We must avoid, however, the common error of attributing the Transcaucasian tombs to the Chaldian kingdom of Van. That kingdom, as far as we know, is subsequent to the prehistoric civilization of Transcaucasia; it adopted, with only slight modification, the culture of Assyria.

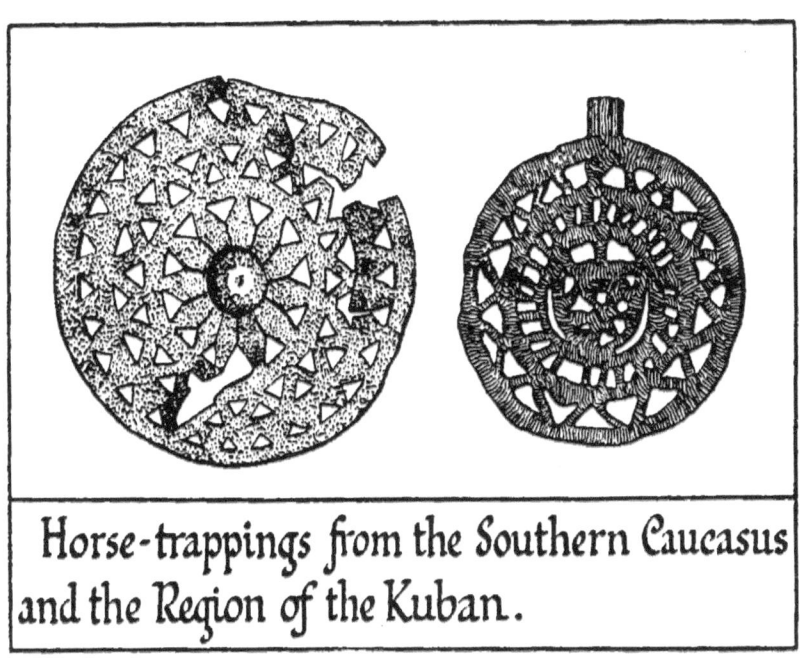

Horse-trappings from the Southern Caucasus and the Region of the Kuban.

Fig. 6.

It is more difficult to class the animal style of objects from the sixth-century Scythian tombs, both in the Kuban and elsewhere. It evidently presents distinctive and very primitive features. We shall discuss the question later; but it should be observed that several of these features reappear in Asiatic art. I would mention certain Hittite figures among the Sinjirli sculptures, the tails of which end in birds' heads. For the animals with reverted heads—a convenient attitude for filling a given space, particularly a circular one—I will quote, in addition to the examples mentioned by Reinach in his paper on the flying gallop, the Assyro-Chaldaean weight found at Susa, in the form of a recumbent wild ass, a form which frequently recurs on old plaques and bridle ornaments from South Russia, especially during the archaic period. Iranian antecedents can be found for the custom of representing animals with their foreparts turned in one direction and their hind-quarters in the other, as on the sword-sheath found near the mouth of the Don, and in several figures, from horse-trappings, found on the Kuban: the motive occurs later in a great number of objects from prehistoric and Sarmatian Siberia. An example is the axe from Hamadan in Persia, now in the British Museum (pl. XI, B): it belongs to a whole series of Persian axes, decorated in the animal style, which are connected by their shape and ornamentation with a group of axes from protohistoric Elam, from Babylon and from Assyria. The British Museum axe has its back part in the form of a Persian lion-headed griffin, winged and horned, with its head reverted: the motive appears as early as Babylonian times on cylinders representing a hero fighting with a lion. The whole series bears a conspicuous resemblance to the objects found in the tumuli of the Kuban. The treatment of the animals is the same as in the heads and figures on the pole-tops of South Russia. Curiously enough, on an axe from Khinaman near Kirman in south-western Persia, close to the frontier of Baluchistan, we find the apotropaic eye which forms the principal decoration of the archaic standard, already mentioned, from the Kuban (pl. XI, E). The most remarkable specimen of this Iranian series, and the one which offers the most striking analogy with kindred objects from South Russia, is the axe from Bactria, of bronze inlaid with silver, recently published by Sir Hercules Read: a symplegma of three animals, a lion fighting with a boar and trampling on a wild goat (pl. XI, A). Apart from the technique of inlay, derived from the process current in Sumerian Babylon, I must draw attention to the combination of three animals in one group, a motive which was taken up by South Russian as well as by Ionian art, and to the reverted heads of the lion and the goat, the prototype of that antithetic arrangement of the animal body which I mentioned above. I reserve a more detailed discussion of the Scythian animal style for my eighth chapter; but I was obliged, before proceeding farther, to point out that this style, albeit very distinctive and very original, only established itself in South Russia after a long period of contact with Assyro-Persian art, during which it was subjected to very powerful influence from that quarter, leading to the amalgamation of motives from both styles which we notice at Kelermes, in the battle-axe and in the lion pectoral with amber inlay.

PLATE XI

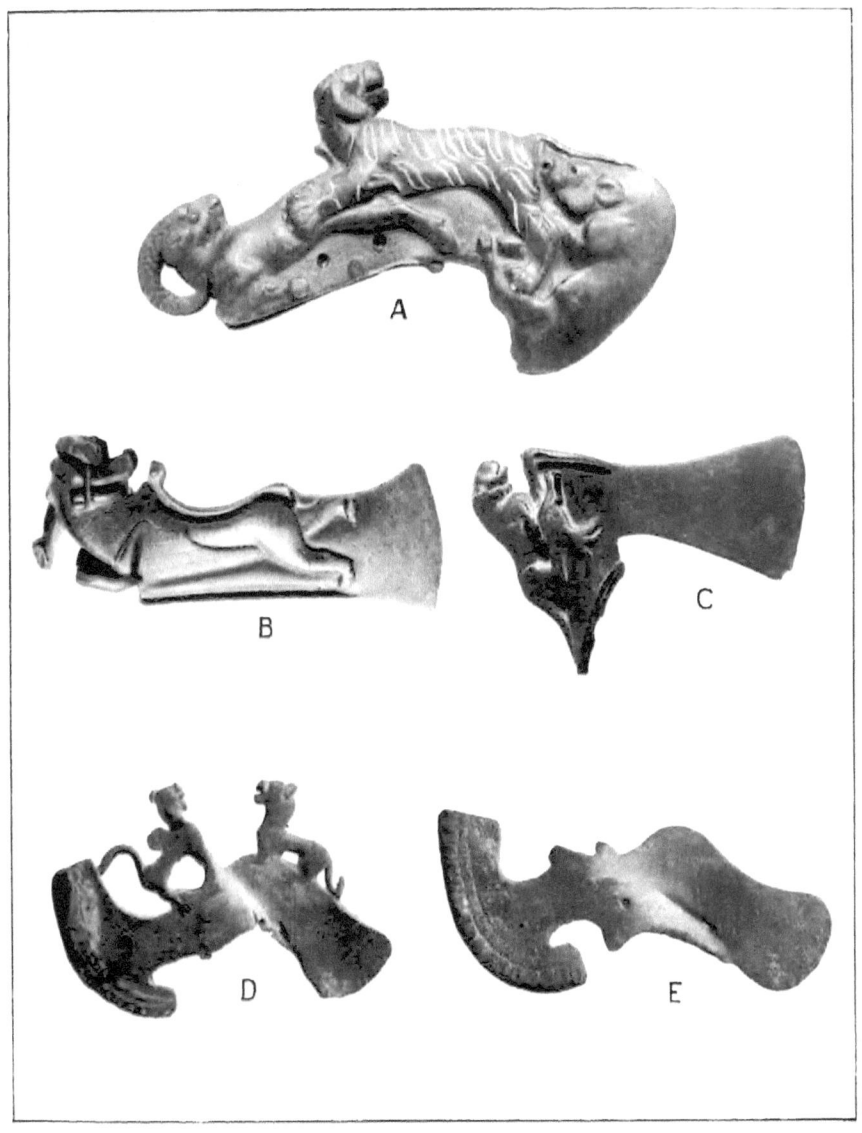

A. BRONZE CEREMONIAL AXE FROM BACTRIA
B. BRONZE CEREMONIAL AXE FROM HAMADAN, PERSIA
C. BRONZE AXE FROM VAN, ARMENIA
D, E. TWO BRONZE AXES FROM PERSIA
British Museum

The Oriental aspect of Scythian civilization in the sixth and fifth centuries could be demonstrated by means of other parallels, and may be taken as proven. We are justified in affirming that Scythian art, at the outset, was a branch of that mixed Iranian art of which hitherto we knew only the Persian branch. The Scyntian branch presents itself on the one hand as a development of motives inherited by Iranian art from the powerful civilization of Mesopotamia and Elam, and on the other as an attempt to combine that art with another, ruder and more primitive, the origin of which is as yet unknown. From the fifth century onwards Scythian art, like Persian, was influenced, more and more strongly, by the Greek art of Ionia. This influence was brought about exclusively by continuous intercourse between the Greek and Scythian world. The intermediaries were the Greek colonies, especially the towns of the Bosphoran kingdom. The subject will be treated at length in the succeeding chapter.

One remark in conclusion. In a general work like the present I cannot dwell in detail on the hotly disputed problem of Scythian nationality. It will have been gathered from the preceding pages, that I believe the Scythians to have been Iranians, although lately several high authorities, such as Geza Nagy, Minns and Treidler, have revived the Mongolian or Turanian theory, which seemed to have been completely disposed of by the judicious observations of Schiefner, Zeuss, Gutschmid, Müllenhoff and Tomaschek. It is difficult to insist on either hypothesis: decisive proofs are lacking on both sides. It has been thought that a conclusive argument in favour of the Iranian theory was furnished by the Iranian names of native or semi-native citizens of Panticapaeum, Tanais and Olbia. But it is forgotten that these names belong to the Roman period, and bear witness to Sarmatian, not Scythian infiltration into the Greek cities. Stress has also been laid on the Mongolian physiognomy of the Scythians as represented on Bosphoran monuments of the fourth and third centuries B.C. But it must be borne in mind that the monuments give two ethnographical types: one Mongolian, as in the gorytus from Solokha, the other Indo-European, as in most of the other monuments. In spite of this I entirely agree with those who believe the Scythians to have been of Iranian extraction, although I readily admit a strong infusion of Mongolian and Turanian blood. My reasons are mainly based on historical, archaeological, and religious considerations, since the study of the language does not provide decisive criteria. Our information about the Ashguzai, who are the same as the Scythians, and about the Sacians; their close affinity with the Sarmatians, whose Iranian nationality is not disputed; and the evidence of Herodotus, confirmed by archaeology, as to the religion of the Pontic Scythians, a matter which we shall discuss later; leave no doubt that the Scythian tribes of South Russia were Iranians, nearly akin to the Medes and Persians, but belonging to another branch of the stock. It is well known that the linguistic evidence, founded on the few Scythian words transmitted to us by the Greeks, is in no way opposed to this hypothesis. But sufficient emphasis has not been laid on the archaeological evidence, which seems to me almost decisive. We have seen that very ancient monuments, which we have every reason for assigning to the Scythians, can only be explained by Iranian parallels; and that it is impossible to define the general character of Scythian art, except by connecting it with Persian art of the same period.

IV.
THE GREEKS ON THE SHORES OF THE BLACK SEA, DOWN TO THE ROMAN PERIOD

I HAVE already spoken of the very ancient relations between the mining districts on the shores of the Black Sea and the peoples of Asia Minor and doubtless of Greece as well. These relations probably date from the same time as the first appearance of iron in what was later the Hellenic world. I have quoted the very old Greek legends as to the origin of iron. Iron and iron weapons were thought to have been the invention of the Chalybians and the Scythians. I am convinced that it was the export of metals from the southeastern corner of the Black Sea which gave rise to the prehellenic, probably Carian, legend of the Argonautic expedition. The Milesian version of the story gave poetic expression to the half-military, half-commercial enterprises of the Carians and other peoples of Asia Minor, sea-raids organized by pirates and intrepid corsairs, always in quest of unknown lands.

It is somewhere about the year 1000 B.C. that we must date two groups of events: the development of the mining industry on the southern shores of the Black Sea, and the first expeditions of Achaeans and Carians in search of iron and of gold. This date is corroborated by a fact which has not hitherto been explained: the complete absence, beyond the straits of the Bosphorus, of that Aegean or Mycenaean influence which is so strong, for example, at Troy. The Cretans of the Minoan epoch, and the Myceneans of the time of Agamemnon, did not frequent the shores of the Black Sea: they had nothing to take them there all their efforts were directed westwards. With the object of procuring an abundant supply of good iron weapons, the heirs of Mycenaean sea-power ventured into the distant Black Sea regions, and opened up the route, later so popular, which led from the Mediterranean, through the straits and along the southern coast of the Black Sea, to the banks of the Thermodon and of the Phasis.

PLATE XII

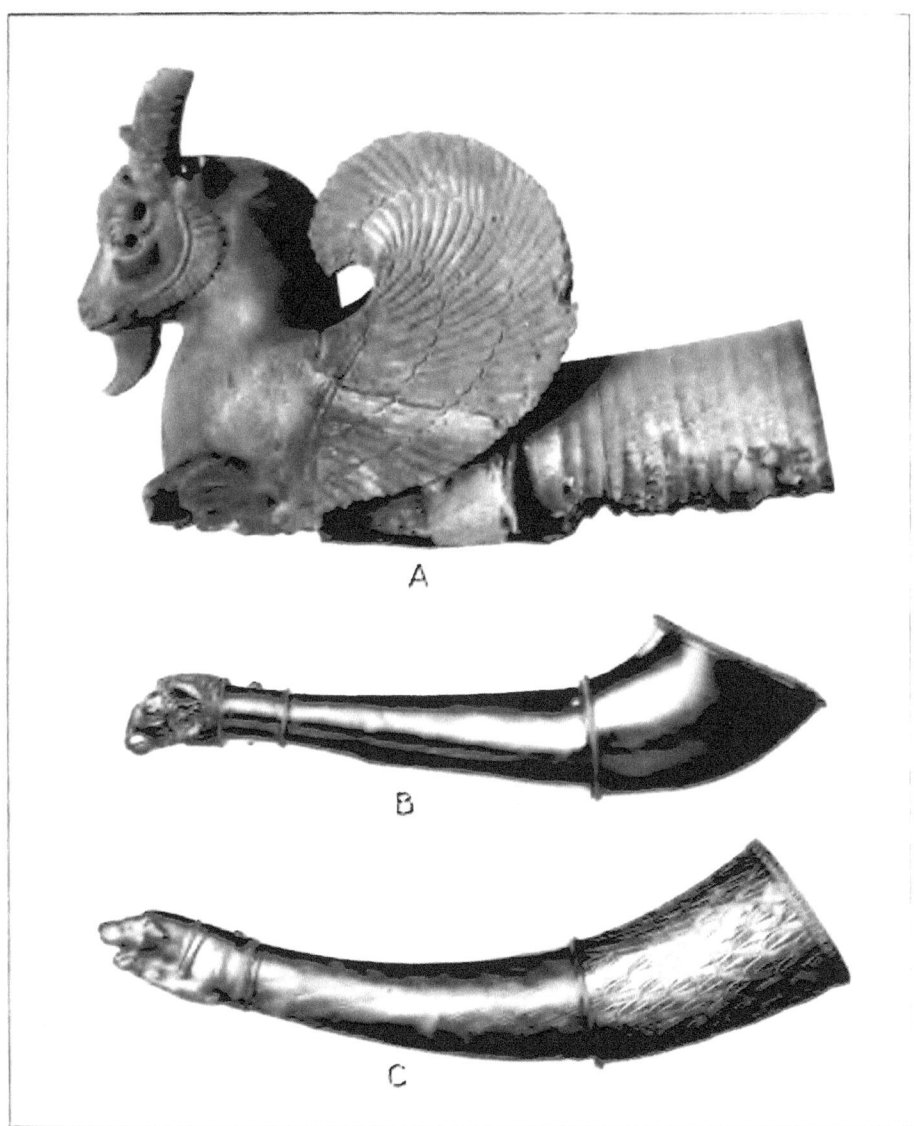

SILVER AND GOLD RHYTA FROM THE 'SEVEN BROTHERS' ON THE KUBAN. V Cent. B.C. Hermitage, Petrograd

The adventurers from Asia Minor soon recognized, that the Black Sea was not only rich in metals, but inexhaustibly rich in fish, and, more important still, that the dwellers on its shores were not ferocious barbarians but fairly civilized people, who had a taste for the products of Asia Minor and were ready to trade. Accordingly they began to found fishing stations on the shores of the Black Sea, advancing slowly, step by step, until they finally reached the heart of the fishing district: the straits of the Bosphorus, and the shores of the Sea of Azov, on the one hand; and, on the other, the mouths of the great Russian rivers. The routes, once open, were never abandoned. The Ionians were the first to follow the example of the Carians, as we can see from the written record. We do not now the Carian version of the Argonautic myth: but we do know the Ionian or Milesian version, which existed as a separate poem and was also incorporated into the story of the hero-mariner Ulysses. I agree with Wilamowitz and Friedländer in believing that the tenth, eleventh and twelfth books of our Odyssey are a reflection of the voyages of Milestian traders and privateers in the Pontus, and that it was the Ionians who compounded that curious medley of Greek myths from various sources, of Ionian sailors' reports, and of those ancient religious and mythical ideas which saw, in the Pontic region and its inhabitants, the world beyond the grave and the souls of departed heroes. I cannot give more than a brief indication of the views which I hold on the numerous difficult and complicated problems suggested by the myth of the Argonauts and the later portion of the Odyssey: I hope to return to them in a special article. But I must insist on the high probability of the theory, pretty generally accepted in the most recent works on the subject, that the adventures of Jason, and part of the adventures of Ulysses, are to be localized in the Black Sea. I do not feel certain that we can go as far as Baer, and lately Maass, who identify the harbour of the Laestrygons with Balaklava, and the island of Circe with the Taman peninsula: but I am persuaded that the land of the rising sun, the Aia of the Odyssey, which seems, at the same time, to be part of the world beyond the grave, is to be placed on the Caucasian bank of the Black Sea. However this may be, it is evident that the only route known to the oldest Ionian navigators was the southern, the same which was used by their predecessors. It is not surprising, that the earliest Ionian stations on this route were at the two places where native centres had long existed: Sinope and Trebizond. Trebizond has always been the best port for the transmission of iron and copper from the Transcaucasian mines, and the terminus of the two great trade routes from south and east. Sinope, as Sir Walter Leaf has recently shown, was the point at which goods brought from Trebizond, on the light vessels which are the only craft plying on that part of the coast, were transferred to big sea-going ships, the Ionian merchantmen. It may be that the Ionians did not stop at Trebizond, but moved along the east coast of the Black Sea as far as the straits of Kerch. We may conjecture that Phanagoria, Hermonassa, and other colonies founded by Teos, Mytilene, and Clazomenai, were pre-Milesian foundations, previous to the hegemony of Miletus in the Black Sea.

But the southern route was neither safe nor convenient. There are no harbours between Batum and Novorossisk (Bata), and the coast teemed with pirates who detested their Greek competitors. It was not only from religious motives that shipwrecked foreigners were sacrificed on the coast of the Crimea. Nor was the coast between Sinope and Trebizond a very hospitable one, to judge from the stories told by Xenophon and by Arrian.

But there were two other routes, one lengthy but commodious, the other shorter. The first ran right along the northern shore of the Black Sea. Nearly every station on this route held out the promise of easy profits and miraculous draughts of fishes. In the course of the eighth and seventh centuries, the mouths of the great fishing rivers on this route, the Danube, the Dniester, the Bug, the Dnieper, were occupied, one after another, by Milesian fishing colonies. I shall not speak of the Danubian colonies: I shall mention only the two great ports, Tyras of the Dniester and Olbia of the Bug and the Dnieper, both at the outset, as may be seen from their coins, almost exclusively fishing stations. A fishing village has been discovered on the island of Berezan near Olbia, full of vases and vase fragments belonging to the seventh and sixth centuries B.C. We may be sure that the village was closely connected with the town of Olbia, which was founded, about the same time, at the mouth of Bug and Dnieper: the village may even be older than Olbia.

The other route was merely a modification of the southern route. Instead of keeping to the perilous coast of the Caucasus, ships leaving the great ports on the southern shore, Amisos, Sinope, and Heracleia, could cross the Black

Sea and head straight for the Crimean coast, from which the coast of Asia was visible in clear weather. On the Crimean coast, an excellent harbour, Chersonesus, received the mariners in perfect safety. It can easily be understood that the Ionian sailors lost no time in seizing this harbour and founding a seaport. It is now known that the city of Chersonesus was not originally a Dorian colony from Heracleia. Archaeological evidence—several finds of sixth-century Ionian vases—suggests that, like the other Black Sea colonies, it was founded by Ionians in the sixth century to be refounded by Heracleotes in the fifth century when Miletus was no longer able to maintain her maritime supremacy in the Black Sea. Chersonesus was only a stepping-stone: the little town produced nothing, the fishing was poor, and the neighbouring Taurians had nothing to sell. But it was a convenient stepping-stone on the direct route, along the Crimean coast, to the straits of Kerch and to the Sea of Azov with its wondrous store of fish. A day or two's sailing along the inhospitable coast of southern Crimea, infested with pirates: then, after these anxious hours, the port of Theodosia, another Milesian foundation, as Ernst von Stern has shown: next, the fine port of Nymphaeum, where the fishing was already plentiful: and so to Panticapaeum, an ancient centre of commerce and of civilization, one of the capitals of the former Cimmerian kingdom, and an excellent port, especially for sailing-vessels. To reach the opposite coast, probably already studded with Greek stations, there was only a strait to cross. Thus the two groups of Black Sea colonies were already established: the numerous eastern group, closely connected with the Caucasus and the southern ports of the Black Sea: and the western, connected less closely with these than with the Greek colonies on the western littoral of the Black Sea. The Milesians soon found means to join the two groups. By skirting the north coast of the Black Sea and the west coast of the Crimea, it was possible to reach the port of Kerkinitis, from which Chersonesus could easily be made. But the voyage was long and perilous, and ships referred to cross direct from the northern coast of Asia Minor to the southern coast of the Crimea.

PLATE XIII

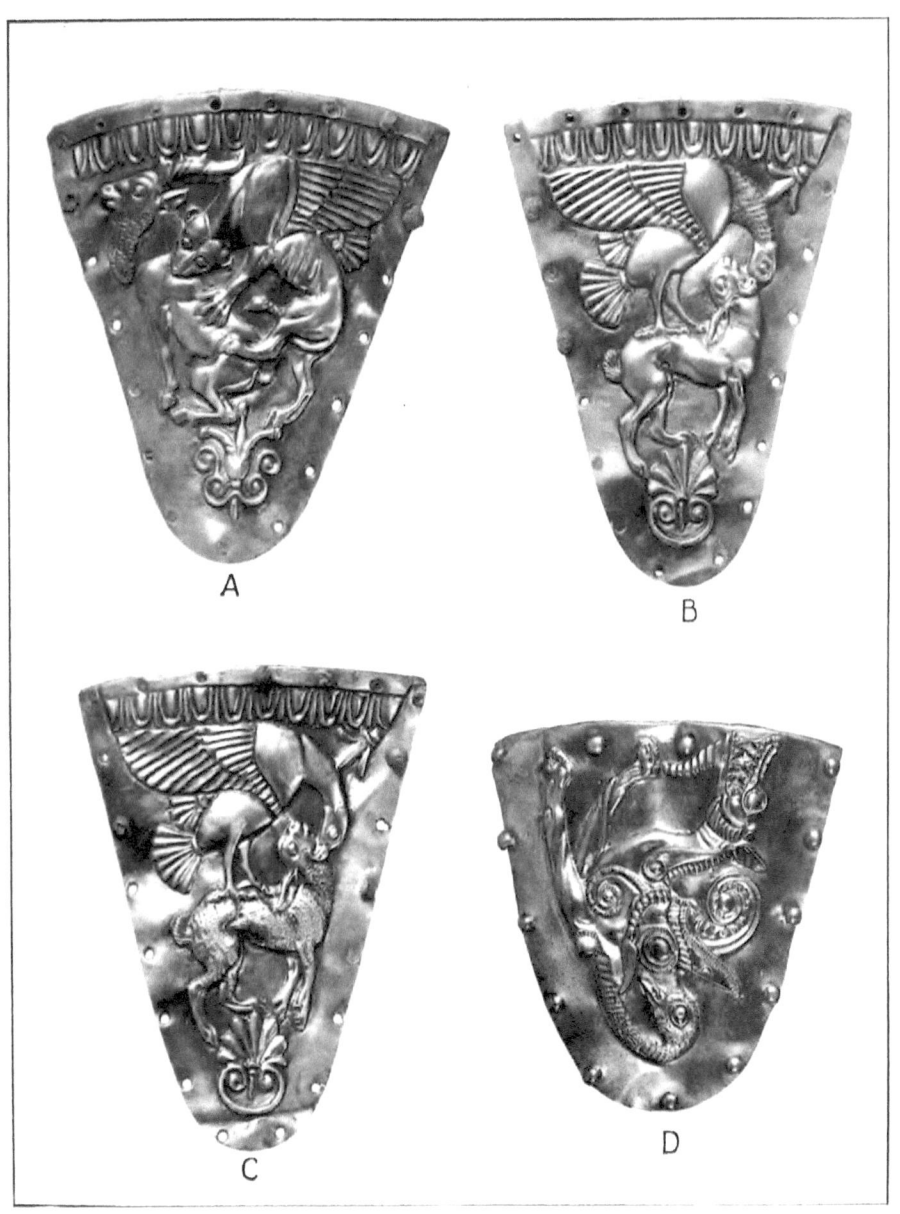

GOLD ORNAMENTS OF WOODEN RHYTA FROM THE 'SEVEN BROTHERS' ON THE KUBAN. V CENT. B.C.
Hermitage, Petrograd

It can easily be seen that the ascendancy in the western group belonged to Olbia. The estuary of Olbia was a calm and spacious lake: ships coming from the Dnieper and the Bug could sail there at their ease. Moreover, big ships could find all they required at Olbia. The Dnieper and the Bug abounded in fish: and the agricultural population of the lower and middle basins was glad to sell its goods to Greek merchants. Finally, the Dnieper and the Bug were always great trade routes joining north with south and bringing southward the produce of the north: furs and slaves, perhaps also amber. The relations of Olbia with north and east are proved by finds in the Kama region. The so-called Anányino civilization, which belongs to the early iron age (sixth to fifth century B.C.), is full of Olbian influences.

The peaceful development of the country was facilitated by the foundation and consolidation of the great Scythian empire. We have seen that from the sixth century onwards, prosperity prevailed among the Scythians and their subject tribes. In Olbia also, the tributary of the Scythian kings, who, as we know from Herodotus, maintained the most cordial relations with the great Greek trading centre. We may recall the Olbian legends of Anacharsis, the wise Scythian, and of King Skyles, who married a Greek wife, paid frequent visits to Olbia, and perished on account of his excessive philhellenism. The excavations of Farmakovski in the archaic cemetery of Olbia, and those of Skadovski and von Stern at Berezan, bear witness to the prosperity of Olbia in the sixth century and to its connexions with almost the whole Greek world. Some of the Olbian tombs were veritable treasure houses of pottery and, even more, of Greek jewellery. The character of the jewellery is purely Ionian.

We can understand how Olbia, protected by the Peace of Scythia, was able to hellenize a number of villages on the lower course of the Dnieper and the Bug, and to send Greek colonists who mingled with the natives and formed a mixed population, the Mixellenes of Herodotus. The mixed civilization of these villages is known to us from the productive excavations of Goshkévich and of Ebert.

The conditions which prevailed in the eastern group of colonies were much more complex. It will be remembered that the inhabitants of the Taman peninsula and the east coast of the Sea of Azov, the Sindians and the Maeotians, possessed a powerful and ancient civilization, that the straits of

Kerch were the nucleus of the Cimmerian state, and that the Cimmero-Maeotian population was never defeated and subjugated by the Scythians. It will also be remembered, that the inhabitants traded regularly with the mining districts of Transcaucasia. We can understand, that in their struggles with the Scythians, the Sindians and the Maeotians welcomed the assistance of Greek colonists from overseas, who brought them metals in exchange for their fish, and who were well armed and ready to defend their profits against Scythian exactions. Archaeological discoveries have shown, that the first Greek towns in the Taman peninsula, dating from the seventh century, were not Milesian colonies: the Carians were followed by the Teians, the Mytileneans, and the Clazomenians, and the Milesians were probably the latest comers. On the other hand, in the sixth century, and most likely in the second half of it, the Milesians founded numerous colonies on the other coast of the Cimmerian Bosphorus, which had certainly been conquered by the Scythians. We have good reason for believing that this colonization was facilitated by the Scythians, who realized, from the example of Olbia, the importance of possessing outlets for their products, and who highly appreciated the tribute paid them by the Greeks.

There existed then in the sixth century two probably rival groups of Greek colonies on the Cimmerian Bosphorus: one in Sindian territory, and the other in the Scythian empire. But it must not be forgotten that geographically and economically the two shores of the strait constitute a single area with similar populations, and that for centuries they had formed a political unit under Cimmerian domination. We must suppose, although it is nowhere stated, that competition led to conflicts between these two groups. Supported by the Scythians; commanding the straits of Kerch by virtue of their geographical position; and possessing the only ports which provided trustworthy shelter for large sailing ships; the Greeks of Panticapaeum seem to have acquired, in the sixth century and at the beginning of the fifth, an ascendancy over the Greeks of the Taman peninsula. The silver coins of the sixth century appear to furnish proof: the number of types is small, and the coins were probably all struck at Panticapaeum.

In the fifth century B.C., especially in the second half, the political situation seems to have completely changed. The Milesians, as we know, lost their maritime supremacy and their connexion with the Persian empire: they became ordinary members of the Athenian league. Athens, after the Persian wars, became the chief political power in Greece, held the command of the seas, and assiduously developed her commerce and her industry. We shall see that the Scythian kingdom, after the expedition of Darius, concentrated its forces on its western frontier, and began to pay less attention than in the sixth century to its struggle with the Sindians. Greek influence increased in the straits of the Cimmerian Bosphorus.

In her external and commercial policy, Athens had to turn her eyes more and more towards the east. Her plan to become mistress of Egypt collapsed, and her relations with Italy encountered stronger and stronger opposition from the Dorians. On the other hand, she needed more and more raw material for her industries, and more and more food-stuffs, corn and fish, for her growing population. The question of food was particularly urgent. Athens, and indeed Greece as a whole, could no longer feed itself. The cities of the Athenian confederation tried to import as much food-stuffs as possible: the other cities did the same. Now the supply of cereals in the market was limited. Owing to Dorian competition in Italy, and to Persian jealousy, it was impossible to count on the west or on Egypt. The only hope of obtaining a sufficient supply of food-stuffs lay in the east, in the fishing and agricultural regions of the great Balkan and Russian rivers. For Athens, therefore, the head of the league, it was a matter of the utmost political and economic importance, to cultivate and develop the commercial relations which Miletus had established with the Black Sea colonies, to foster the colonies, and to make them relatively independent of their old masters the Scythians. But the political interests of Athens demanded more: Athens claimed exclusive control of the export trade, the sole right to dispose of the Black Sea commodities, to collect them at Athens and distribute them afterwards among her allies. This was why the Athenians colonized Amisos and Sinope in the fifth century, and founded military colonies, real fortresses, at the most important points on the straits of the Bosphorus, not in, but beside, the principal Greek cities at Athenaeum near Theodosia, at Nymphaeum near Panticapaeum, and probably at Stratocleia near Phanagoria. Pericles in the year 435, and Alcibiades later, personally inspected this branch of the Athenian imperial system.

PLATE XIV

GREEK BRONZE BREASTPLATE
From Elizavetinskaya on the Kuban
IV Cent B.C. Hermitage, Petrograd

But the Athenian supremacy was of short duration. Some years before the expedition of Pericles, a serious change had taken place in the political life of Panticapaeum. The tradition concerning the Archeanactids, the first rulers of the city, appears to be the work of a forger: but it seems that the city had been governed by an aristocracy and that the government was supplanted by a tyranny, apparently military; in 438, the power was seized by a chieftain with the Thracian name of Spartocos. How can we explain this change and the Thracian name of the tyrant, who was succeeded by other members of the same family, some of whom bore Thracian names, such as Pairisades and Spartocos, others Greek, such as Leucon and Satyros? It has been suggested that Spartocos was the leader of a Thracian military force, engaged by the Panticapaeans for the defence of the town. This is extremely unlikely. Whence came the Thracians, and what route did they take? Did they come by sea, with the permission of Athens? It would surely have been absurd of Athens to import mercenaries who might destroy her cleruchies. Against the will of Athens? No less impossible, for Athens was mistress of the sea. Did they come by way of the Russian steppes? A long and dangerous journey: and what would the Scythian empire have said to it? The Thracians were always enemies of the Scythians. This hypothesis being inacceptable, only one other remains: I have already indicated it in my third chapter. The usurpation of Spartocos was a purely internal change: as in so many Greek cities, a tyranny took the place of an aristocracy which had become an oligarchy. Spartocos must have belonged to a native family which had been incorporated into the aristocracy which governed the town: hence his Thracian name. We have seen that in the prehellenic period the ruling class at Panticapaeum was Cimmerian, and that the Cimmerians were Thracians.

Did this revolution take place with the consent of Athens? I think not. The semi-Thracian aspect of the new dynasty speaks rather for a native reaction against Greek domination, and this theory is corroborated by the title which the new rulers assumed: archons of Panticapaeum and kings of the Sindians and the Maeotians. The fact that among the Sindian princes who ruled at the same period as the tyrants of Panticapaeum, we find Thracian names like Gorgippos and Komosarye, and that the two dynasties probably united shortly after the revolution of Spartocos, seems to show that the principal cause of the political change was the necessity of reconciling the interests of the natives, and especially of the native aristocracy, with those of the Greek population.

It is worth noticing that this phenomenon was not peculiar to Panticapaeum. Similar conditions led to a similar form of government, almost at the same time, at Heracleia on the Pontus, at Halicarnassus in Asia Minor, at Syracuse in Sicily. The same movement gave rise to the Greco-Macedonian monarchy in Macedonia, and later to the combination of city-state and monarchy at Pergamon. But it was only in the Bosphorus that the form of government thus produced was stable: here it lasted for centuries.

The change in the constitution of Panticapaeum was the beginning of a brilliant career for the new state. Possibly one of Pericles' motives for visiting the Euxine was the desire to enter into relations and to come to an arrangement with the new masters of Panticapaeum. The understanding which resulted confirmed the power of the tyrant without sacrificing the military and economic interests of Athens. Athens did not think of withdrawing her garrisons, and the tyrant of Panticapaeum had to accept the status of Athenian commercial agent for the export of corn to Athens alone. All corn had to pass through Piraeus before it could find its way to other Greek cities: an enormous political force in the hands of a state like Athens, which never knew political or moral scruples.

But Athenian monopoly and Bosphoran dependence soon came to an end. The Peloponnesian war, which was decided in the straits of the Thracian Bosphorus, enabled Satyros and Leucon, the successors of Spartocos, to assert their sway over all or nearly all the Greek cities, to reduce the Athenian colonies to impotence and to embody them in their state, to pursue, without restraint, a policy of unification in the Taman peninsula, and to overcome, after a long struggle, the competition of Pontic Heracleia, the powerful Dorian City which was governed, like Panticapaeum, by a tyranny, and which was anxious to secure, not only the port of Chersonesus, but also the town of Theodosia, by nature the principal centre for the corn trade of the Scythian Crimea. Athens was neither able nor willing to impede the development of the Bosphoran state: she probably assisted her semi-vassal in its conflicts with its numerous enemies. The Athenian inscription in honour of the sons of Leucon shows that Athens renounced her exclusive right to purchase the corn from Panticapaeum. Panticapaeum probably received the right of trading freely, on condition of guaranteeing Athens ample privileges in the matter of custom duties. The period of Satyros (433/2-389/8), of Leucon (389/8-349/8), and of Pairisades I (349/8-310/9) was one of great prosperity for the Bosphorus. Leucon was spoken of at Athens as the pattern of a virtuous tyrant. Attic historians wrote about him, as well as Panticapaean. Statues of these tyrants adorned public places in Athens. Pairisades I made bold to attack the Scythians, or at any rate to resist their demand for tribute. It will be remembered that at this period the Scythians were in conflict with the Sarmatians and were slowly retreating towards the Crimean steppes.

The commercial situation remained unchanged. Athens was still the chief customer of Panticapaeum, and in Greece the demand for fish and corn was steadily growing. The Scythians became resigned to the independence of the Bosphorus state, which had organized a powerful army of mercenaries and a regular system of traffic. Great quantities of corn were produced everywhere, and the trade flourished as never before. The fourth century was a period of general prosperity. At Olbia and at Chersonesus, at Theodosia, at Panticapaeum, at Phanagoria, at Tanais on the mouth of the Don, the fourth-century tombs are full of objects of art, especially gold and silver, imported from Greece. We shall speak of these later.

At the end of the fourth century and the beginning of the third, the quiet life of the Bosphorus was disturbed by political disorders. But these disorders were of short duration, and the reigns, as we can now call them, of Eumelos, of Spartocos III (304/3-284/3), and of Pairisades III (284/3-about 252) were comparable with those of their predecessors. It is to be noted that during the reign of Spartocos III Athens not only recognized the complete independence of Panticapaeum, but even concluded with it a defensive military alliance. In consequence of the position in which Spartocos III found himself after the troubles which followed the death of Pairisades I, he was obliged to pay special attention to the recruitment of his army and to alliances with other states.

PLATE XV

1. GOLD BRACELET

2. SILVER BRACELET

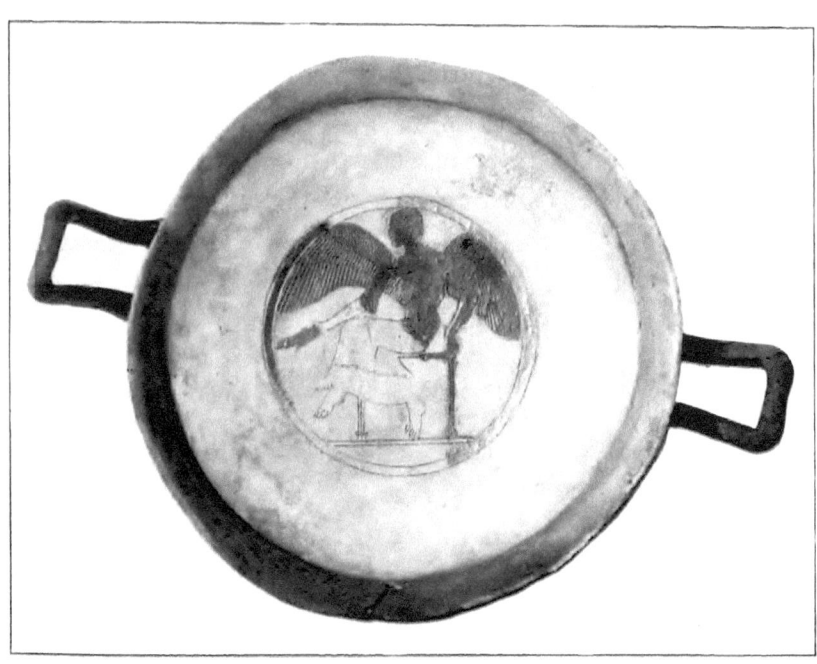

3. SILVER KYLIX WITH ENGRAVED AND GILT EMBLEMA

1 and 3 from the 'Seven Brothers' on the Kuban, 2 from the Taman Peninsula
V-VI Cent. B.C. Hermitage, Petrograd.

It was not until the second half of the third century that economic and political decay set in. During the fourth and third centuries the position of Panticapaeum in the corn trade was an extremely important one. Up to the time of Alexander it had hardly any competitors; after Alexander's conquest of the Eastern world it had to contend with Ptolemaic Egypt, with Asia Minor, and with Macedonia and Thrace, but the competition was not ruinous. The prosperity of the Greek world in the early Hellenistic period, the constant growth of population, the continual foundation of new cities, and the general development of industry, brought about an enormous increase in the demand for the products of South Russia. A close examination of the documents of the period shows that the difficulty for producers was not lack of customers but insufficiency of output. The Ptolemies would never have been able to exercise such powerful influence on the cities of the Mediterranean if they had not employed their corn as a political weapon. We have seen that Spartocos had already used his corn to purchase a military alliance with Athens. No matter how many offers of corn and fish were brought to the exchanges of Rhodes, Delos, and Delphi, customers could always be found.

The decay of Panticapaeum, therefore, cannot have been occasioned by the competition of other producers. The weakness of the Bosphoran kingdom was due to other causes. The output became smaller and smaller. Take the quantity of corn exported by Panticapaeum in the fourth and third centuries: under Leucon I 400,000 medimni by or for Athens alone; and how much besides for the other Greek cities! Compare this with what the whole Bosphoran kingdom paid to Mithridates: 180,000 medimni all told. The difference is enormous. The cause of the decrease was political disturbance in the steppes of South Russia. The Scythian empire was collapsing under the blows of the Sarmatians and of the Thracians. As early as the beginning of the third century, the Gauls, accompanied, it may be, by Germanic tribes, were advancing towards the Danube and ravaging the outskirts of Olbia. Read the inscription of Protogenes, and you will see how precarious was the situation of Olbia at the beginning of the third century, and what anarchy prevailed in the neighbouring steppes. The Bosphorus was in a slightly better position. The Scythian kingdom held out in the steppes between Don and Dnieper, as well as in the Crimea. The valley of the Kuban had not yet been occupied by

Sarmatian tribes. But even so the existence of the Bosphoran kingdom, and of the city of Chersonesus, which depended for its prosperity upon the Bosphorus, became more and more uncertain. The Scythians, driven back towards the Crimea; threatened the cities, demanded, as at Olbia, a heavier and heavier tribute, and neither the Bosphoran kingdom nor Chersonesus was wealthy enough to compete, in the market for mercenaries, with the agents of the Hellenistic monarchs, so as to form a strong hireling army. The army had to be recruited from the citizens and from the subject tribes, as had happened for the first time under Eumelos: production suffered in consequence, and the armed power of the state hardly gained. The people, accustomed to mercenary armies, became discontented, planned revolution, and sometimes carried out its plan. The trade with the Scythians was no longer the same. Constant war, and the invasion of Scythian territory from the west and from the east, crippled the Scythian kingdom and reduced the trade to insignificance. Besides, the Bosphorus was permanently at war with the Scythians. The hour was approaching when the Greeks of South Russia would be forced to renounce their independence and seek the armed protection of powerful friends, whoever these friends might be. What came of this situation we shall see in our sixth chapter.

I have tried to give a survey of the political and economic causes which created the state of the Bosphorus, and which preserved it for more than two centuries as an independent power and as an important part of the whole ancient world. What was the political and social structure of this state? And what kind of civilization did it achieve?

I have tried to show that the state of the Bosphorus was originally a military tyranny and remained one: It grew out of a compromise between the native population and the Greek colonists. For the natives, the ruling dynasty was always a dynasty of kings, since it was kings that for centuries they had been accustomed to obey. The Greeks, in order to preserve their dominant position and the foundation of their economic prosperity, were obliged to abandon their civic liberties and to take for their chiefs the Hellenized barbarians who ruled the native population. For the Greeks, this form of government was a tyranny, although the official style of the tyrant was the constitutional title of archon. This tyranny interests us because it was not a passing incident, like the tyrannies in many Greek cities during the sixth and fourth and third centuries

B.C., but a form of settled government which existed for centuries and which gradually transformed itself into a Hellenistic monarchy comparable with monarchies in Asia Minor: Bithynia with its Thracian population, Cappadocia and Pontus with their semi-Iranian dynasties, Commagene and Armenia with their Hellenized native kings. The only analogies, in the ancient world, to this constitutional form of tyranny which developed into a monarchy, are the tyranny of Pontic Heracleia, and even more that of Syracuse in Sicily. In all three places, a military tyranny based on mercenaries; a strong native element in the population; no council of elders, no boule; a popular assembly, without power; finally, constitutional fictions to disguise the reality.

Still more interesting, the social structure of the Bosphoran state hardly differed from that of the states which we have compared with it. The state was based on an agricultural native population, attached to the soil; a class of great landowners, friends and kinsmen of the king, who was himself a landed proprietor, owning the soil of the whole kingdom; and a very powerful class of Greek merchants, some citizens of the cities in the kingdom, others foreigners, who owned ships and who organized the traffic with the neighbouring semi-independent tribes as well as with the Scythian kingdom. The king himself was undoubtedly one of these merchants. He exported the rain which he received as tribute from his vassals and as contribution from his serfs. We must also reckon with a numerous lower middle class residing in the towns, artisans and small tradesmen; and with a numerous population of slaves, who loaded and unloaded the vessels, laboured in the factories, and so forth.

The same structure is observable wherever a Greek population was obliged to submit to a native, Hellenized, or Greek dynasty whose rule was based on a native population not barbarous but accustomed to monarchic government. Peculiar to the structure of the Bosphoran state is the historical evolution, more easily apprehended here than elsewhere: an Ionian Greek city transforming itself into a Greco-Maeotian state with the Greeks in a privileged position, and gradually changing into a Hellenistic monarchy in which the two elements are confounded, the natives becoming Hellenized and the Greeks gradually adopting the spirit and the habits of the natives. The dualism can be noticed in every department of life. In religion, purely Greek cults are replaced by various forms of native cult, particularly that of the Great Goddess whom we have already mentioned. Nearly every Greek town in the Taman peninsula had a temple of this pre-Hellenic divinity. Two of these sanctuaries have been excavated, one near Phanagoria, where the Great Goddess was identified with the Greek Aphrodite, the other on a promontory in one of the lakes of the Kuban delta, that of Tsukúr, where she was worshipped, as in Asia Minor and in Macedonia, under the name of Artemis Agrotera. We have every reason to suppose that there were temples of the same deity near Hermonassa and in the vicinity of Gorgippia, the modern Anápa. The same cult gradually became predominant at Panticapaeum, and it is well known that the patron goddess of Chersonesus was the Parthenos, who is represented, in the guise of Artemis, on the coins of that city. A significant testimony to the popularity of the Great Goddess in the peninsula of Taman is afforded by her prevalence, as Kore or as Demeter, in the decoration of tomb-furniture from the Taman graves: I would instance the important part played by Demeter in the lady's tomb at Great Bliznitsa. Stephani inferred that the lady had been a priestess of Demeter. I am more inclined to believe that all the queens, or consorts of native kings and princes, for example the queen buried under the barrow of Karagodeuashkh, were priestesses of the Great Goddess, who was sometimes identified with Demeter and sometimes with Aphrodite. The costume which they wore on special occasions during their lifetime, and which accompanied them into the grave, was the ritual costume of the grand priestess, and as such recalled the costume of the Goddess herself. Curiously enough, the Hellenized native queen who was buried under the barrow of Great Bliznitsa had a number of gold plaques sewn on to her clothing which represented the Great Goddess herself. We shall return to them when we come to speak of the goddess worshipped by the Scythians (see page 141). The Great Goddess appears in the form of the Asiatic πότνια θηρῶν: her chthonic character is emphasized by her serpent feet. At the same time, it is shown by certain attributes that she was conceived as the chief goddess of the Bosphoran kingdom, the patron and guardian of the state. In the more explicit of the plaques, her wings terminate in horned and leonine griffin-heads; she masters two eagle-headed griffins; or she holds in her right hand the silen's head which figures on Panticapaean coins and in her left a dagger, and is accompanied by the symbol of Bosphoran prosperity, the ear of corn (see page 168, fig. 17, and pl. XVIII, 4, similar plaques from Kul-Oba and from Chersonesus, compare pl. XVIII, 3—the same goddess represented as

Aphrodite—and 2—the Silen, the national god of vegetation). As we examine these plaques we cannot help recalling the Maeotian legend, mentioned above, of the autochthonous goddess who slew the giants—native deities of fertility— to please Herakles, the Greek or Iranian conquering god. We shall see that the silens and satyrs on the coins of Panticapaeum probably represent those same native gods of vegetation and of reproduction, who are associated with the Great Goddess in the plaques.

The temples on the Taman peninsula, as we learn from an inscription of Roman date, were organized like those in Asia Minor, especially those in Pontus, Cappadocia, and Armenia: a college of priests or priestesses with a grand priest or priestess at its head; vast domains belonging to the goddess; and serfs working for the goddess and for the priests.

There is the same dualism in the material life of the population, especially of the ruling class. For nearly a century excavation, uninterrupted if not always scientific, has been going on in the cities of the Bosphoran state, and most of the city cemeteries have been explored: we can thus form an accurate notion of the civilization and characteristics of the governing class in town and in country.

One characteristic is the opulence of the kingdom in general, and of the urban middle class. The tombs of the Bosphoran Greeks are well constructed, the coffins are often carefully wrought, and the objects interred with the dead are sometimes of high material and artistic value. On the other hand, the urban middle class has kept its character surprisingly pure: Ionian Greek at Olbia and in the Bosphorus, Dorian at Chersonesus. In the Ionian cities, just as in the mother country, cremation and inhumation were practised side by side. The funeral rites are purely Greek; the funerary furniture is no less so; from the sixth to the third century it mainly consists of what may be called athletic objects. Weapons are rare, for the citizens did not serve in the army, but strigils, oil-flasks, and oil-jars are regularly found in the graves of men. Women have mostly jewels and articles of toilet. In purely Greek tombs of this period nearly all the objects are imported. And they are not cheap goods. The Ionian vases are sometimes of the highest quality; the Attic vases, which predominate from the end of the sixth century onwards, often bear signatures of artists: the so-called Phoenician polychrome glass is sometimes exquisitely fine: the gold trinkets probably came from the best-known workshops, and are frequently splendid specimens of the Greek jeweller's art.

PLATE XVI

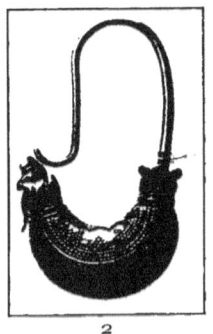

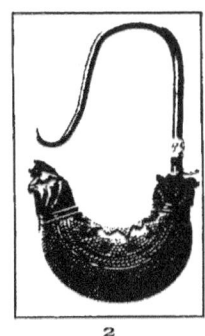
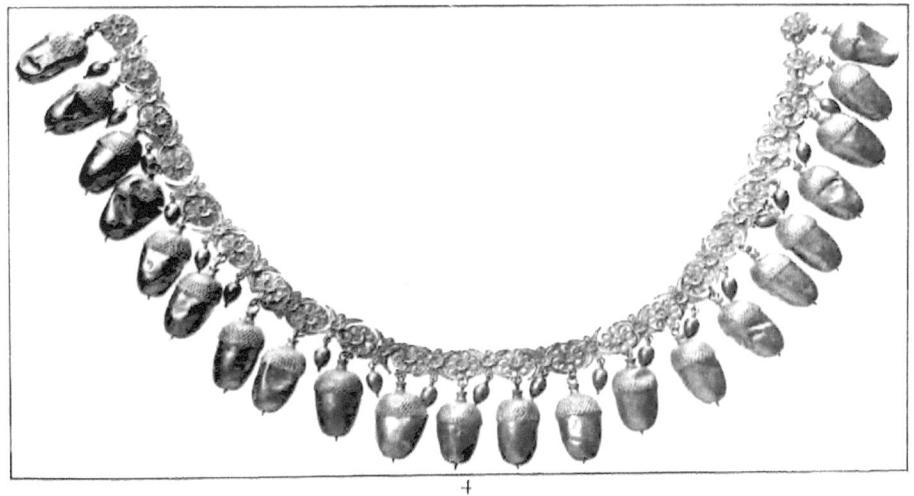

1. Engraved CHALCEDONY SCARABOID, Persian
2, 3. Gold and Gold-plated EARRINGS. 4. Gold NECKLACE
From Nymphaeum, Crimea. V Cent. B.C. Ashmolean Museum

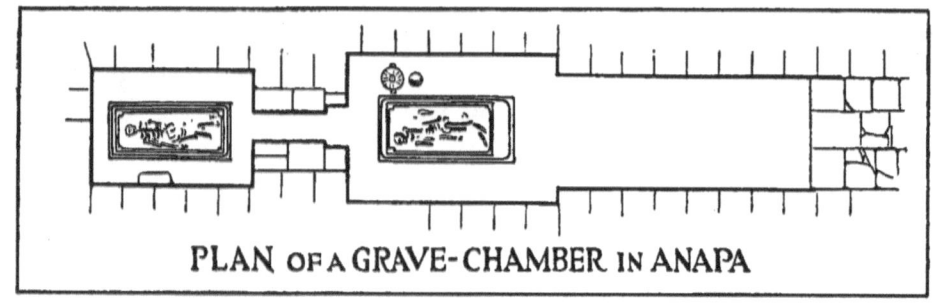

Fig. 7.

But it is not the Greek tombs that captivate the imagination of the visitor to Kerch or to the Hermitage: such tombs, more or less rich, are found in most parts of the Greek world, and the tomb furniture does not vary much from district to district. The most interesting feature of the burial-grounds at Panticapaeum and in the Taman peninsula, is the great tumuli (kurgans) on the summits of Mount Mithridates and Yüz-Oba, two ranges of hills in the neighbourhood of Panticapaeum. There are also tumuli along the roads leading from Panticapaeum to the steppe, and on most of the hill-tops in the Taman peninsula.

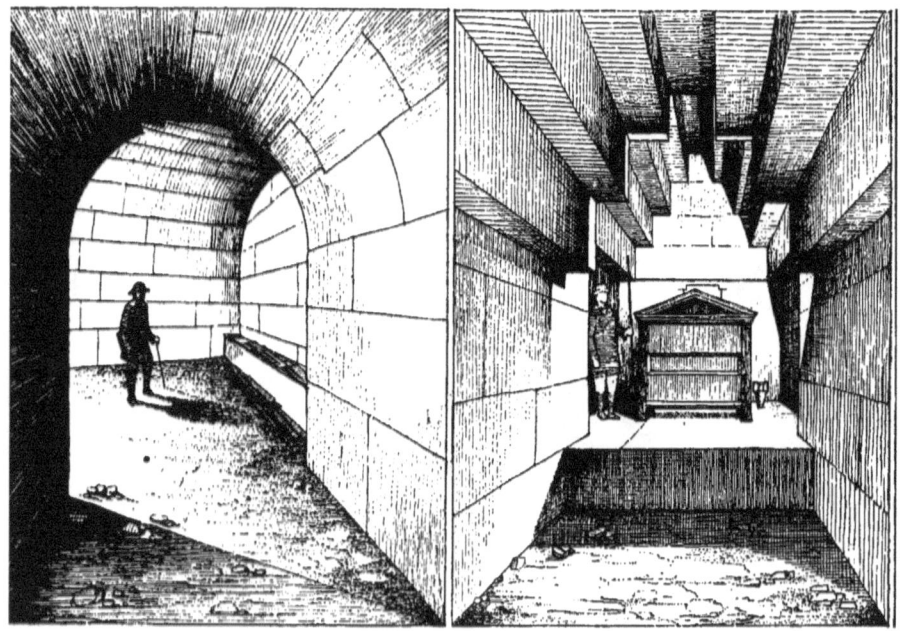

Fig. 8. TWO STONE CHAMBERS IN THE TUMULI OF YUZ-OBA, NEAR PANTICAPAEUM.

The tumulus is carefully constructed and surrounded by a wall of dressed stone (κρηπίς): underneath it is a large sepulchral building, a chamber of dressed stone with a corridor joining it to the circumference of the tumulus (figs. 7 and 8). The chamber and the corridor are vaulted: the vault is often of the corbelled or 'Egyptian' type, round or square, with one course of stones projecting beyond the next; true barrel vaults are occasionally found. Walls and roof were frequently painted, and sometimes lined with costly stuffs: gold plaques were often sewn on to the stuff. In the middle of the chamber was a coffin, usually of wood—rarely of marble—, carved, inlaid, and painted. Several of these coffins have been found: they are marvels of decorative art. Round the coffin were Greek vases of the best fabrics, often not only painted but modelled and gilded as well: one of the best known is the vase with the signature of Xenophantos which represents King Darius hunting. The bodies laid in the coffins wore festal costume; the men had weapons with them, the women jewels.

Some of the graves, which were discovered intact, have yielded superb collections of ancient jewellery and goldsmith's work: engraved stones signed by celebrated artists; necklaces, bracelets, earrings, unequalled in the ancient world. The finest objects in the Hermitage came almost entirely from these monumental tombs. The same opulence everywhere—at Panticapaeum, at Nymphaeum, at Theodosia, in the Taman peninsula, at Chersonesus: but not the same funeral rites. The graves in the Taman peninsula preserve features which recall the native Thracian and Scythian graves, such as bloody sacrifices after the funeral ceremony, and the interment of horses and of funeral chariots.

Such graves are neither purely Greek nor purely native. The Greeks of this period did not bury their dead under barrows, in chambers with Egyptian vaults, in sumptuous coffins. They no longer deposited whole fortunes in their tombs, like the inhabitants of the Bosphoran kingdom. Again, in the funerary ritual and the choice and character of the objects placed in them, the Scythian tumulary graves have nothing in common with the monumental tombs of Panticapaeum. There is no trace at Panticapaeum of the interment of horses, no human sacrifice, and no groups of sacred objects laid beside the dead. We have two completely different rituals: moreover, the Panticapaean ritual influenced the Scythian, not the Scythian the Panticapaean. We cannot claim that the monumental graves of the Taman peninsula were equally independent of Scythian practice: Scythian influence is certain. Although they preserve, in principle, the funerary ritual found at Panticapaeum, which recalls that of heroic Greece, familiar to us from the Homeric poems, with its bloody sacrifices and its funeral feasts, they nevertheless appear to have adopted certain customs from the Scythians, especially the slaughter and interment of the horses which had been harnessed to the hearse. Remains of horses and harness were found in the barrows of Great and Little Bliznitsa and of the Vasyurinskaya Gora, the richest and stateliest tombs in the Taman peninsula. True analogies with the funerary ritual and the sepulchral structures of Panticapaeum are to be found not in Scythian country but partly, as I have said, in the Greece of heroic times, and partly in those barbarian lands which were strongly influenced by heroic Greece. In Thrace, especially, we observe the same characteristics. Besides the barrows in Macedonia, excavated by Heuzey and Kinch, which contain painted sepulchral chambers with barrel vaults, I would mention the sepulchral chambers discovered near Salonica, and near Lozengrad in Bulgaria. The latter is particularly interesting: the mode of construction recalls the Mycenaean tholos, and the plan is exactly like those of the Tsarski tombs and the Golden Tumulus: the date is that of the Panticapaean graves, the fourth century B.C.

Similar monuments have come to light in Asia Minor, especially in Pontus, Caria and Lycia; as well as in Etruria. It must be remembered that Asia Minor was partly peopled by Thracian tribes. Throughout these countries, we come across tumuli, sepulchral chambers of dressed stone, rich coffins, varied and sumptuous tomb furniture. The funerary ritual is almost the same, and here also it vividly recalls heroic, that is to say pre-Hellenic Greece. Everything suggests that the great tombs in the Bosphoran kingdom were built for members of the ruling class, which, as we have already seen, was not of pure Greek origin, but of mixed stock, a combination of native elements with the aristocracy of Greek colonists.

What strikes us particularly in the monumental tombs of Panticapaeum and the Taman peninsula is not the tumuli themselves, for the shape of these huge earthen mounds does not greatly vary from one place or one period to another: much more interesting, both historically and artistically, are the sepulchral chambers of dressed stone. Some dozens of them have been found; not a few are in almost perfect preservation. The chambers of the Golden, Tsarski, and Melék Chesmé tumuli, in the neighbourhood of Kerch, are all three well known: the two latter are accessible and attract a great number of visitors. Not so well known are the chambers of the Yüz-Oba kurgans, near Kerch, which are partially destroyed, those in the Taman peninsula, and those in the vicinity of Gorgippia (see figs. 7 and 8). Some of these can be dated by means of their contents: none are as old as the fifth century: the grandest belong to the beginning of the fourth century B.C., the more summary to the second half of the fourth and the first half of the third. It has been proposed to place the finest examples of the first series, the Golden and Tsarski kurgans, in the fifth century B.C.: but without good reason. The mode of construction is exactly the same as in the sepulchral chambers of Yüz-Oba, which date from the first half of the fourth century. Now we have seen that the fourth century was a period of great prosperity in the Cimmerian Bosphorus, whereas in the fifth century Nymphaeum and the other Athenian cities grew rich at the expense of Panticapaeum. This is shown, on the one hand, by the rich fifth-century finds at Nymphaeum—a mixed cemetery with Greek and Greco-Scythian tombs, and several tumuli—and in the Taman peninsula—the barrows of the Seven Brothers; on the other, by the rarity and poverty of fifth-century tombs at Panticapaeum, not one of which has yielded jewellery comparable with that of the fifth-century tombs in the Taman peninsula and in the cemetery of Nymphaeum; while the vases of severe red-figured style are very poorly represented at Panticapaeum, especially compared with the vases of the sixth and fourth centuries. We have no right to suppose that costly monuments were constructed in Panticapaeum at a time when the city and her rulers were impoverished by dissension at home, by wars abroad, and by complete subordination, if not vassalage, to all-powerful Athens.

I said above, that technically and architecturally, the tomb chambers of Panticapaeum were real creations. The forms are various and elaborate. The roof is sometimes a rectangular corbelled vault, sometimes corbelled but rounded: some architects used the barrel vault, combining it, in the double chambers, with the corbelled vault. It has been conjectured that in constructing tomb-chambers with the so-called Egyptian vault, the Panticapaean architects were following an archaic custom, were imitating heroa and tombs of the Mycenaean period: in short, that they acted like the Augustan sculptors when these carved their archaizing statues. I do not believe this conjecture to be correct. As soon as reek architects learned to construct barrel vaults they put their knowledge into practice, and the barrel vault gradually supplanted the older corbelled vault. But the barrel vault, which apart from the Egyptian vault, is the only suitable method of roofing a sepulchral chamber surmounted by a tumulus several metres high, was not introduced into Greece until the middle of the fourth century. Moreover, the Greek barrel vault is very imperfect compared with the Roman. It must be borne in mind, that in the Bosphoran barrel vaults of the fourth century, the stones are almost always held to ether by metal clamps, a process which the Romans never employed. Now before the Greek architects adopted the Oriental system of barrel vaults, what processes did they know of for constructing a tomb-chamber surmounted by a tumulus? The only process known to them was the corbelled vault, rectangular or circular, the same which was used in the Mycenaean period. I have no doubt, although we possess no examples, that the corbelled vault was continuously employed in Thrace, and in Greece and in Asia Minor as well, from the Mycenaean period onwards, for underground buildings and especially for tumulary graves. All the Panticapaean architects did was to import the technique to Panticapaeum and to perfect it. But they were not servile imitators: they managed to give their buildings an air of grandeur and a distinctive charm: they contrived to find proportions which inspire us with a profound respect for their taste and for their technical acquirement. It surely needed a thorough knowledge of the builder's art to construct a tomb-chamber with an Egyptian vault, which could resist for centuries the enormous pressure of an earthen mound some ten or fifteen metres high! The tomb-chambers of the Bosphoran kurgans are nearly always found intact, though stripped of their contents. If many or most of the Panticapaean tomb-chambers are at present in ruins, it is not the fault of the Bosphoran architects, but of the inhabitants of modern Kerch, who have been attracted by the excellent dressed stone and by the iron and bronze clamps.

I may observe, before taking leave of these buildings, that when I have made my way down the corridor of Tsarski Kurgan, with its Egyptian vault, when I have passed from the corridor to the tomb chamber with its rounded corbelled vault, when I have visited the Yüz-Oba tomb-chambers, I have always been moved by a feeling of deep respect and of lively admiration for the builders of these impressive and mysterious monuments. It is greatly to be regretted that their civil and religious architecture has completely disappeared.

PLATE XVII

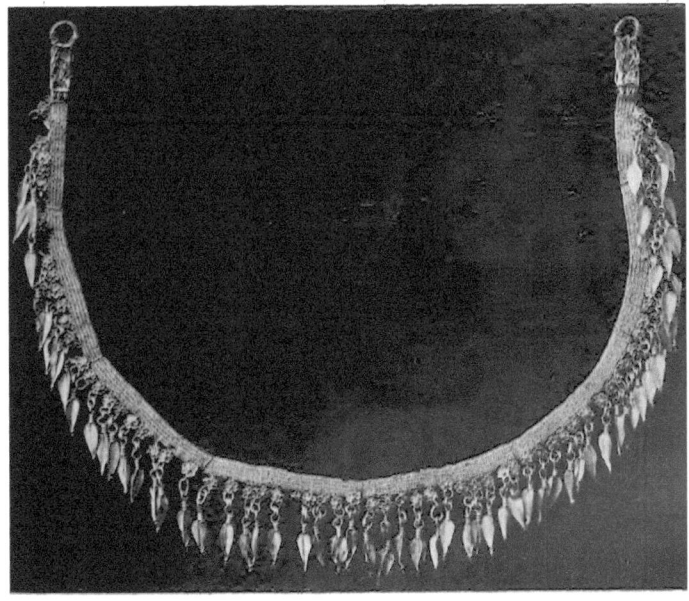

1. PAINTED CLAY VASE FROM THE TAMAN PENINSULA
2. GOLD NECKLACE FROM CHERSONESUS
Late V or early IV Cent. B.C. Hermitage, Petrograd

PLATE XVIII.

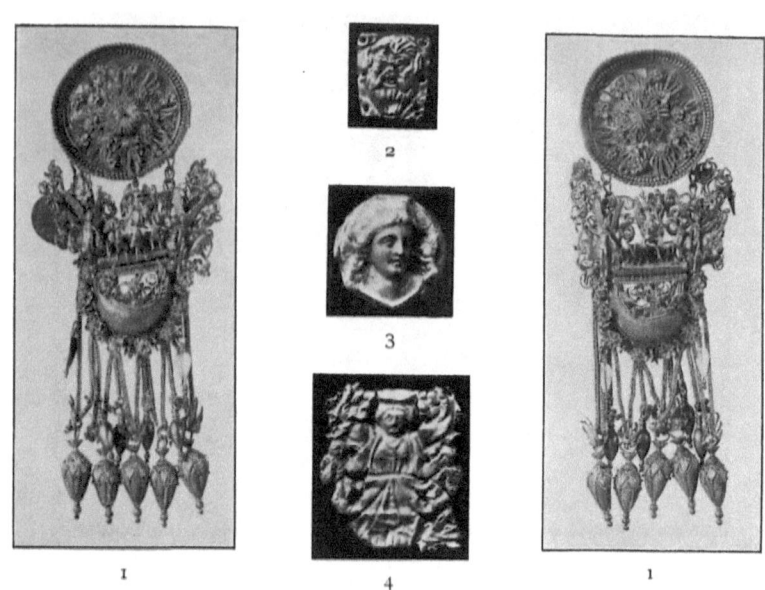

1. EARRINGS FROM THEODOSIA, CRIMEA. Hermitage, Petrograd
2-4. GOLD GARMENT PLAQUES FROM CHERSONESUS, CRIMEA. Hermitage, Petrograd

GOLD COINS OF PANTICAPAEUM. British Museum and Louvre
IV Cent. B.C.

Some of the objects found in these tomb-chambers were imported, from Greece (for instance the silver bracelet, pl. XV, 2; the necklace and earrings found at Nymphaeum, pl. XVI, 2-4; the earrings found at Theodosia, pl. XVIII, 1; the necklace from Chersonesus and the painted vase from Taman, pl. XVII), or from the Orient (the gem from Nymphaeum, pl. XVI, 1); but side by side with these, there are others which are unquestionably local work, and it is these which concern us the more nearly. There is no doubt that the coins of Panticapaeum were struck in Panticapaeum itself. In the sixth and fifth centuries, they differ very little from the coins of the Ionian cities in Asia Minor. The Samian coins, in particular, served as models for the silver of Panticapaeum. But at the end of the fifth, and in the fourth century—the date rests principally on stylistic considerations—probably at the time of the reconstitution of the Bosphoran state, Panticapaean coinage suddenly changes. Gold staters were now struck, and the types of these staters, and of the silver coinage, are quite new. These types are not imitated from the contemporary coinage of other Greek states. The Cyzicene staters offer analogies, but Cyzicus probably imitated the Bosphoran types, not inversely. Doubtless Cyzicus wished to safeguard its monopoly of issuing gold staters, which, until the appearance of the Bosphoran staters, had been uncontested except by Lampsacus; and endeavoured to oust the Bosphoran gold by means of an electrum coinage with similar types. It did not succeed.

The fourth-century coins struck in the Bosphorus are masterpieces of original and forcible art (pl. XVIII, 5). The style is purely Greek. Not so the types. Look at the heads of bearded silens and beardless satyrs. We shall see, in the next chapter, how strongly they influenced the canonical rendering of Scythians in the art of the Greeks. But we can also trace the influence of the Scythian type on these mythical heads. We have been bidden to recognize a representation of the god Pan, and an etymological allusion, in the Greek manner, to the name of Panticapaeum. I cannot accept this suggestion. We are familiar with the type of Pan as it was developed in Greek art. It offers only the faintest of resemblances with the heads on the Bosphoran coins. They are more likely to represent silens and satyrs, but they are not faithful reproductions of the established types. I should be more inclined to take them for heads of some native, probably Thracian divinity, the great god of vegetation who became the Greek Dionysos and who sometimes figures, in the guise of a bearded silen, on coins of Greco-Thracian cities (compare the gold plaques, in the form of a silen's head, found by hundreds in the Crimea and in the Taman peninsula: pl. XVIII, 2). Is it an accident, that one of the Bosphoran dynasts was named Satyros?

The types on the reverse of the Bosphoran coins are also of local origin. The arms of Panticapaeum are not Greek: the griffin treading upon an ear of corn or a fish, the sources whence the rulers and the citizens of the Bosphorus derived their wealth. The lion-headed griffin is the Iranian animal, created in Babylonia, and thence forward common throughout Asia, especially in the Iranian area. I have already mentioned the sculptures from a tomb in Paphlagonia, which belong, it is true, to the archaic period, but which offer many points of comparison with the reverses of Bosphoran coins.

It must be recognized, therefore, that the engravers of the Panticapaean dies were no mere imitators. Masters of Greek craftsman ship, endowed with Greek creative genius, they invented original types which are true emblems of the Bosphoran state, half-Greek, half-Thracian, with strong Iranian influence. In painting, the art is of the same partially local kind. True that those masterpieces of decorative art, the painted wooden and sculptured coffins, may have been imported from Greece or Asia Minor: I do not believe it, but owing to the scarcity of wood-carvings from classical times, I cannot offer proof. But examine the wall paintings in the houses and tombs of this period. We have a whole series of these, partly from Panticapaeum, partly from the Taman peninsula; I have recently republished them in a special work. These paintings are undoubtedly local work; they were executed on the spot by Greek artists. They follow the Greek fashion, and help us to reconstruct the pre-Pompeian system of mural decoration in Greece. But observe them closely. The house decorations are very like those at Delos. Yet there are important differences. At Panticapaeum, the colour is richer and more various, but the architectural effect is poorer: both characteristics of Oriental art. Study the paintings of the two Taman barrows, Great Bliznitsa and Vasyurinskaya Gora. The latter please by their colour: look at the juxtaposition of the dark blue on the roof with the bright red on the walls. The others follow the tradition of the monumental painting in Greek temples: sober ornamentation of friezes and capitals. But the head of Demeter, on the keystone of the Egyptian vault, is not quite Greek. Compare it with the head of the same goddess in a grave belonging to the first century A.D., and the type will be seen to be the same: this is not Demeter, save in name only; it is really a native deity, the Great Goddess, mother of gods and men.

I consider myself justified, therefore, in affirming that the state of the Bosphorus was not by any means a group of little Greek towns lost on the shores of the Black Sea and living on what the mother country could send them. It developed an interesting and original form of life. It had the sagacity to invent a semi-Greek constitution, which held the state together for centuries; it contrived to make this form of government popular in Greece, and by means of propaganda issued by its historians, to install Bosphoran tyrants, such as Leucon and Pairisades, in the great gallery of famous statesmen whose names were familiar in the Greek schools. It succeeded in spreading Greek civilization among its Scythian neighbours, and in saturating its non-Greek subjects with that civilization. For centuries it guaranteed the Greek world a cheap and abundant supply of provisions. It transformed wide tracts of steppe into cultivated fields. Finally, it created a vigorous art, which achieved brilliant triumphs, especially in toreutic, and of which I shall speak further in the following chapter.

In a word, the Bosphorus of the classical Greek period played an important part in the life of the ancient world. The time is past when, in the imagination of cultivated persons, the Greek world was bounded by the shores of Attica and of the Peloponnese. The power of the Greek genius consisted, above all, in its universality, in its flexibility, in its power of adapting itself to unfamiliar conditions, and of constructing, in foreign surroundings, focuses of civilization, in which whatsoever was strong and fertile in the native life was combined with the eternal creations of Greek intelligence.

This is what we see, wherever we look, on the outskirts of the Greek world, long before the so-called Hellenistic age, which merely entered into a heritage bequeathed by the Greeks of the fifth and especially the fourth century. Take Italy, where Samnites, Apulians, Etruscans, and, last of all, Latins, collaborated with the Greeks in producing a Greco-Italic civilization of high achievement: witness the painted vases made in Italy, and the mural paintings in Samnite and Etruscan tombs. Take Spain, with its Greco-Iberian art. Take Celtic Gaul, and the art of the La Tène period, which was strongly influenced by the Greek city of Marseilles, and which has much in common with the

Greco-Iranian art of Panticapaeum, excelling like that art, in toreutic. Little is known of Thrace in the Greek and Hellenistic epoch: but the cemeteries of the Greek cities in Thracian territory, so far as they have been explored, show so many resemblances with those of the Greek cities in South Russia, especially Olbia and her neighbours, that I do not doubt that in Thrace also the Greek artists availed themselves of their contact with the natives and adapted Greek art to the needs and tastes of the Thracian population. The great tumulary graves of Thracian chieftains, with their vaulted tomb-chambers, which have been found in Thrace and in Macedonia, present many analogies with the Bosphoran graves, both in their architecture and in their painted decoration, and bear witness to a close union, just as at Panticapaeum, of local aristocracy and Greek colonists. I feel sure that systematic exploration of the Thracian tumuli will yield the same result as the work of Russian scholars in Scythian tombs. Finally, I am convinced that careful investigation in Pontus, in Cappadocia, in Paphlagonia, in Bithynia will reveal similar phenomena.

One of the most pressing tasks, in the scientific exploration of Asia Minor, is the excavation of the oldest and wealthiest Greek colonies on the southern shore of the Black Sea: Sinope, Amisos, Heracleia.

V.
THE SCYTHIANS AT THE END OF THE FOURTH AND IN THE THIRD CENTURY B.C.

WE have seen how the Scythians spread over the South Russian steppes in the seventh century, how they consolidated their empire and extended it westwards as far as the Danube and even beyond. We are somewhat ill acquainted with their political history, for they have left no written monuments, and the allusions in Herodotus and other Greek writers are few and vague. It is a pity that we do not possess the books of Ephorus in which he related the history of the Scythians in the sixth, fifth and fourth centuries: all we have is a few extracts from his description of Scythian manners and customs.

Notwithstanding the meagreness of our information, we can still trace the general lines along which the Scythian empire evolved. It was primarily a conquering state. Like the Cimmerians before them, the Scythians tended to embody in their empire Thrace on the one hand, and Transcaucasia on the other, so as to have access to Asia Minor, with which they maintained regular commercial relations through the Greek cities. This tendency brought them into contact with Persia, the other Iranian power at this period, which was much stronger and much more highly civilized than the Scythian state, but resembled it in its conquering propensity and in its aspiration to universal empire. The two Iranian movements met in Thrace and in the Caucasus.

The Scythian world was by no means unknown to the Persians. Within their own empire, on their north-west confines, the Persians had to contend with the Sacians and the Scythians of Asia Minor, who were closely akin to the European Scythians. It was not until about 590 B.C. that the Medes, and after them the Persians, were able to substitute their own supremacy for the Scythian in Asia Minor. Even after the final Persian conquest of Asia Minor, there were whole provinces in which the majority of the population, or at least the predominant section, was Scythian. I have already mentioned certain portions of Armenia, Sakasene and Skythene, in which the Scythians undoubtedly formed the ruling aristocracy. We know that even in Hellenistic and Roman times the Iranian families constituted a ruling class, and that the social structure of the country closely resembled the feudalism of the Iranian countries in general. We have no reason to suppose that the Iranian parts of Armenia were differently organized during the period of Persian domination, a domination which was probably only nominal.

It must not be forgotten, on the other hand, that there was constant communication between the two shores, northern and southern, of the Black Sea, and that the existence of a flourishing and independent Scythian kingdom on the northern shore fostered the aspirations of the Scythians on the southern shore. Thus the Scythian kingdom on the Black Sea littoral was not only known to the Persian empire, but dreaded by it.

Darius's project for annexing the whole of Greece was imperilled by Scythian ascendancy in Thrace, and by the chance of a Scythian onslaught at the very moment when his troops were marching on Greece by way of Thrace and Macedonia. If Darius really wished to become master of the Greek world, it was essential for him to protect his rear both in the Caucasus and in Thrace. This is the true explanation of the famous expedition of Darius; in Herodotus' account, the historical facts are almost completely obscured by fable and legend. I cannot think that Darius was bent upon conquest, or that he intended to destroy and subjugate the Scythian empire. He was accompanied by Ionian generals who knew Scythia well and had no motive for deceiving their supreme chief. They were fully conscious of the difficulties which such a plan presented. It is more likely that Darius had the same intention as Philip and Alexander before their expedition to Asia. To make an impressive raid into the Scythian kingdom as a proof of Persian power, to deal one or two heavy blows at the Scythian army, while his Cappadocian satrap Ariaramnes conducted a naval demonstration in the waters of the Greek colonies who were tributary to the Scythians, and along the northern and eastern shores of the Black Sea: this was all that Darius desired to do. I make no doubt that he attained his object. Ctesias states that the expedition of Ariaramnes was completely successful, and that by his raid he not only managed to reconnoitre the country but to capture a member of the Scythian royal family, Marsagetes, the king's brother. What Herodotus gives us is the Greco-Scylthian version of the story; but he cannot conceal the fact, that Darius himself advanced far enough into Scythian territory to terrify the Scythians and to force them to respect the Persian forces. Darius, who was an Iranian like the Scythians, and who had fought the Scythians in Asia, knew beforehand that he had to deal with a mobile cavalry force, and he was doubtless well prepared for those tactics which were afterwards adopted by the Parthians and are hence no less familiar to us than they were to the Persian king. Did he suffer from lack of water? I can hardly suppose so: South Russia is not the Sahara: drinking water is to be had everywhere.

In a word, I believe that Darius succeeded in his enterprise, and that his expedition to Thrace and to Scythia made it possible for him, at a given moment, to invade Greece through Thrace and Macedonia. It is no proof of the contrary, that after this expedition the Scythians executed a raid which carried them as far as the Thracian Chersonese: it is merely another proof, that the Scythian empire was an aggressive power.

The expedition of Darius did not seriously affect the Scythian empire: but it put a stop to expansion southward and westward, and confined the Scythians to the frontiers marked by the Caucasus on the south and by the Danube on the west.

Much more momentous for the Scythian empire were the development of the Bosphoran state, described in our fourth chapter, and the influence of the Athenians in Thrace, where they succeeded in consolidating a powerful native state, that of the Odrysians, which was capable of seriously impeding any attempt of the Scythian kings to renew their expansion towards the west. The Odrysian state, which I cannot discuss at length, existed as a vassal of the Athenian empire until the second half of the fourth century, and presents striking analogies, politically and socially, with the kingdom of the Bosphorus. The kingdom of the Bosphorus, which commanded the mouths of the Don, together with the city of Tanais, founded as an advanced post by Panticapaeum, cut the Scythian empire in two, and the creation of a stable state in the north of the Balkan peninsula closed the door to the west.

But it was not until the end of the fourth century that the position of the Scythians in South Russia became critical. The kingdom of the Bosphorus was richer and more powerful than ever: the Spartocid tyrants, by engaging mercenaries and by mobilizing the native population, got together an army which was probably equal if not superior to the Scythian. On the east, the Sarmatian tribes slowly advanced over the Ural and Orenburg steppes, crossed the Volga, occupied the line of the Don and very likely put an end to Scythian supremacy on the Kuban: we have seen that none of the Scythian graves on the Kuban date from the third century. In consequence the Scythians were obliged to concentrate their attention upon the western and northern portion of their state. We shall see that they contrived to enlarge their empire northwards in the regions of Kiev, of Poltava and of Voronezh, and to plant their civilization in places where hitherto little Scythian influence had been felt.

Let us now turn to the west. Pompeius Trogus furnishes us with precious information about certain events, which took place at the end of the fourth century, and which bear witness to vigorous Scythian expansion towards the west. We learn that the Scythian king Ateas advanced to the southern bank of the Danube and attacked the Histrians: that is to say, he was in process of occupying the Dobrudzha. Philip of Macedon encountered him and defeated him with great loss. As Philip was returning, he was assaulted by the Triballians and had to relinquish all his booty. The story related by Justin is full of suspicious details, romantic and anecdotical, but the fact of the expedition of Ateas and his fight with Philip remains certain. The defeat of Ateas was by no means final. We know from the same author that at the time of Alexander's eastern expedition, one of his generals, Zopyrion, made an expedition to Scythia, probably to cover northern Macedonia: after advancing as far as the walls of Olbia, which may have been held by the Scythians, he perished with his whole army of thirty thousand men. These two events testify to a Scythian policy of westward expansion, resolute, vigorous and systematic. The aim of the Scythians was not only to strengthen their power beyond the Danube, but also to occupy, if possible, the whole western bank of the Black Sea, and to reduce to vassalage the small tribal states in the adjacent part of Thrace. To judge by the expeditions of Philip and of Alexander, the danger was grave, and the Macedonians had great trouble in dislodging the Scythians from Thrace and in driving them back beyond the Danube.

No doubt the Macedonian expeditions weakened the Scythian power, but they did not succeed in destroying Scythian influence on the Danube and beyond it. The Scythians were able to hold out for a long time, perhaps until the Roman period, in the Dobrudzha, where they founded a fairly powerful state, which endured for centuries, outlasting even the ruin of the great Scythian state in South Russia and the retreat of the Scythians into the Crimea. The existence of a Scythian state in the Dobrudzha, resembling that in the Crimea, is attested by archaeological and numismatical evidence. I shall speak later of the silver rhyton found at Poroina, which closely resembles contemporary work of the same class from South Russia, and which points to similar religious and political ideas. I shall also mention the instructive series of coins issued by the Scythian kings of the Dobrudzha, which suggest that the Greek cities of Tomi and Istros were dependants of the Scythian kingdom of the Dobrudzha. No doubt this state was strongly influenced by the Thracian population of the country.

A deadly blow was dealt to Scythian expansion beyond the Danube, not by the Macedonian monarchs, but by the general political situation in Central Europe from the beginning of the third century onwards. In 291, when Lysimachus was trying to strengthen the northern frontier of his Thracian kingdom, the enemies who confronted him on the Danube were not Scythians but Getians. This suggests that Scythian power in the steppes between Danube and Dniester had sustained a serious reverse, no doubt owing to the victorious advance of Celtic and perhaps Germanic tribes, who, about this time, began to invade the steppes of South Russia on their way to the Black Sea.

The anarchy which began to prevail in the Russian steppes, as the result of this advance of Northern tribes, is attested by the facts related in the well-known Olbian decree in honour of Protogenes, a rich citizen and merchant of Olbia. The most interesting feature of the decree is the evidence which it furnishes as to the attitude of the Scythian king Saitapharnes towards Olbia, and the attitude of divers petty kings and princes of adjacent tribes towards the same city. Their demands for tribute became more and more exacting and vexatious. One feels that the little tribes, of different nationality, established in the steppes between Dnieper and Bug, Scythians, Sandaratians, Thisamatians, were mortally afraid of the advancing Galatians and Scirians and were desirous of finding refuge and security behind the Olbian city walls, which Protogenes had helped to build. The anxiety to complete the fortifications of Olbia shows that conditions had greatly changed since the fifth, and probably the fourth century, when the Scythian dynasts lived peaceably in Olbia and built houses and palaces there.

I must state in passing, in order to avoid misunderstanding, that I see no reason to date the Protogenes inscription in the second century or even in the second half of the third. Historical as well as palaeographical considerations are entirely in favour of an earlier date, the beginning of the third century. I also insist on the fact, not generally realized, that King Saitapharnes was the great Scythian king who retired, before the advance of Northern tribes, towards the seat of his power, the steppes in the district of Taurida. It is he who is the King pure and simple, the suzerain of the various sceptre-bearers (σκηπτοῦχοι) who are mentioned in the inscription of Protogenes.

The advance of the Galatians put an end, once and for all, to Scythian ascendancy on the banks of the Danube. The survival of a Scythian state in the Dobrudzha is explained by the geographical situation of the Danube delta, which resembles the delta of the Kuban. Have we more precise evidence as to the Scythian occupation of the lower Danube valley, its duration, character, and vicissitudes? Unhappily we have not. We do not possess sufficient archaeological data, for the archaeological exploration of Bulgaria and Rumania is still in its infancy: and the literary tradition does not deal with these questions. Recent finds, however, made by chance in one or two tumuli in southern Bulgaria, give us a glimpse of the result that may be expected from methodical investigation of the tumuli in Bulgaria and in Rumania. I need not dwell upon these finds, which have lately been published, with a commentary, by Filov, whose conclusions I am unable to accept. Unfortunately, he has not taken the trouble to make a close study of Russian archaeological material, but has contented himself with a few superficial comparisons. Without entering into controversy, I shall briefly indicate the nature of these finds and the conclusions which I draw from them. The most instructive finds are those of Brezovo and of Panagyurishte in the department of Philippopolis: after them, of Bedniakovo in the department of Chirpan and of Radyuvene in the department of Lovech. The objects from the first three places were discovered in tumulary graves. Although the graves were not regularly excavated, the information which Filov collected locally enables us to form a notion of the funerary ritual. It closely resembles the Scythian ritual, and particularly that which prevailed on the Dnieper in the fourth and third centuries B.C.: an Oriental ritual, but here attenuated and unpretentious, compared with that of the great royal tombs by the Kuban and the Dnieper. Characteristic, the burial of the body under a tumulus in a stone chamber, and the interment, beside the body or in the loose earth of the tumulus, of one or more horses with richly ornamented bridles. We may conjecture that the bridle was sometimes laid in the tomb with the body, and the horse slaughtered on the half-finished mound. The tomb furniture, also, is very like that of the Scythian graves: a group of sacred vessels—chiefly paterae and sometimes spherical vases—, amphorae with wine and oil, and various drinking vessels, Greek and local; weapons; rich garments and diadems, loaded with gold; symbols of power—sceptre and ring; lastly, horse trappings, including a richly ornamented bridle. Just as in the Scythian tombs, part of the furniture consists of Greek objects imported from Greek colonies, especially Amphipolis, part of local imitations of Greek work, and part of purely native objects. These similarities cannot all be accidental; they point to close relations between the Scythians and the population of southern Bulgaria, and to strong Scythian influence on the natives. But there is more: we are astonished to find that the horse trappings are almost the same in the Thracian tombs and in the tombs of South Russia. We find the same pieces: frontlet, ear-guards, temple-pieces, nasal; the same Oriental practice of covering nearly the whole bridle with metal plaques; the same system of bits. Further, the two types of bridle ornament: round plaques embossed in the Greek manner; and plaques in the form of animals, cast and incised in the Oriental fashion. Lastly, and this is the most important of all: all the pieces in the animal style find striking parallels in the Scythian horse trappings, from Scythian tombs of the fourth and third centuries, which we shall discuss at length in the course of this chapter some of these are almost duplicates.

Besides these coincidences I may mention the tendency to reproduce local religious scenes on objects made for or by the natives: such scenes are the unexplained representation on the horse's frontlet from Panagyurishte, and the royal investiture, or holy communion, which appears on the Brezovo ring, and is common in objects from fourth-or third-century Scythian tombs in South Russia. We shall see that this tendency is characteristic of Scythian tombs in the fourth and third century, while it is unknown in earlier Scythian graves.

The tombs of southern Bulgaria were no doubt constructed for Thracian kinglets and princes. But it is clear that for their material culture these princes were completely dependent upon Greek and upon Scythian civilization. The horse trappings cannot all have been imported from Scythia: they were probably made in Thrace, but certainly after Scythian models. The local craftsman may well have introduced one or two alterations of detail, but he has preserved not only the principle of Scythian art, but even the features characteristic of western Scythia in the fourth and third centuries B.C. I see no reason for agreeing with Filov in postulating a parallel development of the animal style in Thrace and in Scythia. The Thracian pieces are obvious imitations of western Scythian work of the fourth and third centuries B.C.

How can we account for this Scythian influence, which shows itself not only in the adoption of the animal style, but also in funerary ritual and in political and religious ideas? I can see only one way. The Bulgarian finds all belong to the fourth century B.C. We have seen that the fourth century was marked by considerable Scythian expansion towards the west, and by the enfeeblement of the Odrysian state, which was no longer supported by Athens, and which was a dangerous rival to Macedonia. We must suppose that, profiting by these circumstances, the Scythians established themselves firmly on the lower Danube, influenced the neighbouring Thracian tribes, and probably reduced some of them to vassalage. The Bulgarian excavations show that the expeditions of Philip and of Zopyrion were only the last manifestations of a rivalry which had existed between Macedon and Scythia since the collapse of the Odrysian state, and that these manifestations presuppose Scythian ascendancy, nominal at least, in the regions adjoining Macedonian territory. Can it be presumed, that this ascendancy had continued without interruption from the expedition of Darius and the Scythian inroad into the Chersonese? I can hardly accept the theory: it is contradicted by what we know of the Odrysian kingdom and the anti-Scythian policy of Athens. Further and more systematic excavation in Bulgaria and Rumania will give us more definite information. For the present I incline to believe that the Scythians, driven back by the Thracians with the aid of Athens in the fifth century B.C., resumed the offensive in the fourth, and succeeded in asserting supremacy, for some decades at least, over a number of Thracian tribes. The reverses suffered by the Scythians in the west, during the last years of the fourth century, and the pressure of the Sarmatians from the east, forced them to concentrate their efforts in the central and northern part of their state, the land on the Dnieper and between Dnieper and Don, including the tributaries of these rivers and the rich district of Poltava. We have already spoken of this country as it was in the neolithic, copper and bronze ages: what happened to it in the iron age, immediately before the arrival of the Scythians and after their conquest of South Russia?

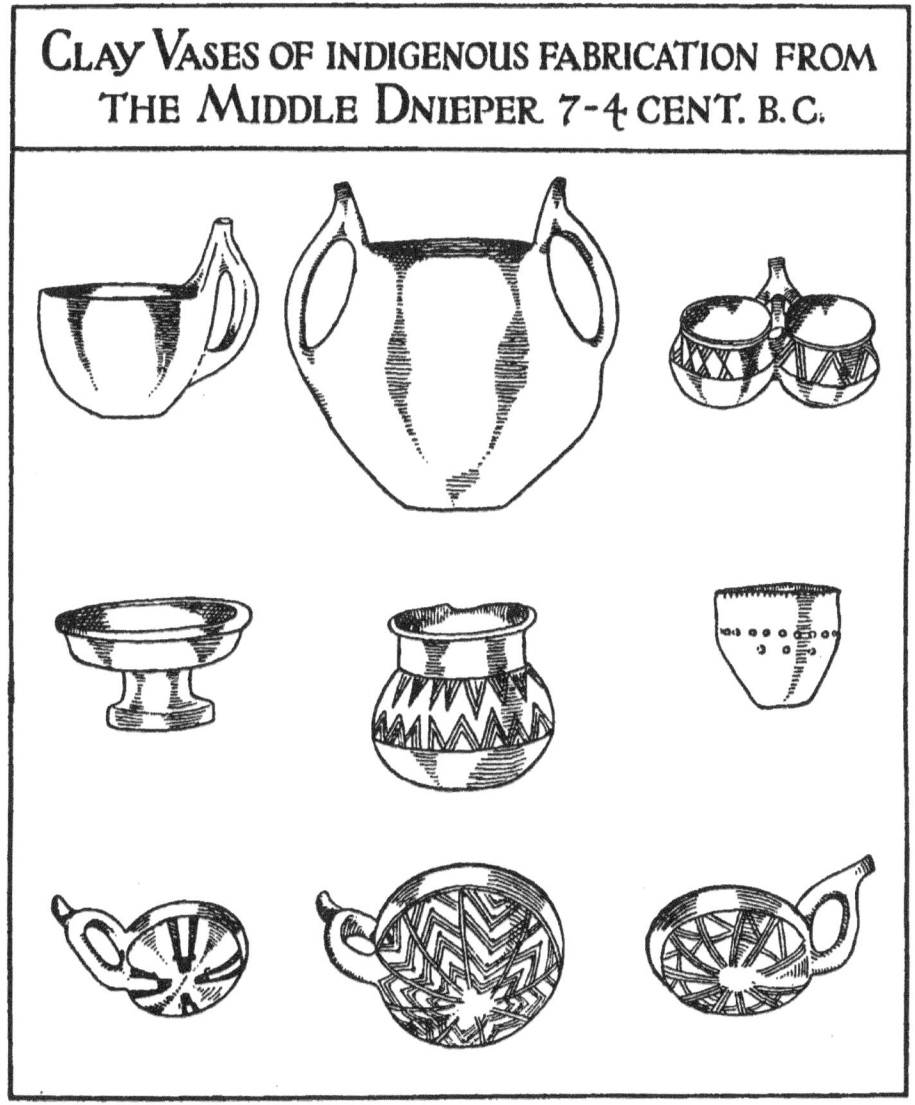

Fig. 9.

We have seen that as far back as the neolithic period, the regions between Dnieper and Bug and farther west were agricultural regions. Excavation in the ruins of the fortified settlements which are common enough in these parts—for example the excavations of Spitsyn in the gorodishche (ruins of a town) of Nemirov in Podolia, and those of Chvojka and of Bobrinskoy in the districts of Kiev and of Poltava—and archaeological investigations in the adjacent cemeteries, have shown that the conditions remained the same, even at the period when the mixed civilization of the tribes which brought the Spiral and maeander pottery and of those which constructed tumulary graves with contracted skeletons, gave place to an iron age civilization, probably introduced by conquering tribes. It was these tribes who first acquainted the western part of South Russia with the use of iron weapons, in shapes which remind one of the Hallstatt culture, for instance, the sword with antennae, and with a quite distinctive pottery which cannot be connected either with the spiral and maeander ware, or with the pottery of the graves with contracted skeletons. The pots are of black clay, with incised ornament filled in with white the ornament is exclusively geometric and is very primitive. The commonest and most typical shape is a cup with a big handle which is sometimes horned (fig. 9). This pottery recalls, most of all, the Bronze Age pottery of Hungary, also Trojan pottery of the so-called Cimmerian period, and the Hallstatt pottery of Central Europe. Unfortunately it has never been properly studied, although the Russian archaeological museums are full of it and the most interesting varieties have frequently been published.

The graves and settlements distinguished by iron weapons and the pottery just described are usually attributed to the Scythians: wrongly in my opinion. We have seen the culture brought with them by the Scythians: a mixed culture, purely nomadic and purely Oriental. In the eastern part of the Russian steppes, the tombs yield neither iron weapons of Hallstatt type, nor pottery of the kind described above. It is true that purely Scythian graves have been discovered in the steppes between Dnieper and Bug, for example the grave in a tumulus excavated by Melgunóv in the eighteenth century, which presents notable affinity with the finds at Kelermes. But these are exceptions. The majority of the graves in this region belong to a different type, both in structure and in contents (fig. 10). There is a certain superficial resemblance between the purely Scythian graves and those of the Dnieper region, which has misled scholars into ascribing the Dnieper graves to the Scythians. In both groups we have tumuli, and wooden structures under the tumuli. But in the Russian steppes, the tumulus, as a grave monument, does not begin in the Scythian period: it is much older: and the wooden funerary structure in the basin of the Dnieper is quite different from that on the Kuban. It is not a nomadic tent, but a farmer's house, a 'kháta', made of planks and tree-trunks it is not imitated from the type used in the nomadic graves, but derived from the type current in the district as early as the copper age. The funerary ritual of these graves differs from that of the Kuban basin in several essential points. There is no trace of hecatombs of horses, or of human sacrifice. The furniture of the tumulary graves in the Dnieper region, from the sixth to the fourth century, is rich and varied, and of a mixed description, just as in the Kuban graves. But the general aspect is very different from that of the Kuban tumuli. First of all, we must notice that the Dnieper graves are not exclusively those of ruling warriors, of nomadic chiefs: there are rich and poor graves, large and small. That implies a different social system.

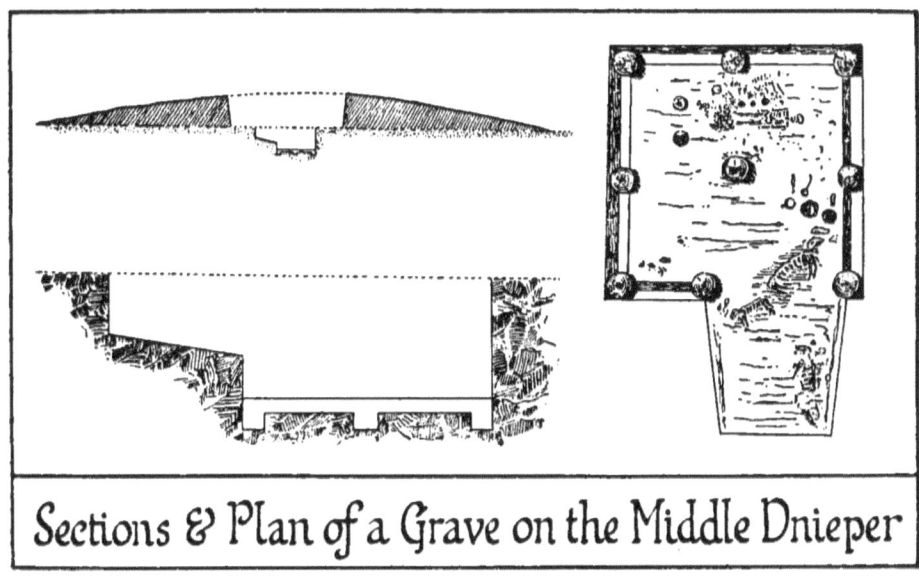

Fig. 10.

Again, the tomb furniture is not composed of the same elements on the Dnieper as on the Kuban. To judge from the excavations in the settlements and in the oldest raves, Greek influence set in long before Oriental influence, that is, long before the Scythian conquest. In the deepest, oldest strata of the settlements between Dnieper and Dniester, we regularly find heaps of native potsherds mingled with less numerous fragments of Greek seventh-century vases; also weapons and objects in bronze, iron and precious metal, of Hallstatt type: but no articles of Oriental origin. So likewise in the oldest so-called Scythian graves in the Dnieper region. Unfortunately; these graves have never been carefully studied and arranged in chronological order. The task is a difficult one, and I cannot undertake it here: it could only be executed on the spot, above all in the great archaeological museum of Kiev. But to judge from the reports published by Bobrinskoy, Brandenburg, Samokvásov and Chvojka, and from the objects reproduced in the works of Bobrinskoy and Khanenko, it seems that the oldest graves in the Kiev region do not differ from the oldest strata of the settlements, that is to say, they present the same mixture of Greek and Hallstatt objects.

The uniform culture of the eighth and seventh centuries B.C. changes towards the end of the seventh century and even more in the sixth. We find at this period, in the steppes of western Russia, certain graves of purely Oriental type which resemble those of the Kuban region. I have already spoken of them. Again, in the common graves, side by side with Greek and Hallstatt things, which are still very plentiful, there are products of Oriental art and industry, some of them decorated in the animal style. Towards the end of the sixth century, these products become more and more frequent, but in the fifth century they are gradually ousted by objects imported from Greece. But the staple of the furniture remains native. Down to the fourth century B.C., native pottery predominates and Hallstatt weapons outnumber Greek and Scythian.

The predominance of native and Hellenic elements in the west is an extremely characteristic and important feature. We have found nothing like it in the region of the Kuban, where the material culture of the native was completely absorbed, first by Oriental, and then by Greek civilization.

One is tempted to ask, whether racial difference may not account for the difference of archaeological aspect. What was the nationality of the tribes with the black pottery and the Hallstatt weapons? From the parallels which we have adduced, western South Russia would appear to have been closely connected, in material culture, with the portions of Europe and of Asia Minor peopled, both then and in the later neolithic and the copper ages, by Thracians. It was conceivably tribes of Thracian stock which invaded the western steppes of Russia, perhaps for the second time, in the iron age. But I prefer to abstain from ill-founded hypotheses. We must wait until Rumanian, Bulgarian and Serbian scholars can give us more methodical information as to the prehistory of the central and northern parts of the Balkan peninsula.

Meanwhile we have a consistent picture: the continuous evolution of a distinctive material civilization in the western portion of the Russian steppes: a powerful native civilization, in touch with the Greeks from the seventh century onwards, and an Oriental element which becomes more and more prominent from the end of the seventh century and the beginning of the sixth.

This archaeological picture accords very well with the historical data quoted above. It is clear that from the seventh to the fourth century the sovereignty of the Scythians in the western part of their empire was neither very powerful nor very oppressive. It made little alteration in the social and economic order which prevailed on the Dnieper and the Bug before the arrival of the Scythians. The Scythians no doubt contented themselves with exacting tribute from the conquered peoples and repressing their attempts to regain their freedom. The tribute from the agricultural districts, and the furs delivered by the hunters in the forests, enabled the conquerors to conduct a profitable traffic with the Greek city of Olbia. The centre of Scythian ascendancy did not lie in the western part of the kingdom. Being nomads, the Scythians needed the freedom of the steppes, for their cattle, and for their military training: hunting, wild rides, and warlike exercises. We have seen that their centre, from the sixth to the fourth century, was somewhere in the steppes between Dnieper and Don, probably near the coast of the Sea of Azov.

In the fourth century, the events which I have already mentioned considerably modified the circumstances of the Scythian state, driving it westward and northward. I have spoken of the Scythian advance towards the west: we must now turn to the archaeological evidence as to the organization of the principal part of the Scythian empire, the part between Don and Dnieper, especially along the Dnieper and its tributaries, after these events, that is to say in the fourth and third centuries B.C.

When archaeologists began to explore the tumuli, often of enormous size, in the region east and west of the lower Dnieper, they were dazzled by the magnificence of these truly regal sepulchres. So rich were the tumuli of Chertomlýk, of Alexandrópol, of the Tsymbálka; the Ogüz, Dêev and Chmyrëva barrows; the Sêrogózy and Známenka groups; and, above all, the now famous tumulus of Solókha, and the tumulus explored by myself in Count Mordvínov's estate, the Black Valley, Chërnay Dolina: that explorers were led to identify this whole vast region with the half-mythical locality of Gerrhoi, mentioned more than once by Herodotus. But quite apart from the question, whether Gerrhoi was a real place at all, the chronology of these tumuli was not taken into account. I maintain, and I have often essayed to prove, that they form a chronological unit, that they all belong to the same period, that none of them is earlier than the end of the fourth century or later than the second half of the third, a period of a hundred years more or less. I cannot repeat all my arguments: I will indicate them briefly.

The unity of the group is proved by the following facts: first, the type of sepulchral structure is the same; secondly, the funerary ritual is the same; thirdly, the composition of the tomb furniture is almost identical; fourthly, the style of the objects is the same; fifthly, duplicates are often found in different tombs, especially duplicates of the gold plaques sewn on to garments: the plaques were produced and sold in large quantities.

The chronology of the group has been hotly disputed. According to some scholars, some of the tombs date from the fifth century: Farmakovski and others place some of them in the second century B.C. Both dates are impossible. Comparison of the contents with dated objects, especially of the garment plaques with the Greek coins from which they were imitated; analysis of the pottery found in some of the graves; and other considerations which I cannot specify here, lead me to place the whole group at the end of the fourth and the beginning of the third century.

Now if I am right, if the whole group is much later than Herodotus, it is not possible to identify the region with Herodotus' Gerrhoi. In the period between the sixth and fourth centuries, Gerrhoi, as I have already pointed out, must have been situated farther east, corresponding to the political centre of the Scythian kingdom in the time of Herodotus. On the other hand, ours are certainly royal sepulchres. They can only have belonged to members of the dynasty of the great Scythian kings. They prove that in the fourth and third centuries B.C. the political centre of the Scythian empire was no longer where we supposed it to have been from the sixth to the fourth century, but farther to the west, nearer to the Dnieper on one side and the Crimea on the other. The transference can easily be accounted for by the events to which I have alluded above. Forced to concentrate west and north, especially north, the Scythians moved westwards, with their capital covering the route to the Crimea, their last refuge in case of retreat. Their main task was to command the Dnieper and to keep in contact with their northern provinces: otherwise they would have nothing to sell to the Greeks. It was impossible to command the Dnieper without bringing their political and military head-quarters nearer the river and disposing their armed forces along its banks. If they remained concentrated on the Sea of Azov, they could not face attacks delivered from the west and aimed at the wealthy agricultural regions on the middle and lower Dnieper and the populated nuclei in that district, including Olbia. Nor could they pursue an active policy on the Bug, the Dniester and the Danube, unless they moved their main forces in that direction.

The archaeological and historical considerations, which lead me to postulate a transference of the Scythian centre to the lower Dnieper and the approach to the Crimea, are confirmed by further archaeological evidence. We have seen that, during the period in which the Scythian centre lay in the eastern part of the steppes between Dnieper and Don, Scythian culture exercised comparatively little influence on the region of the Dnieper. But from the fourth or third century onwards, the aspect of things alters appreciably in this part of the Scythian state. Henceforward, on the middle course of the Dnieper and westward in the fertile country between Dnieper and Bug, as well as in the regions east of the Dnieper, on its eastern tributaries, the Sula, the Psël, the Vorskla (the district of Poltava) as far as the middle course of the Don (the district of Vorónezh), we find a goodly number of purely Scythian graves, belonging to the same period and presenting the same characteristics as the already-mentioned graves on the lower Dnieper and in Taurida. The large and sumptuous tombs of Ryzhanóvka, of Dárievka, of Ilyintsý, of Novosëlki, in the districts of Kiev and Podolia; a number of tombs in the great tumulary cemeteries belonging to the native settlements—big fortified towns—of Romny; finally, the tumulary cemeteries of the middle Don: all these recall, feature by feature, the kurgans of the lower Dnieper and of Taurida. The ancient funerary ritual of the natives is still retained, but considerably modified by the purely Scythian ritual. Even the traditional wooden structure is sometimes abandoned, and replaced by the tomb-chambers of the lower Dnieper. Horses are now sacrificed the funeral car appears, the canopy, the canopy poles with rattles atop surmounted by figures of animals and of deities. At the same time the tomb furniture also changes. There is no longer any native pottery, and hardly any weapons of Hallstatt type. The whole furniture assumes a marked Oriental character, and the Greek objects imported from Olbia give place to objects which seem, as I shall show at the end of this chapter, to have been produced in Panticapaeum. Particularly characteristic is the repetition, in both groups of graves, of the same types of caparison plaque. It is important to notice, that on the middle Dnieper, in Poltava and in Voronezh, the plaques are always imitations, sometimes very coarse, of the plaques on the lower Dnieper: we found the same in Bulgaria. Still more characteristic: some of the objects from this area are duplicates of objects found in the Crimea and on the lower Dnieper; thus a replica of the celebrated Chertomlýk gorytus was found at Ilyintsy. Gold garment-plaques, from tumuli in the districts of Kiev and Poltava, find counterparts, made from fellow dies, on the lower Dnieper. The habit, which distinguishes, as we shall see, our group of tombs, of decorating artistic objects with scenes from Scythian life, and of adorning jewels with figures of local deities, is general in the region which we are studying. Take the silver vase from the Voronezh tomb, decorated with scenes from Scythian camp-life: it is not a duplicate of the famous electrum vase from Kul-Oba, but it obviously originated in the same artistic area. Take the earrings from another tomb in Voronezh, with figures of the great local goddess: certainly native work, but imitated from Panticapaean models. Take the silver plaque from the same tomb. Take, lastly, the gold ornaments from the tiara of the lady buried at Ryzhanovka, which find exact parallels at Chertomlýk and elsewhere.

These resemblances cannot be fortuitous. We cannot but recognize that in the fourth and third centuries, the Scythians endeavoured to install themselves, as a ruling class, in the northern regions of their empire, to transform their suzerainty into a real domination, and to extend that domination as far as possible to the north. It will not be denied that this

Scythian expansion, hitherto unnoticed, is an historical fact of the first importance, for it must be remembered, that the middle Dnieper, with Kiev, was the cradle of the great Slavonic state from which modern Russia sprang.

These archaeological data agree most admirably with the history of the Scythian state from the fourth to the third centuries B.C., as I have set it forth above. I will repeat my conclusions. Weakened in the east, the Scythian power tried to extend westward and northward. Its western conquests broke down under the pressure of the Macedonians and the Thracians, and the Gallo-German invasion created a very difficult situation in the steppes between Danube and Dnieper. But the Scythians maintained themselves between Dnieper and Don, and were able to wield vigorous sway in the adjoining regions north ward, on the middle Dnieper and the middle Don. Not for long, however. Towards the second half of the third century, the Sarmatians crossed the Don and advanced on the Dnieper; the Scythian provinces on the middle Dnieper fell into anarchy and were partially invaded by Germanic and perhaps Slavonic tribes. The Scythians were driven back into the Crimea and towards the shores of the Black Sea, they were confined within narrow limits and reduced to comparative indigence. The great Scythian empire collapsed for ever.

Nevertheless the fourth and third centuries were a period of great prosperity for the Scythian state. The loss of the eastern provinces was counterbalanced by acquisitions in the west and by the strengthening of Scythian power in the agricultural region of the middle Dnieper and the middle Don. Scythian trade flourished. It must not be forgotten, that this period corresponds to the great conquests of Alexander and the formation of the Hellenistic states. In an era of political expansion, which witnessed the development of a really world-wide trade and the creation and amplification of a modern industrial system, the Greek world needed enormous quantities of food-stuffs and of raw material. The supplies were absorbed eagerly, and gladly paid for with the gold which Alexander had brought from conquered Persia and put into circulation. No wonder, therefore, that the period of Scythian political decay was a period of great material prosperity. It was not otherwise in the Greek cities on the Black Sea. The kingdom of the Bosphorus, as we have already seen, was never so flourishing as at this time. Even Olbia, which passed through many anxious ours, remained rich, although wealth passed more and more into the hands of one or two families, like that of

Heroson and Protogenes: these families succeeded in equipping a fleet which was sufficiently large and powerful to give them the monopoly of the Scythian trade. Read the inscription of Protogenes, and similar inscriptions from the Greek cities on the western shore of the Black Sea, and you will be astonished by the great wealth of certain families, and by the poverty of the city itself, crushed by debts and exactions.

It is therefore not surprising that in this period of political decay, the Scythian tombs are full of gold and silver, of superb works of art, of jewels and of precious stones. Apart from the sixth century, the Scythian tombs were never so rich as in the fourth and third centuries B.C.

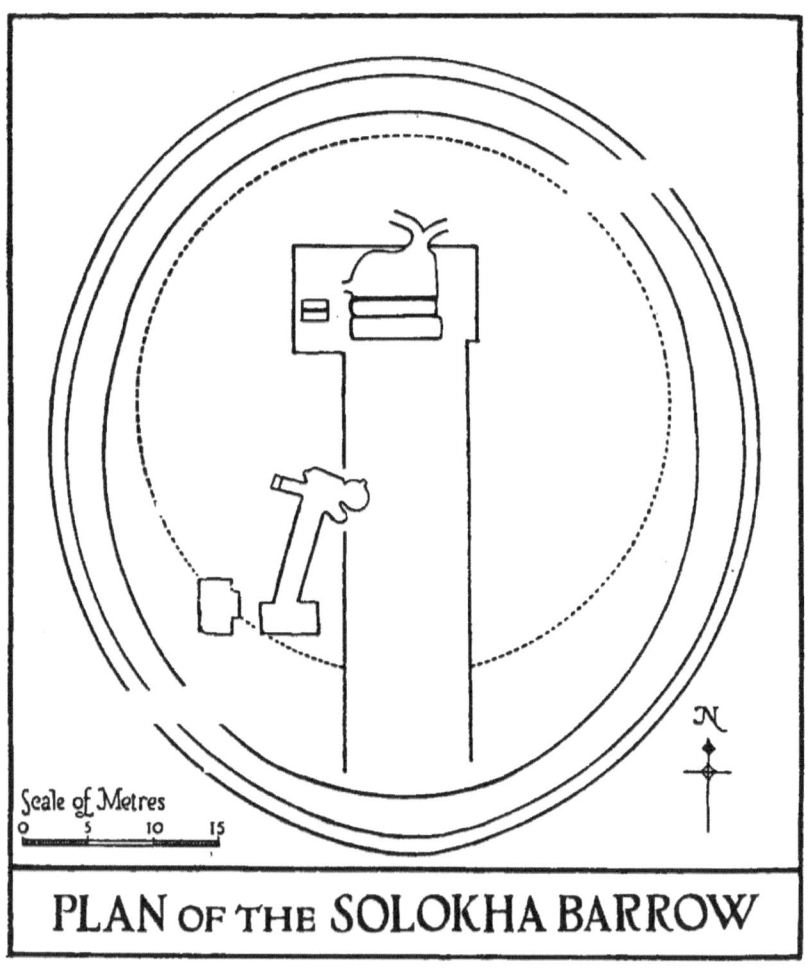

Fig. 11.

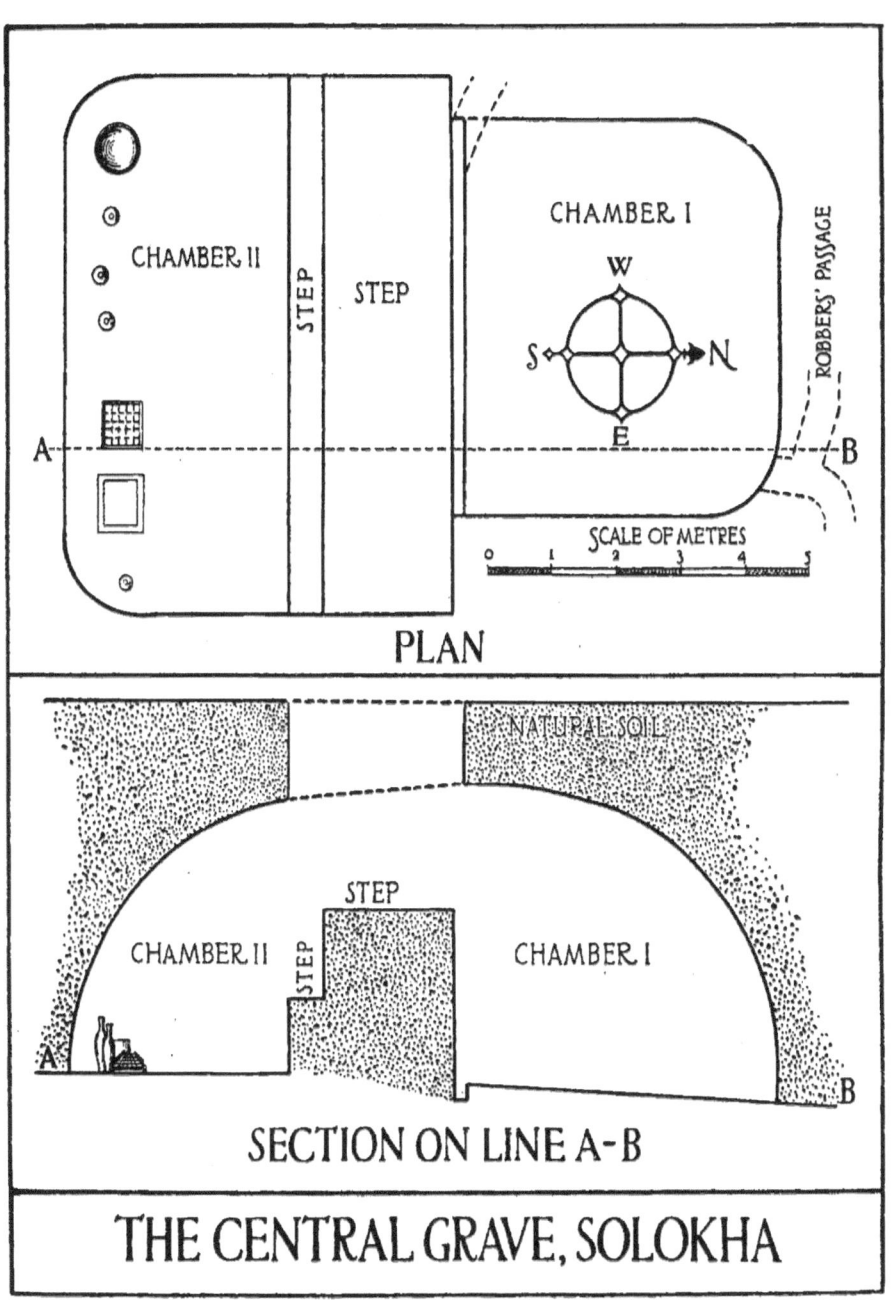

Fig. 12.

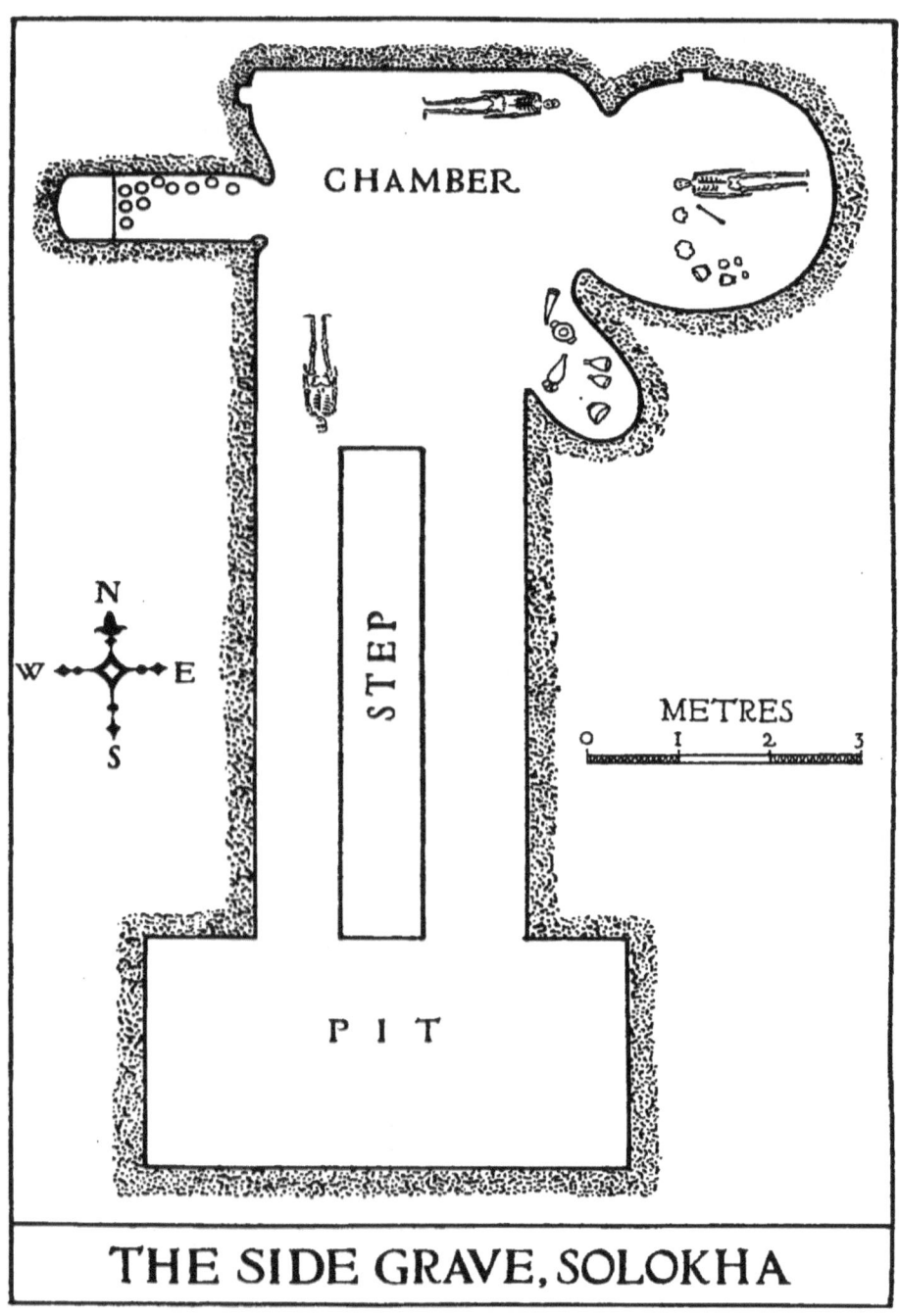

Fig. 13.

These graves are not essentially different from the Kuban graves: the same type of nomad chieftain's tomb, the same stately ritual, the same heavy profusion of gold, silver, and other precious objects. There are modifications, however, due to various geographical and economic causes. First of all, the structure beneath the tumulus is no longer of wood: it is replaced by a chamber or chambers dug in virgin soil inside the walls of the sepulchral trench (figs. 11, 12). The change was undoubtedly occasioned by the lack of forests in the immediate neighbourhood of the steppes adjoining the Crimea. Again, horses are no longer slaughtered in great numbers. It is clear that owing to agricultural development in the riverine and coastal districts it became more difficult to keep large herds of horses: their value increased, and oxen were preferred for the purpose of sacrifice. It was now considered sufficient, to slaughter the horses which drew the funeral car, and the dead man's parade horses: in the poorer graves, the sacrifice was merely simulated, by the interment of the horse's bridle. Lastly, under the single tumulus, not one, but two sepulchral chambers were made, one subsequently to the other, the second always after the construction of the tumulus. The second chamber sometimes accommodates a woman: but by no means regularly. In the Solokha kurgan, the additional chamber was reserved for a man, who was buried with enormous wealth beside him (figs. 11-13).

With these exceptions, the funerary ritual remains the same. The funeral cars, the canopies with poles crowned by rattles and figures of animals and deities, the bells on the canopies, the funeral repast, the sacrifice of servants and of horses: all these are found on the Dnieper as on the Kuban.

The tomb furniture is no less rich, perhaps richer, than in the period between the sixth and fourth centuries. The contents of the Kul-Oba tumulus, mentioned in my first chapter, are well known and have often been published. It is typical tomb furniture of the period. To give an idea of the wealth of such furniture, I shall enumerate the objects which were buried with the dead in the lateral grave at Solokha (fig. 13) and which recur, with slight modifications, in all the tombs of our group. Arms: two swords, one with gold-plated sheath and guard; a quiver plated with silver gilt (pl. XXI, 1); a bronze helmet; a scale corslet of bronze; bronze greaves; a number of copper weapons or sceptres. Ornaments: a gold torc, a necklace or chain of gold tubes, with gold pendants, five bracelets of solid gold, more than three hundred gold garment-plaques; a solid gold comb (pl. XIX). Vessels: a gold patera (pl. XX, 3), seven silver vases (pl. XX, 1, 2), some wooden vases plated with gold, three large copper cauldrons, and several amphorae for wine or oil.

PLATE XIX

GOLD COMB FROM THE 'SOLOKHA' TUMULUS
IV Cent. B.C. Hermitage, Petrograd

Still richer were the tombs of Chertomlýk and of Alexandropol, and those of the Chmyrëva Mogila and of the Sêrogozy group: for not only the king's grave but the queen's grave was found as well. The jewels worn by the women were extremely rich and various, and usually very heavy and costly. Their festal costume was loaded with gold, especially the great conical tiara, of Irano-Greek type, which I have lately reconstructed by means of fragments from a number of different graves.

We must notice that nearly all these objects were artistic works covered with figures and ornaments in relief: sometimes artistic works of the highest order. Let us compare the funeral inventory with that of the Scythian tombs on the Kuban. The superficial aspect has not altered. Side by side with pure Greek work, made for Greeks but sold to Scythians, a series of Greek objects made for Scythians, and a series which seems pure Scythian, especially some jewels, the bridle decoration, the ornaments of the funeral canopies, and those of the funeral cars. But if we look more closely we detect a notable change, particularly in the second class of products. We have seen that as early as the fifth century, Greek artists adapted themselves to Scythian taste, fashioned for them weapons and ornaments of regular Scythian type, and endeavoured to please them by decorating these articles in the animal style which the Scythians loved. But while they thus consulted the taste of their customers, they remained Greeks. They ennobled the shapes, and they partly substituted the animal style of Asia Minor for the Scythian. But their art remained purely decorative: religious subjects are rarely found, and that only on pure Greek objects brought to the Russian steppes by chance.

In the fourth and third centuries there is a significant change. There is still importation from Iranian lands: for instance, one of the Chertomlýk swords, and some engraved gems. But most of the objects are the work of Greek artists. They still produced the same kind of weapons and ornaments. But the mode of decoration is quite different. The animal style is no longer predominant, but confined to subsidiary positions. Scenes with figures now prevail: and strange scenes! Partly representations from Greek mythology, taken almost at random from the plentiful repertory of the Greeks, and employed, more or less successfully, to decorate surfaces for which the originals were never intended: examples are the celebrated gorytus of Chertomlýk, a replica of which has lately been discovered at Ilyintsy, and one of the sword-sheaths from the same tumulus. But the great majority of the objects are decorated with subjects which are completely new to Greek art, subjects borrowed from the religious and social life of the Scythians themselves. The scenes are studied in every detail. The minute rendering of Scythian costume and equipment corresponds exactly to the originals found in the tombs. The religious scenes are so peculiar, and so foreign to Greek ideas, that we must accept their correctness *a priori*. Some of them are like illustrations to Herodotus. The scenes from social life are slightly idealized, the types also. Here we can trace the Stoic tendency of Ephorus, who desired to substitute, for the real Scythians, Scythians idealized according to Stoic theory. But the idealization does not go very far. One can see that the Scythians themselves, under Greek influence, wished the Greek artists to provide them with objects reproducing Scythian scenes: scenes from their religious, from their economic and social life. Precious documents for reconstructing the life and the religion of the Scythians: let us try to profit by them, as briefly as we can.

PLATE XX

SILVER CUP AND GOLD PATERA FROM THE 'SOLOKHA'
TUMULUS
IV Cent. B.C. Hermitage, Petrograd.

PLATE XXI

1. 'GORYTOS' (bow and arrow case) covered with silver, from the 'Solokha' tulumus. IV Cent. B.C. Hermitage, Petrograd
2, 3. SILVER AMPHORAE from the 'Chertomlýk' tumulus (lower Dniper). III Cent. B.C. Hermitage, Petrograd

The religious scenes are mainly concerned with Scythian ideas about the connexion of the royal power with divinity. The chief subject is the rite of the holy communion, a rite which occurs later in the Irano-Pontic cult of Mithra, and which played a considerable part in the Christian religion. On the rhyton from Karagodeuashkh, we see the supreme god offering the holy communion to the king, by means of a rhyton filled with the sacred drink. Both king and god are represented on horseback, like the god Mithra on a number of Pontic coins and sculptures: under their horses' feet they trample the prostrate bodies of their enemies, the forces of evil: a valuable instance of the dualism of the Iranian religion. It is important to observe, that the same subject recurs, six centuries later, on Sassanid gems. Still more interesting, that the holy communion reappears on a great many other monuments, in which the administering divinity is not the great god Ahuramazda, but the Great Goddess whom we may call Anaitis. In the queen's grave at Karagodeuashkh, a scene like that on the rhyton is figured on the great triangular gold plaque which adorned the front of the ritual tiara (pl. XXIII, 1). The goddess is seated on a throne, clad in a heavy ceremonial garment, and wearing a tiara on her head: behind her are two priestesses with their heads veiled. A young Scythian noble, no doubt a prince, approaches the goddess on the right, and she offers him the holy communion in a rhyton. On the other side, a strange figure, a beardless man clad in a woman's garment, advances towards the goddess with a round vase, probably containing the sacred beverage, in his right hand: he must be a servant of the goddess, a priest: his facial features and his costume suggest that he is a eunuch. Now Herodotus states that among the Scythian aristocracy there was a special class of persons who were afflicted with a mysterious malady; they changed their male clothing for female and consecrated themselves to the worship of the goddess Herodotus calls them Enareans. Whatever the cause of the malady, whether that alleged by the pseudo-Hippocrates, or another, we may take it that the Enareans fulfilled the same function among the Scythians, in the worship of the Great Goddess, mother of gods, of men and of animals, as the eunuchs elsewhere. Above the communion scene is a figure of a god in a chariot; the type is influenced by the type of Helios, but the god, unless I am mistaken, is the great Iranian sun-god, the Sol Mithra of the Roman Empire. Lastly, in the uppermost row is a figure of a Greek Tyche which I should identify with the Iranian Hvareno. Whether my interpretation of the two upper rows be right or wrong, the scene in the lower row is certainly a religious one. The same scene is reproduced, over and over again, on the gold garment-plaques in the tumuli of our group (pl. XXIII, 4). A kind of contamination of the scenes on the rhyton of Karagodeuashkh and on the tiara is engraved on a rhyton from a tomb near the village of Merdjany, where the king, on horseback, is receiving the holy communion from a goddess seated on a throne and holding the round sacred vessel in her hands, while the king holds the rhyton (pl. XXIII, 2). An interesting detail is the sacred spike with a horse's skull on it, which stands near the goddess, indicating the sacrifice of horses to her.

It is very important to notice, that the same religious and political conceptions found their way into Thrace, part of which, as we have seen, was ruled by Scythian conquerors in the fourth century. Among the objects, already mentioned, from Brezovo in southern Bulgaria, is a gold ring engraved with the counterpart of the Merdjany representation: a king on horseback receiving the holy communion, in a rhyton, from the goddess standing in front of him.

A similar subject appears on the gilded silver rhyton found at Poroina in Rumania and published by Odobesco. It has the same sturdy proportions, and terminates in the same massive bull's head, as another rhyton, found at Contzesti in Rumania, and now preserved in the Hermitage, together with other objects from the same place, including a sceptre resembling that of Brezovo. Both sides of the Poroina rhyton are ornamented with figures in relief. We see the same goddess seated on a stool, holding the round vase in her right hand, and in her left a rhyton of the same shape as the Poroina rhyton itself. Facing the goddess is a priestess or worshipper raising her right hand in the gesture of adoration. The scene is given twice, on the upper part of each side. It is not possible to date the rhyton: it is unquestionably the work of a native artist, and consequently barbarous in style. One would be inclined to consider it much later than the Merdjany rhyton, which can be dated, by the objects found along with it, in the third century B.C.; but the style of the representations on the Merdjany rhyton, if one can speak of style in such uncouth works, does not differ from that of the Poroina rhyton. It must also be noticed, that the goddess who adorns the centre of the famous Petrossa phiale seems to be closely akin to the Great Goddess worshipped by the Scythians of South Russia.

This whole series of religious representations shows the sacred character of the vases which are regularly found in Scythian tombs of our period: the round vase and the rhyton, two very primitive forms which go back to the earliest stages of civilized life. The two Scythians on the girdle or diadem from the barrow of Kul-Oba, one of whom bears the rhyton, the other the round vase, must be devotees of the supreme goddess.

We are now in a position to understand the ceremony of the sacred oath, described by Herodotus (iv. 70): 'When the Scythians make a treaty, they pour wine into a great clay cup, and the parties prick themselves with a needle or cut themselves with a sword, and mingle their blood with the wine; and they dip into the cup a scimitar, and arrows, and a battle-axe, and a javelin. Then they pronounce a long curse, and they drink, the parties, and their principal followers.' This is the same ceremony of holy communion. It was reproduced on the clasp (?) of the Kul-Oba girdle or diadem, mentioned above (pl. XXIII, 3): the representation included the figures of Scythians with round vase and rhyton, taking part in the ceremony described by Herodotus. Many such figures have been found and are to be seen in museums: they were set to left and right of the central group, the Holy Communion, on the girdle or diadem. The same in the Solokha tumulus, on gold plaques attached to the king.

In Scythian religion the great god has been almost totally eclipsed by the Great Goddess. It is she who is the great divinity, the divinity above all others. It is she who presides at oath-taking, who administers the holy communion, and who initiates the royal Scythians into the mysteries of her religion. We have observed the part which she played in the religion of the Maeotians and of the Sauromatians: we have mentioned her temples in the Taman peninsula. At Panticapaeum, as we shall find, she became the chief goddess of the Bosphoran state in the Roman period. But we have just seen that she was deeply venerated by the Scythians as well. What can be the reason? Did the Scythians bring the cult with them from their eastern homeland? It is possible, nay probable. But the development and prominence of the cult can only be accounted for by supposing that here, as in Asia Minor, the Iranians inherited the worship of the Great Goddess from the native population, that it was the primitive worship of the natives. This view is confirmed by the list of Scythian deities in Herodotus (iv. 59): 'they worship these deities and no others: first, Histie, after her Zeus and Ge, then Apollo and Heavenly Aphrodite, Herakles and Ares.' Later he says: 'they call Histie in their tongue Tabiti, and Zeus, I think, Papaios, Ge Api, Apollo Gaitosyros, Heavenly Aphrodite Argimpasa, Poseidon Thagi masadas.' At first sight it is strange to find, in a list of Iranian divinities, a goddess with the un-Iranian name of Tabiti occupying the highest place, while the supreme god has the second place only. But it is not surprising on the hypothesis which I have formulated. Herodotus' list is a mixed one, a list of the divinities who were revered by the native population primarily, the neighbours of the city of Olbia. We can understand, therefore, that the Great Goddess should be mentioned first, and after her a god with a name which is Thracian rather than Iranian, Papaios.

The Scythian legends collected by Herodotus corroborate my theory. Remember the story of the autochthonous goddess of the Dnieper region, half-woman, half-serpent, who dwelt in a woodland cave near the mouth of the Dnieper. Herakles, the conquering god, had to come to terms with her, and she bore him the three eponymous heroes of the peoples in the Russian and Thracian plain, the Gelonians, the Agathyrsians and the Scythians. The legend reflects the history of the country. Conquerors who were servants of a warrior god; and a native population devoted to the worship of an earth goddess, a serpent goddess. It is worth noticing that a similar tale was current in Sakastan: the part of Herakles is played by the hero and demi-god Rostahm. The legend reported by Herodotus is confirmed by the archaeological monuments. The same group of tumuli, those of the fourth and third centuries B.C., have furnished several representations of a serpent-footed goddess: she appears on the horse's frontlet from Tsymbalka; on gold garment-plaques (pl. XVIII, 4, and see page 168, fig. 17); and in plaster on Panticapaean coffins of the Roman period. The serpent-footed goddess is an old Ionian type, a variant of Medusa. It is rare in archaic Ionian monuments: I know but two examples, an archaic vase-handle of bronze in the Museum at Nimes, its fellow in the British Museum, and a well-preserved archaic vase, with the same kind of handles, in Berlin. But the type was adapted by Greek artists to the beliefs of the Scythian and Maeotian tribes, and became extremely popular in the Russian steppes and nowhere else.

PLATE XXII

ELECTRUM VASE FROM THE 'KUL-OBA' TUMULUS, NEAR KERCH
IV-III Cent B.C. Hermitage, Petrograd

PLATE XXIII

1. GOLD PLAQUE OF THE TIARA FROM THE 'KARAGODEUASHKH' TUMULUS ON THE KUBAN
2. FRAGMENTS OF THE RHYTON OF MERDJANY IN THE KUBAN REGION
3. GOLD CLASP OF A BELT OR DIADEM FROM THE 'KUL-OBA' TUMULUS, NEAR KERCH
4-6. GOLD PLAQUES SEWN ON GARMENTS, FROM VARIOUS TUMULI ON THE LOWER DNIPER
IV-III Cent. B.C. Hermitage, Petrograd

To conclude our survey of the religious scenes, I will mention the plaques representing the Great Goddess accompanied by her sacred animals, the raven and the dog (pl. XXIII, 5), and the plaque with a wrestling contest between two Scythians, no doubt in honour of the same deity (pl. XXIII, 6). In a word: we see that in the hands of Greek artists, the aniconic Iranian religion, as described by Herodotus, becomes peopled with divine images, created by the Greek artists and no doubt accepted by the Scythian devotee. In creating these images, the artists seem to have been inspired by very ancient representations of Oriental divinities, such as the seated goddess with a vase in her hand, a type which is found in Babylonia from the remotest times.

Let us now pass to social and economic life. The warlike activity of the ruling class was a favourite subject with the artists who worked for the Scythians. Battle scenes are common everywhere: fights between Scythians and their enemies, Scythians of other tribes, Thracians, Maeotians: enough to cite the Solokha comb (pl. XIX) and the gorytus from the same grave (pl. XXI, 1). Hare-hunts, and hunting in general (pl. XX, 1, 2), are no less frequent: this was the most usual form of sport among the Scythians: it trained them to hit a moving adversary at full gallop. More interesting are the scenes on two spherical vases; one, of silver, from Vorónezh, the other, of electrum, from Kul-Oba. The scene on the Vorónezh vase is a peaceful one: Scythian warriors in conference; an old warrior instructing a youth in the use of the bow, the principal weapon of the Scythians: a Scythian camp on the eve of an expedition. The Kul-Oba vase (pl. XXII) shows the same camp after the battle: the king receiving a report from a messenger, wounded warriors attended by their comrades—a leg-wound being dressed, an operation for a mouth wound. Both vases are interesting for their style and their inspiration: they provide, as it were, illustrations to the account of Ephorus, who was the first to idealize the Scythian social system, as an example of communism on a democratic basis: the same motive recurs in the Scythian dialogues of Lucian. The two scenes might be described as realistic idylls in the manner of Theocritus. It must be remembered that they are the oldest Greek monuments which attempt to give realistic illustrations corresponding to the ethnographical treatises which were especially common about the time of Alexander the Great.

I should like to conclude this series of racial representations with the famous Chertomlýk vase (pl. XXI, 2). Once more the Scythian camp on the eve of battle. The warriors are scattered over the steppe, catching the horses which they will ride on the morrow. I shall not dwell upon the artistic power with which the artist has seized the type of the horses (pl. XXI, 3), of the Scythian warriors, and even of the landscape. The whole atmosphere is that of the Russian steppe: the artist must have known the steppe, must have studied the life of a Scythian camp, and must have been thoroughly well-acquainted with the little horse of the steppes, dry and muscular, quite unlike the horses of Greece or of Asia Minor. The Chertomlýk vase is a masterpiece, even compared with the vases of Vorónezh and Kul-Oba, which must belong to the same artistic school.

What was the artistic school that created these marvels of realistic, slightly idyllic art, an art which devoted itself almost entirely to the study of a nation, and which was able to catch the characteristic features of a national life? The artists cannot possibly have been Athenians: Athens produced nothing similar, and the nature of Athenian art was opposed to such ethnographical realism. Artists of Asia Minor? But where could they have obtained their profound knowledge of Scythian life, of Scythian religion, and of the Russian steppe? Impossible for artists residing at Ephesus, at Miletus, nay, at Cyzicus; even supposing that they had visited Russia. But why go so far afield? Have we not admired the masterpieces of Greek toreutic produced at Panticapaeum, particularly the gold and silver coins of the fourth century (pl. XVIII, 5)? Compare the three-quarter face of the old silen with the head of the Scythian whose teeth are being operated upon, compare the silen's head in profile with the profile head of the Scythian on the Solokha gorytus, compare the beardless heads of the young satyr with the young Scythians on the same, compare, finally, the realistic horse on the silver didrachms of the third century with the horses on the Chertomlýk vase. Is the style not the same; a style derived from Scopaic art, a forerunner of the style of Pergamon? Nowhere will you find more striking and more convincing analogies. This is the dawn of Hellenistic art, the art which we find later in the Hellenistic kingdoms; which was influenced by the interest taken by science and literature in the hitherto barbarian peoples who were now entering into the great family of civilized, that is, Hellenized nations; which, like the idylls of Theocritus and the mimes of Herodas, was at once idyllic and realistic. An art which was glad to place itself at the disposal of foreign nations, and which gave birth to new masterpieces of pure Greek type, inspired, however, by the strange and exotic spectacle of a life both foreign and familiar to the artists.

One more reason for insisting on the Panticapaean origin of the artistic objects found in the tumuli of this group, is the geographical distribution of the tumuli themselves. The tumuli which lie nearest Panticapaeum are likewise the richest in artistic objects of Bosphoran work. One of the most splendid is the barrow of Kul-Oba, which stood in the cemetery of Panticapaeum, but which undoubtedly contained the body of a Crimean prince of Scythian blood, a vassal of the great king; one, who like Skyles of old, the neighbour of Olbia, loved to spend his days in the wealthy and hospitable Greek city. It cannot be doubted that this prince was strongly Hellenized, and that he had a regular business connexion with the tyrants of Panticapaeum. The tumuli of Karagodeuashkh and of Merdjany, situated on the Kuban close to Bosphoran territory, belong to the same category. These also were the graves of petty kings, princes of Scythian extraction, who, even after the collapse of the great king's ascendancy over the region of the Kuban, retained their local authority for some time, just like the Scythian dynasty in the Dobrudzha. Finally, there is the stately group of tumuli in the districts of Taurida and Ekaterinoslav on the lower Dnieper; which are closely akin to the barrow of Kul-Oba. I have no doubt that the vast wealth of these tumuli belonged to the family of the Scythian great kings, the overlords of the petty kings and princes mentioned above. This group, also, lies very near the kingdom of the Bosphorus. The royal family seems to have maintained a steady and intimate connexion with the Bosphoran state. In more distant places, on the middle Dnieper and on the Don, Bosphoran influence is much fainter. Local products, of which we shall presently speak, prevail.

The question will be asked, what is the reason for the powerful influence exerted by Bosphoran art and commerce? Why did the Scythian kings not fetch their weapons and their jewellery from Olbia? The answer is simple. We have seen that Olbia suffered terribly from its exposed position and from the pressure of the Scythians upon their vassal city. Some of the Olbian families were still able to carry on a flourishing trade and to accumulate great wealth, but the conditions were not favourable to the development of local industry and art, which demand a calmer atmosphere and greater security and tranquillity. Olbia was content to act as intermediary between Greece and

Asia Minor on the one hand, Scythia on the other, and perhaps to manufacture a few simple, rude objects for export to the Scythian provinces on the middle Dnieper.

It appears then, that the masterpieces which I have described above were the work of Bosphoran artists, a Bosphoran school of metalwork closely connected with the artistic schools of Asia Minor. Compare the Bosphoran productions, especially the two silver vases from Solokha (pl. XX, 1, 2) and the gold patera from the same place (pl. XX, 3), with the Lycian tomb sculptures and the sarcophagus of Alexander, and the affinity is immediately apparent. It must be remembered that it is the artists of Asia Minor who have transmitted to us the detailed and authentic studies of Persians on the sarcophagus of Alexander, on the great mosaic from Pompeii, and on a number of reliefs recently discovered in Asia Minor: moreover, that it is Lycian artists who have provided us with scenes from the social and religious life of semi-Hellenized Asia Minor, scenes which closely resemble, in their artistic character, the contemporary representations of Scythian life produced at Panticapaeum.

Side by side with the artistic products of Panticapaeum, we find hundreds and thousands of others which by their rudeness and primitiveness present a strong contrast to the refinement of Panticapaean work. Some of these are rough imitations of Greek jewellery, such as a number of necklaces, diadems, bracelets and earrings found in the region of the Dnieper and the Don: others are objects decorated with local mythological scenes, coarse versions of Panticapaean objects of the same type; such as the earrings from Vorónezh, with figures of the Great Goddess, and the Merdjany rhyton described above: others are objects, mostly of bronze, which served to ornament the horses' bridles and the funeral cars. The third class is the most interesting. The Scythian animal style, always employed for such purposes, shows a rich development. On the one hand, we find the specific motives of the style combined in infinite and fantastic variety: heads of eagles (fig. 21, E; compare the pole-top from the Kuban, pl. X, A), griffins, lions and other savage beasts grouped with highly complicated barbarian refinement: on the other hand, a marked Greek influence, attempting to ennoble the style and at the same time robbing it of its vigour, by combining it with motives, borrowed from Greek vegetable ornament, which are completely alien to the animal style. The effect of the combination is not very happy.

It is very difficult to say where these objects were manufactured. Some of them may have been produced by local workmen or by Greek immigrants in the native settlements, others by itinerant craftsmen wandering with their tools from place to place, working here and there to order, and using the raw material provided by their customers. In any case, the quantity of objects bears witness to the importance of the industry and to the wide circulation of its products.

VI.
The Sarmatians

THE Sarmatians are first mentioned by Greek writers as a people which advanced to the middle Don in the second half of the fourth century. Since little was known about the new-comers at the time, and since their name closely resembled that of the Sauromatians, who had long dwelt on the lower Don and on the shores of the Sea of Azov, Greek historians and geographers were misled by the similarity of appellation into identifying the two peoples, a confusion which has given rise to countless misunderstandings.

Herodotus and the pseudo-Hippocrates give descriptions of the Sauromatians. Of the Sarmatians, the historians of the Roman period, who knew them on the banks of the Danube and in the Caucasus,—Tacitus, Valerius Flaccus, Arrian, Pausanias, Ammianus Marcellinus—have left us a picture which though fragmentary is highly finished in parts. Now the two descriptions are completely different, and precisely in the most important and characteristic points. The Sauromatians impressed the Greeks by a notable peculiarity of their social system: matriarchy, or rather survivals of it: the participation of women in war and in government, the preponderance of woman in the political, military and religious life of the community. Among the Sarmatians, as far as we know, there was nothing of the kind. They were a warrior tribe like the Scythians, nomads with a military organization; hunters and shepherds. They fought many a battle with the Roman legions: but it is nowhere said that women appeared in the ranks of their army, or that women played any part in their political life.

We may take it, then, that the Sauromatians had nothing to do with the Sarmatians, that the Sauromatians were probably conquered by the Sarmatians and then disappeared from history, only surviving in historic tradition: writers like Ammianus Marcellinus attempting to combine literary references to the Sauromatians, with later accounts of the warlike Sarmatians, formidable opponents of Imperial Rome.

When first we meet them, the Sarmatians appear as a series of separate groups moving westward in uninterrupted succession. With the details of the movement we are but ill acquainted, for the references in the historians of the Roman republic and empire are few and sometimes exasperatingly brief: these references enable us, however, to reconstruct, in its general outline, the Sarmatian invasion of the South Russian steppes.

The Sarmatians, like the Scythians, belonged to the Iranian group of Asiatic peoples. They may have been closely akin to the Scythians; may have belonged, like them, to those Iranian peoples who were generally called Sacian, to distinguish them from the other branch of the Iranians, represented by the Medes and Persians, who were bitter enemies of the Sacians. That the Sarmatians were of Iranian extraction has been definitely established by the study of the Ossetian language: the Ossetians are known to be descended from the Alans, the strongest and most numerous, as we shall see, of the Sarmatian tribes. Ossetian, although it contains an admixture of heterogeneous elements, is unquestionably an Iranian tongue, nearly related to Persian.

We do not know the origin of the general term Sarmatian, applied by Greeks and Romans to the succession of tribes which gradually dislodged the Scythians from the steppes of South Russia. The earliest writer to speak of Sarmatians was the pseudo-Scylax: he, and Eudoxos of Cnidos, had heard of Συρμάται on the Don in the fourth century, about 338 B.C. Was this the name of a tribe, the first to arrive? Is it not conceivable, that the resemblance of the word Συρμάται to the familiar Σαυρομάται, and the amalgamation of the newcomers, proved, as we shall find, by archaeological evidence, with the Sauromatians long established on the Don, led to the transformation of the name Συρμάται into Σαρμάται, and to the permanent confusion of two distinct peoples in our historical tradition? However that may be, from the time of Polybius, who mentions the Sarmatians, in 179 B.C., as enemies of the Crimean Scythians, the name of Sarmatian was in general use among the Greeks and Romans, to designate those Iranian peoples, who, in the third and especially in the second century B.C., were advancing from east to west towards the Danube and western Europe. The employment of this generic designation for all the variously named tribes which supplanted the Scythians in the steppes of South Russia, is evidence that these tribes were closely interrelated.

Whence came this Neo-Iranian wave, which re-enacted the story of the Cimmerians and the Scythians? We have little information about the history of Central Asia in that tangled and difficult period, the Hellenistic. Chinese records speak of an important movement during the Ts'in and Han dynasties: Mongolian tribes were pushed westward by the vigorous defence of the Chinese frontier, and by the construction of the Limes which we know as the Great Wall of China. This movement probably displaced a number of Iranian tribes in Central Asia and in Turkestan, who turned northward and westward, as the Scythians had turned before them, and made for western Siberia and the Ural and Volga steppes to the north of the Caspian: the southern road being barred by the kingdom of Parthia. I have no doubt that the events which took place in Central Asia during the third and second centuries were much less elementary and more complicated than the Chinese sources make them out; although the Chinese account is by no means so simple as the version given above. For further details we must wait until the results of recent exploration are better known and better digested: Russian, German, French, British and Japanese exploration in Chinese Turkestan, Seistan and Baluchistan. The new data, linguistic, archaeological, and historical, will perhaps afford a clearer view of Central Asiatic history in the last centuries before and the earliest after Christ. This much we can already affirm, that the flow of Sarmatian tribes towards the South Russian steppes was due to the political and economic condition of Central Asia between the fourth and the second centuries B.C.: a symptom of which was a movement of Mongolian tribes towards the west, and a corresponding movement of Iranians.

The second century B.C. seems to have been the critical period of Sarmatian expansion in South Russia, although archaeological evidence and a few historical passages indicate that long before this period Sarmatian tribes had been slowly moving towards the west. But the earliest certain notice of Sarmatians in the South Russian steppes dates from the second century B.C. I have already quoted the evidence of Polybius, proving the presence of Sarmatians between Don and Dnieper in 179. From the part played by the Sarmatian king in the political events of this period it is clear that by 179 Sarmatian power was firmly established between Dnieper and Don, counterbalancing the Scythian power, which, as we have seen from the archaeological evidence treated in the last chapter, centred in the Crimea. To judge from the chronology of Scythian tumuli, it was in the second half of the third century that the Sarmatians crossed the Don and invaded the steppes between Don and Dnieper. This date is confirmed by Strabo. The authority used by Strabo for his seventh book, Artemidorus of Ephesus, who wrote at the end of the second century, bears witness that about this time the advance guard of the Sarmatians, the Iazygians, reached the steppes between Dnieper and Danube, while the next in order, the Roxalans or White Alans, were between Don and Dnieper and figured on the political stage in the war which Mithridates the Great was waging in the Crimea. Behind the Roxalans, another of Strabo's informants, the authority used for the eleventh book, Theophanes of Mytilene, a contemporary of Pompey and his biographer, alludes to Aorsians as occupying the left bank of the Don and the shores of the Sea of Azov, and to Siracians as holding the valley of the Kuban. Farther east we must suppose that the Alans were supreme: it is not long before they appear as the dominant tribe in the eastern steppes of South Russia.

The earliest reference to the Alans belongs to the year A.D. 35. Josephus, who mentions them, leads us to suppose that they had held the Kuban valley for some time, and were trying to force their way, through the passes of the Caucasus, to Iberia and Armenia, with the ultimate intention of fighting the Parthians. It seems, however, that their attempt was frustrated, that they turned aside and followed the other Sarmatian tribes towards the Don and the Dnieper. In A.D. 49, during the troubles which arose in the Cimmerian Bosphorus, the immediate neighbours of the Bosphoran kingdom were Aorsians and Siracians, not Alans. But these tribes seem to have been gradually invaded by the Alans and to have combined with them to form a unit which was thenceforth known by the name of the dominant tribe, the Alans. The continual advance of the Sarmatians soon carried them beyond the Dnieper in the direction of the Danube. In A.D. 50, we find the Iazygians between Theiss and Danube, and the Roxalans beyond the Dnieper.

The Sarmatians now became an imminent danger to Roman power, which was threatened from two different quarters. The provinces and vassal kingdoms south of the Caucasus daily anticipated a flood of conquerors from the steppes beside the Kuban, while the Danubian provinces were already feeling the pressure of the Sarmatian vanguard. Little is known about the conditions on the Dnieper at this period, and between Dnieper and Danube. The region seems to have been the meeting-place of several currents: a Thracian current of Getians or Dacians, who took Olbia in the middle of the first century B.C.; a Celto-Germanic current of Galatians and Scirians in the third century, and later of Bastarnians, who appear to have occupied at least a portion of the Dniper basin; and, lastly, the Sarmatian current. What matters most to us, is that from this period, the first century B.C., the Iranians maintained regular and sometimes cordial relations with the Germanic and Thracian tribes, and that they dwelt side by side with them in the succeeding centuries.

From the first century B.C., therefore, Rome had to face a new enemy on her frontiers: the Sarmatians. Time would fail me, nor is this the place, to tell the whole story of the long and sanguinary struggle between Roman and Sarmatian which was waged in the Danubian provinces and especially in Lower Moesia. A brief sketch must suffice. The Sarmatian advance beyond the Danube compelled the Romans to take the offensive. In 62-63, Nero's general, Plautius Silvanus, dealt a heavy blow at the forces of the Thracian, Germanic and Sarmatian tribes, and hurled them back across the Danube. The same Plautius Silvanus tried to reinforce the Greek oases in the Scythian world by relieving them of the danger which threatened them from the Scythians in the Crimea.

It is generally believed that the Sarmatians destroyed or completely absorbed the Scythians. This is one of the many historical figments invented by modern historians. The Scythians continued to exist as long as the Romans were supreme on the Black Sea: explicit evidence is furnished by the Bosphoran inscriptions of Roman imperial date. The Scythians only disappear with the arrival of the Goths in the third century B.C., or rather with the destruction of the Gothic state by Mongolian nomad tribes. It is true that the Scythians were conquered by the Sarmatians and had to retire before them. But the Sarmatians never managed to dislodge them from their last refuges, the Crimea in the east, and the Dobrudzha in the west. We shall see in the next chapter that for centuries the Scythians maintained a strong monarchical state in the Crimea, with its centre in the neighbourhood of Simferopol, and were powerful enough to persist in their claim to supremacy over Olbia and the Greek towns of the Crimea.

The expedition of Plautius Silvanus opened the eyes of the Roman government to the Sarmatian peril. Hence Nero's project for attacking the Alans in the very seat of their power, the steppes of Northern Caucasus. It seems to have been Nero's intention, to concentrate his forces in the kingdom of the Bosphorus, which was to be made a Roman province for the purpose, and thence to open an offensive against the Sarmatian armies; the Sarmatian empire would be cut in two, and the Caucasus and the Danube preserved from incessant attacks from north and east. As a subsidiary measure, Pontus was to be transformed into a Roman province. Owing to the dethronement of Nero, the plan was never carried out. The period of civil war which followed the death of Nero laid the Danubian provinces open to Sarmatian assaults. This period over, it cost the Romans many efforts and much blood to arrest the triumphal march of the Sarmatians and their Thracian and Germanic allies. The famous wars on the Danube, begun by Vespasian, and continued by Domitian, Trajan and Marcus Aurelius, though they led to the temporary annexation of Dacia, were primarily defensive wars with the object of interposing an effective barrier between the Danubian provinces and the combined attacks of Germans and Sarmatians.

In the Crimea and in the Caucasus, the Romans pursued the same defensive policy. We shall see that after Nero the kingdom of the Bosphorus was re-established as a vassal kingdom, and entrusted with the duty of defending the Crimea and Olbia against the Scythians, and of keeping watch in the Taman peninsula and on the Don to preserve the Greek colonies in that region from complete occupation by the Sarmatians. The kingdom of the Bosphorus proving unequal to the task, the Roman government, from the time of Hadrian onwards, was forced to protect the rear by drawing a line of fortresses, manned by Roman troops round the territory of Chersonesus Taurica; in fact, it had to resume that military occupation of part of the Crimea, which had been taken in hand by Claudius and by Nero. Roman policy in the Caucasus was the same. The kingdom of Iberia which covered the Caucasian passes, was guarded, at its most vulnerable points, by fortresses and Roman troops: Armenia also, from the second century A.D. The military bases, on which these two groups of advanced posts depended, were the province of Lower Moesia for the Crimea, and for the Caucasus the province of Cappadocia and the legions re-installed there by the Flavian emperors.

The Alans, by themselves, were never able to cross the barriers set up by the Romans. In 73-74, they tried to invade the Parthian kingdom from the east: in Hadrian's time, in 135, they attempted to cross the Caucasus and to invade Armenia from the north. Both enterprises failed. The invasion of 135 was repulsed by the governor of Cappadocia, the historian Arrian, whose treatise on his tactics and order of battle against the Alans throws valuable light on Alan military organization. The invasion of 73-74 collapsed before the might of Parthia. On the Danube also, the Sarmatian advance was arrested, once and for all, by the vigorous defensive measures and counter attacks of the second-century emperors.

In the third century A.D., the situation changed. We have already observed, that from their first appearance on the Dnieper, the Alans maintained constant relations with the Germanic tribes, and often joined hands with Germans and Thracians to fight the Roman legions. What shape these relations assumed we do not know: nor what was the character of the association, formed in South Russia during the third century, between the Alans and the Goths, who were Germanic tribes from the Dnieper. Was it a conquest of Alans by Goths, or an alliance, or both? Again, we know little about the fusion of other Germanic tribes, Suevians and Vandals, with the Alans. What is certain is that this epoch was one of inestimable importance for the history of the whole world. Iranians and Germans combined to invade the kingdom of the Bosphorus, the Crimea, and the Greek towns in the Taman peninsula, destroyed Olbia and Tanais and the Roman fortresses in the Crimea, passed to Asia and to Greece, dealt formidable blows at the Roman empire on its Danubian frontier, and finally succeeded in effecting a temporary conquest of Italy herself, of Gaul, of Spain and even of Africa. The Iranian tribes—especially the Alans—who had remained in Asia and in the eastern portion of the Russian steppes, were drawn once more westward, by the Huns: leaving, however, strong, almost independent detachments on the Kuban, and, united with the Goths, in the Crimea and in the Taman peninsula. I cannot examine this period in detail: it has often been treated, and it lies outside the chronological limit which we have prescribed. But I must lay stress upon the participation of the Alans in the conquest of the Roman empire, and upon the extreme importance of the Iranian element in the conquering armies of Goths and Huns. The union of Iranians and Germans is mirrored, to take a single instance, in the legend about the origin of the Emperor Maximin, who was said to have had a Gothic father and an Alan mother.

Again, it must be borne in mind, that if the Germans exercised a powerful influence on the Roman state and the Roman army from the fourth century onwards, so did the Sarmatians, whose influence, moreover, was much older. From the time of Hadrian, Roman cavalry tactics were affected by the distinctive tactics of the Alans: the Sarmatian element played an increasingly important part in the Roman army, and we may go so far as to say, that in the third and fourth centuries some Roman corps, like that which figures on the arch of Galerius at Salonica, were almost entirely Sarmatian both in composition and in armament.

This historical survey, incomplete as it is, shows that from the second century B.C. till the third century A.D., the Sarmatians, and particularly the Alans, were the predominant force throughout South Russia and western Asia, especially in the central and eastern regions, where they were unhampered by their dangerous rivals and confederates, the Thracians and the Germans. From the third century onwards, they had to share their supremacy with the Goths or even yield it to them, but they still formed a very important factor in the governing class and in the army of the Gothic tribes. What do literary documents and inscriptions teach us about their state, their manners and their beliefs?

Very little. They were doubtless governed, like the Aorsians and the Siracians in 49, by princes or kings. But nothing is known, either about the power of these rulers, or about the social structure of the state. To judge from a few words in Arrian, the system was tribal and feudal, the component parts of each tribe being governed by sceptre-bearers, σκηπτοῦχοι. We would gladly know, if the Alans succeeded, as the Scythians succeeded, in creating a united state with a hereditary dynasty: but it is doubtful, whether they did or not.

We learn a little more about their attitude towards the Greek towns. Like the Scythians while the Scythians were masters of the Russian steppes, they had never any intention of vanquishing or annihilating the Greek cities. Even Olbia, which was destroyed by the Getians, weak as she was and exposed on every side, was never occupied by the Sarmatians. From the first to the third century A.D., her enemies were not the Sarmatians, but the Scythians of the

Crimea. It is true that after the union of the Sarmatians with the Goths, the united tribes altered their method and began to conquer and destroy the Greek cities, such as Olbia and probably Tanais. But even then they preserved Panticapaeum with its social and political structure intact. We shall see in the following chapter that they preferred to percolate into the populations of the Greek cities and to Sarmatize them gradually, adopting, however, the Greek language and some of the Greek customs. This must be taken into account in our estimate of Sarmatian civilization.

As to the Greek cities as such, the Sarmatians were content to preserve them and to use them as commercial agents. Like the Scythians, they had a high opinion of Greek civilization, and of Greek goods: wine, oil, jewels, pottery, glass and metal vases. The Greek towns on the Black Sea kept their position as centres of production and exportation. They continued to work for customers in the South Russian steppes.

The Sarmatians, as described by Greek and Roman authors, did not greatly differ from the Scythians. They were Iranians, as we said above: perhaps of purer blood than the Scythians, who had probably incorporated certain Mongolian tribes into their political and military organization.

The affinity between Scythians and Sarmatians is demonstrated by common features in their clothing, armour, ethnographic type, and social and political structure: it is generally accepted, and I shall not dwell upon it. More interesting are the differences between the two peoples: which show that the Sarmatians had had no regular dealings with the Scythians; that they had developed, independently of the Scythians, somewhere in Central Asia; and that they came as conquerors to the steppes of South Russia, bringing with them a body of distinctive customs, and a material culture peculiar to themselves. Their equipment and their military tactics were un-Scythian. The Scythians were primarily bold archers: their principal weapons were bow and arrows. It was only after they had broken the enemy's resistance by a succession of attacks at long range, by a continuous bombardment of arrows, sometimes poisoned, that they advanced in wedge formation for a final assault, a hand-to-hand struggle in which they used their short daggers.

The tactics of the Sarmatians, especially the Alans, were very different. Their principal weapon was a long, heavy lance, such as was carried by mediaeval knights. Covered, horse and man, with corslets of scale- or ring-armour, or sometimes of cast iron, they charged in masses and broke resistance by the weight of this heavy cavalry attack: the formation may be compared to a mounted phalanx. The lance attack was followed by hand-to-hand fighting in which they used long swords with sharp points. The part played by bow and arrows was quite secondary. Conical helmets of iron, and stirrups, both unknown to the Scythians, completed the Sarmatian outfit. There was the same difference between the Parthians, mobile archers, and the Sassanid Persians, mounted hoplites. We seem to be witnessing the dawn of the Middle Ages, with their ironclad knights.

Very little is known about Sarmatian religion. From such insufficient evidence as we possess, the Sarmatians would seem to have been fire-worshippers. The sacrifice of horses appears to have been prominent in their ritual.

This is virtually all we can gather about the Sarmatians from our written sources. But the Sarmatians inhabited the Russian steppes for more than five centuries, and the eastern branch of them dwelt for ages in the steppes between the Sea of Aral and the Caspian Sea and in the adjacent steppes of Siberia. They must have left many traces of their sojourn. Nevertheless, the works on the archaeology of South Russia provide no clue to the archaeological material illustrating the life and manners of the Sarmatians. Yet such material abounds: if it has not been utilized hitherto, the reason is that no one has taken the trouble to arrange it systematically in chronological order, to date the several finds precisely, and to make a historical analysis of the groups.

In a general work like the present I cannot undertake a task so lengthy and so minute. But I would draw the reader's attention to certain phenomena which have never been observed or explained, and which are of the highest historical interest. The data are by no means complete, nor even very copious: but they form an unbroken series which lends itself, in my opinion, to an historical explanation. No methodical excavation has ever taken place in the vast steppe-land of the Ural valley: in the districts of Ufá and Orenburg, in the country of the Ural Cossacks, in the region of Turgai and the district of Samára. The area is bounded on the north by the Ural mountains, on the south by the Caspian Sea: eastward and westward it lies open. It is traversed by a large river, the Ural, which is navigable and rich in fish. Clandestine excavations, verified and sometimes completed by competent persons, and investigations by amateurs, have furnished a quantity of valuable material, which I have collected and reproduced in a special memoir. The graves of 'the Orenburg region', the name which I shall give to the whole area, are tumulary like the Scythian. Apart from the few prehistoric graves, belonging to the neolithic and bronze ages, they date from a period which corresponds to the sojourn of the Scythians in South Russia: that is to say, the sixth century B.C. and onwards. But in funerary ritual, in sepulchral construction, and in tomb furniture, they differ considerably from the Scythian graves of the time. I know but one find which bears a certain likeness to those from the Scythian tumuli; it came from the village of Pokróvka near Orenburg, and probably belongs to the fifth century B.C.; it includes a number of triangular arrow-heads, some bronze plaques in the animal style from the trappings of a horse, and a boar's tooth with a gold mounting like the tooth from the Seven Brothers on the Kuban. But first, triangular arrow-heads were very common, all over the world, between the sixth and third centuries B.C.; secondly, the griffin-head plaques from Pokróvka find no convincing analogies in the Scythian tumuli, and there is nothing quite like them in the fifth-century tumuli on the Kuban and in the Crimea: lastly, the boar's tooth from the Seven Brothers does not square with the other finds from the same grave and seems to have been imported. On the other hand, there is no difference, either in the mode of burial, or in the general aspect of the tomb furniture, between the Pokróvka tumuli and the rest of the Orenburg group: we notice the same absence of Greek imports, and the same Iranian influence: one of the sepulchres yielded a Persian seal, and gold plaques, probably imported, in a style which is not far removed from the Assyro-Persian. We shall see that these are just the features which distinguish the Orenburg group as a whole.

In characterizing this group I shall take as my principal guide the finds recently made in four tumuli near the village of Prókhorovka. Although the objects came from clandestine excavations, the reports of the excavators seem to be perfectly accurate: they were verified on the spot by a competent archaeologist, Rudenko, and the complementary excavations which he carried out have given us full particulars about the funerary ritual and the structure of the tombs. The Prókhorovka excavations may therefore rank as scientific, and round them we can group others which gave closely similar results.

The funerary structures in the Orenburg region are very unpretentious (fig. 14). A square, oval, or circular trench dug in the soil, sometimes with a small pocket in one of the walls. The corpses were not put in coffins, but wrapped in mantles of leather or fur, occasionally, perhaps, with mats or turf beneath them.

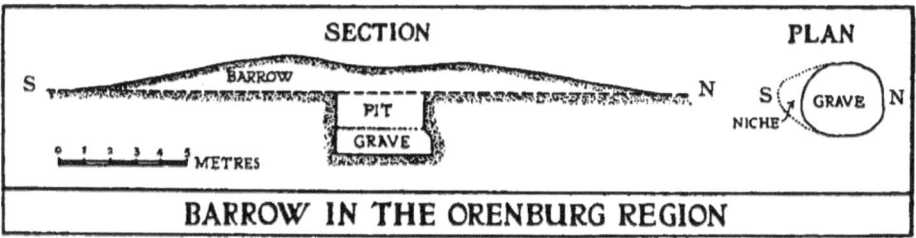

Fig. 14.

The funerary ritual is quite different from the Scythian. There were no wooden structures, no funeral cars, and no sacrifices of horses or human beings. The ritual was no less primitive than the Scythian, the dead being provided with everything necessary for the life beyond the grave: but it was much simpler.

The classes of objects buried with the dead are the same as in the Scythian graves: arms, sometimes horse-trappings, garments, precious articles, pottery. But one characteristic is immediately obvious: the total absence of Greek imports. No Greek vases, no Greek jewels. Imports are not lacking, but they are Oriental, generally Persian: I may mention the two silver cups, of Persian work, with Aramaean inscriptions from one of the Prókhorovka graves (pl. XXIV, 1), and the Persian seal, engraved with a figure of a king fighting with a lion, from a grave at Pokróvka. The people which established itself in the steppes of Orenburg was not in touch with the Greeks or with the Scythians: but it maintained regular relations with the eastern Iranian world, especially with the Persian kingdom. The principal weapons are a long heavy lance and a long sharp-pointed sword. A heavy corslet of cast iron was found in one of the tombs. Like the Scythians, the warriors of Orenburg and their wives were fond of gold and silver articles. But these articles differ widely from the

Scythian. The animal style is rare: the geometric style predominates. There is a strong tendency to polychromy, rarely observable in the Scythian kurgans. A gold-plated dagger-sheath, from a third-century grave at Prókhorovka, is covered with floral and geometric ornaments, embellished with enamels in a technique which already brings to mind the cloisonné of the so-called Gothic period (pl. XXIV, 4). The gold torcs from the same find are particularly interesting (pl. XXIV, 2,3). The use of torcs for the neck is common to several races and peoples, but the shape varies. At Orenburg the shape is purely Oriental: a thick wire of solid gold, twisted twice or thrice, and ornamented at either end, in Eastern fashion, by an animal or an animal's head—the well-known dragon with the characteristic crest, large ears and sharp teeth. We shall come across the same type in the South Russian steppes during the last centuries before Christ and the first centuries of our era. Scythian torcs, of which we have many specimens, are almost all Greek work, and the shapes are very different.

The jewels, which are somewhat rare, are clumsy and primitive the shapes are purely Oriental. The gold garment plaques differ greatly from the Scythian forms, and their prototypes must be sought in the Assyro-Persian world.

Speaking generally, the furniture is extremely rude. To a few imported articles, we have a great number of local products: iron weapons, and objects in bone. Both classes of local products present striking analogies with certain objects, of the same shape and purpose, found in the Altai Mountains and in eastern Russia, especially on the Kama. These belong to the earliest iron age.

It is impossible to assign an exact date to this group of tombs. As far as we can judge from the imports, the oldest tombs belong to the sixth, the Pokróvka group to the fifth, and the Prókhorovka to the fourth and third centuries B.C. Others are certainly later: some of these may be placed in the last centuries before and the earliest after Christ. From first to last, and this is important, there are few changes: the group is homogeneous and distinctive: the civilization which it reflects is a primitive civilization of nomadic warriors, whose only relations were with east and north, and who were not in regular contact with their neighbours beyond the Volga.

PLATE XXIV

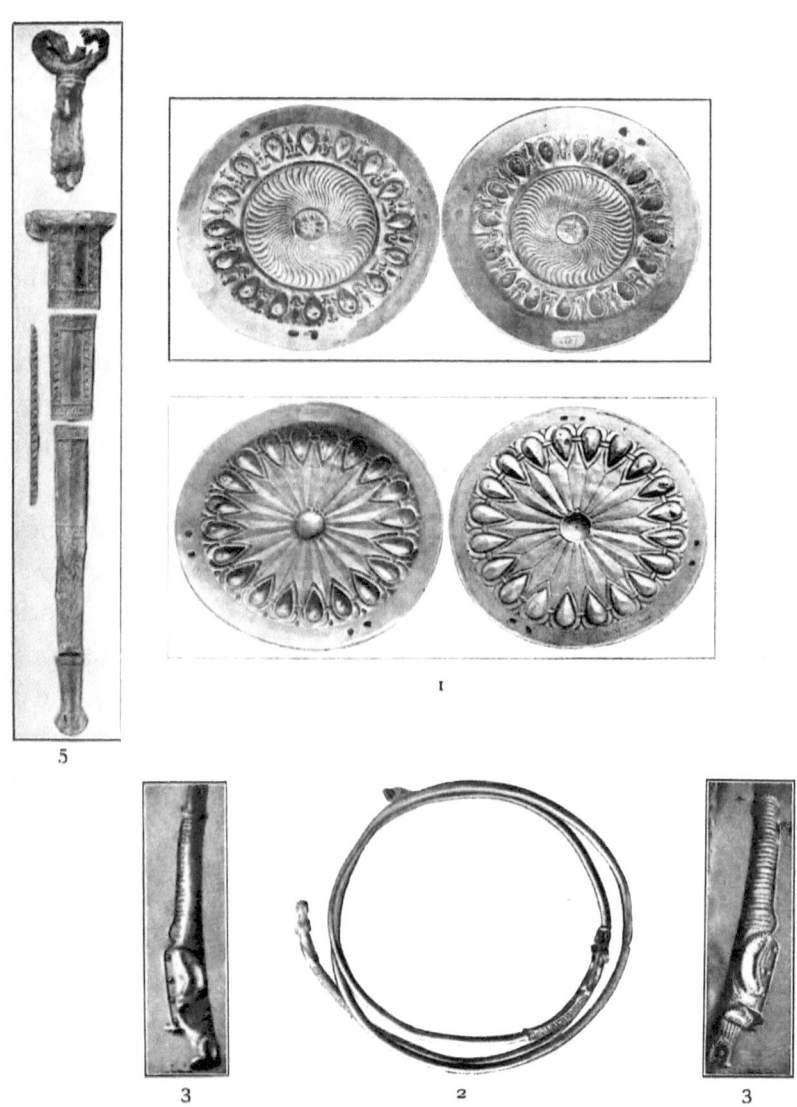

1-4. SILVER PATERAE, GOLD TORC, AND GOLD-PLATED
SCABBARD
From Prokhorovka, Orenburg. Orenburg Museum
5. GOLD-PLATED SCABBARD
From the tumulus Buerova Mogila (Taman Peninsula). Hermitrage, Petrograd
III Cent. B.C.

Of almost the same date as the Orenburg group are the tumulary graves which were excavated by Alexander Miller in the vicinity of Elizavétovskaya Stanitsa, a village in the Don delta. The civilization which the reveal is a curious one: it differs widely from the Scythian, and closely resembles that of the Orenburg region: it lasted on the Don for more than three hundred years, from the end of the fourth to the first century B.C. The shape of the graves—simple trenches lined with reeds—is almost the same as in the Orenburg region, and totally different from the Scythian types. The funerary ritual is far simpler than the Scythian: the dead man is buried by himself, sometimes with his horse or its bridle. The arms of the warriors are not the same as in Scythia: just as in the Orenburg group, the principal piece is a long heavy lance. But the Don graves differ from the Orenburg group in containing a large quantity of Greek objects and a number of weapons and other objects of the forms used by the Scythians. In a word, a cemetery of half-nomadic warriors, closely akin to the Orenburg type, but noticeably modified.

Much closer to the Orenburg graves are those which have been discovered on the Volga, in the neighbourhood of Sarátov and of Tsaritsyn, and the great find from the valley of the upper Kuban, near Stavrópol, which has recently furnished a whole series of torcs and bracelets in solid gold, closely resembling those from Orenburg, and probably of the same date.

At the same period, in the third century B.C., we notice a marked change in the furniture of the native tombs in the Taman peninsula and on the Kuban. The tombs of this time are characterized by a taste for polychromy, which is confined to this period and to graves with a particular type of furniture. It chiefly shows itself in the gold objects interred with the dead, which are set with precious stones and many-coloured enamels. For example, the grave at Buerova Mogila yielded a gold-plated sword-sheath (pl. XXIV, 5), which in its shape and in its geometric, probably polychrome decoration, is remarkably like the Orenburg sheath described above. Very characteristic, also, the graves in the villages of Kurdzhips and Beslenêevskaya. Both are dated: the former by engraved gems and by a bronze vase with scenes from the myth of Telephos, of the third or second century B.C.: the other by engraved gems of the second or first century B.C. Both retain some of the traditional features which distinguished the native tombs of the Taman peninsula in the preceding period: gold garment plaques of circular form jewels with delicate, purely classical decoration; and so forth. But at the same time there are novelties, unknown in the fourth or third centuries B.C.: gold jewels set with precious stones; fibulae, especially a round type with a figure of a lion, whose body is set with stones, biting his tail; necklace pendants of geometric type; bronze fibulae, the shapes of which are forerunners of the so-called Gothic fibula. Wherever we turn, we find a new world, which brings with it, as it advances, tastes and habits unfamiliar to the Greco-Scythian world of South Russia in the fourth and third centuries B.C.

In the first century B.C. and later, we witness the triumph of those elements which, in the graves of the transitional period, were only beginning to appear. The new civilization, hitherto represented by scattered objects, difficult to date, was first revealed and rendered intelligible by the explorations of Veselóvski in the region of the Kuban.

In 1895 Veselóvski began to excavate a series of kurgans in the Kuban valley. The shape of these kurgans was peculiar: they were mostly small, flat tumuli with an oval ground plan, quite unlike the Scythian tumuli (fig. 15). The graves which they contained were sometimes very rich and remarkable. Several graves of this type were found in barrows which had originally been constructed or prehistoric burials with contracted skeletons.

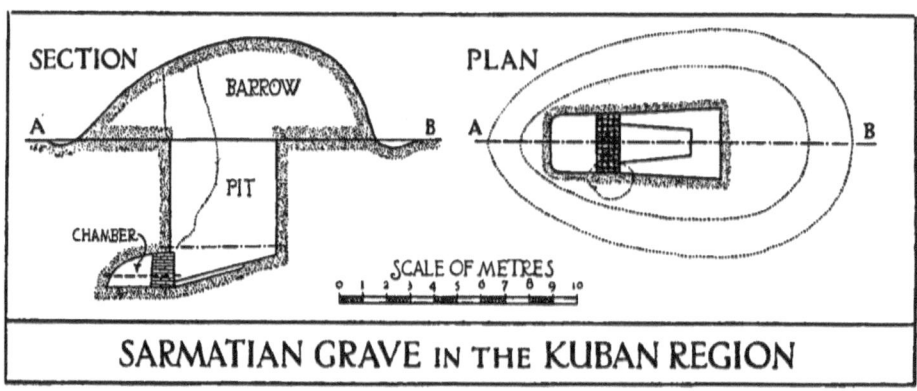

Fig. 15.

Veselóvski excavated some dozens of these kurgans, but there are hundreds or even thousands in the valley of the Kuban. They are all of one type, and the graves which they contain are uniform. The funeral structures under the barrows are very simple, and resemble those in the Orenburg steppes: they regularly consist of a sepulchral trench and a small cave in which the corpse was deposited. The funerary ritual recalls the ritual at Orenburg and on the lower Don: the graves are those of warriors and their wives, who were buried separately: but there were neither funeral cars, nor sacrifices of horses or of human beings.

No Greek or Roman coins have been found in these graves: but they nearly all contain objects exported from Greece, and these enable us to date the graves with accuracy. To begin with, the total absence of Greek vases with black glaze, and of the various classes of Hellenistic pottery, provides a lower chronological limit. But besides this negative evidence, we have a good deal of positive, by means of which we can arrange the graves in three chronological series. The first is dated by its pronounced predilection for glass vases, either cast or hewn out of solid blocks of glass (fig. 16, 1-3). In shape, they reproduce the metal vases of the late Hellenistic and early Imperial epoch. It is well known that cast- and cut-glass vases preceded blown-glass vases, and belong to the first century before and the first century after Christ. Such vases have been found in about a dozen tumuli, the contents of which are uniform: the richest graves were discovered in the kurgans of Zúbovski, Akhtanízovka, Vozdvizhenskaya, Yaroslávskaya, Tiflísskaya and Armavir. The jewels which are regularly found in these graves are distinctive both in shape and in technique. The artists have a fondness for filigree decoration, the motives being almost without exception geometric. But the technique is no longer the true granulation of classical times, but an imitation of it, pseudo-filigree, which consists in dividing a gold wire into a row of grainlike sections, so as to give the impression of a row of separate grains. The artists also obtain a rich and varied polychromy by using precious stones and pieces of coloured glass (see fig. 16, 4 and 5—the two gold fibulae from Zubov's farm, with Alexandrian coloured glass in the centre; and the enamelled earring, which is very popular at Kerch in the later period). The first group, then, may be dated in the first century before and the first after Christ.

The second and largest group can be dated by a series of objects which belong to the end of the first and to the second century of our era: a profusion of blown-glass vessels, with the typical shapes of the period; engraved gems; clay vases in the form of animals and of human heads; Roman fibulae; fragments of terra sigillata; and the like. It is in these Kuban tumuli that the fibula appears for the first time in South Russia. Fibulae are rare in the tombs of the first period and become common only in the second. Again, in the tombs of the first period, nearly all the fibulae belong to one or other of two types: one type, usually in gold, is derived from the well-known fibula of the La Tène period, and has all the characteristics of the tendril fibula, the 'fibula with foot turned over' of the Germans, the forerunner of the so-called Gothic fibula; the other is in the form of a brooch or of an animal, sometimes a grasshopper; the material is again gold, richly embellished with precious stones. The second period offers fibulae of the various types which are current in the Roman empire, but also develops the tendril fibula, which comes nearer and nearer to the so-called Gothic type.

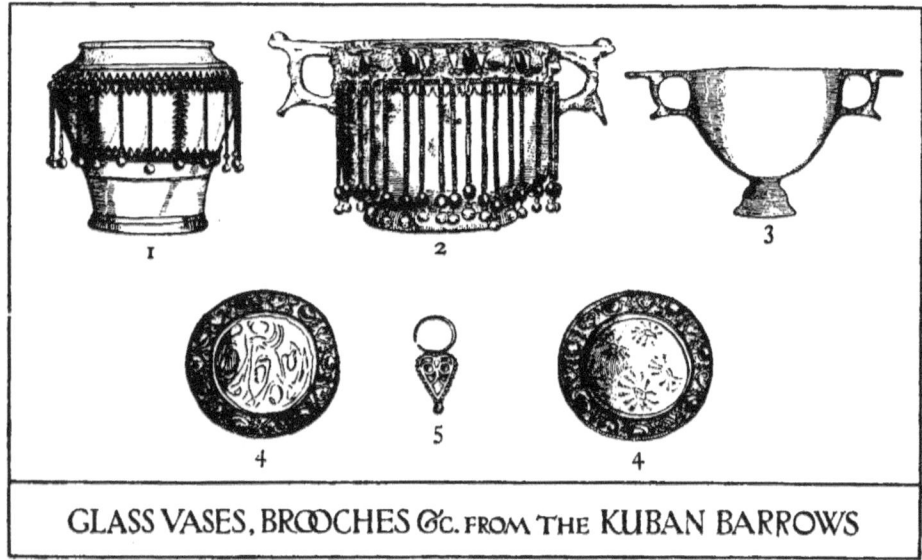

Fig. 16.

The third and last group of graves may be dated in the third and fourth centuries A.D.: they present remarkable analogies with the Kerch graves of the same period, which we shall describe in the next chapter.

One more observation: in certain tombs which belong to the first division of the group, notably in a grave at Zubov's farm, and in another at the village of Ust-Labínskaya, objects were discovered which are much earlier than the grave as a whole: a Greek phiale in the former grave, with the inscription Ἀπόλλωνος Ἡγεμόνος εἰμὶ τομ Φάσι, and a bronze candelabrum in the latter, unquestionably belong to the sixth century B.C. I have no doubt that the objects were looted, in the course of a tribal raid beyond the Caucasus, by the warriors who were buried in these graves: the phiale must have been a sacred vessel belonging to the temple of Apollo at Phasis. Consequently the objects have no bearing on the date of the tombs but they furnish valuable evidence as to the character of the builders.

Although they extend over a period of more than four centuries, the tombs of the Kuban valley from a coherent group. The construction of the graves, the funerary ritual, and the class of contents, are the same throughout. The contents are especially interesting. It is true that there are many features in the tomb furniture which recall the furniture in Orenburg and at the mouth of the Don, but there are others which are quite new and which point to an original and independent civilization. The tomb furniture consists, as I have said, of the objects usually found in nomadic graves: arms, horse-trappings, remains of clothing, jewels, vessels. Many of these are imports, made in Greece or even in Italy. But the general character of the furniture is neither Greek nor Italian. It is pure Oriental, and, further, widely different from what we observed in Scythian tombs.

A noteworthy change has taken place in the arms. The Scythian sword—the acinaces with its characteristic sheath and hilt—is nowhere found. It has been supplanted by a long sword with a remarkable hilt, a type which was also adopted, in the first century, by the citizens of Panticapaeum. The wooden hilt is oval in section, and in itself extremely simple: but it is regularly topped by a round or square knob, of onyx, agate or some other precious stone, or by a wooden knob plated with old and adorned with gems. The guard or the upper part of the sheath is often made out of one large piece of semiprecious stone. The only parallels, as far as I know, are the swords of the second Assyrian empire, the hilts of which are surmounted by a knob of bone or bronze, and some Chinese swords of the Han period. The Scythian gorytus is also absent: indeed the part played bow and quiver is much less important than in the Scythian graves. The lance seems, with the sword, to have been the favourite weapon of the warriors buried in the tumuli of the Kuban. The scaled corslet was replaced, towards the end of the first century, by the corslet of ring-armour; and a helmet, often conical, is sometimes found in such tombs as have not been despoiled.

The horse-trappings are no longer the same as in the Scythian tombs. There are a few specimens of bar-bridles, bridles with ψάλια, rods, but the psalia have not the rich and manifold forms of the Scythian examples; they degenerate fast and are gradually replaced by simple rings. We do not find the distinctive pieces of the Scythian bridle, frontlet, cheek-pieces, ear-guards, nasal, and the rest, with their varied forms in the animal style: instead, round phalarae, of silver or gold, with embossed ornaments, usually geometric, sometimes in an animal style, but in an animal style which is not the Scythian, and which recalls the corresponding styles of the second Assyrian empire and of archaic Ionia. The normal material of the horse-trappings is silver: the silver phalarae are often gilt. Here also we notice a return to Oriental tradition, to the tradition of the late Assyrian period, in which the bridles were commonly decorated with round phalarae of metal. It is in these tombs that we find the first stirrups.

We do not know much about the costume of the Kuban warriors and their wives. But the introduction of the fibula points to a great change, and the appearance of the class of fibula derived from the La Tène type, and of a Celtic fibula of the Augustan period with the name of the maker Aucissa, is a proof of regular relations with the Celtic, and probably with the Germanic world.

Still more important is the complete change in the forms of the gold ornaments sewn to clothing and shrouds. In the East, at all periods, clothes had been ornamented with metal plaques sewn on to the material. We have seen that the mode prevailed in South Russia in the period of Scythian ascendancy: in that period, the plaques were nearly always round or square: they were fairly large; they were covered with embossed decoration in floral or animal style; they were often imitated from Greek coins, and in the fourth and third centuries, religious scenes were sometimes represented. The Kuban graves have yielded hundreds of garment plaques, but never of a type known from the Scythian tombs: they are now very small and thin, and the shapes are geometric, roundels, billets, fleursdelys, crescents, voided triangles, rosettes and the like (fig. 17). All these shapes belong exclusively to the Oriental repertory: exactly similar plaques have been found in Assyria: the same ornaments appear later in Sassanian and Arabic art.

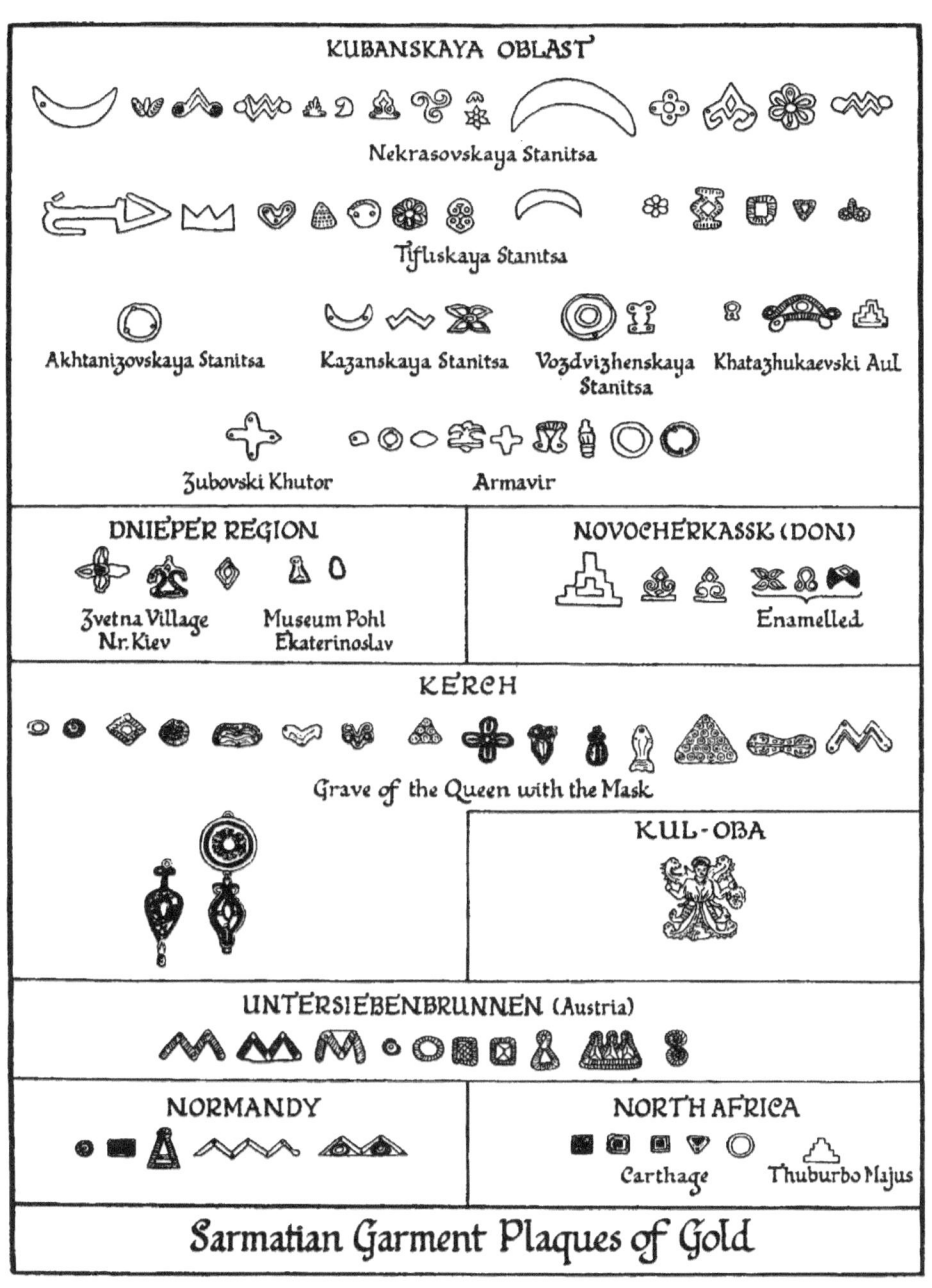

Fig. 17.

The vessels, numerous in the Kuban graves, are sometimes of metal, sometimes of clay. The metal vases, of silver or bronze, are almost all importations: the shapes are those current in late Hellenistic and Roman

Imperial times. Most of the clay vases are also imported: some are local imitations of classical models. But there are also native products: the large Asiatic cauldrons of bronze or copper, which we found in the Scythian tombs, are very common on the Kuban as well. The general form of these cauldrons remains the same, but there are alterations of detail which link the Kuban vessels with those found in the tombs of the period of migrations. Several of the Kuban vessels bear signs which are undoubtedly alphabetical: this alphabet, as we shall find, was in use at Panticapaeum in the second, and third centuries A.D. The same signs occur on certain pieces of caparison.

I would also suggest an Oriental origin for the small round bottles of gold—recalling the spherical vases of the Scythian tombs—which are frequently found in the graves of women. The bottles are always studded with gems (fig. 18, 1, 2).

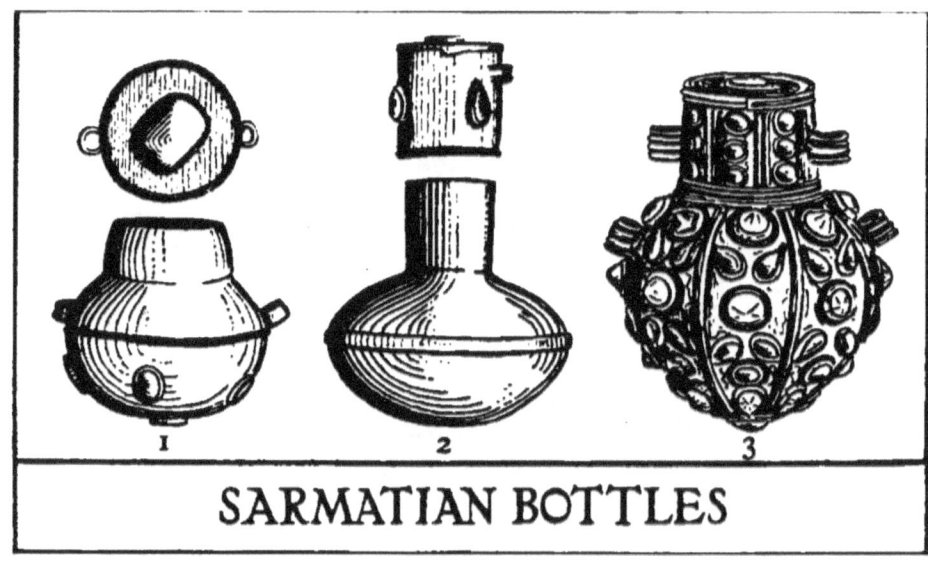

Fig. 18.

One word more. The torcs and mirrors in our tombs are beyond doubt local work. Both torcs and mirrors were constantly found in Scythian tombs: but the forms have now changed. The torcs are massive and rude, of the type which we noticed at Orenburg and at Stavropol. The mirrors are no longer of bronze, like the Scythian mirrors, nor have they bronze handles ending in figures of animals: they are now made of a special alloy, silvery in colour, are considerably smaller, and have a wooden handle, or a knob in the centre for suspension. Both shape and alloy are purely Asiatic, and are widespread in Asia, especially in Central Asia and in China. Speaking of the relation between the Kuban tombs and China, I would also mention a small amber figure of a lion, found at Armavir in a grave of the first century A.D.: it reminds one strangely of the Chinese lions familiar from our museums of Chinese art.

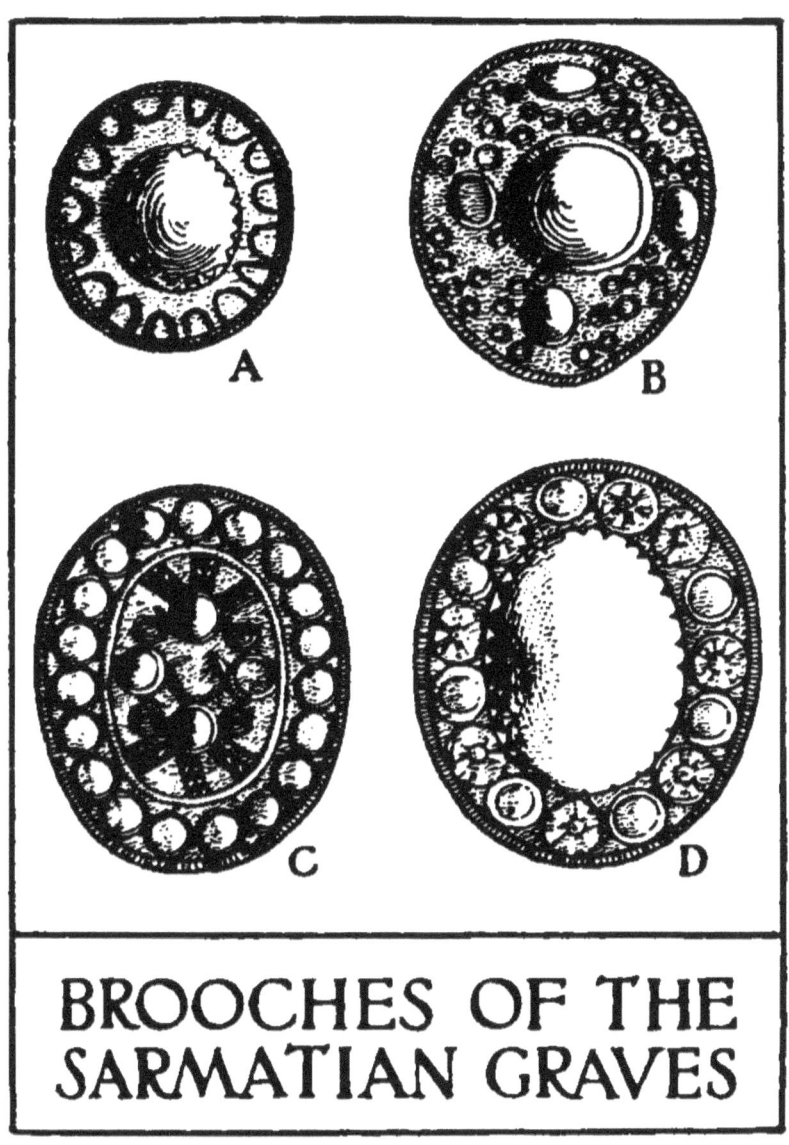

Fig. 19.

The jewellery and goldsmith's work is particularly characteristic in the Kuban tombs of the Roman period: torcs, diadems, gold plating for weapons and for glass vases, belt clasps, and so forth. The most remarkable feature is the complete abandonment of the principles of Greek jewellery. What interests the artist is no longer delicacy of form, proportions, or artistic modelling, but, above all, richness and polychromy in the surface decoration. Historical, mythological and religious subjects have been almost entirely suppressed: geometric and floral motives, and the animal style, hold the field. The technical processes employed are embossing, and ornamentation by means of gold wires and granulation: as I said above, true granulation begins to die out, and is replaced by pseudo-granulation, a variant of the gold wire technique. But the decoration is entirely subordinated to the colouring. The artist's chief object is to vary the coloration by inserting precious stones wherever he can; by filling with stones the spaces which the geometric or floral decoration leaves free. There was a great demand for vases cut out of blocks of solid glass, in imitation of stone and metal vases. But the elegant shape of the vase did not satisfy the inhabitants of the Kuban valley in the Roman period: they required a casing of gold enriched with stones and enamels (fig. 16, 1, 2). The gold diadem or bracelet must present a combination of gold and of precious stones: a fibula or a belt clasp must be gay with inset coloured glass and gems (fig. 16, 4—Alexandrian coloured glass in the centre—, and fig. 19, D—transparent white glass). I shall speak presently of the openwork plaques with coloured filling. I would also mention a vase found in the Caucasus: the vase itself is of coloured glass, the openwork casing of silver.

It is interesting to notice the revival of the polychrome style, rejected by Greek art but popular throughout the East. Greek art furnishes no parallels to this rude and vivid polychromy: in the East, however, the tradition flourished without interruption. The Kuban polychromy is very closely akin to the Persian goldsmith's work which is represented by the Oxus treasure in the British Museum and by the finds from Susa in the Louvre. The processes, the principles, the shapes are the same, but the Kuban work is ruder and more primitive.

The goldsmiths who worked for the Kuban valley revived a form of polychrome toreutic which became highly developed in the Western Europe of later times: openwork objects, the voids of which are filled with coloured substances. They were mentioned above when we were studying the sixth- and fifth-century Scythian tombs on the Kuban. I drew attention to the openwork plaques which adorned the horses' bridles, and I pointed to the original models, the bronze plaques of Transcaucasia in the earliest Iron Age (fig. 6). It is curious to find the same plaques used for belt clasping in the tombs on the Kuban. Every one knows that the technique was very popular in the metalwork of the Roman Empire, and that it probably exercised a strong influence on the cloisonné enamel of the Middle Ages. The famous golden vase from Petroasa certainly goes back to these openwork polychrome jewels, characteristic specimens of which—earrings—are found on the Kuban in the fifth century B.C. and in the Persian graves of Susa in the fourth.

This polychromy profoundly modified the animal style of ornament, of which the inhabitants of the Kuban valley in the Hellenistic period were no less fond than the Scythians. The animal style of the graves on the Kuban is doubtless poorer in motives than the Scythian. But in certain objects it shows exceptional vigour and charm. On a belt clasp of silver gilt, recently discovered at Maikop, and now in the Hermitage (pl. XXV, 1), the familiar scheme of a beast of prey devouring an animal is handled in a most remarkable way. The animals are subordinated to their decorative and practical purpose, to form a belt clasp, but the powerful feeling expressed in the swoop of the griffin, and in the head of the dying horse, contrasts strangely with the fantastic position of the griffin's body and with the treatment of the horse's hind-quarters, reversed to fill a space which would else be vacant. And how rich the colouring is! The artist has studded the animals' bodies with gems and cut garnets, and enclosed the whole design in a richly modelled and gaily coloured frame; this frame is the body of the belt itself, formed of rows of wings, the compartments of which are filled with enamels. The technique, notice, is already that of cloisonné enamel, although the date cannot be later than the second or first century B.C. The same combination of polychromy and animal style is frequent in the jewellery of the Sarmatian period: for example, in the belt clasps, already mentioned, adorned with figures of lions biting their tails. We shall come across the same tendency in the contemporary and kindred jewellery of western Siberia, which I shall presently discuss.

PLATE XXV

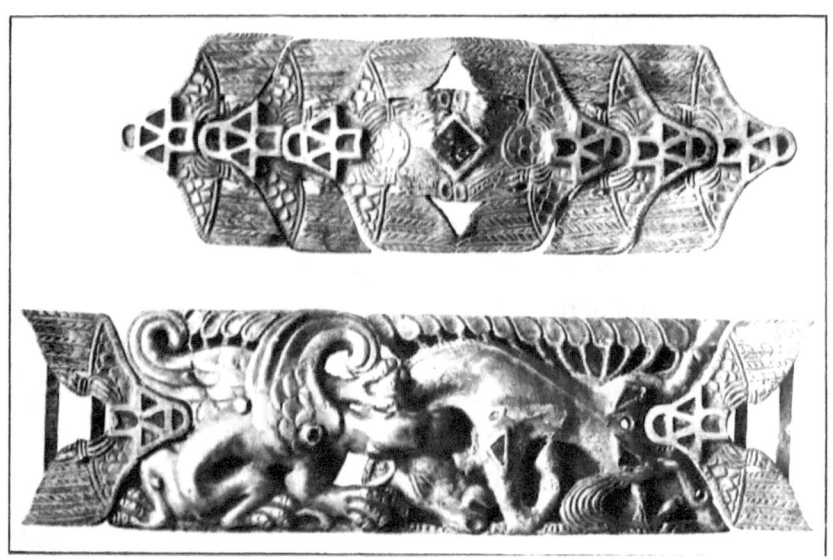

1. SILVER-GILT BELT WITH INSET STONES
From Maikop. II Cent. B.C. (?). Hermitage, Petrograd

2. GOLD PLAQUE WITH INSET STONES
From Western Siberia. I Cent. A.D. Hermitage, Petrograd

PLATE XXVI

1. CROWN

2. PERFUME BOTTLE

 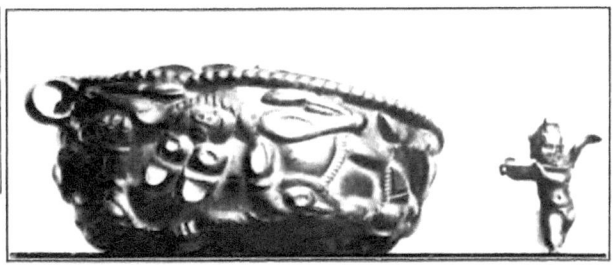

3. PERFUME BOTTLE   4, 5 CUP AND STATUETTE OF EROS

THE TREASURE OF NOVOCHERKÁSSK (ALL GOLD)
I Cent. B.C. to I Cent. A.D. Hermitage, Petrograd

The group of Kuban graves which I have just described is by no means isolated. Similar graves occur in most parts of the South Russian steppes, and we find a flourishing development of the same civilization in western Siberia. The most remarkable parallel to the Kuban culture appears in the valley of the Don. I would mention, in especial, the celebrated treasure of Novocherkássk, which resembles, feature for feature, the furniture of the Kuban tombs; and the less sumptuous find from Golubínskaya Stanitsa. The gold diadem from Novocherkássk (pl. XXVI, 1) is a characteristic specimen of the strange jewellery described above. The shape is Greek; Greek the cameo which adorns the front of the diadem; and the pendants attached to the lower part of the diadem are imitations of the pendants which are common in Greek jewellery and widespread in South Russia during the fourth and third centuries B.C. But the upper part of the diadem is in a pure animal style, and reminds one of motives which we shall find in Siberian jewellery. Lastly, the polychromy of the diadem as a whole, the pearls, the amethysts and garnets, large and small, with which the entire surface is studded, takes us back to the valley of the Kuban. It is there also that we find perfect parallels for the gold perfume vase (pl. XXVI, 3), decorated in the animal style and set with stones; for its lid, which recalls, with extraordinary vividness, the belt clasps from the tombs on the Kuban; for the golden vase covered with figures of animals and set with stones (pl. XXVI, 4); and above all, for the hundreds of little gold garment plaques, some of them encrusted with tiny pieces of blue or pink enamel, pink coral, or turquoise (fig. 17). The same spirit prevails in the curious perfume-tube, in the form of a lion whose body is replaced by an onyx tube (pl. XXVI, 2). I cannot speak of all the objects which make up this splendid treasure: but I must insist on their close resemblance to the finds from the tombs on the Kuban. The Novocherkássk find forms a kind of bridge between the Kuban and Siberia. The date has been hotly disputed: but if we consider that the cameo set in the diadem is probably a late Hellenistic work, that pendants like those of the diadem never appear in the jewellery of the Roman period, that the small gold statuette of Eros (pl. XXVI, 5) is late Hellenistic, that the Kuban analogies point to the period of the first group of tombs we must date the treasure in the first century B.C., or at latest the first A.D. A little later is the gold vase found at Migulinskaya Stanitsa, which bears the names of the owner, Ξηβανόκου, and of the artist, Ταρούλας ἐποίει, with an indication of the weight, λ(ίτρας) χρ(υσοῦ) ΜΗ (forty-eight ounces): a closely similar vase, uninscribed, forms part of the treasure of Novocherkássk. The inscription is valuable, for it shows us where the vase was made: I have pointed out, in a special article, that both names are Thracian, common at Tanais and even at Panticapaeum in the Roman period. Let us bear this important fact in mind.

From the same region of the Don and the Donets comes a peculiar group of silver gilt plaques, mostly from horse-trappings, which belong to the earlier part of the same period (pl. XXVII, 4). The decoration of these phalarae, which have recently been published by Spitsyn, is sometimes identical with that of similar plaques from the region of the Kuban. The most interesting of those found on the Kuban is the bronze phalara, excavated at Vozdvizhenskaya Stanitsa in 1899, representing a goat devoured by a hydra with six heads, all eared and nearly square. Large finds of plaques have been made at Siverskaya Stanitsa in the Taman peninsula, at Taganrog, Fedúlovo and Starobêlsk in the region of the Don and the Donets, at Yanchekrák in the district of Taurida: that is, between the Caucasus and the steppes of the Dnieper. The style of the plaques from Akhtanízovka is different, and appears to be purely Greek: the Akhtanízovka phalarae were probably either imported, or made by Greek artists in South Russia. The Siverskaya find dates from the second or first century B.C.: the others from about the same period. Some of the plaques are decorated with patterns only, and in these the ornamentation is purely Iranian; just as in a plaque found in 1901 at Tiflísskaya Stanitsa on the Kuban. Others, at Starobêlsk for instance, bear figures of animals (fig. 20) or mythological scenes. The animals have nothing in common with the animals of Roman provincial art: a similar style prevails in the painted tomb discovered by Stasov at Kerch and presently to be described: a pure Iranian style; derived, as I have proved in my work on decorative painting, from the art of which one branch is Parthian art; and perhaps presenting a certain analogy with the earliest stage of the Ionian animal style, which was borrowed from the East. Two gilded silver plaques in the Cabinet des Médailles at Paris (pl. XXVII, 1, 2), which are said to have come from Pontus, although the provenience is not certain, show a style and a technique which are almost identical with those of the plaques from South Russia. The Oriental style of the Paris plaques was recognized, and their date established, by Drexel and by Reinach, but neither scholar noticed the numerous and convincing analogies from South Russia. It is well known that in their artistic development Pontus and South Russia were always closely associated. But it may be that the Paris plaques reached Constantinople, where they were purchased, from South Russia. The engraved inscription, in spite of Drexel's arguments, I believe to be false: it looks as if it had been made in Russia, where Mithridates is even more popular among forgers than Saitapharnes: the Pontic provenience would be subsequent, and occasioned by the inscription.

I should like to draw special attention to the second, fragmentary plaque, which is published here for the first time, by kind permission of Mr. Ernest Babelon, director of the Cabinet des Médailles, and from a photograph supplied by him (pl. XXVII, 2). The Indian elephant's head in the centre, and the three stags, show all the peculiarities of later Iranian style. It is worth noticing that the scales which cover the body of the central animal in the first plaque are very similar to the scales of the archaic lion on the plaque from the Golden Tumulus near Simferopol (see page 70).

Still more interesting are the plaques with mythological subjects. On the Siverskaya plaque (pl. XXVII, 4) there are two scenes, on the left the triumph of Dionysos, on the right Athena mastering a giant. Both scenes, however, have undergone a quaint transformation which recalls some of the Greco-Indian monuments from Gandhara. For instance, the costumes are purely Oriental, and the panther on which Dionysos is seated has an almost human head. The curious technique of the plaque, especially the strewing of the ground with incised dots, is constant in the monuments of our series. The plaque from Yanchekrák has a half-length, frontal figure of a sun god, with wings of the recurving Oriental type, holding a solar disk, a plate or patera with an eight-petalled rosette, in his right hand. These mythological plaques remind one strangely of a number of monuments which exhibit the same technique and the same treatment of mythological figures. Some groups of them have been found in Bulgaria. The earliest group, that of Panagüríshte, which belongs to the third century B.C., consists of a horse's frontlet in silver and four circular phalarae of the same metal. The frontlet has the regular form of the third century frontlets from South Russia, for instance, the frontlet from the Tsymbalka tumulus: the phalarae remind one of the phalarae from Alexandropol, which show strong affinities with the whole group of phalarae which we are discussing. But the style of the figures—Herakles mastering a boar, a siren with a lyre and two griffins—which represent, under borrowed forms, deities of the local pantheon, has the same characteristics as the above-mentioned plaques from South Russia, those of the second and first centuries B.C. The same may be said of the animals and the floral motives in the circular phalarae from Panagürishte. The best parallels are provided, on the one hand by the phalarae found at Alexandropol, and on the other by the phalara from Starobêlsk (fig. 20). Still closer is the analogy between the South Russian phalarae of the Sarmatian period and the recent find of silver-gilt phalarae at Galiché in the district of Orêkhovo on the Danube, which I shall describe and analyse in the Memoirs of the Bulgarian Archaeological Society. The phalarae are all circular, and the forms correspond closely to those of the phalarae from South Russia mentioned above. The technique is the same in both groups: I would instance the habit of covering the whole ground with incised dots. The floral ornaments are oriental, as in South Russia, and have nothing to do with classical floral patterns. Here also we find mythological figures which recall the most popular figures in the Greco-Iranian pantheon of South Russia: the bust of the Great Goddess flanked by birds (compare pl. XXIII, 5), and a corresponding figure of a native prince on horseback (pl. XXIII, 2). Even the great torcs which cover the necks of both figures find a parallel in the numerous torcs of the same type found at Anapa, Stavropol, Akhtanizovka, and on the Kuban, which belong to the third or second century B.C. Another good parallel to the Bulgarian mythological phalarae is presented by many of the objects which compose the rich find of Petroasa in Rumania, to be dealt with in my eighth chapter: for example, the torcs, and above all the large gold patera mentioned in the preceding chapter. Here again we have a local pantheon in classical disguise.

Finally, the same style and the same main ideas appear in certain finds from Germanic lands. I am thinking of the phalarae from Raermond in Holland (pl. XXVII, 3), with a frieze of animals and a figure of Hercules strangling a lion which presents the same peculiarities—beardlessness, local costume—as the Hercules of Panagürishte: and of the famous cauldron from Gundestrup. I agree with Salomon Reinach and Drexel in attributing these monuments to a peculiar branch of art which they call Irano-Celtic: but I am convinced that this art grew up, not in Pontus or Cappadocia, but in South Russia; that it began to develop as early as the final period of Scythian domination, the third century B.C.; and that it was brought to completion by the Sarmatians in the second and first centuries B.C. It was indebted to the Sarmatians for the strong Iranian tone both in the representation of human beings and animals and in the Iranian floral motives; Greco-Scythian art contributed the semi-Greek travesties of Iranian gods; the Celts certain technical peculiarities and in the treatment of human and animal figures a peculiar touch borrowed from archaic Ionian art at the time when their own art was just beginning. A few special traits may have been added by the native Thracian population. There is nothing astonishing in the mixture; nor in the wide diffusion of the style, which even reached Germany. I would remind the reader of what I said about the advance of the Celts in South Russia in the third century B.C., where they encountered first the Scythians—Posidonius, in Strabo, knew of Celto-Scythians on the Black Sea—and afterwards the Sarmatians, who were evidently familiar to the Gaulish tribes, especially to the Scordiscans who infested the Balkan peninsula in the second and first centuries B.C. Through the Bastamians, the phalara and the cauldron of Gundestrup may very well have passed from hand to hand until they reached Germany. I would invite the reader to compare the Gundestrup serpents with those on the plaque from Vozdvizhenskaya Stanitsa, and the gods with those on the Siverskaya and Yanchekrak plaques.

Fig. 20. THE PHALARA FROM STAROBÊLSK.

PLATE XXVII

1, 2. SILVER-GILT PHALARAE FROM THE SHORES OF THE BLACK
SEA. Cabinet des Médailles, Paris
3. SILVER PLAQUE FROM RAERMOND (HOLAND). Rijks Museum,
Leyden
4. SILVER-GILT PLAQUE FROM THE SIVERSKAYA STANITSA,
TAMAN PENINSULA. Historical Museum, Moscow II Cent. B.C.

These products of the Irano-Celtic art of the last centuries before Christ probably represent the achievement of those groups of Sarmatian tribes which first came into contact with the western peoples. It is noticeable that they consist almost exclusively of horse-trappings, the bearers of them being conquering horsemen whose lives and successes depended upon the speed and training of their horses. They show close kinship, of course, with the objects from the Kuban, from the Don and from Siberia, especially with those of the earlier period, the third and second centuries B.C.: but in general they are characteristic of the western, earlier group alone. The specifically Sarmatian products are the objects, described above, from the Kuban, from the Don, and from Siberia: these belong to the last century B.C. and the first A.D. and probably represent the special culture of the strongest and latest of the Sarmatian tribes—the Alans. But the ethnographical problem will be discussed later. Let us now proceed to the analysis of the archaeological evidence.

Finds like those of the Kuban are not lacking farther west. Gold plaques in geometric shapes have been discovered in the barrows of the Kharkov district. A characteristic find, with small gold plaques shaped like the Kuban plaques, came to light at Tsvêtna in the district of Kiev: and another near Odessa. From Olbia come two little gold perfume bottles, exactly similar to the bottles from Ust-Labinskaya Stanitsa on the Kuban and in the treasure of Novocherkássk; one of these Olbian bottles presents a striking resemblance to the gold vases from Novocherkássk and from Migulinskaya Stanitsa, by reason of its animal-shaped handles and the lion on the lid: like the cauldrons from the Kuban, it bears an alphabetical sign.

We now come to the old objects brought from western Siberia to the Hermitage in the eighteenth century. I have no space to discuss them at length. That they came from Siberia cannot be doubted: yet at first sight one is almost tempted to follow Veselóvski in assigning them, one and all, to the region of the Kuban. Compare the Maikop belt-clasp, described above, with the gold plaque in the Hermitage (pl. XXV, 2): they agree in the composition, in the attitude of the horse, and in the expression of the dying animal: one would be inclined to attribute the two plaques to a single artist, were it not for a marked difference of execution. The plaque from the Kuban is full of life, the Siberian probably reproduces an oft-repeated motive and consequently lacks the pathos of the plaque from the Kuban. Other Siberian plaques are coarser and clumsier. But some of them are real masterpieces, vying with the finest pieces in the Oxus treasure and in the Persian tomb at Susa. Take the eagle attacking a goat, or the statuette of an eagle grasping a swan. In composition, the Siberian eagle is a worthy rival of the celebrated plaque from the barrow of the Seven Brothers, and in polychromy it is unequalled. Take the Siberian torc lately published by Pridik. The griffin is the familiar Persian and Panticapaean animal. But the living force of head and body, the leonine leap, the rich and cunning polychromy, make it far superior to the griffins of the Oxus treasure. There is a marked contrast between these masterpieces and the rude figures of fantastic animals peaceably devouring victims no less fantastic and no less peaceable. It is as if we had originals from a master's hand and travesties by barbarian imitators. But there can be no doubt about the origin of the Siberian objects and of the motives which they exhibit: they came from the Iranian world, either directly or through South Russia. There remains the question of date. It is natural to suppose, that most of the objects in the Hermitage, together with those which were brought to Holland by Witsen and which have completely disappeared, came from a single great find or from a few contemporary tombs in a single cemetery. If this is so, great importance must be attached to the Roman coins of Galba and Nero published by Witsen and probably discovered along with the objects which he carried off. There is no reason to suspect Witsen's good faith: and where could Roman coins have been found in Siberia, except in such tombs? These considerations, and the contemporaneousness of the Siberian finds with the finds from the Kuban and from Novocherkássk, lead me to believe that the greater portion of the Siberian objects are to be assigned to the first century A.D.; some, perhaps, being earlier than this date; others, it may be, later.

 This civilization then was widespread. I shall show in the next chapter that it profoundly influenced the Panticapaean civilization of the second and third centuries A.D., and we shall see that it left strong traces all over Europe, in Austria, in Italy, in France, in Spain, and in Africa.

 It will possibly be asked, whether we are justified in speaking of a civilization, whether the predilection for polychromy may not be explained by influence from the Roman empire, where the polychrome style took root, in more than one province, about the second century A.D. I do not deny an influence from without, nor the presence, among the Kuban finds, of objects imported from Asia Minor and from Syria, where the same tendency to polychromy produced articles which took the fancy of the Sarmatian customer. But I think that after the preceding demonstration, no one will dispute the existence of a very distinctive Sarmatian civilization. We see before us the development of a purely Oriental civilization by a nomadic people, which brought the germs of this civilization with it and developed them locally, while in uninterrupted contact with the Greek colonies of South Russia. The polychrome style is only one of the characteristics of this civilization: but its appearance is easily intelligible. The whole civilization was Iranian; in part, it was directly based on the productions which marked the last period of cultural development in Babylonia and Assyria. We have little information about the story of Iranian art outside of Persia. We have seen that it influenced the earliest Scythian art. We now see that its development did not cease in the succeeding centuries, and that it invaded the Russian steppes, for the second time, in the Hellenistic age. Moreover, this Iranian art of Central Asia did not remain stationary during that obscure period: it made progress, keeping, however, to the same lines as in the seventh and sixth centuries, when the Scythians first introduced it into South Russia. Just as before, it has a decided taste for polychromy, chiefly known to us from its jewellery, for few save metal objects have survived to our time, but doubtless manifested in other arts as well. The jewels from Kelermes, with their amber and enamel inlay, exhibit the same tendency as the jewels from the barrows on the Kuban, on the Don, and in Siberia. Another feature of this Iranian style is its fondness for the animal style. In essentials, this animal style, as we have already noticed, is the same in the first centuries before and after Christ, as it was in the sixth century B.C.: a propensity to pure ornament still shows itself, in the arbitrary disposal of animal bodies, in associations, sometimes fantastic, of several animals, in the formation of extremities as animal heads, in the love of fabulous creatures, especially griffins. But between the Scythian animal style and that of our finds there are great differences. The chief reason is that our style is more closely connected with the Assyro-Persian animal style, and apparently less influenced by northern elements, although these do appear in the monuments from Siberia and from the region of the Don. The style of our finds seems to have been almost unaffected by the Scythian animal style as the Scythians had developed it, mainly under Greek influence, in South Russia.

Where were the objects made, which are found in the tombs of the Kuban, of the South Russian steppes, and of western Siberia? I think we may say that, just as in the Scythian period, some of the objects are imports from the East, some imports from Greek colonies, and some neither the one nor the other. Among our finds there are several pieces of goldsmith's and jeweller's work which offer a curious mixture of Greek and Oriental motives and technique. Take the diadem from Novocherkássk, the bracelets and the round fibulae from the Kuban, the glass vases encased with gold and precious stones, the silver openwork vase, with hunting scenes, from the Caucasus, the gold perfume-bottles, and other articles. Here there is such a mixture of elements that the objects cannot be defined except as Greco-Oriental. The Maikop belt, the griffin torcs, the eagle and a number of old statuettes from Siberia, are surely Oriental importations. But the hand of a Greek artist is traceable in the diadem of Novocherkássk and the other works mentioned above. The answer to our question is given by the gold vase from Migulinskaya Stanitsa, and by parallels, found in Panticapaean tombs of the first to the third centuries B.C., to the objects from the tumuli on the Kuban. It was a native artist of Tanais who made the Migulinskaya vase, and Panticapaean artists who furnished the warriors of the Kuban region with most of their gold and silver articles. The gold bottles from Olbia appear to be the work of an Olbian. Now as before, the Greek artists or Hellenized natives who lived in the Black Sea cities worked for the neighbouring peoples and adapted themselves to their tastes and requirements. Was it such artists who made the barbaric objects from Siberia? I do not know. There may have been a local industry which imitated the articles imported from the East and from the Greek cities on the Black Sea.

If we proceed to ask ourselves, now that we have described and analysed this civilization, whether it can be associated with a particular people, the answer appears to be easy. It is a purely Oriental civilization, which is closely connected with the Iranian; which slowly advanced from Central Asia and gradually invaded the steppes of South Russia and Siberia in the first and second centuries A.D.; which exerted a profound influence, as we shall show in our seventh chapter, on the Greek colonies of the Black Sea. The furniture of the tombs which we have examined shows that the warriors buried there were nomads, mounted hoplites, whose principal weapons were lance, sword and dagger, whose defensive armour consisted of a helmet and a corslet of scales or rings, and who were already acquainted with spurs.

All these data correspond to what we know of the Sarmatians, who occupied part of the Russian steppes about the end of the fourth century, who advanced slowly westwards and settled down for a long while in the basin of the Kuban. I do not hesitate then to identify the bearers of this civilization with the Sarmatians, especially the Alans, Iranian tribes who were at the height of their political development in the first and second centuries A.D., precisely the time at which this civilization flourished. We can now complete, with the help of archaeological evidence, the historical picture which we outlined at the beginning of the chapter.

Setting out from Central Asia, the Sarmatians moved both westward, occupying the steppes in the Ural region; and northward, to the Siberian steppes. At the end of the fourth century B.C., they appeared, as we know from the pseudo-Scylax, on the Don. At this period, we found near Tanais a civilization mixed in character but certainly belonging to nomadic warriors and very different from the Scythian. Some have supposed, that the cemetery of Elizavetovskaya, excavated by A. Miller, belonged to the pre-Roman city of Tanais. I cannot subscribe to this theory. The city of Tanais was founded by Greek colonists from Panticapaeum. Its cemetery, in consequence, in the fourth and third centuries, must have been like that of Panticapaeum: it must have been a Greek cemetery. Now the cemetery of Elizavetovskaya, in all its features, is the cemetery of a population which was originally nomadic, a population of mounted warriors, which settled near the mouth of the Don so as to watch the Greek city of Tanais and to collect tribute from it.

From numerous inscriptions, all of the Roman period, discovered on the site of Tanais, we know that the city then presented a semi-Iranian aspect. The names of the citizens, who belonged to the aristocracy of Tanais, are partly Iranian and partly Thracian. The population, therefore, was a mixed population of Hellenized Iranians and Thracians, which gradually supplanted the original Greek inhabitants. The process of supersession, the result of which we see in the second century A.D., the time to which most of the inscriptions belong, was necessarily a protracted one: the native infiltration into a heterogeneous society, and the complete Hellenization of the native elements, can only have been accomplished in the course of long years of peaceful cohabitation. The Iranian names, studied by V. Miller, of the second century Tanaites, and the type of the Tanaites as we gather it from funerary statues and votive reliefs of the period, approximate to the names and type which we know to be Sarmatian. It is among the Ossetes that we find most of the analogies with those Tanaite names which have been recognized as Iranian: the armour of the Tanaite horsemen on the funerary reliefs and statues corresponds exactly with the Sarmatian, as described by Tacitus and portrayed in Roman reliefs. All this leads me to believe, that as early as the fourth century an advanced tribe of Sarmatians came and settled on the banks of the Don. It drove the Scythians across the river and opened relations with the kingdom of the Bosphorus and the colony of Tanais. The Sarmatians kept an eye on the colony, and it paid them a regular tribute. They also absorbed the native population of the country, the Sauromatians, and art of the former masters of the Don steppes, the conquering Scythians of old. In this way a mixed population grew up at the mouth of the Don; it gradually became Hellenized, and supplanted the old Greek population of the city. Established on the river and constantly reinforced from the Ural and Volga steppes, the Sarmatians, held in check by the Scythians at the barrier of the Don, naturally spread southward, towards the valley of the Kuban and the mountains of Caucasus, in the fourth or third centuries B.C. and later. I observed in the third chapter that after the end of the fourth century there are hardly any Scythian graves in the valley of the Kuban. The Scythians were probably obliged to leave the Kuban valley when they decided to resist the advance of the Sarmatians at the barrier of the Don. The Kuban valley was gradually occupied by the Sarmatians. The Siracians were probably the first tribe to arrive, and it was probably they who expelled the Scythians. If the name of the Siracians is correctly restored in a corrupt passage of Diodorus, they took an important part in the struggle of two pretenders, Eumelos and Satyros, for the tyranny of the Bosphorus, in the year 309. The advance of the Sarmatians from east to west was comparatively slow; towards the second century B.C., they occupied the whole valley of the Kuban, with the exception of the delta, that is, the Taman peninsula; and even penetrated into the peninsula in the first century. They thus became immediate neighbours of the Bosphoran kingdom, with which they entered into relations. Thence they moved still farther west, and subdued the whole of South Russia. We have seen that the valley of the Don preserves numerous archaeological traces of their prolonged sojourn on the Don and between Don and Dnieper in the second and first centuries B.C.

On their arrival in the valley of the Dnieper and the Bug, the Sarmatians were faced by a much more complicated situation. In the second century B.C., when the first Sarmatian tribes appeared, the ethnological and political aspect of the region between Dnieper and Danube was extremely varied and complex. As early as the third century B.C., Celtic tribes possessed themselves of a number of districts in South Russia, and advanced as far as the Black Sea. German tribes followed at their heels. Moreover, the revival of a Thracian state, that of the Dacians, in the first century B.C. and the first A.D., led to constant invasions of South Russia by Thracians. One of these brought about the capture and sack of Olbia. The Sarmatians also settled in the same localities. The varied ethnographical character of the steppes between Dnieper and Danube is reflected by the archaeological finds. The period in which Scythian influence predominates, the fourth and third centuries B.C., with its sumptuous tombs of Scythian chieftains, is succeeded, in the steppes of the Dnieper region and in the wooded country northward, by a period in which the raves gradually lose their Scythian stamp, and in which a number of new strains are observable, very different from the Scythian. A great number of objects have recently been discovered in the basin of the Dnieper, which certainly belong to the civilization of La Tène: bronze and clay vases, and weapons. I have already referred to the appearance of the fibula of the latest La Tène period. These are the remains of the Galatians, a portion of whom, the Celto-Scythians of Posidonius, settled on the shores of the Black Sea. There is also a series of graves which closely resemble the Orenburg graves and which probably date from the third century B.C.: these are perhaps to be assigned to the first Sarmatian arrivals, the Iazygians and the Roxalans, the bearers of the silver phalarae described above. Other finds are exactly analogous to the Kuban finds of the first century A.D.: including, for example, the characteristic gold plaques. We may assign them to the Alans. At the same time, a new civilization is asserting itself on the middle Dnieper. It is marked by a new mode of burial: the tumuli disappear, and their place is taken by vast crematory cemeteries, the urn fields, which date from the first and second centuries A.D. Many writers have pointed out the resemblances between these urn fields and contemporaneous phenomena in Germany, especially South Germany. Arné may be right in supposing an advance of Germanic tribes, carrying with them, as they advanced, a number of Slavs.

In a word, the archaeological evidence as to the region between Don and Dnieper does not conflict with the historical. A closer study of the archaeological data than has hitherto been attempted will give us clearer insight into the difficult questions which are raised by the early stage of the period of migrations. The details of the subject cannot be discussed in a book about Iranians and Greeks.

It thus appears that such knowledge of the Sarmatians as we derive from ancient writers, is completed and amplified by archaeological evidence. Far from being destructive barbarians, the Sarmatians were a fresh wave of Iranian conquerors, who brought to Europe the new achievements of Iranian culture in the home of the Iranian people. Like their predecessors, the Scythians, the Sarmatians did not aim at abolishing the centres of Greek civilization. They fought with the Greeks, but never because they were bent on destroying or subduing the Greek cities. Even remote Tanais, and unprotected Olbia, continued to exist, commercial intermediaries to the Sarmatians, as they had been to the Scythians. But unlike the Scythians the Sarmatians showed great power of penetration. They contrived to make their way into the Greek cities and to Iranize them almost completely.

This process will form the subject of the next chapter.

VII.
THE GREEK CITIES OF SOUTH RUSSIA IN THE ROMAN PERIOD

THE political life of the Greek cities on the Black Sea was profoundly affected by the appearance of the Sarmatians in the South Russian steppes.

As long as the Scythian kingdom held the Sarmatians in check on the banks of the Don, the political and economic situation of the Bosphoran kingdom suffered little change. The hard times began, both for the Scythians and for the kingdom of the Bosphorus, in the third or second century B.C., when the Sarmatians crossed the Don, penetrated far into the region of the Kuban, and invaded the Taman peninsula. The Scythians were forced to seek shelter in the Crimean steppes, and consequently began to exert stronger and stronger pressure on the Greek cities of the Crimea. Chersonesus and the Bosphorus were compelled to fight the Scythians for their independence, and at the same time the Greeks of the Bosphorus had to defend the Greek cities of the Taman peninsula against the advancing Sarmatians. Life in the Greek cities became more and more precarious and uncertain. The Greeks tried to resist, they paid heavy ransom to the Scythian and Sarmatian armies, they mobilized their citizens and fortified their towns, but the hostile pressure increased, and the resources accumulated during centuries of prosperity rapidly diminished. They still exported corn, leather, fish and slaves, but, while the land routes became more and more unreliable, the sea routes became quite insecure. Piracy prevailed as at the dawn of Greek civilization. Athens, enfeebled as she was, and 'allied' with the Romans, could offer no remedy. Rhodes, who had policed the seas in the third and second century B.C., lost her importance at the end of the second century, and Rome, the new mistress of the world, engaged in internal struggles of increasing ferocity, had neither time nor leisure to provide for the security of the Aegean and the Black Sea, and took not the least interest in the affairs of the Pontic Greeks. The position became critical at the end of the third century B.C., when a strong Scythian state was formed in the Crimea under the sceptre of King Skiluros. In order not to succumb to the Scythians, the Greek cities of the Crimea, Chersonesus foremost, had no choice but to look for a powerful protector who would turn his attention to the northern shore of the Black Sea.

Pontus and the Crimea had been closely connected from the earliest times. In both regions, there was a strongly Iranized native population, and in both, Greek cities which made their living by exploiting native vassals or bondmen. It will be remembered that Pontic Heracleia recolonized Chersonesus; the relations between the two cities never ceased. As long as the Bosphorus, with the help of Athens and of its own abundant resources, was able to maintain an army and a navy strong enough to defend the whole Crimea, Chersonesus availed itself of the services of its neighbour and ally. But when this protection failed, and the Bosphorans themselves were groaning under hostile pressure, the Chersonesans turned once more to their ancient allies, the Greek cities of Pontus. The precarious position of Chersonesus, as early as the third century, is illustrated by the decree in honour of Syriscos, a young scholar who belonged to one of the good Greek families in the city. He had recounted, in an historical treatise, the miraculous appearances of the Parthenos, the patron goddess of Chersonesus, and also more prosaic matters, the diplomatic intercourse of Chersonesus with the Bosphoran kings, which had assured it military protection. The combined assistance of the miracles and the Bosphoran armies was rarely adequate to defend the city from the growing fierceness of the Scythian onslaughts. We can well understand, that in this difficult plight the Chersonesans sought allies wherever they could hope to find them.

But the Pontic cities, the natural allies of Chersonesus, were no longer free. A monarchical state had formed itself in Pontus during the third century, and the Pontic kings, who were only slightly Hellenized, had contrived to subjugate the Greek cities. It was to these kings, therefore, that the Chersonesans addressed themselves when they were at the end of their resources. By the second century B.C., their prayers became more instant, as we know from an inscription, recently discovered, which testifies to a military treaty between Pharnaces I of Pontus and the city of Chersonesus. But even the kingdom of Pontus was only a Hellenistic monarchy of the second class, entirely dependent on the Roman Empire; so that its intervention did not greatly alter the position in the Crimea.

This position changed with the accession of Mithridates, surnamed the Great. Every one knows of his conflict with Rome, and that in his campaigns against the Romans, he found a safe base on the northern coast of the Black Sea. But it is not sufficiently recognized, that it was only against their will, and of bitter necessity, that the Crimean Greeks summoned Mithridates to their aid. Their fortunes had sunk so low, that they must either become the Subjects of the Scythians, or accept the assistance of the Pontic king. It was certainly not from any liking that they approached him. The generals of Mithridates conquered the Scythians in three campaigns, took possession of the Bosphoran kingdom, and established Pontic garrisons in all the cities on the northern shore of the Black Sea, including Olbia. For the Greeks, accustomed to freedom, especially the Chersonesans and the Olbians, the domination of Mithridates was a heavy burden. It became intolerable, when they realized that the philhellenism of Mithridates was merely superficial, and that his true purpose was to unite the native populations, especially the Iranian tribes, under his banner, and to lead them to the conquest of the Roman Empire: the Greeks being useful only as a source of revenue. The Scythians, indeed, were vanquished by Mithridates, and the Crimea was nominally embodied in the Pontic kingdom, but it nevertheless remained independent and powerful, and Mithridates hastened to enter into amicable relations with the Scythians: it is well known that he made himself popular by marrying his sons and daughters to Scythian princesses and princes. He also adopted a friendly policy towards the Maeotian, Sarmatian and Thracian tribes. He thus succeeded in arousing a strong feeling of sympathy in these warlike races, who looked upon Mithridates as a descendant of the Achaemenids and the founder of a new and great Iranian power. We pointed out, in preceding chapters, that neither the Scythians nor the Sarmatians were in any wise barbarous peoples. If large numbers of Greek objects found their way into their fortified camps, if they valued Greek representations of native myths and of native military and religious life, they must certainly have learned from the Greeks the history of the Iranian world and of the universal empire of Persia.

It is not surprising, therefore, that the tribes of South Russia lent their aid to Mithridates. When he found a last refuge in Panticapaeum, after his defeat by Lucullus and Pompey in Asia Minor, and tried to organize a new army to march against Rome, it was not the Iranian and Thracian tribes who betrayed him, but the Greeks, first at Phanagoria and then at Panticapaeum. He perished in a rising of his Greek subjects, who were apprehensive of his alliance with their secular enemies and preferred the lordship of Rome to that of an Iranian king. The same story as in Asia Minor.

It must also be remembered, that Mithridates brought into the Greek towns of the Bosphorus, besides his garrisons, a great many colonists from Paphlagonia, Pontus, and Cappadocia, especially after he had been driven out of those regions by the Romans. We may conjecture that the first Jewish colonists of Panticapaeum were introduced by Mithridates: so many more competitors for the Greek population of the kingdom.

It was the war with Mithridates which opened the eyes of Rome to the political and economic significance of South Russia. As early as the second century B.C., the Romans had occasionally interested themselves in the affairs of the Greek colonies on the northern shore of the Black Sea, since the Crimea was connected with Pontus, and the Romans had to dictate their wishes to that Hellenistic monarchy. But it was only after the Mithridatic war, in which the Romans had to face almost the entire forces of Iranian expansion, that they realized the enormous importance of South Russia, which was still one of the principal producing centres, and which at any moment might become a rallying point for the Iranian tribes, the most dangerous enemies of the young Roman Empire. It is for this reason that from the second half of the first century, South Russia always played a very considerable part in the foreign policy of the Roman Empire. It was some time before the Romans formed a definite policy for dealing with the Greek colonies and the Iranian tribes in South Russia. In the middle of the first century B.C. Rome herself was in a critical situation. Civil war was raging in Italy and in the eastern and western provinces. The Romans were too busy to think of such distant countries. Pompey, bestowing freedom with one hand on the Greek cities of South Russia, confirmed with the other the authority of Mithridates' villainous son, Pharnaces. Pharnaces, we have reason to believe, was only another Mithridates: his ambition was to conquer Asia first, and then Rome. But he lacked both the genius and the resources of his father, and he miscalculated the opportunity presented by the Roman civil war. He attempted to reconquer Pontus, but was bloodily defeated by Caesar at Zela. He tried to shelter himself in Panticapaeum and to reconstruct his forces. But the governor whom he left in the Crimea, Asandtos, refused to recognize him, and Pharnaces fell in a hopeless struggle.

We do not know who Asandros was, or what title he had to the Bosphoran crown. His Greek name tells us nothing. But we may suppose that he was a citizen of Panticapaeum, half Greek like most of the citizens of the Greek cities in Pontus at the time. His haste to marry a daughter of Pharnaces, Princess Dynamis, suggests that this marriage was probably the sole legitimate title with which he could confront Mithridates of Pergamon, a Pergamene Greek who called himself a bastard son of Mithridates the Great and who was one of Caesar's favourites. Caesar owed it partly to the younger Mithridates, that he was not assassinated at Alexandria: he assigned him the kingdom of Pharnaces as a reward. Asandros would not submit to this decision. With the help of his subjects he defeated Mithridates, who perished in the conflict.

It is curious that after this stroke, Caesar, who never forgot a friend, did not think of expelling Asandros and punishing him for his treason. But Caesar had hardly time. On his return to Rome after the final defeat of his opponents in Spain, he was not able to carry out his plan for an eastern expedition to destroy the Thracian empire of Boerebista and to prepare his decisive blow at Iranian power in the east. That he concentrated his army at Apollonia, and that he intended to begin his Parthian campaign, like Alexander the Great, by a war on the Danube, proves that he would have settled the affairs of the Bosphorus before opening the great struggle with the Iranian forces. An inscription from Chersonesus, discovered recently and studied by myself in special articles, shows that he was deeply interested in the fortunes of that colony, that he had friends there, and that he pursued a definite policy in South Russia. But Caesar was assassinated at Rome on the eve of his departure for the east, and Asandros contrived, no doubt by paying money, to obtain recognition from Antony as archon and later as king of the Bosphorus.

As ruler of the Bosphorus, Asandros governed the enfeebled kingdom with a strong and resolute hand. He managed to re-establish order, to defeat the pirates, and to secure his frontiers against Scythian and Sarmatian invasions. He was sixty years old when he ascended the throne, and he remained king to an advanced age. The end of his reign was troubled. A usurper, one Scribonius, who claimed to be descended from Mithridates, and who probably belonged, like Mithridates of Pergamon, to the Greco-Oriental aristocracy of Asia Minor, enlisted Asandros' subjects against him, wedded Queen Dynamis, and ejected the aged king. It is not impossible that Dynamis, daughter of Pharnaces and wife of Asandros, took part in the rising. She certainly profited by it, for in 17 B.C. she was the recognized ruler of the Bosphorus, and she struck coins with her own effigy and the insignia of Mithridates. Scribonius was probably only her tool, to be discarded at the first opportunity.

Henceforth the dominant figure in Bosphoran history is the energetic and unscrupulous Queen Dynamis. Augustus, and his counsellor for eastern affairs, Agrippa, had to reckon with her. They could not allow her to remain sole governor of the Bosphoran kingdom. The risk was too great, that the story of Mithridates would be re-enacted. But they did not venture simply to expel her: she seems to have had considerable support from the subject population. Accordingly they tried a compromise. They compelled Dynamis to marry Polemon, a Greek of Asia Minor, in whose hands the kingdoms of Pontus and of the Bosphorus were to be united. Polemon was a forcible man who was not prepared to play Scribonius: he quarrelled with Dynamis and married Pythodoris, daughter of Pythodoros of Tralles. This marriage has been supposed to show that Dynamis had died. I think not. Numismatical and epigraphical evidence, which I have studied in a special memoir, proves that Dynamis not only survived Polemon's marriage, but deprived him of his kingdom. It seems most likely that when the marriage took place, she fled to the steppes of the Kuban; found support among the Sarmatian and Maeotian tribes, who were probably kinsfolk of her mother; wedded a Sarmatian or Maeotian, Aspurgos, son of a native prince, Asandrochos; and possessed herself of a number of fortified places in the Bosphoran kingdom. Polemon offered stout resistance, but he was enticed into a trap and slain, by a tribe, probably Sarmatian, which bore the significant name of Aspurgians and was probably the tribe of Dynamis and of Aspurgos.

The disappearance of Polemon opens a new era in the history of the Bosphorus. Dynamis had conquered, but she could not reign without recognition from the Roman Government. Now Augustus, in 9-8 B.C., was neither able to intervene with an armed force, nor inclined to countenance a power which was not controlled by himself and his agents. On the other hand, Dynamis could not make her throne secure without Roman support: the principal resources of the Bosphoran kingdom were the revenues from traffic with the Aegean, and that traffic was impossible without the permission of Rome. A compromise was effected. Dynamis was recognized, but as a vassal queen, who must acknowledge the supremacy of Rome and the independence of the Greek cities. This was the opening of a period, in which the kingdom of the Bosphorus was virtually incorporated in the Roman Empire, although it preserved its dynasty and a nominal independence.

I have dwelt at some length upon the beginnings of Bosphoran vassalage, first because the period has usually been misinterpreted by our historians of the ancient world, and secondly, because unless we understand it, we cannot understand the political and social life of the Bosphoran kingdom in Roman times. I shall add a word or two about the political vicissitudes of the Bosphoran kingdom down to the third century A.D. On the death of Dynamis, Aspurgos succeeded to the throne and reigned peacefully till his decease. His second wife was a princess with the Thracian name of Gepaepyris, who bore him a son Cotys. His son by Dynamis was Mithridates. After the death of Aspurgos, the two sons naturally quarrelled. The elder, Mithridates, occupied the throne as co-regent with his stepmother and his younger brother. He conceived a high ambition: he wished to reconstitute the kingdom of Mithridates the Great. Betrayed by his brother, and probably betraying his mother, he fell in a desperate struggle, in which he was assisted by Sarmatian tribes against a Roman army sent to attack him.

After his death, the dynasty of Cotys established itself, and ruled the Bosphorus right down to the arrival of the Goths: the loyal servant of the Roman Empire. It is not this Thraco-Iranian dynasty that interests us, but the views and designs of the Roman Empire: without the Roman Empire the Bosphoran kingdom could not have endured. The main lines of Roman policy towards the kingdom of the Bosphorus were fixed, once and for all, by Augustus and Agrippa. They were both well aware, that it was impossible to enlarge the Roman Empire beyond the Danube and to take in the whole of the Pontic coastland. Nero was the only Roman emperor who seriously contemplated such expansion and prepared an expedition for the purpose. More sensible emperors saw that the Roman forces were not sufficient to conquer the Iranian portion of the world. The Sarmatians and the Parthians remained dangerous enemies, to be averted, if possible, from the Roman frontiers, and to be closely watched. The same policy was adopted towards the Germans after the defeat of Varus. To weaken and to watch, these were the two objects of Roman policy towards the Iranians. But how?

The safest way was to strengthen the non-Iranian elements on the Black Sea, to keep alive the fires of Greek civilization which still smouldered in the ancient Greek colonies. There were economic as well as political reasons: the Greeks of the Aegean, as well as the Greeks on the southern shore of the Black Sea, could not exist without the produce of South Russia. Now the most powerful organization on the Black Sea was the kingdom of the Bosphorus. That kingdom must at all costs be preserved. Otherwise it would be impossible to keep close watch over the movements of the Sarmatian tribes, and to bring up the necessary forces, when the Sarmatians threatened to swallow up the Greek settlements on the Black Sea. Moreover, the kingdom of the Bosphorus was still a great centre of supply, not only for famished Greece, but, still more important, for the Roman armies stationed in Pontus, Cappadocia, and Armenia to prevent a Parthian advance. The kingdom of the Bosphorus must therefore be assisted and upheld, especially in its perpetual conflict with the Scythians of the Crimea, who were still dangerous opponents. The Black Sea trade routes must also be kept clear, so that the merchant fleets could sail from the Cimmerian to the Thracian Bosphorus and to the southern shore of the Black Sea. These objects the Romans attained by various devices. The first was an annual subvention to the kings of the Bosphorus for the maintenance of an army and a fleet, which were supervised, as we know from Trajan's correspondence with Pliny, by the vigilant eye of the Governor of Pontus. The subvention was probably made on the understanding that the kingdom should provision the troops and cities of the Pontic provinces. Another device consisted of military measures. The principal object of the Roman administration was the reservation of peace on the seas. Now the fleet which maintained this peace needed a secure and ample harbour. Chersonesus was the only harbour safe enough and well enough situated to become the centre of a naval police force. Accordingly, when the emperors saw that the Bosphorus could not defend the whole Crimea unaided, and at the same time keep guard on the sea, or rather, when they understood that the assignment of such a mission to the Bosphoran kingdom would make it over-strong and perhaps imperil Roman prestige, they sent a

Roman squadron to Chersonesus and garrisoned the city with troops from their armies on the Danube. The fort of Chersonesus once occupied, the Romans were obliged to defend the city and its territory, and to patrol the coast between Chersonesus and Panticapaeum. The defence of the city meant the fortification of the passes leading from the region occupied by the Scythians to the territory of Chersonesus: the patrolling of the coast involved the erection of forts and naval stations at prominent points. Chersonesus seems to have been first occupied in the time of Claudius and Nero, when the formation of a new province, Scythia Taurica, was being seriously considered. But this occupation did not last long. Domitian and Trajan preferred to reinforce the kingdom of the Bosphorus, and to entrust it with the entire defence of the Greek colonies, including Olbia, which soon recovered after its destruction by the Getians, and Tanais, which had been almost annihilated during the war between Polemon and Dynamis. But this policy was not successful. Hadrian, and after him Antoninus, Marcus Aurelius, Commodus, and Severus, saw that it was impossible for the Greek cities of the Black Sea to hold out without Roman troops. The pressure of the Scythians and the Sarmatians was too heavy: the frontier was too long for the Bosphoran army to defend. Accordingly Hadrian and his successors reoccupied the Chersonesan part of the Crimea, and garrisoned Olbia and probably Tyras as well. At the same time the gave these cities their freedom, in other words they relieved them of the Bosphoran protectorate and conceded them the status of Roman provincial cities. The Roman fortress, recently excavated on the promontory of Ai-Todor, was one of the points of concentration for Roman troops from the army of Moesia.

This state of things lasted for nearly two centuries, and the kingdom of Bosphorus throve. The change came in the third century A.D. The dynasty of the Severi was the last which was able to preserve order on the northern shore of the Black Sea. The revolutions which succeeded one another at Rome in the middle of the third century, the internal policy of violence and extortion gradually adopted by the emperors, rendered the Roman Empire incapable of maintaining its frontiers and compelled the government to abandon the outposts of empire to their fate. It was from this cause alone, that the Bosphorus had to capitulate to the combined forces of Sarmatians and Goths, and lost, almost completely, its rank as an outpost of Greek civilization and of

Roman policy. The lot of the other colonies was worse still. Olbia became a small and struggling fishing village: so did the other cities on the coast. Chersonesus alone was defended by the Romans, and preserved its Greek culture to the end of the Byzantine period. Panticapaeum did not disappear: it continued to exist for centuries, down to our own time if you like, but it was no longer a real Greek city. Hellenism in Panticapaeum was perishing daily.

Here we may stop: but let us not forget, that the seeds of civilized life were never entirely destroyed in the Greek cities on the Black Sea. If Panticapaeum was no longer a Greek city, it remained a very important centre of culture, and it was one of the homes of the Christian religion. Its civilization was not Greek, but the life which its inhabitants led was a civilized one, and its neo-Iranian culture radiated over an enormous area. The Byzantine Empire did its best to gather up the threads of Roman policy, and to preserve a breath of cultivated life in the ancient Greek centres: not only Chersonesus, but at times Panticapaeum, and certain new settlements in the Crimea, served as starting-points for the civilizing mission of Byzantium in the Russian East.

We said above, that the two centuries of the Roman Empire were a most prosperous period in the kingdom of the Bosphorus. But it was no longer the old kingdom. Its life had greatly altered. We have already noticed, that the Bosphoran state was a mixed state from the very outset: but we also observed, that in the cities the Greeks succeeded in retaining their nationality and their civilization: it was only the aristocracy and the rural population that showed a strong native admixture. In the Roman period, the Iranization spreads to the townsfolk, and the Greek element receives a strong native infusion.

This can be seen at every turn. Let us look first at the political system.

The ruling family had not a drop of Greek blood in its veins. What its origin was we have seen. A Sarmato-Pontic or Maeoto-Pontic woman, Dynamis, married a prince whom we have every reason to suppose a Sarmatian or a Maeotian, that is, an Iranian or a semi-Thracian: Aspurgos. Aspurgos, in his turn, married a Thracian princess. These persons were the ancestors of the Bosphoran rulers, whose names are mainly Thracian, Cotys, Rhescuporis, Rhoemetalces, or else recall their Maeotian or perhaps Sarmatian affinity, such as Sauromates: we know that historical tradition tended to identify Sauromatians and Sarmatians. The preponderance of Thracian names may be thought curious, seeing that the kings were Thracian only through Gepaepyris the second wife of Aspurgos. But it must be remembered that there had always been a strong Thracian strain in the population of the Bosphorus, and that the Thracian royal names in the Roman period were but a revival of a very ancient historic tradition, the tradition of the Spartocids. The name of Sauromates, highly popular in the Bosphorus from the first to the third century A.D., did not necessarily mean the Sarmatian origin of the dynasty: it may equally well be referred to the Sauromatians, the Maeotian tribe of which we have frequently spoken. Dynamis, the warrior queen, reminds us of the Maeotian and Sauromatian queens, Tirgatao and Amage. Pontic reminiscences, on the other hand, are rare: one of the kings, and only one, was called Eupator; it is doubtful whether after Mithridates Eupator or not. The vassals of Rome may well have been chary of commemorating the great enemy of the Roman Empire.

The same mixture is observable in the religious traditions of the Bosphoran monarchy. On their coins and in their inscriptions, the Bosphoran monarchs liked to evoke the memory of Herakles; he, and through Eumolpos, Poseidon, were considered to be the ancestors of the royal house (see, for example, the coin pl. XXX, 3, second row, fig. 2). The tradition is clearly the same as the legend (invented by the Athenians to glorify their allies) which attributed an Athenian origin to the Odrysian kings. But Herakles plays a great part in the coinage of Mithridates VII, the son of Dynamis, who was in no way related to the Thracian dynasty; Mithridates seems to have been thinking of the Maeotian legend mentioned in a previous chapter: the Hellenized Maeotian aristocracy, to judge from the legend, believed itself to be descended from the god Herakles and the Great Goddess of the natives. On the other hand, Herakles was extremely popular with the Roman emperors of the second century owing to the Cynic and Stoic theory of imperial power: Commodus, it will be remembered, believed himself to be Hercules ἐπιφανής. This fashion no doubt influenced the kings of the Bosphorus, who like Herakles had to combat malefic forces, the Scythians and the Sarmatians. We can also understand the combination of Herakles and Poseidon which was introduced by Mithridates VII. We have seen that Poseidon figured in Herodotus' list of deities venerated by the Scythians. Asandros invoked this god, Poseidon Σωσίνεως, together with Aphrodite Ναυαρχίς, to celebrate a naval victory, probably over the pirates of the Black Sea; the pair seems to have been worshipped by the natives at Gorgippia from the earliest times. Further, it was natural that these monarchs should venerate the sea-god and wish to identify themselves with him: they were warriors and traders, whose prosperity depended on their command of the sea. An odd mixture of religious ideas derived from divers sources.

We have already noticed that, even under the last Spartocids, the power of the Bosphoran rulers was no longer a compound of a Greek magistracy and a native kingship. It gradually took the form of a Hellenistic monarchy. In the time of Asandros, an attempt was made to revive the old dualism: which would suggest that at the outset he was supported by the Greek population of the Bosphorus, anxious to resuscitate the Spartocid tradition. But Asandros hastened to assume the more convenient and more brilliant title of king. Henceforward the Spartocid dualism was dead, and the rulers of the Bosphorus adopted, once and for all, the title of king, in its Irano-Hellenistic form King of Kings, a style which was no doubt inherited from Mithridates the Great, and which was tolerated by the Romans, in view of its popularity with the natives, who constituted an important part of the kingdom. This would lead us to suppose, that the Greek cities in the Bosphoran kingdom did not long retain the autonomy which Pompey had granted them, and which Augustus had confirmed. The last autonomous coins issued by the cities of the Bosphoran kingdom are the bronze coins of Agrippea and Caesarea, the new names imposed by Augustus, as Orêshnikov has seen, on the two capitals of Queen Dynamis' kingdom, Phanagoria and Panticapaeum. And I feel convinced, that the goddess, whose head is represented on these coins, is no other than Queen Dynamis herself. It is possible that even at a later period the city of Phanagoria preserved some vestiges of this fictitious and titular autonomy. The fact is, that under Roman domination the Bosphoran kingship was a Hellenized Oriental autocracy, like the kingships of Commagene or of Armenia. But in the course of its three centuries of Roman protectorate, it underwent gradual but significant alterations. We can follow the changes by studying the inscribed stones and the types and legends of the royal coinage. During the first and second centuries, both in their inscriptions and on their coins, the kings emphasize their vassalage, their dependence upon Rome and the Emperor. On the stones, they regularly style themselves Φιλορώμαιος and Φιλόκαισαρ, according to the custom of Roman vassal kings;

they assume the prenomen and gentile name of the Caesars—Tiberius Julius—and the priesthood of the imperial cult. Under Eupator, a Capitol was even constructed at Panticapaeum, as if the city had become a Roman colony. From the period of Augustus to that of the Flavians, with a few brief intervals, the gold coins of the Bosphorus show heads of the emperor and of a member of the imperial house: from the time of Domitian onwards, the emperor's head on one side and the king's on the other; again a sign of vassalage. Lastly, in their bronze coinage (pl. XXX, 3), the Bosphoran kings make a special parade of their vassalage and of their loyalty, as well as of the military services rendered to the empire and to their subjects. On the bronze coins, as on the coins of other vassal kings, the king is represented sitting on the curule chair, with the image of the emperor on his crown, and the emperor's head on his sceptre: or else in the garb of a Roman general, riding to attack the enemy, a type which recalls the contemporary coinage of Thrace. The reverses commonly figure the complimentary gifts of the Roman emperors: the selection of gifts is traditional, but it well expresses the dominant ideas of the Roman Empire in its dealings with Oriental vassals. The Bosphoran kings received the curule chair; the royal crown, probably embellished with the image of the emperor; the sceptre surmounted by the imperial bust; and the complete armour of a Roman knight, he met, spear, round shield, sword, and sometimes battle-axe. The intention was always the same everywhere: the king was to be a loyal vassal, and a good soldier. The triumphal types which are used by certain kings are imitated from the corresponding imperial coins, and give expression to the military character of the Bosphoran kingship.

In the course of the second century, however, the enthusiasm for vassalage dies down, and the types of the Bosphoran bronze sensibly alter. Henceforth religious types predominate. At the end of the second century the image of the Great Goddess reappears (pl. XXX, 3, second row, fig. 3): it had already played a considerable part in the coinage of Dynamis and her heirs and successors. The goddess is figured in her Hellenized form, in the guise of Aphrodite. Further, the martial representation of the king charging the enemy is gradually replaced by another type, influenced by the statues of Roman emperors from Marcus Aurelius onwards (pl. XXX, 3, first row, fig. 4). The king, who is bearded, sits on a heavy charger, wearing a corslet of scale armour, a flying cloak, trousers, and soft leather shoes: a diadem encircles his head; in his left hand he holds a long sceptre, without the image of the emperor; his right hand makes the gesture of adoration, either to the supreme God, whose bust sometimes appears, as a subsidiary type, on the same side of the coin; or to the Great Goddess, who is regularly represented on the reverse. A totally new type, then, which bears witness to the thorough Iranization of the dynasty, and to its increasing religiosity. The type recurs, at the end of the second and the beginning of the third century, on gold funerary crowns. The religious and political character of these representations is even more strongly marked than on the coins. I have republished these crowns, with a commentary, in a special treatise: we shall return to them.

We have every reason to suppose that the power of the king was absolute. There is no evidence that the Greek citizens of the kingdom had any share in the government. The administration, also, is purely monarchical. The king was surrounded by a court, the members of which bore pompous, Oriental titles. It was the courtiers who filled the public posts, who acted as military governors in the provinces, as financial officers, and the like. The system of administration was probably modelled on those of the Iranian kingdoms, the Parthian, the Armenian and the rest. It was very likely inherited from Mithridates the Great. Roman influence can occasionally be traced: for instance in the creation, during the Trajanic period, of a kind of praetorian prefect or, let us say, grand vizier.

The social and economic system had not greatly altered since the later Spartocid period. Two classes are to be distinguished. On the one hand, the governing class, the citizen aristocracy, which served at court and in the army, and which provided the king with agents and officials: landed proprietors, merchants, owners of industrial establishments. On the other, the governed, the serfs and slaves. The sole owners of cultivated land appear to have been the king, the city aristocracy, and the temples. I can hardly believe that a peasant-farmer class, of the Greek type, existed or could exist in the Bosphoran kingdom. Agricultural conditions did not lend themselves to a system of small proprietors. The territory of the kingdom, theoretically vast, since it covered the whole of the Crimea and the Taman peninsula, was actually very modest. The Crimean plains were in the hands of the Scythians, the mountains were inhabited by the Taurians. The cultivable and cultivated portion of the Taman peninsula was still smaller, for to judge from what we know of the

Aspurgians, the Sarmatians had seized the greater part of the country. The precariousness of agriculture in the Bosphoran territory is illustrable by archaeological evidence. Both from ruins, and from representations of fortified cities on coins (pl. XXX, 3, second row, fig. 4), we learn that in the Roman period the cities of the Bosphorus, large and small, were transformed into so many fortresses. A group of small strongholds, belonging to the Roman period, has been discovered in the Taman peninsula: these must have been fortified refuges for the agricultural population. Moreover, the Bosphoran kings, like the Chinese emperors, had to erect lines of forts, to protect the cultivable land in, the peninsulas of Kerch and of Taman. Strabo mentions a wall constructed by Asandros: whether it is one of those that still remain we cannot tell. It may be that this system of defences dates from the change in Scythian policy towards the Greek cities: but this is doubtful. In any case the three parallel lines in the peninsula of Kerch, and a similar line in the Taman peninsula, as far as they have been studied, seem to date from the Roman period. Lastly, certain pictures in Panticapaean tombs of the first or second century give us a good idea of agricultural life at the time. The dead are frequently represented as heroized beings, in the usual Greek schemes, the funeral repast, and the combat. The Panticapaean artists, who painted the scenes on the walls of the tombs, were not content merely to reproduce the old types: they transformed them into scenes from the social life of the deceased. In one of these tombs, which belongs to the first century A.D., the scene is an idyllic one (pl. XXVIII, 1). The dead man, armed, and followed by a retainer, is riding towards his family residence, a tent of true nomadic type. His household, wife, children, and servants, are assembled in the tent and beside it, under the shade of a single tree; beside the tree is his long spear, and his quiver hangs from a branch. The interpretation is easy: the gentleman is a landed proprietor, who spends most of his time in town: in summer, during the harvest season, he goes out to the steppes, armed, and accompanied by armed servants; taking his family with him. He supervises the work in the fields, and defends his labourers and harvesters from the attacks of neighbours who live beyond the fortified lines: Taurians from the mountains, ferocious foot-soldiers; Scythians from the plains, horse men and landowners. Who knows? perhaps he raids a little himself. Fights between neighbours are often represented in Panticapaean tomb-paintings of the first or second century

B.C. We see the Panticapaean chief, followed by his little army, battling with a black bearded Taurian or with shag-haired Scythians, the same bold archers and horsemen whom we knew in the sixth, and down to the third century B.C. (pl. XXIX, 1-3). When he moves house, he uses heavy wagons to transport his tent, his furniture, and his family. Clay models of these wagons have been found in Panticapaean tombs of the first century A.D.

I infer from all this evidence, that the Bosphorans of the Roman period adopted the customs and the land system of nomadic peoples. Their land system must have been taken from the Scythians: the Sarmatian system cannot have differed much from the Scythian. Owing to the uncertainty of life in the steppes, the Greek method of tilling the soil was out of the question. The labourers and harvesters had to be protected by a military force, and the only persons who could provide this military force were the great landed proprietors. Their armed retainers guarded the herds in winter and summer. In spring, master and servants went out to the domain, to protect the natives, who lived a miserable life in caves or huts, and to enable them to work on the land. The harvest was shared between master and serfs: the master carried off his share, the serfs hid theirs in grain pits.

This land system presupposes a social structure of feudal type, a state composed like the Scythian of a king, an armed aristocracy with armed followers, and a more or less numerous body of serfs. We must suppose that the precariousness of life, in the later Hellenistic and the Roman periods, gradually reduced the Bosphoran state to this primitive and barbarous condition. I have no doubt that the Bosphoran army chiefly consisted of separate contingents under feudal chiefs, which were supplemented by forced levies from the serf farm-labourers, who were probably the native population of the country. Apart from the feudal lords, the only great landowners were the gods and the temples. I have already cited an inscription from Phanagoria which proves the existence of extensive domains belonging to the gods and cultivated by serfs. The priests who looked after the serfs probably did not differ greatly from the other feudal lords already described. Strabo gives a similar account of the economic and social conditions in the great temples of Pontus and Cappadocia.

PLATE XXVIII

WALL PAINTINGS IN TWO GRAVES AT KERCH
The first now destroyed. I-II Cent. A.D.

PLATE XXIX

WALL PAINTINGS IN A GRAVE AT KERCH
I-II Cent. A.D.

The serf-reaped harvest passed into the hands of the kings, priests and great landowners: after feeding the city population, they exported the remainder, on the Bosphoran merchant fleet and on foreign trading vessels, to Greece, and especially to the Greek towns on the southern shore of the Black Sea. The traffic between Panticapaeum and the cities of Pontus and Bithynia was livelier than ever before, as we know from the numerous Panticapaean inscriptions which mention citizens of Amisos, Sinope and other cities, domiciled at Panticapaeum. We should naturally suppose that the chief exporters of corn were the shipowners. But they were not alone. The kings and the rich landowners also maintained a considerable merchant fleet. From an inscription recently discovered at Gorgippia in the Taman peninsula, we learn that a religious corporation of naucleroi existed in this city, its honorary president being the king himself. The royal president bestowed a gift upon the corporation: it consisted in a large quantity of corn, reckoned in Persian artabai.

The corn which was exported did not come exclusively from the territory of the kingdom. It is highly probable, that the Bosphoran naucleroi played the middleman between the foreign purchaser and the neighbours of the Bosphoran state, the Scythians of the Crimea and the Sarmatians in the district of the Kuban. Considering the political situation from the first to the third centuries A.D., I question whether the Don and Dnieper regions still produced a great quantity of corn for export. As early as the time of Polybius, who had the Dnieper region particularly in mind, the export of corn through Olbia and Tyras was by no means regular, the Scythian power, which protected agriculture, having disappeared. It is possible, of course, that circumstances changed in the first century A.D. and subsequently the geographer Ptolemy mentions scores of cities on the lower Dnieper, which shows that Olbia, under Roman protection, was able to recover part of the Dnieper trade. In any case, the existence of a firmly-established Scythian state in the Crimea, and the prolonged supremacy of the Sarmatians on the Kuban, created conditions in both places which furthered extensive production and active commerce. We must remember that these are the richest agricultural districts in modern Russia, and that they had been tenanted, from the earliest times, by a sedentary agricultural population, which changed masters, but itself remained unchanged. The constant efforts of the Scythians, in the first three centuries of our era no less than in the three preceding; to get possession of the Greek cities on the shores of the Black Sea, efforts which led to the appearance of Mithridates in the Crimea, to the expedition of Plautius Silvanus to rescue Chersonesus, to the military occupation of part of the Crimea by the Romans, to the war of Antoninus Pius with the Tauro-Scythians for the liberation of Olbia, to innumerable contests between the Bosphoran kings and the Scythian state in the Crimea, show how anxious the Crimean Scythians were to rid themselves of these middlemen and to open direct relations with the purchasers of their corn. We have no right to suppose, that the Scythian state of Skiluros' successors was a nomadic and barbarous state. Ruins of a fortified town near Simferopol belong to the Roman period: to judge from Greek inscriptions found in the town, it was the centre of the Scythian kingdom as early as the first century B.C., and was even then in regular communication with the Olbian exporters. The ruins suggest that the Scythian kingdom of the Roman period did not greatly differ from the Bosphoran kingdom, except that it preserved its independence. The cemetery is full of Greek imports dating from the early centuries of our era, which show that the town had a Hellenized population and traded with the coastal cities. The Greek objects can hardly be due to Roman military occupation: for there are no inscriptions of Roman soldiers, such as we find in the fortress of Ai-Todor.

Again, we have convincing evidence that life on the Kuban was not unlike life in the Crimea. A Bosphoran historian, used by Diodorus' authority, gives a picture of social life among the Siracians on the Kuban. The Siracians were a Sarmatian tribe, and it was probably they who dislodged the Scythians from the Kuban valley. Unhappily the reading in the text of Diodorus is corrupt: it was Mueller who proposed to read Σιρακῶν, whereas Boeckh corrected the Θρηκῶν of the manuscripts into Θατέων. Speaking of the struggle between Eumelos and Satyros, the rival claimants to the Bosphoran throne in 309-308 B.C., the historian describes the fortified capital of King Aripharnes. The centre was occupied by the fortified palace of the king, which was surrounded by a wall, perhaps of stone. The palace was situated on a tongue of land formed by the River Thates. The town itself lay in the river marshes; it was a settlement of the lacustrine or paludal type, supported by pillars and encircled by a wooden fortification. Diodorus also mentions another town of the same sort, Gargaza, and a number of less important towns and villages. The country, then, had a sedentary population, which was no doubt agricultural.

The description is confirmed by another eye-witness, the same who furnished the authority used by Tacitus with his account of the expedition of Aquila against King Mithridates VII in A.D. 49: the primary source is probably Aquila's own official report. This witness speaks of the same tribe, the Siracians, and describes the fortified town of King Zorsines, Uspe: again the same type of fortified royal residence. The most characteristic feature of the story is the proposal of King Zorsines to deliver ten thousand 'slaves' to the conqueror in return for the lives of the 'freemen': these slaves were no doubt native serfs who worked for Sarmatian masters.

This information explains the finds in the Sarmatian cemeteries, described in the last chapter. As soon as they arrived in the region of the Kuban, the Sarmatians, as I have pointed out, established regular commercial relations with the Greek towns on the coast, Tanais, Phanagoria, Gorgippia. They bartered their corn, cattle and fish for the products of the Greek workshops. In a number of inscriptions, we read the names of merchants from Greek cities, who traded in the towns and villages of the country subject to the Sarmatians. Some of these merchants died there.

The ports of Theodosia and Chersonesus served as outlets for the produce of the Crimea; Tanais, and the ports in the Taman peninsula, for the produce of the Sarmatian countries. We must bear in mind what Strabo expressly tells us about Sarmatian commerce, in particular that the great trade route from the East, which passed through the Russian steppes, was still used under Sarmatian supremacy. We may be sure that it was the merchants of the Bosphoran kingdom who acted as middlemen between the caravans from Central Asia and the Greco-Roman world.

Here was another source of wealth for the inhabitants of the Bosphorus. As long as the Bosphoran state, with the help of the Romans, controlled the Black Sea, the Scythians and the Sarmatians were necessarily dependent upon it, for they had neither navy nor merchant fleet.

Agriculture and commerce, then, enriched the citizen aristocracy of the Bosphoran state: but the inhabitants of the kingdom had other means of acquiring wealth besides these. We have seen that the finds in the Sarmatian cemeteries point to a fairly prosperous industrial activity in the Bosphorus. We cannot affirm with certainty, that it was the workshops of Panticapaeum and other Bosphoran towns which supplied the Sarmatians with their pottery and their cut and blown glass. These may have been imported, although the examples of Gaul, Germany and Britain suggest that wherever there was a demand for such articles plenty of local workshops arose to meet it. But we cannot doubt that the goldsmith's work exported by the Bosphoran cities was of local make. I have shown that goldsmiths flourished at Panticapaeum in the Spartocid epoch and produced large quantities of articles for the Scythian market. I am convinced that the same workshops continued to supply the Sarmatian demand. I shall return to the question when I come to discuss the Panticapaean tomb furniture in this period.

The wealth of the city population, therefore, was derived from agriculture, from commerce and from industry. We are pretty well acquainted with this class from inscriptions in tombs, from grave stelai and from lists of members of corporations. The city class was undoubtedly a real force. We are particularly struck, in examining its records, by its high organization and by its parade of Hellenism. The members were proud of belonging to the Greek race, and did their best not to forget the language, the literature, and the traditions of Greece. This is what impressed Dio Chrysostom at Olbia towards the end of the first century A.D., this is what we can gather from the Tristia and the Pontic letters of Ovid, who was forced to dwell, a needy exile, in the 'Greek' city of Tomi, in the heart of the Dobrudzha, which, as we have already seen, remained a Scythian kingdom, like the kingdom of the Crimea, until it was occupied by the Romans.

We find the same spirit at Panticapaeum and in the other cities of the Bosphoran kingdom. Wherever we turn, we are impressed by the societies formed by a population proud of its Hellenism. These Bosphoran colleges have been classed with the other colleges which were founded all over the Greek world. A grave error. I cannot discuss this important question in detail, but I must lay stress on certain significant points. The synods (σύνοδοι) or brotherhoods (συναδελφίαι) which existed in all Bosphoran towns, especially those which were most exposed to attacks from their neighbours, Tanais, Gorgippia and Panticapaeum, present themselves to us, first, as religious fraternities centring in the official cult of the Great God and probably in that of the Great Goddess; secondly, as unions of a limited number of families, that is, as aristocratic and purely citizen unions; thirdly, as clubs closely connected with the royal family and the court; fourthly, as military and political organizations, the members of which are always represented in military costume and armed as infantrymen or mounted hoplites, often on horseback, attended by a squire; fifthly, as colleges which provided their members, especially the younger ones, the νεανίσκοι, with a Greek education in gymnasia and palaistrai; colleges comparable with those of the Juvenes and νέοι in other parts of the Greek world; this effort to provide Greek education, in a town surrounded by barbarians, for the Greek or Hellenized youth, finds an interesting parallel in Egypt, where the class which had been educated in the gymnasium formed the city aristocracy and enjoyed a number of privileges; sixthly and lastly, as burial societies, an important function in view of the military organization of the colleges: one is struck by the number of members who died young, defending their country on the field of battle. I am certain that these colleges were a product and a curious one, of the historical development of the Bosphoran kingdom. The constant penetration of heterogeneous elements into the citizen society in the Greek towns, the perpetual danger of being submerged by their Scythian and Sarmatian neighbours, the economic and social situation which raised the Greeks to the position of a dominant class with hundreds of natives working for it, led the city populations to rally closely round the throne, in order to defend, if not their nationality, at least their civilization and their privileges. I am not quite sure that the form of these exclusively masculine colleges was borrowed wholesale from the Greeks. It seems very likely that colleges of young men existed in Italy, and among the Celts and Germans, from prehistoric times, and retained, though reconstituted by Augustus to suit his views and aims, a considerable measure of their primitive structure. It may be that the origin of the Bosphoran colleges was similar, that there was an institution of the same sort in the Iranian world. But this is not the place to examine this difficult and controversial question.

It is clear, then, that the citizen class in the Bosphoran kingdom was highly organized, and formed an aristocracy which was principally responsible for defending the kingdom from foreign attacks. These citizens probably formed the army of the Bosphoran kings. We do not know how the army was organized: perhaps in contingents furnished by the great landowners and by the various colleges in the towns: but we cannot be certain. The nucleus was composed of citizens; but we may take it for granted that the Bosphoran kings tried to obtain assistance from semi-independent subject tribes and from 'allied' tribes, that is to say, tribes which would serve for pay. The practice, which was adopted by Eumelos and Satyros in their fratricidal struggle, and later, by Dynamis and Aspurgos and by Mithridates VII, must have been continued by the Bosphoran kings from the first to the third century A.D.: when fighting the Scythians they had Sarmatian and Maeotian allies; and inversely. The same system was employed by the Romans from the third or fourth century A.D., and regularly in the Hellenistic monarchies. A peculiar political and social organization, with a strange mixture of elements.

I said above that the citizens of the Greek towns on the Black Sea were very anxious not to be confused with the barbarians. They counted themselves Greeks, and did their best to appear Greek and to be Greek. Greek was the only language used at Panticapaeum for public and private inscriptions and on coins. The citizens received a Greek education and were proud of it. Dio Chrysostom speaks of the reverence paid to Homer and Plato at Olbia. At Panticapaeum we have many funerary inscriptions in verse, which were assuredly composed in Panticapaeum itself. One of the finest commemorates the services rendered to the city of Nymphaeum by Glycaria, wife of Asandros, perhaps his first wife while he was still a private citizen: it was found in the sea near Nymphaeum and has been published recently by myself and by Škorpil. Another inscription praises the scientific and educational attainments of a young Bosphoran.

In spite of all this, the Hellenism of the citizen population in the Bosphorus seems to have been no more than a veneer, which wore thinner and thinner. It is true that the inscriptions are all Greek. But from the second century onwards we notice traces, even on official monuments, of a new system of writing which was probably used for texts in the native language. We observed, in the last chapter, that a number of objects from Sarmatian tombs are decorated with alphabetical signs of heraldic appearance, monograms which made one think of badges or coats of arms. From the second century B.C., we find the same signs, accompanying the names of kings, on stones with official inscriptions, on public documents, on inscribed tombstones, on certain coins, on horse trappings, on belt clasps, on strap mounts, and so forth. The strap mounts are in the openwork technique normal in Sarmatian objects of the kind. It is certain that these signs are private monograms, personal, family, or tribal devices. But elsewhere we have complete texts written in signs which are partly identical with and partly similar to the signs described above: so on two funerary lions found at Olbia; so on the entrance of a tomb at Kerch, where the inscription is placed on a lower layer of plaster, which was covered with an upper, painted layer. I have no doubt that these are the first stages in the development of a Sarmatian system of writing. Let us remember that the Hittite hieroglyphic writing developed in the same manner out of badge-like signs: this has been shown by Sayce and by Cowley, and de Linas has already compared the Bosphoran signs with Persian. A significant testimony to the importance of the Iranian element in the citizen population: for it was the Bosphoran nobles who built these sumptuous carved and painted tombs.

The testimony is confirmed by an analysis of the proper names at Panticapaeum, at Olbia, at Tanais, at Phanagoria, at Gorgippia. It would not be difficult to produce statistics, which would show the rate at which, in the Roman period, native names gradually supplanted the Greek names which predominated in pre-Roman times. But a glance at the college lists and at the names of members of colleges on tombstones, will suffice to prove that the population was losing its Hellenic character. It is curious that the Bosphorans become less and less inclined to substitute Greek names for their native names, and that the reverse was probably the rule: native names were substituted for Greek ones. The native names have been studied by Vsévolod Miller: he shows that they are mostly Iranian, and explicable by comparison with Ossetian. But I have lately drawn attention to an equally significant fact: side by side with the Iranian, we have a group of names which are undoubtedly Thracian, both in formation and in type. Others are typical of Asia Minor: but these are very few. It appears, therefore, that the Greek citizen population was gradually submerged by Iranian and Thracian elements. The Iranians were the Scythians, of the Crimea and, even more, the Sarmatians: the Thracians must have come from the Maeotian tribes, which as we have seen, had been strongly Thracized by the Cimmerians. It was unquestionably the aristocracy among the Sarmatians, Scythians and Maeotians, which was attracted towards the former Greek centres. Remember Lucian's descriptions of life at the Bosphoran court in the Hellenistic and Roman periods: a kaleidoscopic picture of Scythians, Sarmatians, and Bosphorans, intermarrying, making friends, quarrelling. We may be sure that the citizen aristocracy acted like the others, and that there was constant coming and going between the cities of the Bosphorus and the neighbouring tribes, interrupted by frequent but by no means sanguinary wars. The difference between the Bosphoran kingdom, as I have already pointed out, and the Scythian or Sarmatian kingdoms was not very great; but the life of the Greek cities had a strong fascination for the Iranians, who came to trade, to make agreements, to visit kinsfolk, and the like.

It was natural, under these conditions, that the city population rapidly became Iranized. It is unfortunate that we know very little about the costume of the Panticapaeans in the pre-Roman period: the stelai of this period are few, and they never bear the effigy of the dead. But we have every reason to suppose that their costume was Greek like their names and their tombs. In the Roman period the material becomes very plentiful, especially in the first and second centuries A.D. A series of carved and sometimes painted funeral stelai (pl. XXX, 2), and an equally rich series of tombs with painted walls, present us with hundreds of portraits of Bosphoran citizens, in civil and in military costume. Their garments at this period are far from Greek. They wear trousers, soft leather shoes, leather or fur doublets, and long cloaks probably of wool: just like the Scythians and the Sarmatians on monuments of the fourth or third century B.C. Ovid at Tomi, Dio Chrysostom at Olbia, can hardly recognize the descendants of the ancient Milesian colonists.

The armour is no longer Greek. No doubt the mercenary armies of the Spartocid period were armed like the Greek hoplites, peltasts and cavalrymen of the time. But as early as the third or second century B.C., when the mercenaries were mainly recruited from the barbarian tribes, a change took place: it affected even the armour of the citizen troops, which now began to play an important part. A number of clay statuettes from this period, found exclusively at Panticapaeum, and undoubtedly made there, represent soldiers of the citizen army (pl. XXX, 1): their costume is Thraco-Iranian, their shields Gaulish. In the first and second centuries A.D., we have an abundance of documents for the armour of the citizen troops and of the contingents recruited among the native population. Hundreds of stelai reproduce the heroized dead in complete armour (pl. XXX, 2): mural paintings in tombs, the battles of the Bosphoran army with the Scythians and the Taurians (pl. XXIX). The armour is the same everywhere. The cavalryman, and the Bosphoran nobles are almost always cavalry, has a conical metal helmet; a corslet of scale- or ring-armour; a long lance; a dagger fastened to the leg, with a ring on the top as in the Kuban tombs; a sword with a round stone pommel and a stone guard; a bow; a gorytus; and a shield, small in the cavalry, large in the infantry: a combination of Scythian and Sarmatian panoply, with predominance of the characteristic Sarmatian weapons, as they are represented on Trajan's column and on the arch of Galerius at Salonica. Infantry plays little part in the Bosphoran army. It consists of peltasts, generally without corslets, armed with lances, javelins, shields and sometimes bows. The tactics are also Sarmatian. Heavily armed warriors, cataphracts, fighting tourney-wise in single combat, or phalanx pitted against phalanx: harbingers of the Middle Ages. The same armour is found in the tombs of the period.

Our principal source of information for the material culture of the Bosphoran citizens is as usual the tombs. Thousands have been excavated. They bear witness, first of all, to great prosperity on the Bosphorus during the first two centuries of our era. The sepulchral structures are varied and sumptuous. There are three main types. One continues the old Greek tradition: a tomb dug in the earth; the body was enclosed in a wooden coffin or a stone sarcophagus and deposited in the tomb. The walls of the trench sometimes have a revetment of dressed stone, and dressed stone is used for roof and floor. I know very few certain examples of cremation: inhumation is the rule. The trench was covered with a small mound which was topped by a carved and painted stele. These stelai mostly belong to the first century A.D., some to the second, none, as far as I know, to the third. Nearly all the stelai were used again, and have been found embodied in funeral structures of the second and third centuries. There are slight variants of this type: I shall not discuss them.

The second type of grave was introduced in the latter half of the third century B.C., but is rare in the Hellenistic period: it appears to be of Pontic origin. In the soft rock on the chain of Mount Mithridates at Panticapaeum, or in the clay elsewhere, a tomb chamber was cut, sometimes with double berths, both berths cut in the rock or clay. The chambers were approached by a shaft, sometimes very deep, and a corridor. The bodies were placed in the berths, often enclosed in wooden coffins. The graves are always family graves and were frequently re-employed. The walls of the tombs were often coated with stucco and painted.

PLATE XXX

1. CLAY STATUETTE OF A PANTICAPAEAN SOLDIER
I Cent. B.C. Hermitage, Petrograd
2. GRAVE STELA FROM KERCH. I Cent. A.D. Kerch, Royal Tumulus
3. COPPER COINS OF THE BOSPHORAN KINGDOM
I-II Cent. A.D. Hermitage, Petrograd

The third type takes up the old Spartocid tradition: monumental tumulary chambers, of dressed stone, with barrel vaults. They are often sculptured without and painted within. These also were family graves, belonging to Bosphoran aristocrats. We know the occupants of some of them. The dead were laid in wooden coffins, in sarcophagi of dressed stone, or in hermetically sealed sarcophagi.

All these types of tomb must have been very costly and show that the inhabitants were wealthy. The same types appear in the cemeteries of the other Greek cities on the Black Sea; the tumulary graves at Olbia more than elsewhere, but fewer and less rich than on the Bosphorus.

The funerary ritual is everywhere the same as before. In all three types, the tomb furniture is astonishingly rich and varied. Unhappily, the tumulary and chamber graves have almost always been pillaged, and it is only the trenches that are usually found intact. The dead were furnished with everything that might be useful in the other world. Garments; mortuary crowns; jewels; baskets of fruit, especially nuts; baskets of eggs, the funerary significance of which is well known; toilet boxes; terra-cottas, often quaint representations of strange beings, probably evil geniuses—perhaps personifications of diseases—like those found in contemporary Chinese graves; toys and games, for instance a complete set of duodecim scripta; coins; gold plaques struck from coins; and so forth. Weapons are sometimes found in men's tombs, but chiefly from the second century A.D. onwards. It is significant that from the first century A.D. metal bridle pieces are found in a number of tombs: the custom is thoroughly Sarmatian.

As before, most of the objects buried with the dead are imports. But some are certainly local work. We shall begin with the tombs themselves. The grave stelai, and the decorative sculpture of the tombs, were certainly executed in Panticapaeum and the other Greek cities. The art of the sculptors is not purely Greek: the style is decadent Ionian, at once heavy and dry. There is a notable propensity towards naturalism and realism, which shows itself particularly in the care with which every detail of costume and armour is rendered. I do not know, whether the same can be said of the racial type. As before, the tomb chambers were decorated with painting, and sometimes the stone sarcophagi and stelai as well. The paintings are assuredly local work, and are very interesting. I have discussed them in a special treatise and I shall say only a few words about them here. The old Greek style of mural decoration was retained in the first century: the architectural style. But from the second half of the first century onwards, its place was taken by two Oriental styles: one, the floral style, probably came from Egypt; the other, the incrustation style, was purely Asiatic; heavy, richly coloured, pompous, a style created in the palaces of the Asiatic monarchs, a style in which architectural form, variety of hue, and fineness of detail are all killed by colour. Artists began 'to paint with marbles' (*marmoribus pingere*), and to imitate this painting in paint. This style was to conquer the Roman world, and it was in this style that the Christian churches were to be decorated.

The tombs were painted with figures and scenes: but look at the scenes. The art is no longer Greek. Animals, plants, real and mythical persons, can only be compared with Parthian and Sassanid monuments (pl. XXX, 2, 3).

Characteristic, also, of the Bosphoran tombs, are the coffins, boxes, and other objects of wood. The finest specimens may have been brought from Asia or Syria, although it is not very likely. But even if they were imported, these objects will always have a singular value, as almost unique specimens of the once flourishing art of marquetry. More well-preserved examples have been found in South Russia than anywhere else. It was an old custom at Panticapaeum to bury the wealthy and noble dead in wooden coffins worthy of them, carved, gilded and painted. We found such coffins as early as the Spartocid period. It is to be regretted that Hellenistic and Roman marquetry has never been properly studied. Watzinger, who published a book on the subject, says hardly anything about this period. It is interesting to find, in the Hellenistic and Roman times, especially in the first century B.C. and the first A.D., a process which has been common in the East down to our own day: the insertion of ornamental inlay of a different colour, in wood, glass, stone or metal, into the plain surface of the wooden object. In the first century A.D., sarcophagi were hardly ever painted or decorated with figure subjects. Painting is replaced by incrustation, figure subjects by geometric and floral ornaments. The old fashion was revived much later, in the second century A.D.; very ugly coffins, decorated with plaster or clay figures glued to the sides. I do not know the origin of the incrusted sarcophagi: in any case they help to show that there was a pronounced taste at Panticapaeum for rich and varied polychromy: further evidence will be furnished by the jewellery.

I now proceed to speak of Panticapaean jewellery in the Roman period. The Panticapaean tombs are as rich as before in gold and silver objects. It is difficult to distinguish the local jewels from the imported. But I have already pointed out, that the existence of a school of goldsmiths at Panticapaeum in Greek and Hellenistic times suggests that a large proportion of the jewels were local work and not imported. From the second century B.C., what distinguishes Panticapaean and, in general, Bosphoran goldsmith's work, is the taste for polychromy. This taste is already very noticeable in a find which is certainly as old as the second, if not the third century B.C., the sumptuous tombs at Artyukhov's farm in the Taman peninsula; in graves of the same period at Gorgippia; and in a group of finds at Panticapaeum, which cannot be enumerated here, but which date from the second, perhaps even from the end of the third century B.C. Thenceforth the series is uninterrupted.

I spoke of the taste for polychromy in the last chapter. It is general all over the ancient world in late Hellenistic and Imperial times, but the South Russian finds are richer, more numerous, more varied and more ancient than any others. I do not wish in the least to suggest, that the polychrome style in jewellery arose and developed in South Russia, and spread thence over the Roman Empire. The love of polychromy prevailed throughout the classic East, in Egypt as well as in Mesopotamia, Syria, and the Iranian world. The Orientalization of taste, the result of the later Hellenistic period, and the participation of non-Greek races, eastern and western, with their love of brilliancy and pomp—observe the affection of the Celts for polychrome ornaments—in the civilized life of the Greco-Roman world, led to that change of psychology which has been well characterized by Alois Riegl. But I do maintain that South Russia was one of the centres, in which polychromy developed early, and independently of the other centres of ancient jewellery; and assumed special forms which brought about the new style commonly called Gothic.

Even after what I said in the preceding chapter, I shall allow myself to return once more to this question, because it is extremely important for us, if we wish to appreciate the part which the Bosphorus played in the history of civilization during the period of the migrations and the early Middle Ages.

The characteristic feature of the polychrome style at Panticapaeum and in the Sarmatian world—for the same objects are found in both places, and it cannot be doubted that the Bosphoran workshops furnished the Sarmatian world with most of its jewellery—is not merely the use of precious stones to adorn jewels, or rather the predominance of the stone in the goldsmiths art, which is now principally concerned with providing artistic settings for one or more gems; but something more important and more distinctive. The speciality of Panticapaean and Sarmatian jewellery does not lie in providing settings for precious stones, but in the incrustation of gold objects, in ornamenting the surface with gems and cut stones, occasionally enamels. The surface gradually loses its independence and becomes no more than a field for incrustation, for the production of polychrome effects. The goldsmith uses inset gems of various shapes and sizes; the same stones cut to the required shape; and glass and enamel of various hues. The result is a kind of carpet made of precious stones, in which the scheme and arrangement of colours is all, while the form of the objects themselves, and their geometric, floral, or animal ornamentation, play hardly any part. Polychrome effect is now the alpha and omega of the Panticapaean jeweller.

This tendency in jewellery, as I have already pointed out, is by no means new. It is to be observed in South Russia during the archaic period. The Kelermes find, the finds of Vettersfelde, of Tomakôvka on the lower Dnieper, of the Golden Tumulus in the Crimea, furnish characteristic specimens of this Oriental style, in which enamel and precious stones are employed side by side to enliven the surface of gold objects. But at this period the polychrome decoration was subordinated to the form and ornamentation of the objects themselves. Towards the fifth century, this style disappears in South Russia: a few survivals, discreet touches of colour, occur in some jewels of the fourth and third centuries: but these are exceptions. The style as such develops in the East, in Iranian lands, as we see from the Oxus and Susa treasures. It returns to South Russia with the Sarmatians. It reappears in the Orenburg steppes during the fourth century B.C., and influences Panticapaean jewellery by the third, witness the Taman and Kuban finds just described, and the others analysed in the preceding chapter. The enamelled sword sheath from Buerova Mogila in the Taman peninsula (pl. XXIV, 4), the round brooch from the grave at Artyukhov's farm, the gold roundels, dotted with precious stones, from Kurjips, the gold openwork mounting of a vase or rhyton from Beslenêevskaya: all these lead on to the finds of the first century B.C., and of

Roman imperial times, from Panticapaeum and from the Russian steppes, in which the polychrome style eventually triumphs, and incrustation prevails over the form and decoration of the object. The result of this victory we have already seen in the finds from Novocherkássk and from western Siberia. But the same phenomenon may be observed at Panticapaeum.

To ascertain the true nature of Panticapaean jewellery in the Roman period, we must make a rather closer examination of certain very characteristic finds which have often been quoted but never thoroughly investigated. In the first century A.D., and in the earlier part of the second, the tombs of Panticapaeum present almost the same picture as contemporary tombs elsewhere. I have already observed, that the citizens of the Bosphorus, notwithstanding the progress of Iranization, were strongly attached to their Greek nationality; the objects which they liked to take with them into their tombs were such as bore hardly any local stamp: those which did were reserved for export. In the second century, however, a profound change takes place. Iranization has borne its fruit. The tomb furniture comes more and more to resemble that of the tombs in the valleys of the Kuban and the Don. By the third century, one might be in the heart of Sarmatian country. These tombs can often be dated by imprints of coins on gold funerary crowns.

I shall first speak of three exceptionally rich tombs discovered in 1837 and 1841. The two tombs of 1841 were stone chambers surmounted by tumuli: the third, of 1837, found in the same district but under another tumulus, was a marble sarcophagus, not interred in the virgin soil, but in the soil of the tumulus: the lid of the sarcophagus was shaped like a pediment with an acroterion. To give an idea of the wealth of the furniture, I shall briefly enumerate the objects of which it consisted, adding references to the publications. In the 1837 tomb, the tomb of the Queen with the Golden Mask: a grave-mask of gold (*Antiquités du Bosphore Cimmérien*, pl. I); a silver sceptre (pl. II, 5); a gold funerary crown (pl. III, 4); a pair of gold ear-pendants; a gold circlet like that on plate XI, 6; two gold bracelets (pl. XIV, 4); three gold rings (pls. XV, 3 and XVIII, 19); a simple pin, of gold; a distaff (pl. XXX, 8); a bridle (pl. XXIX, 1-7); a red leather purse, with a figure of a bird cut out of leather and applied; two small fibulae, one of gold, the other of bronze; beads of glass and of cornelian; a gold bottle (pl. XXIV, 25); a number of garnets mounted in bezels; a gold medallion (pl. LXXXV, 8); several hundreds of small stamped plaques in gold (pl. XXII, 1, 3, 4, 6, 22, 25; pl. XXIII, 10-12 and 14). A great quantity of silver plate; two vases with reliefs (pl. XXXVII, 1 and 2); another, plain; two cups with feet and without handles; a large covered cup; a pyxis for cosmetic; two spoons (pl. XXX, 3 and 5); a round plate (pl. XXX, 11). In bronze: a basin (pl. XLIV, 2); a bell (pl. XLIV, 8); a round seal; two small bells (pl. XXXI, 1); a small pilaster (pl. XLIV, 15); two lion's paws, feet of a vase; remains of a dagger, and of a knife with a gold filigree mount.

One of the stone chambers discovered in 1841 had a stepped vault, the other a barrel vault. As far as can be ascertained from the drawings published by Ashik (*Bosphoran Kingdom*, ii, pls. IV and V), neither chamber was constructed for its ultimate occupant: they were both built in the fourth century B.C. and re-employed; this explains the discovery, in the second tomb, of a painted vase with reliefs, of an alabastron, and of a mirror, which belong to the fourth century B.C., and resent a strong contrast to the furniture found in the coffin. In the first tomb, which was a man's, a wooden coffin, plated with lead, was found intact, and the furniture complete. The furniture consisted of a gold funerary crown, a counterpart to the Queen with the Mask's (*A. B. C.* pl. III, 3); a tunic embroidered with gold; a sword, a long spear, a knife blade, with remains of a gold mount, a dagger (pl. XXVII, 7), a whetstone, a bridle like that of the Queen with the Mask (Ashik, *Bosphoran Kingdom*, iii, fig. 209 a-e), a gold plaque (pl. XXIV, 16), and two gold imprints from a coin of Rhescuporis II (A.D. 212-29). The other chamber contained a woman's body, also in a wooden coffin: a gold funeral crown (pl. III, 5), a necklace (pl. X, 3), bracelets of gold wire, gold lion's head earrings, two gold rings, one set with a garnet, and the painted vase, mentioned above, belonging to the fourth century B.C. (pl. LVIII, 6, 2).

I must also mention the tomb excavated in 1910, which contained a gold crown exactly similar to those in the grave of the Queen with the Mask and in the man's tomb of 1841. If we look closely at the three tombs, we see that they must have belonged to members of one family. The objects certainly came from the same workshops. First of all the crowns: the crowns of the warrior and of the Queen with the Mask make a pair, and the workmanship is exactly the same: the representations on the plaques in front are likewise pendants, as I have shown in a special article. The crown in the woman's tomb of 1841 is of the same work as the others, and has the same square plaque in front although the ornamentation is different. The two bridles, the Queen's and the warrior's, are almost identical: the same badge-like monogram appears on parts of the gold plating; it was probably, as I said above, a kind of family device. The gold circlet of the Queen with the Mask closely resembles the bracelets of the woman in the tumulus of 1841. And so forth. It cannot be doubted that the three tombs belong not only to the same period but to the same family.

The date of the tombs was established by Ashik and Stephani at the time of the discovery. The tomb of the Queen with the Mask contained the famous silver plate with the words βασιλέως Ῥησκουπόρει (=Ῥησκουπόριδος, the genitive in -ει being common in the Bosphorus) incised in dots, and the indication of the weight, finally deciphered by Zahn with the help of information supplied by Pridik and myself. The plate belonged, then, to King Rhescuporis. The date of the king is fixed by the monogram engraved in the centre and round the rim of the plate: it is composed of the letters ANTB. Instead of Ἀντ(ιόχου) β(ασιλέως) which would give a date incompatible with the style, Zahn proposes to read Ἀντ(ωνείνου) β(ασιλέως). I entirely agree with this reading, especially as the monogram seems to me to contain all the letters of the name Ἀντ(ωνείνου) or Ἀντ(ωνεῖνος). The Antoninus meant is undoubtedly Caracalla, as Zahn saw, and the plate is one of the regular gifts which the Roman emperors presented to their Bosphoran vassals. The lady buried in the tomb of 1837 was therefore a member of the family of King Rhescuporis II, Caracalla's contemporary: perhaps she was the king's wife and died before him. The date is corroborated by imprints, found in the tomb of 1841, from coins of the same king. I am inclined to think that this lordly tomb, though built in the fourth century for some one else, was the tomb of the king himself: his second wife or his concubine being buried beside him. I have laid stress upon this date, because Kubitschek has recently questioned it; he wishes to assign the three tombs to a much later period, the fourth century A.D. His arguments are extremely flimsy: he is clearly anxious to confirm his own dating of the Siebenbrunnen tomb, which I shall discuss later. He accordingly attributes the Kerch tombs to the Gothic epoch. But there cannot be the least doubt that they are pre-Gothic, that the first belongs to the period A.D. 212-29, and the two others to A.D. 229, the date of the death of Rhescuporis II: that is, some decades before the appearance of the Goths.

The furniture of these tombs is astonishingly similar to that of the Sarmatian tombs on the Kuban. The funerary ritual is the same, the bridle occurs in both, and the objects have the same shapes. Look at the gold bottle, which recurs at Ust-Labinskaya, at Novocherkássk and at Olbia (fig. 19, 1-2 from the Kuban; 3, from the grave of the Queen); the characteristic gold garment plaques, regular in Sarmatian tombs (fig. 17); the bracelets and torcs, of the same type as the Sarmatian; the distinctive armour of the king, with the great spear predominating; the shape and decoration of the dagger. The clasp of the necklace, in the form of a ram ornamented with false filigree, reappears in many of the tombs on the Kuban: the type of bridle, with rings, is the same; the monogram devices also; the same technical processes are used, embossing and pseudo-granulation combined with inlaid stones. Finally, a highly developed style of polychrome jewellery. I must also notice the striking resemblance between the funeral crown of the lady in the tumulus of 1841, and the crown from Novocherkássk. The plaque in front of the lady's crown is divided into nine compartments, which are decorated with embossed geometrical patterns, very primitive and very characteristic of Sarmatian art as a whole; seven of the compartments are embellished with inlaid precious stones, three of which are chalcedony cameos of the first century A.D. The Syrian garnet, with a female head, which forms the centre-piece of the lady's necklace, may belong to the third century and may represent the deceased herself.

Let us now examine the polychrome style of the gold objects found in these tombs. It is much richer and much more highly developed than in the Kuban finds, and vies with the polychrome style at Novocherkássk and in Siberia. Stones are inlaid everywhere, even in the funeral crowns. Compare the gold bottle of the Queen with the Mask and the gold bottle from Ust-Labinskaya: the Queen's bottle is thickly studded with precious stones. Look at the two bridles: embossed work like that on the crown described above, and precious stones inlaid all over it.

But there are two other features to which I would draw attention. The king's dagger was richly ornamented, like the knife in the same tomb and the dagger of the queen. The hilt is coated with gold foil, and bears the same monogram device as the bridle: it is studded with carnelians fixed in bezels. The flat pommel is a chalcedony with a gold rosette in the middle: the rosette is enriched with enamel and coloured pastes forming a mosaic design. The same combination, then, of proto-cloisonné and inlaid stones as is typical of the Gothic style.

The other feature is the entire absence of decoration in the animal style, which we found abundantly represented in Siberia and at Novocherkássk, and much less abundantly on the Kuban. The western variety of the polychrome style is developing before our eyes: it will presently start from Panticapaeum to conquer the world.

It has always been recognized that the Kerch finds which I have just analysed are of the greatest importance for determining the origin of the Gothic or Merovingian style of jewellery. The close affinity of the two styles is undeniable. No one will dispute the significance of the conclusions which we have now reached: first, that the finds analysed date from the beginning of the third century, that is, from the pre-Gothic period; secondly, that they are connected with a series of much more ancient finds, which we have every justification for assigning to the Sarmatians, and which go back as far as the fourth century B.C. and form an uninterrupted sequence.

Let us now return to Bosphoran civilization. The tomb furniture of the second and third centuries A.D. agrees with the rest of our evidence in pointing to progressive, almost precipitate Iranization at Panticapaeum and in the Bosphorus generally. It is difficult to think of the family tombs of Rhescuporis II as belonging to persons who spoke Greek, and called themselves Greeks. These persons were Iranians, Sarmatians, with a veneer of Hellenism. It was mainly in the second century that the transformation took place. This is proved by a number of tombs which I have no time to describe. I refer the reader to Ernst von Stern's careful description of one of these monumental chambers, or to Ashik's of a chamber with fourteen wooden coffins, one of which contained a crown with an imprint from a coin of Marcus Aurelius (A.D. 173), and a number of typical Sarmatian plaques: or to the account of the chamber discovered by Karéysha in 1842, which is dated by an imprint from a coin of Commodus. He will receive the same impression everywhere: Hellenism, still strong in the first century A.D., was now in complete decline: the Iranian world was overwhelming the Greek.

It remains to say a few words about religion and worship in the Bosphoran kingdom during Roman times. I have already spoken of the power wielded by native, especially Maeotian cults, in the Asiatic portion' of the Bosphorus during the Greek and Hellenistic periods. I have mentioned the cult of the Great Goddess, which in Greek disguise continued to be the principal cult among the Greek and native population. With this cult, as we have seen, was associated that of the Great God. The only native names of these deities which are preserved are Sanerges and Astara, names which remind us of Hittite Asia Minor: they appear in a Hellenistic inscription.

In the Roman period, the part which the Great Goddess plays in the coinage of Dynamis points to a resurrection or a fresh manifestation of the ancient beliefs. I pointed out that the old sanctuaries of the Goddess never ceased to exist, and that they were protected by the sovereigns of the Bosphorus. At Panticapaeum, as everywhere else, the Roman epoch was a period of religious syncretism. But through all this syncretism the Great Goddess preserves her dominant position. It is true that Demeter and Persephone were chthonic divinities above everything else, and it is not surprising to find them in tombs, as defenders of the dead in the world beyond the grave. The presence of Orphic influence is also natural, considering the importance of Orphism in the Roman period. Nevertheless, it may well have been due to native influence, to the cult of the Great Goddess, that the scenes depicted in the tombs are taken almost exclusively from the Eleusino-Orphic cycle. At the period when native influence in the Bosphorus becomes strongly marked, in the second and third centuries A.D., there was a vigorous revival of the cult of the Great Goddess in the official religion. We have seen that the Great Goddess, the patroness of the kingdom, appears on the reverse of nearly all Bosphoran bronze coins from the third century onwards. At Chersonesus we find the same.

But side by side with the worship of the Great Goddess, the worship of the Great God increases in importance, and is coupled with a noticeable tendency towards monotheism. The chief divinity revered by the official colleges was the supreme God, Θεὸς Ὕψιστος. He appears in the barbarous tomb paintings of the third century A.D., accompanied by orgiasts engaged in ritual acts. It has been proposed, on the strength of analogies from Asia Minor, to attribute this cult to the influence of the Jewish and Thracian religions, to see in it a syncretism of Sabaziasts and Sabbathiasts. It is true that there was a powerful Jewish colony in the Bosphorus by the first century A.D.: it probably came from Asia Minor. But here as everywhere, the Jewish colony kept to itself. Hardly any Jewish names occur in the college lists: and yet it was the members of the colleges who were the principal votaries of the Great God. I believe, therefore, that in South Russia the cult of the Θεὸς Ὕψιστος was related, first and foremost, to the cult of Sabazios, the supreme god of the Thracians, especially as it has recently been shown, that the Sabbathiasts themselves had nothing to do with Jewish religion, but were connected with a cult of the Great Goddess of Asia Minor and her consort. The arguments of Schürer and of Cumont fail to convince me that the Jewish beliefs exercised a dominant influence on the Bosphorus; the tendency to monotheism, and to moralization of the gods, was general at the Roman period, especially in the East. On the other hand, the figure of Sabazios appears in the Bosphoran tombs described above, his cult is found in the Caucasus, and it was probably he who gave rise to the Bosphoran coin types of the fourth century B.C., the silen and the satyr. Moreover, there was a powerful Thracian element in the Bosphoran population, and the deity who has most affinity with the god Sanerges is along with Sandas of Asia Minor, god of wine and prosperity, the mystic Thracian god Sabazios. I consider, therefore, that the Θεὸς Ὕψιστος of the Bosphoran inscriptions, is the supreme god of the native population, a syncretism of the Iranian Ahuramazda and of the Thracian Sabazios, who was influenced, in his turn, by the consort of the Great Goddess of Asia Minor.

In conclusion: our study has shown, that the Roman period was a period of real renaissance in the Bosphoran kingdom and in the Greek colonies on the Black Sea. Under Roman protection, Hellenism, which had been almost stifled by Iranism, began to revive and to prosper. But Iranization, undefeated, returned to the attack and took possession of the Greek city life in all its branches. The Iranian world exercised a powerful effect upon the political and social life of the Greek colonies, upon their religion, their art and their industry. By the time that Roman protection ceased to be the principal factor, the process of Iranization was almost completed. But the fusion of Iranism and Hellenism did not involve the suppression of Hellenism: it was a true fusion, and the outcome was a mixed civilization of singular complexity and interest. The northern tribes who mingled with this world in the third century A.D., and who had long been penetrating into its midst, were faced by a civilization which was far higher than theirs. They naturally learned from it and made it their own. We must not forget, that there is no evidence of the Sarmatians having been conquered and subjugated by the Goths. The relation between the two was rather that of co-operation and alliance: in military matters, the Goths were the stronger; the Sarmatians were the cultivated element. The result of this fusion will be made clear in the next chapter.

VIII.
THE POLYCHROME STYLE AND THE ANIMAL STYLE

MY purpose in writing this chapter is not to compile a history of the polychrome and animal styles. The task could only be accomplished by a specialist, in a comprehensive and copiously illustrated work of several volumes. My own task is a much more modest one. I wish to indicate, in a few pages, the influence exerted upon Central Europe by Greco-Iranian South Russia, during the formation of two styles which are of the utmost importance for the historian of mediaeval art: the polychrome style of the period of migrations, and the animal style of the Germanic North.

Much has been written on these problems. The steps in the evolution of the two styles, from the Fourth century A.D. onwards, have been established: of the objects which exhibit these styles, especially the fibulae and the clasps, from a much earlier period. The origin of the styles has often been discussed. There are several conflicting theories about the polychrome style. One theory, that it is of purely Germanic origin, is almost abandoned. The theory of Oriental origin, proposed by de Linas and Odobesco, was stated in such vague terms that it has hardly affected the discussion. The third theory, the most widely current, is Riegl's: he attributes the appearance of the polychrome style to a general change of taste, of stylistic feeling, of artistic psychology, in the Roman world of Imperial times. Certain discoveries at Kerch, which I have not mentioned hitherto, gave rise to a modification of this theory. Ernst von Stern, Ebert, Reinecke, and Kossinna believed that the new feeling was particularly strong at Panticapaeum; it was at Panticapaeum, they maintained, that the Goths encountered it, adopted it, and created the polychrome style of the Middle Ages, which they carried with them into Central Europe, altering it and perfecting it as they went.

In the study of the animal style, Salin's book marked a new epoch. Salin made a thorough study of the evolution of this style, especially from the fourth century A.D. onwards: he pointed out the various stages by which it was transformed into a geometric style, taking the fibulae and clasps of the Germanic countries as his principal guides. On the question of origin he is less explicit, but he is inclined to think, that the chief motives of the northern animal style were mostly borrowed from late Roman art. I cannot discuss all these theories here: I shall merely adduce certain facts which may prove useful to future investigators.

Let us begin with the polychrome style. Polychromy had never died out in the East: and from the Hellenistic period onwards, as we have already seen, there was a powerful revival of polychromy in the Iranian world. A similar revival took place in Semitic and Egyptian quarters at the same time. It is among the Sarmatians that we can best follow the revival of the polychrome style in its Iranian branch. Among the Sarmatians, who were in touch with the Greeks of South Russia, the style flourished with a vigour and an originality unequalled, as far as we can see, in any other part of the Helfenistic world. All the jewellery becomes polychrome. Various processes are employed: cloisonné, where the stones are enclosed by metal partitions; open-work, where the coloured substance is inserted into a metal network champlevé, where the stones or other coloured materials are let into hollows: the first is the usual process, the others are less common. Coloured enamels are sometimes, but seldom used as well as stones. The variety of this style which we find in the valley of the Kuban is more sober and more classical, and not so closely connected with the animal style. In the valley of the Don, and in western Siberia, the objects are more gaily coloured and more barbaric: the polychrome style takes possession of the animal style and unites with it.

There is every reason to suppose that most of this polychrome jewellery was manufactured, for export, in the workshops of various Bosphoran cities. The Bosphoran artists adopted the Oriental fashion, and used it to decorate the particular articles which their barbarian customers required: pieces of armour and of horse trappings; glass and metal vases personal ornaments, such as crowns, torcs, necklaces, bracelets, metal-plated belts, fibulae and brooches, garment plaques, and the like. In the Greek towns themselves the new fashion was slow in establishing itself, and the objects in the polychrome style are almost exclusively imports, probably from Greece, Asia Minor and Syria, where the same period saw a great revival, under Persian and Egyptian influence, of the polychrome style in jewellery. In these imports, the principle of the polychromy, the technique and the whole spirit are not the same as in the articles manufactured by Bosphoran artists for Sarmatian customers: the Greco-Oriental branch is more refined and more moderate, it makes more use of enamel, less of coloured stones. But from the end of the first century A.D., certain objects, hitherto peculiar to the Sarmatians, come into use among the Greek inhabitants of the Bosphoran cities: and these are ornamented in the characteristic Sarmatian manner. Arms in the first place: also fibulae. Until the first century B.C., fibulae were virtually unknown to the Iranians of the Russian steppes and to the inhabitants of the Greek cities: they now become more and more common: tendril fibulae, round and oval fibulae, animal-shaped fibulae, and so forth. From the very beginning they are decorated in the polychrome style. In the second and third centuries A.D., the adoption of Sarmatian customs and of the Sarmatian style becomes more and more pronounced. Thenceforward it is not only in Sarmatian country, in the steppes of Europe and Asia, that the objects in the polychrome style prevail: they appear, in steadily increasing numbers, in the Greek cities as well.

I have already mentioned, in the preceding chapter, the most interesting of the second- and third-century finds at Panticapaeum, which bear witness to the change of taste and habits. We saw that the tomb of Rhescuporis II belonged at latest to the year 229. A recent find, which has been acquired by the Louvre, and which I hope to publish before long, contains imprints from coins of the Emperor Pupienus (A.D. 238), and consequently belongs to the last decades of the first half of the third century. It has become customary, in archaeological works, to consider that coins comprised in a find possess no more than a relative value for the purpose of dating the tomb. But the special circumstances of each case must be taken into account. When discussing the tomb of Rhescuporis II, I showed that the chronological evidence afforded by the coin imprints was perfectly accurate. So in the Louvre find: I cannot think that if the tomb were much later than the single year of Pupienus' reign, it would have contained imprints of his coins, which cannot have had a wide or a prolonged circulation. Now the Louvre find presents the same peculiarities as those which are dated by the reign of Rhescuporis II: the same arms, the same clasps, the same system of polychrome decoration. It is worth noticing that it includes a golden fibula of the same shape as the fibulae found in the region of the Kuban, a fibula with flat back and tendril foot. Throughout the third century, that is to say, the period immediately preceding the arrival of the Goths, we have an almost continuous series of similar finds. The most characteristic are those of 1874, published in the *Compte Rendu* for 1874, pp. x-xi, and 1875, p. 26. One of these is dated by imprints from coins of the Emperor Gordian (A.D. 238-44) and undoubtedly belongs to his time; two others by coins of Maximian (275-307) and of his contemporary, the Bosphoran king Thothorses (278/9-308/9). The two latter are particularly distinctive. The second includes an iron sword of purely Bosphoran type, silver clasps, and beads and garment plaques like those from the tomb of Rhescuporis II. A great number of similar plaques were found in the tomb dated by the coins of Gordian. It is clear, therefore, that down to the end of the third century and the beginning of the fourth, the civilization of the Bosphorus retained that purely Sarmatian character which it had assumed in the second century A.D. In the third century, just as in the time of Rhescuporis II, the majority of the objects from Panticapaean tombs are exactly similar to those from Sarmatian tombs, of the first and second centuries A.D., on the Kuban.

This continuous series leads directly to the fourth-century finds at Panticapaeum, which are no less numerous. The richest and most important are the contents, now in the Hermitage, of two tombs which were pillaged about 1904. They can be accurately dated by two dishes, one from each tomb, which were gifts from the Emperor Constantius II (337-61), to the persons buried in the tombs also by imprints from coins of Valentinian I (364-75) or Valentinian II (375-92), of Sauromates II (174-210) and of Gordian (238-44). As the finds probably belonged to a number of consecutive burials, a frequent practice at the time, I have no hesitation in assigning part of the objects to the third, and part to the second half of the fourth century A.D. Now, in the nature of the tomb furniture, these finds do not differ from third-century finds. There are the same funerary crowns, with gold medallions taken from Roman and Bosphoran coins; the same solid gold torcs, terminating in heads of fantastic animals, eared and fanged, with a long squarish snout; the same custom of burying horse trappings with the dead; and so forth. But there are novelties both in the character and in the decoration of the objects. The shapes of the arms, especially of the swords, are new: new arms are introduced, such as the shield with egg-shaped boss. The fibulae are more numerous, larger, more massive and more complicated: the types remain the same, but the forms are exaggerated. Lastly, in the system of decoration, the predominant process is the diversification of the surface by means of garnets cut to geometric shapes and surrounded by golden cloisons: although the older practice is by no means abandoned, that of stones inlaid in hollows and surrounded by a wire in pseudo-granulation. It cannot be doubted that a new wave has spread over the almost wholly Sarmatian culture of Panticapaeum. This was unquestionably the Germanic, the Gothic wave. What did it bring with it?

The introduction of the new arms, and the modification of the old, were certainly due to the military and conquering spirit of the new-comers. I will not deny that they brought with them the new variety or varieties of fibula, which they had developed elsewhere, out of the same type, however, as was current at Panticapaeum, the tendril fibula. Nevertheless these new forms of fibula were now deeply influenced by Panticapaean art. I would instance the introduction of the animal style into the ornamentation—the use of bird's heads, the lion fibula from Szilagy-Somlyó, and so forth—; and the constant occurrence of fibulae in the shape of animals, such as were widespread in the Bosphorus from the first to the third centuries A.D. But I see no novelty in the technical processes of the jewellery, or in the decorative system. The Goths adopted all the processes which were employed in the Bosphorus before their arrival: embossing; false filigree, cloisonné. They also appropriated the polychrome style of decoration with all its rules. Their predilection for the garnet is nothing new. Before their time, the garnet was the most popular of precious stones with the Sarmatians, no doubt because it was the cheapest and the easiest to work. Lastly, the development of cloisonné combined with cut garnets was merely the natural outcome of principles which had been observed in the Bosphorus long before the arrival of the Goths: witness the Maikop belt. It must also be noted, that the fourth-century style of jewellery at Panticapaeum was not greatly affected by the animal style: we said the same about the western branch of the polychrome style as a whole, the branch of the Kuban valley and the Bosphoran kingdom.

The fourth-century finds just mentioned are by no means isolated. We have several of them, and some later ones as well. They are not confined to Kerch; like the Sarmatian art of the previous age, they are spread all over the Russian steppes. I may cite the finds, published by Tolstóy and Kondakóv in the *Antiquities of South Russia*, from Chúlek near Taganrog in the region of the Don, from Kudinétov in the Tersk province in Northern Caucasus, the great fibula from Nêzhin in the district of Chernígov; and the excavations unknown to these writers, in the cemetery of Suúk Su near Gurzúf in the southern Crimea. The Gotho-Sarmatian civilization, therefore, developed uninterruptedly in South Russia and covered the same area as the Sarmatian. Every one knows that it did not stop at the frontiers of modern Russia. It spread, through the region of the Danube, all over the western Roman provinces and even over Italy itself. Products of this distinctive art, which was very closely connected with the Gotho-Sarmatian, are found on the Rhine, in Merovingian France, in the English county of Kent, in Spain, and in North Africa. The carriers of the art were certainly not the Goths alone, who in so short a space of time cannot have formed a class of craftsmen familiar with all the technical details of this complicated kind of jewellery, but more than any one else, the Hellenized Sarmatians or Sarmatized Greeks who took an active share in the expeditions of the Goths. This is the reason why the spread of the new style was not only not checked, but even assisted by the conquests of the Huns: it is well known that the Huns, like the Goths, were accompanied by Sarmatian tribes.

I cannot give a list here of all the finds which illustrate the development of this style in the various quarters into which the Goths and the Sarmatians introduced it; I should like, however, to mention one or two, to show the stability of type in the objects which we have proved to be wholly and exclusively Sarmatian.

A special position is occupied by the celebrated find at Petrossa or Petroasa in Rumania, to which I have made several allusions already, and which has been sumptuously published by Odobesco. I cannot deal with it in detail: but I would draw attention to certain important points. It is remarkable that the Petroasa treasure contains a number of objects which strangely recall the Siberian finds and the treasure of Novocherkássk, that is to say, the northern branch of the polychrome style. I have already mentioned the gold patera, which reminded us, by its semi-classical form and figures, of the silver phalarae from Sarmatian South Russia. I would lay special stress on the tendency, in both groups, to give the gods of the native Pantheon a classical guise. This tendency is observable in South Russia from the fourth century B.C. It never leads, however, as in the Roman provinces, to the substitution of a classical for the native deity. The native deity preserves his attributes and his individuality. I would also point to the similarities in technique, and in the forms of the animals.

Let me also draw attention to the two openwork paterae, with handles in the shape of panthers, covered with precious stones; and to the fibulae in the form of eagles studded with gems. These Objects are in the same style as the best things from Siberia, and their Oriental character cannot be denied. One would like to assign them a fairly early date. Whatever its date may be, it is certain that the treasure of Petroasa is closely connected with the finds from Siberia and from the region of the Don. I do not know whether we can ascribe it to the Goths. The runes on the torc may be later than the objects themselves, and the whole find may have been seized by the Goths from some Sarmatian or Thracian prince.

The new find at Siebenbrunnen in Austria is of a different nature. Kubitschek, who published it, recognized the close affinity between the Austrian graves and the tombs, already mentioned, of the family of Rhescuporis II. Astonished at this affinity, and convinced that the Siebenbrunnen things were Gothic, he wished to assign the Kerch finds to a post-Gothic date: this we have shown to be quite impossible. The affinity is even closer than Kubitschek supposed. The little gold garment plaques from the Austrian find are of exactly the same shapes as the Sarmatian plaques from tombs on the Kuban, at Kerch, on the Don, and on the Dnieper (see fig. 17). It is not surprising that they occur in the Danube region as well. The gold bracelets terminate in the same heads as the torcs from Orenburg, from Stavropol, from the regions of the Kuban and of Kerch. The mirrors are closely connected with the mirrors of the Kuban. I do not wish to discuss the date of the Siebenbrunnen find. But whether it dates from the fourth or from the fifth century, it is nearly allied to the finds of pre-Gothic South Russia. I do not see why the Siebenbrunnen graves should not have belonged to a Sarmatian woman and child.

Kubitschek himself noticed the kinship between the Siebenbrunnen find and a find made at Valmeray in the commune of Moult in Calvados (Normandy). The tomb was that of a young girl; it contained, besides a fibula decorated with inset stones, 'one hundred and sixty small gold fragments, weighing 37 grammes in all, consisting of linear borders forming a succession of triangles, of solid triangles with little balls at the angles, of rectangles ornamented with three raised lines of six dots each, of circles with a ball in the centre, and lastly of double, conjoined triangles, like the solid triangles already mentioned, but set with small garnets' (E. de Robillard de Beaurepaire, *Bulletin de la Societè d'Antiquaires de France*, viii (1878), p. 155). These plaques, like the plaques from Siebenbrunnen and from South Russia, were undoubtedly sewn on to garments. The Norman plaques, then, offer a striking resemblance to the South Russian finds mentioned above (see fig. 17).

Others have been found at Nordendorf in Germany, according to Brenner, whose references I have been unable to verify; and in North Africa, in a Carthaginian tomb of the Vandal period which I hope to publish before long. The plaques from Carthage have the same shapes as the Sarmatian plaques, but their purpose was perhaps different: they may have formed a necklace.

Half-way between these finds, which go with the Bosphoran, and the treasure of Petroasa, stands the celebrated find of Szilagy-Somlyó, published by Pulszky and Hampel, which undoubtedly belongs to the same period as the Kerch finds of 1904, the period of Valens, Valentinian and Gratian. Let us look at the fibulae. One class of fibula is enriched with cabochons, which are set in cavities surrounded by granulation or false filigree, and is ornamented with granulated geometric patterns—double spirals spectacle-shaped, eight-shaped, or triangular: the whole decoration, therefore, is of the same type as in the Sarmatian polychrome objects. In another class of fibula, the granulated ornaments are partly replaced by, partly combined with, the embossed work which is frequent on the Kuban. It is with this class that we must connect the large fibula in the form of an oval brooch a common shape on the Kuban. A third class finds remarkable analogies among the Sarmatian objects from the Don and the Dnieper, and in the treasure of Petroasa: the most characteristic specimen is a fibula with the body in the form of a couchant lion, geometrically stylized, and embellished with precious stones. The figure of the lion is strangely reminiscent of the Scythian animal style pure and simple, modified to suit the fashion of polychrome decoration. The tail of the fibula is adorned with an embossed griffin. Curiously enough, the incisions on the lion's body are extraordinarily like the incisions in the field of the plaque from Siverskaya Stanitsa. Still closer to the Sarmatian plaques or phalarae, with their vegetable, animal and mythological decoration, are the boss-shaped fibulae: the boss is decorated with two embossed friezes of animals: the work, though barbarous, is exceedingly like that of the South Russian phalarae.

Before leaving Szilagy-Somlyó, let me point out another queer coincidence. The gold vases of Szilagy-Somlyó have triangular plaques, studded with gems, attached to their mouths. This strange system of decoration can be explained with the help of Scythian monuments: the rhyta, of horn or wood, from the kurgans of the Seven Brothers, the wooden vases from Solokha and from other tombs of the same group. In these objects, the golden triangles fastened to the mouth have a technical justification: in the Szilagy-Somlyó vases, they are decorative survivals and nothing more. I have no doubt that the Szilagy-Somlyó vases, which are very primitive, were imitated from wooden originals. It is not surprising that the ornamentation in triangles reappears on the well-known drinking-horn from Taplow Barrow in Buckinghamshire, now in the British Museum, a work of the Anglo-Saxon period.

It would be easy, if space permitted, to multiply these comparisons between Sarmatian art and the art of the Merovingian epoch. To conclude my study of the polychrome style, I should like to draw attention to a matter which has hitherto, I fancy, escaped notice. We have followed the development of the round or oval brooch in Sarmatian art (figs. 16 and 19): the characteristic feature of the decoration appeared to be the combination of the simplest geometric motives—circle, spectacle-shaped spiral, double spiral in the form of an eight—carried out in granulation or in filigree, with a rich polychromy effected by the use of precious stones, transparent or coloured glass, and enamels. Embossing is sometimes employed for the ornaments instead of granulation. Very few specimens of these brooches have been found in the Roman provinces, and such as have been found are comparatively late. The British Museum, for example, has only two (Marshall, Nos. 2863 and 2864, pl. LXV): they came from Antarados in Syria, and belong to the third or fourth century A.D. We have seen that these brooches are common on the Kuban, where the earliest go back to the second or first century B.C., the date of the finds at Artyúkhov's farm, at Akhtanizovka, at Siverskaya, at Zubov's farm. Now just at the period of the migrations these brooches become common in Western Europe: we find them in Italy, in France, on the Rhine, and in Anglo-Saxon England. In England they are confined to Kent, where they exhibit an interesting and original development, and are characteristic of the rich civilization which flourished there from the fourth to the sixth century. Compare the South Russian brooches which I have reproduced with the selection given by Baldwin Brown (*The Arts in Early England*, iv, pls. CXLV-CXLVII): particularly the Frankish fibula in the museum at Rouen (pl. CXLVII, 2); the fibula from Kent, formerly in the Mayer Collection and now in the Liverpool Museum (pl. CXLVII, 1); or the Maidstone and Dover fibulae (pl. CXLVI, 1-2): ornament and technique are the same as in South Russia. Another testimony to the persistence of the types created or adopted by the Sarmatians, and to the wide diffusion of these types at the period of the migration of the Sarmatian tribes.

The conclusion which follows from these facts and these comparisons is one which must be taken into account in all future investigation. The polychrome style which spread over Central Europe at the period of the migrations is totally different from the polychrome style which was current in the Roman provinces and in Italy during the first and second centuries A.D. The provincial and Italian style has nothing to do with South Russia: it is the outcome of the Syrian polychrome style on the one hand, and of the ancient Celtic polychrome style on the other. The Syrian style aims at providing a handsome gold setting for one or more precious stones, the Celtic at ornamenting objects, chiefly bronze objects, by means of coloured enamels in champlevé. This brief characterization must suffice: but I would gladly be corrected, if my definitions of the Syrian and Gaulish styles are beside the mark.

The aim and the character of the North Iranian polychrome style, as I have already noticed, are quite different. The problem which it sets itself is a more difficult one: it endeavours to transform the gold or silver surface into a field for colouristic display, for a symphony of sheer colour: the ground itself serves merely as a foil for the stone, providing a shining monochrome frame to intensify the play of tints. Accordingly the technical processes which this style prefers are the insertion of gems or cut stones into cavities surrounded by filigree; the arrangement of cut stones and gems, by means of cloisons, in geometric patterns; and the instalment of cut stones and pastes in openwork frames of gold.

This style, which originated in the East, and was highly elaborated in Iranian art, established itself in the steppes of South Russia and Siberia during the Hellenistic period: here it underwent considerable modification at the hands of Greco-Iranian artists, and when the Goths came, it was adapted by the Sarmatians to the objects which the Goths introduced into South Russia from their northern home.

Down to this period, the Iranian polychrome style, developed by Sarmatians and Greeks in South Russia, was virtually confined to the Russian steppes. A few specimens were brought by the Sarmatians to the Danubian provinces. But when the Goths, with Sarmatians and Greco-Sarmatians in their train, poured into Central Europe, and spread thence to Southern Europe and Northern Africa, they took with them the Sarmatian art which served to decorate their arms, their fibulae, their garments, their vases: the shapes of these objects remaining, partially at least, Germanic. Since the use of the Syrian and Celtic polychrome styles was already widespread in Central Europe; since, under the influence of imports from the Syrian East, the artistic taste of the population was turning more and more towards polychromy; and since Europe was being gradually transformed into a group of states in which the dominant classes were Germanic: it is not to be wondered at, that the whole of Central and Southern Europe now adopted the Irano-Sarmatian polychrome style, and substituted it for, or combined it with the Syrian and Celtic styles, which were much poorer, and over refined for the taste of the conquerors of Europe. Naturally enough, in each of the new European and African states, the style was modified and associated with the local art varieties of the polychrome style thus arose, the Lombard, the Vandal, the Spanish, the Frankish or Merovingian, the Anglo-Saxon. But the source of the style should not be forgotten: nor need it astonish us, that the style continued to flourish in its original homes, in Sassanid Persia, and in South Russia; and there, perhaps, with greater splendour than anywhere else.

One more remark, to finish our sketch of the polychrome style. It was not through conquest only that the style was propagated. It was mainly through commercial intercourse that the polychrome style penetrated to northern Europe, especially central, eastern and northern Russia and the Finnish and Germanic north: above all, through the constant communication between southern and central Russia, along the great Russian rivers; and between the Germanic tribes settled in Russia, and those which had remained in the north. Thus the northern branch of the polychrome style arose. It differs from the central and southern European branch in being an offshoot of the northern branch of the Sarmatian style, the branch which preserved a close connexion with the animal style.

Let us now turn to the animal style. Its history is much more difficult and complicated. I have spoken of the animal style several times in the course of this work: but I must recapitulate the principal features of its evolution, to make its development in South Russia clear, and to indicate the channels by which it made its way into western Europe. Unfortunately no one has ever examined the general evolution of the animal style, from the artistic and historical point of view. Special aspects have been dealt with, but no comprehensive study exists. Yet I am convinced that without such a study it is impossible to elucidate the many complex problems which are presented by the animal style of the Middle Ages.

What is the origin of the animal style? Which came first in order of time, the animal style or the geometric? I do not know that a definite answer can be given. I do not believe that the evolution proceeded on the same lines everywhere, or that everywhere, as at Susa, the animal style preceded the geometric and enriched it with new motives. Without committing ourselves to ill-founded theories, we may affirm that the animal style is very ancient. I will not speak of the palaeolithic period: but as early as the neolithic period, it plays, in some regions, a predominant part in the ornamentation of clay vases and other objects. The classic example is the neolithic pottery of Susa.

In the Copper Age, as we have seen, the place of the animal style in decorative art was an exceedingly important one. We find the animal style at every turn, especially in carved and engraved objects of metal, bone, or stone. The system of decoration is very primitive, and recalls the palaeolithic system. The surface of the object is covered with naturalistic figures of animals, sometimes broadcast, sometimes arranged in horizontal or vertical rows.

In Mesopotamia, a number of radical innovations were made, which introduced certain new principles of decoration. These principles were of the highest importance, and have remained classic down to our own time. Side by side with the arrangement of animals in series, and with their haphazard distribution over the surface, the Sumerian Age in Mesopotamia employed all the schemes which afterwards became normal in the animal style generally. The heraldic combinations of two or three animals; of two animals and an inanimate object; of two animals and a human figure; or of two human figures and an animal. The combination of two or three animals in a close-knit group, where one of the animals may be replaced by a human figure: the favourite scheme being that of a fight between two animals, or between a human or divine being male or female, and one or two animals. The contortion of an animal figure to suit a given space:—crouching animal with head reverted; couchant animals forming a frieze or even a circle, a motive taken from the cat tribe. A continuous succession of animal figures, so that the space is filled with a close network of animals, one attached to the other, the hunting motive being the commonest. Lastly, the termination of objects by figures of animals or animal heads.

Each of these schemes might be illustrated by a number of examples from the Sumerian period: I shall not linger over the matter, but merely refer the reader to Heuzey's great works, and to the excellent analysis recently published by Professor Ludwig Curtius.

These schemes of naturalistic animals were accompanied by another very important innovation: the introduction into decorative and symbolic art of special symbolic and fantastic creations formed by the amalgamation of favourite animals of the period with each other and sometimes with human beings: lions, eagles, snakes, bulls, perhaps sheep and goats; mostly winged. It was thus that the popular types of fantastic animals with a religious significance arose: the two types of griffin—with a horned lion's head, and with an eared eagle's head, both crested; the two types of dragon—with a snake's or a crocodile's head, horned or not; the well-known type of the sphinx. All these types spread far and wide, eastward, westward and northward. I cannot dwell upon this subject either. I must point out, however, that the Sumerian innovations exercised a powerful influence upon the entire ancient world. This influence can be observed everywhere, in Egypt, in Hittite Asia Minor, in Babylonia and Assyria, in the Aegean and Mycenaean world in Cyprus and in Phoenicia, in Phrygia, Lydia, Cappadocia, Paphlagonia, Lycia, in Etruria and in Sardinia, and finally in continental, island and colonial Greece.

In Greece, the style flourished during the archaic period, but gradually gave way to other decorative conceptions, richer and more subtle. It persisted, however, in the East. In Assyria, above all, it underwent a remarkable development. Assyria, and the countries dependent on Assyria, retained all the schemes mentioned above, but introduced a number of rather important alterations. The animal ornamentation becomes more and more purely decorative: the animal figure loses all reality, and comes to be used as a mere ornamental motive, like vegetable and geometric motives. On Assyro-Persian sword-hilts in the Louvre, and from Carchemish in the Ashmolean, the very ancient scheme of a lion devouring a goat is reduced to a lion attacking the head of a goat: the next stage is the gradual transformation of both lion and goat's head into a collection of lines, and the fantastic combination of them with floral ornament. This is but one example; many could be given.

The Iranian world was strongly influenced by Assyria and its civilization, especially in the first millennium B.C. But at the same time it certainly had a civilization of its own, and a comparatively independent art. The Iranian world probably created the animal style usually called Scythian. I shall examine this style in some detail, for the animal style nowhere attained so high a development as in South Russia during the period of Scythian ascendancy. All the varieties of the Oriental animal style are represented, the most archaic as well as the most elaborate. From the sixth century B.C. onwards, we find objects strewn all over with figures of animals, such as the axe from Kelermes (pl. VIII, 1), the stag from Kul-Oba, the fish of Vettersfelde: objects decorated with groups of fighting animals; heraldic combinations animals and groups of animals forming a dense network which covers the whole surface of the object, as in the phiale from Solokha (pl. XX, 3); and so forth. Several of these motives were borrowed directly from Oriental art, others were transformed by Ionian artists and reached South Russia in a modified, Ionian form. By the sixth century, three main currents are observable in the animal style of South Russia: an Assyro-Persian current, an Ionian current, and a current which may be called Scythian. These currents influenced each other and gave rise to hybrid forms.

The purely Scythian variety, the only one which is used to decorate horse trappings, though affected by the two others, preserves a pronounced individuality and is always readily distinguishable. The animal style was never so purely ornamental as in the variety which established itself in South Russia at the Scythian epoch. It would be an embarrassing task to catalogue all the features of this style and to classify all its variants. We notice, first of all, that the general tendency is the same as in the classical East. The animal figure is subordinated to its ornamental purpose: hence it is often treated arbitrarily and fancifully. The attitudes are sometimes wholly unnatural: The common Eastern motive of the animal with reverted head is frequently exaggerated; the hindquarters being turned in the opposite direction to the forepart (fig. 21, F, H). A round space is decorated with a circle of lions or other felines: a common modification is to make the animal bite its own tail (fig. 21, C). Sometimes two animals biting each other's tail are grouped together (fig. 21, B). The artist is quite ready to cut the animal into pieces and to use the head, or even the flanks, foreleg, or hindleg as a separate motive. The favourite heads are heads of birds of prey (figs. 21, E and 22, B), lions (fig. 22, F), elks (fig. 22, A, C), reindeer (fig. 22, H), wild goats (fig. 21 D), boars, wolves (fig. 22, D). The heads or foreparts are frequently grouped in pairs or in triangles, or even form a complete wheel, oddly reminiscent of the solar wheel (fig. 21, D, E). Heads of birds or griffins lend themselves particularly well to fantastic combinations. Remember the standard from the Kuban, in which the bird's eye plays an important part: we find the same procedure in fourth and third-century plaques from the region of the Dnieper (fig. 21, E). The lion's head is also in regular use. It goes without saying that the bird's heads, griffin's heads, and lion's heads are reduced to their essential elements and geometrically stylized. All that remains of the bird's head is a beak and huge eye; of the lion's head, the ears, the eyes, and a vestige of the muzzle.

The *horror vacui*, it has been said, is strongly pronounced in Scythian art. Not more, I should say, than in decorative art elsewhere. What makes our objects look so strange, is that the voids are filled almost exclusively with animals or parts of animals. The artist likes to give the object the shape of an animal: but he does not hesitate to cover this animal with other animals or parts of animals.

Still more peculiar is the tendency to shape the extremities of animals as animals or parts of animals. Look at the lion of Kelermes: each paw has the form of a lion with reverted head; the tail is composed of a row of such lions (pl. IX, 1). The heads used for this purpose are generally bird's heads or griffin's heads. In works decorated in the Scythian animal style, the paws, the tail, the ends of the horns, the ears, seldom retain their natural form: they are usually transformed into birds' heads (e.g. fig. 22, C and E). In figures of horned beasts, stag, elk, reindeer, wild oat, the propensity has particularly free play. Oxen, we may remark, hardly ever appear, sheep rarely. The style looks as if it had been invented by a race of hunters.

HORSE TRAPPINGS – ANIMAL STYLE – VI-III CENT. B.C.

Fig. 21.

I have already referred to the choice of animals. Side by side with the favourite animals of Oriental art as a whole—the cat tribe, especially the lion; and fanciful creatures—we find others which are not familiar to Greek or Oriental decorative art: reindeer, elk, wolf and horse. The animals of the Ionian animal style appear chiefly on objects which show strong Ionian influence or were actually made by Ionian artists.

The motives of the Scythian animal style are sometimes combined with floral motives, especially palmettes (fig. 22, A-C). Still more interesting, palmettes are occasionally made out of purely animal motives. Here is an elk's head, in which the horns, wildly exaggerated, form a real palmette (fig. 22, H). Here, a stag at rest, whose horns make a sort of floral ornament above its head (fig. 21, G). So in fanciful animals also, for example in the griffin, with stag's antlers, figured on fig. 21, H. Sometimes the bodies and heads of heraldic animals compose a palmette, a kind of arabesque in which the bodies are lost and only the ornament appears (fig. 22, G—two lions; fig. 22, I—two stags): at other times the palmette is composed of the heads alone, set on excessively long necks (fig 22, F).

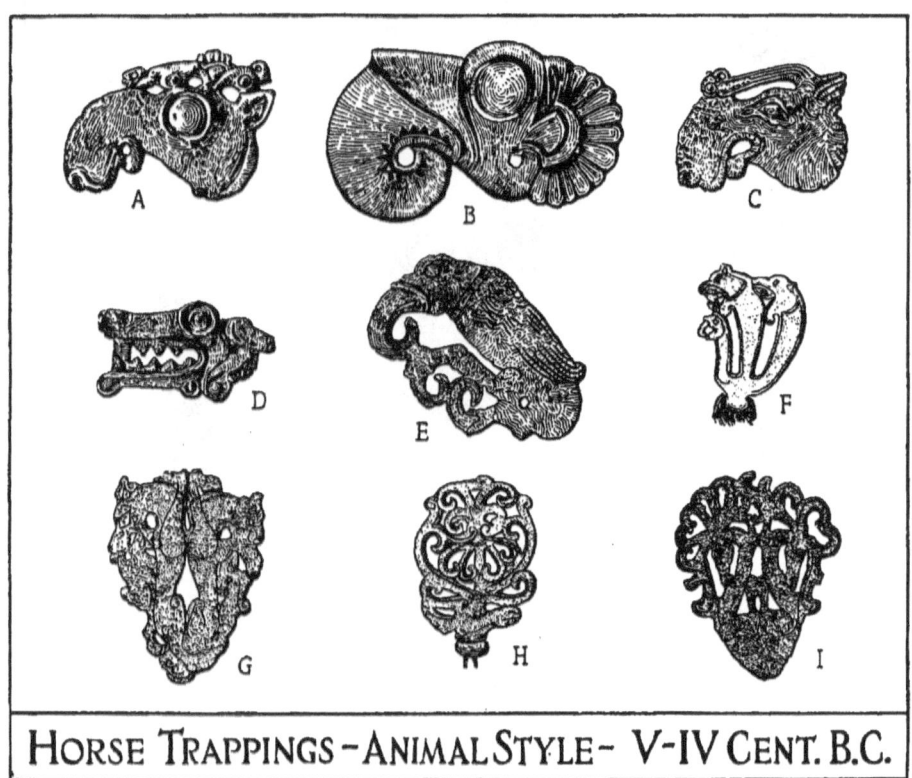

Fig. 22.

I cannot enumerate all the variations of the Scythian animal style. It would be well if a complete repertory of the motives were compiled. They are at present scattered in publications which are not always easily procurable. Moreover, the greater part of the objects have never been published: the initial task would be to collect and photograph them. Hundreds of variants would come to light.

The variety of the animal style which I have briefly described is not a product of South Russia. As early as the sixth century B.C. we find it fully formed. Historical analysis shows, that apart from the pieces which show strong Greek influence, this variety finds remarkable analogies in the contemporaneous art of Iranian Asia, and is thereby connected with the late Assyrian animal style. But it also contains elements which are northern rather than eastern. The elk and the reindeer are entirely foreign to Mesopotamian and Persian art. The appearance of the northern element has been accounted for by supposing that the style arose in western Siberia, in the region of Minussinsk. True, that in this region, from the Bronze Age onwards, we find a similar style. But first, the Minussinsk style shows no signs of evolution: it remains almost stationary, and is much poorer in motives than the Scythian animal style. And secondly, the Siberian style, though very awkward, clumsy and rude, is by no means primitive. It is a decadent and a derivative style. It bears marks of Assyrian influence, but this influence was indirect: the Assyrian elements reached Siberia through another medium, and were distorted before they arrived.

The only theory, which really accounts for the genesis of the Scythian animal style, places its origin in a country which roughly corresponds to modern Turkestan, but which also comprises the mountain region of Altai, rich in metals, where tombs have been discovered which resemble those on the Kuban. It was here that an Iranian people, the Sacians, in constant intercourse with Assyria, formed the animal style which they afterwards brought with them to South Russia.

The theory of the Central Asiatic origin of the South Russian animal style is not new. But I have found no definite proof of the theory in any work on the subject. Such a proof, as far as I can judge, is furnished by the following considerations. It is well known that the animal style, in conjunction with the geometric, forms the basis of the ornamental style of the earlier Chinese art. The early system of ornamental art in China is a topic which I cannot discuss at length: I have devoted a special article to it: 'South Russia and China, two centres of the animal style'. But I should like to lay stress upon certain peculiarities of earlier Chinese art which, as far as I know, have never been properly emphasized. By earlier Chinese art I mean the art of the Chu dynasty (1122-250 B.C.). From the mass of archaic Chinese objects, many scholars have tried to separate a group of monuments earlier than the Chu dynasty. But there is no possibility of dating these objects, as no systematic excavation has ever been conducted in China, and the Chu dynasty is our only landmark. This matter, however, is of little importance to us, for the system of decoration in the earlier group coincides, in the main points, with the system of the Chu dynasty.

The chief fact which issues from the study of early Chinese art is this. Even in the earlier monuments, we find a definite, well characterized system of decoration: a combination of decoration in the animal, and in the geometric style. Which is the more ancient we do not know. The basis of the decorative system is of course the animal style. But the closest study of the monuments fails to establish the priority of the one or the other style. All that can be proved is that the animal decoration cannot be traced back to the geometric. Let me now describe briefly the peculiarities of the Chinese animal style.

(1) The principle of decoration consists in a combination of motives of the animal and of the geometric style, the animal motives forming the foundation. The geometric motives—mostly combinations of ribbons—serve to connect the animal motives, and assume very primitive forms, mostly primitive spiral and maeander patterns. The ribbons often end in heads of animals.

(2) The scale of the animal motives does not greatly vary. Complete figures of naturalistic animals are exceptional: half-stylized tigers, fishes and perhaps snakes.

(3) The leading part in the ornamental system is played by fantastic, symbolical animals of four types: (*a*) a griffin with a horned lion's head, the head being usually adorned with a crest; (*b*) a griffin with an eagle's head, the head being eared and crested; (*c*) a dragon or snake-griffin, with the head horned, toothed, sometimes eared, and sometimes crested; (*d*) the same dragon, but hornless. It goes without saying that these types were not invented in China. All four, as we know, were favourite types in Babylon-Assyrian art, which had inherited them from Sumerian art. It is impossible to suppose that such peculiar creations were invented independently by Sumerians and later by Chinese: for we find very primitive forms of these fantastic beings in Sumer, and the lion, for example, was quite unknown to Chinese art throughout the period of the Chu dynasty.

(4) Complete figures of animals, whether realistic, like the tiger, or fantastic, are rare. The chief basis of Chinese decoration is constituted by *parts* of these animals, especially heads.

(5) The heads are used both in naturalistic reproduction, giving all the details, and in geometric schematizations, where the heads are reduced to their most characteristic and most prominent features. The head of the lion-griffin appears as a combination of geometrized crest, horns, eyebrows, eyes, ears, and muzzle; the head of the eagle-griffin as a combination of beak and eyes, both occasionally assuming the form of a primitive spiral; the tiger-head is reduced to the same elements as the lion-griffin's head, excepting the crest and the horns. I need not remind the reader that these peculiarities are the peculiarities of the Scythian animal style as well: compare the pole-top from Ulski on the Kuban (pl. X, 1).

(6) Just as in the Scythian animal style, the eyes and beak of an eagle-griffin are very commonly used to replace the extremities of parts of an animal body.

(7) The various bronze vases, which are the most characteristic products of Chinese art under the Chu dynasty, very often take the shape of the fantastic animals mentioned above, or of a combination of such animals.

I will not support my definition of the main features of Chinese art in the Chu dynasty by references to particular monuments. A glance at the illustrations in Münsterberg's history of Chinese art will suffice. But I should like to describe one of the most characteristic and at the same time one of the richest and most elaborate examples of the animal style in China, the beautiful bronze vase in the collection of Mrs. E. Meyer at New York, which is at present exhibited on loan in the Metropolitan Museum, and which is reproduced, with the owner's kind permission, on pl. XXXI, 1. A vase which is almost a pendant of Mrs. Meyer's is in a private collection in Japan; it is reproduced, insufficiently, by Münsterberg in his *Geschichte der Chinesischen Kunst*, ii. 132, fig. 204.

The vase takes the form of six combined foreparts of fantastic animals. The upper part of the front of the vase consists of the head and neck of a lion-griffin with sheep's horns; the lower part, of the head, crest and forelegs of an eagle-griffin, the head being reduced to the beak, the big eyes, which are shaped like spirals, the ears and the crest. The legs are those of an eagle and cover the forelegs of the vase. The surface of the vase is covered on both sides with three figures of dragons, the bodies of which are shaped like broad ribbons and form primitive maeanders. Under the back of the eagle-griffin we notice the wing and leg of an eagle-griffin. The cover of the vase, that is, the back of the horned lion-griffin, is adorned with realistic figures of beasts—two tigers turned to the left, with reverted heads, two fishes and two snakes (?). The back of the vase and the handle each consist of two superposed foreparts of fantastic animals. The back shows two superposed heads: the head of a lion-griffin with horns in the form of two fishes, heraldically arranged and another, more geometrical head of the same, with enormous eyes, ears and horns. The hindlegs of the vase have the form of two geometrized human figures. The handle consists of a tiger's head issuing from the mouth of the lion-griffin's head which constitutes the upper part of the back of the vase: the mouth of this tiger's head holds the lower part of the handle—the forepart of a dragon with two legs in the form of human legs with two large eyes. The whole surface of the vase is covered with a net of minute geometric ornaments in the form of spirals and maeanders.

The vase is truly a strange combination, a rich symphony of motives of the animal style. But to us, who have studied the Scythian animal style, there is nothing in it unfamiliar. Objects in the form of beasts' heads are common in Scythia: common also the geometrization of the heads, the tendency to cover the surface of the objects with figures of other animals, the predilection for the symbolic animals of the Assyro-Babylonian repertory, the idea of giving the parts of an animal the form of other animals (compare the fishes on our vase with the fishes which make the wings of the fantastic creatures on the scabbards from Kelermes and Melgunov's barrow, pl. VIII, 2), the use of parts of the body for separate ornaments (the wings on the Maikop belt, pl. XXV, 1; compare the Chinese vase, of the same type and time as Mrs. Meyer's, in a Japanese collection, Münsterberg, ii, p. 132, fig. 203); and so forth.

I would draw attention to one more feature of the Chinese animal style, not represented in the New York vase, but common both on Chinese vases of the Chu dynasty and in the Scythian animal style. I refer to the combination of floral and animal motives, that is, the treatment of the extremities of animal and parts of animals as quasi-floral patterns, often combined with eagles' beaks and eyes.

These striking coincidences between the Scythian and the Chinese animal style cannot be accidental. The fact that motives borrowed from Assyro-Babylonian art are paramount in both speaks for itself. I have not the slightest doubt that both countries received the animal style from a common source: I mean Iranian Central Asia. The Chinese adopted the elements of this style, dealt with them freely, in accordance with their artistic temperament, and formed a new and peculiar decorative style: the Scythians developed their style in close connexion with Persian and Greek art. This explains why the two styles, in their final shape, are utterly different. But their common origin is evident. We shall see later a repetition of the phenomenon in the China of the Hellenistic epoch—the period of the Han dynasty.

The Scythian animal style endured for centuries in South Russia. It came under various influences, especially Greek influence; and developed in several directions of its own accord. There were two branches of the style in South Russia. One, the eastern, clung to the old traditions and produced interesting developments of them. This branch probably maintained regular relations with Central Asia, the original home of the Scythian animal style. This is shown by recent finds on the Kuban, those of the 'Seven Brothers' and of the barrows at Elisavétinskaya, which belong to the fifth or fourth century B.C. It was this branch which devised the ingenious motives of the horns and the animal palmettes, and which adapted the heraldic pair of animals for the purpose of ornament. Nothing of the sort is to be found in the western portion of the Scythian state, on the Dnieper and the Bug, during the period of its prime, the fourth and third centuries B.C. In western Scythia the animal style was by this time moribund: proof meets us at every turn: there are no new forms, no token of creative power, nothing but dry repetitions of ancient designs. Take for example the gold-plated sword-sheath from Solokha. The native artist has chosen the ancient motive of the lion devouring the deer, in its Ionian form. But see how he has treated it: the lion has become a mere conglomeration of strokes, without modelling and without plastic value; the deer, like the earlier deer in Persian art, is reduced to a schematic head. The decadence is complete. And so in thousands of other objects.

PLATE XXXI

1. CHINESE BRONZE VASE OF THE CHU DYNASTY
First Millennium B.C. Collection of Mrs. E. Meyer, New York
(*Copyright Mrs E Meyer, New York*)

2, 3. TWO BRONZE PLAQUES FROM A CHINESE GRAVE OF THE
HAN DYNASTY. Metropolitan Museum, New York

The Sarmatians, who succeeded the Scythians, adopted and cultivated the animal style. It is hard to say whether they borrowed it from their predecessors or not. On the one hand, the Sarmatian style shows a fondness for motives which are by no means favourites in the true Scythian animal style, the style which was uninfluenced by Ionian art. The Sarmatian repertory consists chiefly of fights between animals, and of separate animals, naturalistically rendered, arranged in rows and sometimes grouped with human beings. There is also a tendency, in the Siberian examples, to place the animals and men in a landscape setting, a tendency foreign to the Scythian style, which is essentially ornamental. The inference is that the Sarmatians brought with them a stock of animal motives which differed from the Scythian stock, and which had been constituted under the influence of a Hellenized Oriental art. The nearest analogy is the art of Parthia and Sassanid Persia.

On the other hand, it is probable that the development of the Sarmatian animal style was strongly influenced by Scythian art: for the Sarmatians took over most of the peculiarities of the Scythian style, and adapted them to their own cherished and traditional motives. In the Sarmatian style, as in the Scythian, we find animal extremities formed as heads or figures of animals; horns converted into ornament; contorted animals; and so forth; in the Siberian group, a predilection also for northern fauna.

All these considerations lead me to suppose, that the Sarmatian animal style originated in a stock of motives brought by the Sarmatians from their old home; and that the style developed under the influence of the Scythian animal style, in particular of its northern and eastern branch, the branch which we know from the monuments of the Kuban on the one hand, and those of Minussinsk and the Altai mountains on the other.

A distinguishing feature of the Sarmatian animal style is its polychromy. The Scythian animal style is almost entirely monochrome. We have already spoken of Sarmatian polychromy, and need not discuss it here. It is possible that polychromy formed an integral part of the Sarmatian animal style from the outset.

We noticed above that there were two branches of Sarmatian jewellery: the southern, on the Kuban and in the state of the Bosphorus; and the northern, on the Don and in Siberia. It was the northern branch which cultivated the animal style, of which there are only vestiges in the southern branch. These vestiges it carried with it into western Europe, in particular the use of birds' heads for ornament. Birds' heads, as we know, played an important part in the so-called Merovingian and Gothic style of jewellery. The Scytho-Sarmatian animal style left a few other traces in the Gothic jewellery of the West. For example, the combinations of birds' heads, the friezes of crouching animals, and the like. More significant, but more difficult to determine, is the influence of the northern branch of Scytho-Sarmatian jewellery, the branch which preserved its love for the animal style.

I spoke of the northern branch in my sixth chapter. I showed that there was a powerful revival of this style on the Kuban, and to some extent in Siberia. In its finest products, such as the Maikop belt or some of the plaques from Siberia, it reached a very high artistic level. Some of the Siberian plaques exhibit a tendency towards a naturalism and an ethnographic realism which are different from the naturalism and realism of Roman art. The same quality is observable on silver phalarae from the South Russian steppes. But it was not this tendency which carried the day. The old ornamentalism asserted itself once again, and the majority of the Siberian plaques show as great a fondness for purely ornamental composition as the creations of the Scythian animal style on the Kuban. We find the same contracted attitudes in the animals, the same decoration of the animal's body by means of other animals, the same animal stylization of the extremities, the same ornamental exaggeration of the horns. All these peculiarities occur together in the figure of an elk found at Verkhneudinsk (Minns, p. 275, fig. 192). The body of the elk is surcharged with a figure of a griffin and with the head of an eagle devouring a ram's head: the end of the tail is shaped as an eagle's head: the antlers form a kind of nimbus, and each tine terminates in the head of an eagle or a griffin.

It is clear, then, that the eastern and northern branch of the Sarmatian animal style had a career of great brilliance and intensity. Like the southern branch, it doubtless exercised a powerful influence on its neighbours. Its influence, however, did not spread westwards, but mainly to east and north. The Chinese world was deeply affected by it. The most characteristic features of Chinese life, especially Chinese military life, in the Han dynasty (206 B.C. - 220 A.D.) cannot be explained without assuming profound Iranian influence. It is to the credit of B. Laufer that he was the first to lay the proper stress upon this truth. Had he known the Sarmatian antiquities published by myself, he would certainly have been able to point out many other coincidences which are perhaps more remarkable than those which he noted. I shall deal with this topic at length in my article, already mentioned, on the relations between China and South Russia: for the present I will confine myself to a brief summary of the results of my investigation. I maintain that the whole military life of China was reorganized by the kings of the Han dynasty on Iranian lines. The Iranian influence reached China, not directly from Parthia or Bactria, but through the medium of the Sarmatian tribes, many of which, beyond doubt, took part in the Hunnish assaults upon China. The Huns had no culture of their own. They borrowed everything, especially in their military training, from a more cultivated race, the Sarmatians, and particularly the Alans. The indebtedness of China, in military matters, to the Sarmatians, is fully proved by the following facts. Laufer has shown that the new heavy cavalry of China was armed and trained on the same model as we described when we were speaking of the military life of the Sarmatians. But I must add, that the Chinese adopted not only their scale and ring armour from the Sarmatians, their heavy spears, and their conical helmets, but their arrows, with the characteristic triangular head, their short ring-headed daggers (almost identical with those found in Sarmatian graves on the Kuban and those represented in the figures of semi-Sarmatian warriors on the funerary stelai of Panticapaeum and Tanais), their horse-trappings, which during the Han and succeeding dynasties in China are purely Iranian, and last but not least their long swords, in which the guard, the pommel and the bottom of the scabbard are of jade, just as in the South Russia of the Sarmatian period. These jade ornaments, found both in China and in South Russia (scores of specimens have been found in Panticapaeum and in Sarmatian graves, often with remains of the iron swords), are almost identical in the two countries, and are made of the same material, the jade of Central Asia. But Sarmatian influence was not restricted to the military life of Han China. I have every reason for supposing that the habit of interring dozens of clay figures with the deceased, to represent the funeral procession, and the type of funeral procession itself, were borrowed by the Chinese from the nomadic peoples of Central Asia (compare the description of Scythian funeral processions on pp. 45, 49, 99). It is noteworthy that the clay figures of the gods of Death, regularly buried with the dead in China, are Iranian: one of these figures reproduces the type of the Iranian horned lion-griffin; the other—a half-human, half-leonine figure, the head of which is covered with the skin of an elephant (usually, but wrongly, called a unicorn), reminds one of the portraits of Alexander the Great wearing the elephant helmet, of the symbolic figure of Egypt with the same head-dress, and of the portraits of Bactrian and Tibetan kings. One more coincidence: strange figures of clay are commonly found in the graves of the inhabitants of Panticapaeum in the first and second centuries A.D., the period of strong Sarmatian influence: fantastic half-human, sometimes grotesque creatures of various types; a puzzle to archaeologists. Exactly similar figures are found by the dozen in Chinese graves of the Han dynasty. Laufer considers them to be personifications of various diseases.

Here I must leave the subject. The relationship between China and South Russia is not new to the scientific world. As early as 1896, Reinecke pointed to similarities between certain Scythian and Sarmatian objects and certain Chinese. Some of his comparisons are not convincing: but some remain: the same rattles in Chinese and in Scythian graves; the same forms of mirror in Sarmatian and Chinese graves; similar shapes of cauldron. But Reinecke's explanation of the resemblances is certainly wrong. The phenomena which we have observed in the military and religious life of China under the Han dynasty show that we have no right whatever to speak of Chinese influence on South Russia, on the Scythian and Sarmatian world. The opposite is true. The Chinese of the Han dynasty, remodelling their life and their civilization to meet fresh requirements, borrowed many features from their Central Asiatic neighbours. A measure of Sarmatian influence is also noticeable in the art of the Han dynasty. It is shown, first and foremost, by the hundreds of belt-plaques and plaques for horse-trappings which the Chinese of the Han dynasty manufactured for themselves on Sarmatian models. Many such have been found in Chinese graves of the Han period, and many have been published by Chinese archaeologists in their archaeological albums. The best specimens are reproduced in pl. XXXI, 2 and 3. Both plaques were found in Northern China, near the Chinese Wall, in a grave of the Han period they are now in the Metropolitan Museum of New York. One of them reproduces, feature for feature, the dead horse of the Maikop belt and of the Siberian old plaque in the Hermitage (pl. XXV); the other has a figure of a horse, in the same scheme, killed by two beasts—a lion, and a bear or perhaps a lioness.

Other equally remarkable coincidences have been observed by Sir Hercules Read and by Minns. The motives of these plaques are entirely foreign to Chinese art of the Chu dynasty. They must have been seen by the Chinese on Sarmatian warriors, and reproduced by Chinese artists as forming part of the new equipment, which was almost wholly Sarmatian. But the main stream of Chinese art in the Han dynasty was not influenced by these plaques. In Chinese art they remained an accident. This does not mean that Chinese art of the Han dynasty was unaffected by the influence of the Iranian animal style. But that influence did not affect the composition of the ornamental symphonies, and it is more noticeable in details than in the general scheme. In the details, however, the influence was exceedingly strong: I may mention the motive of the head and eyes of the eagle-griffin, a motive which is constantly being employed for ornamentation by the Chinese artists of the Han period; the use of vegetable forms for the extremities of animals; the use of figures heraldically confronted; the freedom with which the animals are treated for ornamental purposes: all these features are characteristic both of the Chinese animal style in the Han dynasty, and of the Sarmatian. We should also notice the spread of landscape elements in the decoration of varnished clay vases these elements were probably borrowed directly, together with the figures of warriors and hunters, from Parthian art.

I cannot develop my ideas on this subject more fully in this place. It is enough for my purpose to have proved the diffusion of Sarmatian culture and art to the East. It is no wonder that this powerful art spread to the West as well; and, particularly in its eastern, purely Oriental form, to the North, to the forests and swamps of Northern Europe.

I have already referred to the influence of the Scythian animal style upon the Iron Age in central and eastern Russia. The objects found at Ananyino and at Zuevskoe reproduce many of the motives which are characteristic of the Scythian animal style in the fifth and fourth centuries B.C. Later finds, of the Hellenistic and Roman epoch, in the region of Perm, give token of the same influence, which evidently spread along the Russian rivers to North Russia and the Baltic Sea. The animal style of North Russia preserves all the peculiarities of the eastern and northern branch of the Sarmatian animal style: animal extremities terminating in heads and beaks of birds or griffins; animal motive piled on animal motive, often in strange combinations; motives repeated in continuous series, sometimes forming a kind of fantastic lattice-work which immediately recalls Sarmatian art (fig. 23).

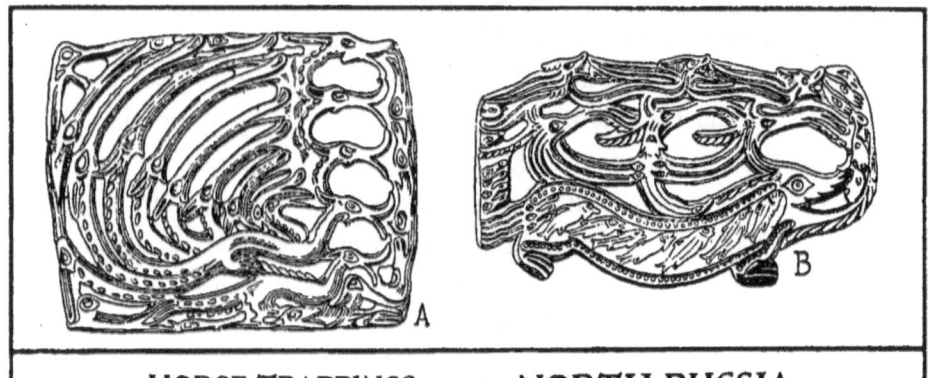

HORSE TRAPPINGS FROM NORTH RUSSIA

Fig. 23.

Now in examining this style, one cannot fail to recognize the remarkable analogies which it presents with the animal style of the Scandinavian countries.

I am not a specialist in the art of northern Germany and Scandinavia. I have studied the works on the subject, especially the classic work of Salin; I am acquainted with the articles and books of Goetze and others on Gothic art; and I took advantage of a stay, lasting several months, in Sweden and Norway, to scrutinize the specimens of the style exhibited in the museums of those countries. I formed the impression, that from the third or fourth century A.D., this art was strongly affected by Oriental influence. I regard the Germanic animal style as a very original development of the South Russian animal style; presenting all the peculiarities of that style; but schematizing and geometrizing it. Look at the evolution of the ornamentation on Scandinavian fibulae. There is the same fondness for the fanciful animals of the East; the same use of animal heads, especially beak and eye of griffin or bird of prey, to form extremities; the same treatment of the animal body as an ornamental motive; the same dislocation of animal bodies, with forepart turned in one direction, and hindquarters in the other.

When I had the opportunity of inspecting the Viking funerary ship, recently discovered at Oseberg near Christiania (pl. XXXII), and the funeral furniture belonging to it, many features of that rich and luxurious art brought the Scythian animal style vividly before my mind. The carver of the sledges and wagons found in the ship took almost all his motives from the animal style. The animals which he used to create his Oriental symphonies were not the fauna of the north—there are no reindeer or elks, and very few deer—: but mainly the creatures of Oriental fancy, lions, griffins bird-headed or lion-headed, and sphinxes. When he has a large surface to cover, he uses an intertexture of various fantastic figures, with curiously contorted bodies, treated in a purely Oriental manner. Sometimes this intertexture forms regular palmettes, and just as in the Scythian animal style, the original animal motives can hardly be made out. Sometimes the animals, on which the decoration is based, suggest the fantastic fauna of Scythian, Sarmatian and Siberian art, and of the objects from Perm. But when the Scandinavian craftsman sets to work on a separate head, he does his very best, and produces real gems: but Orient gems. I cannot dwell longer on this topic, but I am convinced that it is impossible to understand the Scandinavian art of the first millennium A.D., without previous study of the objects in the Scythian animal style. There have indeed been scholars, who have turned their attention to the Scythian monuments, in the hope that these would shed light on Scandinavian art. But they have never studied the subject thoroughly: they have been content to select and analyse a few isolated monuments, and compare them with Scandinavian works. I am sorry to say that they have done their cause more harm than good. We must apply ourselves to the complete series, and study it historically.

That Scandinavian art should be derived from the Oriental art of South Russia is not surprising. We have seen that the South Russian style spread to North Russia by way of the Russian rivers. We must remember, that the arrival of the Goths in the South Russian steppes was neither the first nor the last appearance of Germanic tribes in South Russia. Excavation in the Dnieper valley has given proof of strong Germanic influence in those quarters as early as the first century A.D. From that time the Germanic tribes steadily advanced southwards, and entered into contact with the Scytho-Sarmatian civilization. It is no wonder that the Scytho-Sarmatian civilization spread north-west as well as north-east.

PLATE XXXII

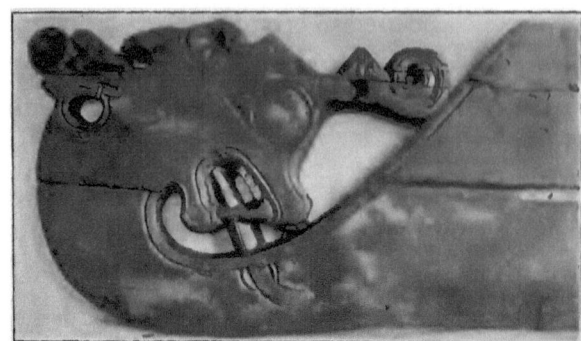

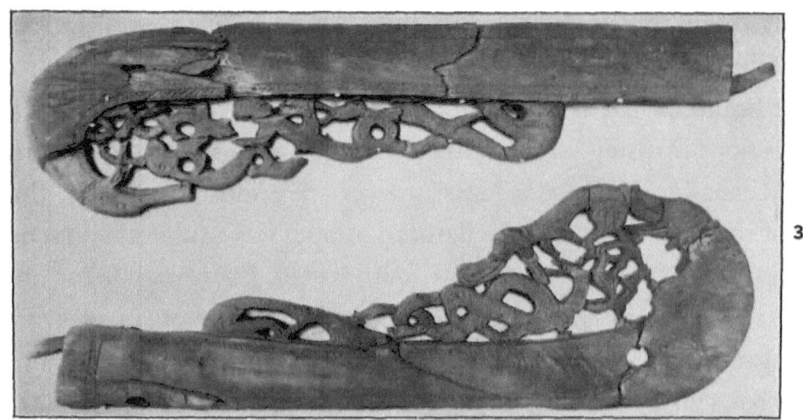

WOODEN ORNAMENTS OF THE FURNITURE OF THE OSEBERG
SHIP FROM NORWAY
Museum, Christiania

Much more intricate is the question of the relation borne by Romanesque and so-called Gothic art to the Oriental animal style. I cannot venture to discuss it: but I will say that I have noticed more than one curious and significant coincidence.

My task is drawing to a close. I will sum up the principal ideas which have guided me in my investigation. The characteristics of South Russian civilization are the same in the classical period as in subsequent centuries: and the types of phenomena are the same. South Russia was always one of the most important centres of civilization. Three main currents are traceable: an eastern current, proceeding from both Iranian and Mesopotamian Asia by two routes, the Caucasus route, and the Russian steppe route; a southern current from Asia Minor and Greece, which brought with it the splendid civilization of Greece; and a western and northern current, by means of which Russia partook in the civilization of central and northern Europe. The three currents met in the Russian steppes, coalesced, and formed a great civilization, quite independent and extremely original, which influenced, in its turn, central and northern Russia, and central Europe as well. The sudden development of Russian civilization, in the ninth century A.D., on the banks of the Dnieper, and its rapid diffusion over the whole of Russia, have been counted a very extraordinary thing: the princes of Kiev, in constant intercourse with Byzantium and the East, appear to us, from the very beginning, as enlightened monarchs who succeeded in founding a great centre of civilization and art at Kiev. It all seems natural enough, if we remember that the State of Kiev was only one member of a long series of civilized states in South Russia that it was not the first state to establish close relations between South Russia and Greece lastly, that long before, other states had paved the way for the advance of southern civilization over the country which later became Russia, and that even the intercourse between the Dnieper and the Germanic north, and the intercourse between the Dnieper and the region of the Danube, were already very ancient in the ninth century. I am convinced that it is wrong to make the history of Russia begin in the ninth century. In Russia, as in all European countries, the date must be put back many centuries: the history of modern Europe should begin in the protohistoric and classic period.

IX.
THE ORIGIN OF THE RUSSIAN STATE ON THE DNIEPER

IN the ninth century, when the Russian annals first begin to give us a systematic record of the Russian people and its princes, Russia appears as a well-developed body, as an organized state possessing its own peculiar political, social and economic structure and endowed with a high and flourishing civilization. Russia of the ninth century consisted of many important commercial cities situated partly on the Dnieper and its tributaries, partly in the far north on Lake Ilmen, and partly in the east on the upper Volga. Each of these cities possessed a large territory populated by various Slavonic tribes, and had its own self-government with a popular assembly, a council of elders, and elected magistrates. To defend its flourishing trade, the population of each town issued an invitation to a special body of trained and well-armed warriors commanded by a prince; this prince was also entrusted with the tasks of collecting tribute from the population and of carrying out certain administrative and judicial duties. These princes with their retinues were generally of Germanic blood, and chiefly Norsemen, who were called in Russia Varangers. One of these ninth-century princes succeeded in uniting all the Russian cities under the rule of one dynasty, and in forming out of them a single, though not very firmly established state, with its capital on the Dnieper—Kiev.

Nothing similar to this kind of federation of large commercial self-governing cities, ruled by an invited, that is, a hired dynasty, existed at that time in Western Europe with its well-known feudal structure. In the history of the formation of the Russian state everything is peculiar and original: the exclusively commercial character of the cities, the wide extension of Russian commerce, which reached Constantinople in the south, Central Asia, China and India in the east, and the Baltic and White Seas in the north, the sharp distinction between the self-government of the cities and the primitive tribal organization of the country, the contrast between the prehistoric manner of life in the country population and the high standard of civilized life in the cities, and, last but not least, the unparalleled combination of foreign military power and well-organized self-rule in the frame of a single city state.

All these peculiarities of Russian origins and the extraordinary differences between Russia and western Europe are still unexplained. Why should Russia begin her evolution with commerce and city life and western Europe with agriculture and the so-called feudal system? Why is it that Russia developed a feudal system much later, not earlier than the thirteenth century, when western Europe had already begun to abandon that system? Why even then did Russian feudalism assume peculiar and original forms which bear little resemblance to the corresponding phenomena in western Europe?

In spite of many attempts by both Russian and western European scholars to solve this problem, it remains unsolved. The main reasons for this failure are as follows. It is a mistake to begin the history of Russia with the Russian annals in the ninth century, that is, to confound the history of Russia with the history of the Slavonic race. The history of Russia as an economic and political organism is much more ancient than the earliest references to the Slavonic race. Russia as a country existed long before the ninth century, and formed part of the civilized world even in the classical period and in the period of migrations. At this epoch the main lines of future evolution were already laid down. We must therefore treat the history of Russia not as the history of the Slavonic race but as the history of the country of Russia. I am convinced that, if we treat the history of Russia from this point of view, many of the alleged difficulties will disappear at once, and the history of Russia in general will appear before us in an entirely new light. Let me go more into detail and try to explain from this point of view the political and social structure of the Kievan princedom in the ninth and tenth centuries.

In the preceding chapters I have tried to show what were the conditions of life in the steppes of South Russia before it was occupied by the German tribes. Let me summarize once more the main features of the social and economic life of this period. During this whole period the leading part was played in the steppes of South Russia by different nomadic tribes. One replaced another: the Cimmerians were driven out and conquered by the Scythians; the Scythians gave up their sovereignty under the pressure of the Sarmatians; but the main structure of the states successively formed by these tribes was almost the same. A small minority of nomads with a strong and effective military organization ruled over a large majority of conquered peoples and tribes. Some of these tribes were themselves nomads, but most of them were agriculturists established on the rich plains of South Russia or half-nomadic hunters and bee-keepers in the forests and marshes of Central Russia. The relations between the rulers and the ruled were of the simplest description: the ruled paid their masters a tribute in kind (money was not used either by the subjects or by the masters; in the graves which belong to the pre-Sarmatian, that is to say, the pre-Roman period, we never find coins), and were probably forced to serve them in their military expeditions. The fact that so many 'Scythians' were sold in the Greek colonies of South Russia and went abroad as slaves (for instance, the 'Scythian' archers who formed the police force of Athens in the fifth and fourth centuries B.C.) seems to bear witness to a free disposal of the conquered population by the conquerors, to a kind of potential slavery. I must emphasize, by the way, my conviction that most of the slaves sold to the Greeks under the name of Scythians did not belong to the ruling tribes of Iranian conquerors but to the conquered native pre-Scythian population. The name 'Scythians' for the whole population of the Scythian kingdom was in general Greek use during the fifth and fourth centuries B.C., and so in the fourth book of Herodotus.

These political and social conditions explain the peculiar economic life of South Russia during the Greco-Scythian and the Greco-Sarmatian periods. The main foundation of the strength and the wealth of the ruling Scythian tribes was not their productive activity, which was very primitive. As pure nomads they produced only milk, butter and meat for themselves, and hides for commerce. The whole wealth of the Scythian kings and princes, as shown by the enormous riches buried with them in their graves, depended on their *commercial* activity, on the active part which they took in the international trade of the period. The objects which are found in the Scythian and Sarmatian graves and which have been analysed in the preceding chapters offer eloquent testimony to the importance of Scythian commerce, and enable us to determine the great commercial routes which were used by the Scythians in their international commercial relations. The main route was, of course, the route of the great South Russian rivers to the Black Sea. The Greek merchants paid regular visits to the Scythian trading centres on the Bug, the Dnieper and the Don, and carried with them to the Greek harbours on the Black Sea enormous quantities of food-stuffs and raw materials. These food-stuffs and raw materials were partly the tribute paid by the subjects of the Scythian kings: grain and fish which were furnished by the settled population of the banks of the great rivers and their tributaries, hides paid by the nomads, furs, wax and honey by the hunters and bee-keepers of the forests. But part of this merchandise was itself the product of the lively commerce which naturally grew up between the inhabitants of the Scythian kingdom and the independent Finnish tribes of Central and Eastern Russia, who dwelt on the middle and upper courses of the great Russian rivers: Volga, Oká, Kama, Don, Donets, Dnieper, Pripet, Desná. Moreover, products of the Far East were brought to South Russia by the caravans which started from Central Asia and Western Siberia and made for the shores of the Black Sea. The merchants of Central Asia and Siberia were doubtless obliged to sacrifice a proportion of their merchandise as tribute or custom duties to the Scythian rulers of South Russia, who retained part for their own use, and sold part to the Greek merchants. Here again, a traffic between these merchants and the inhabitants of South Russia was bound to grow up.

The age-long existence of such commerce, protected by the military forces of the Scythian state, contributed on the one hand to increase of productivity in the Scythian state itself and in the neighbouring countries, and on the other hand to the development of numerous commercial centres of the city type on the banks of the Russian rivers. The Greek geographers of the fourth and third centuries B.C. do not tell us the names of these cities, as they had no independent knowledge of South Russia and mostly repeated the data of the Ionian geographers of the sixth century B.C. But the geographers of the Hellenistic and Roman epoch, especially Ptolemy, enumerate scores of such places on the banks of the Bug, the Dnieper, the Don and the Kuban. The half-Greek city of the Gelonians, mentioned by Herodotus, was undoubtedly of this type. I have already mentioned the remains of such cities, partially but unsystematically excavated by Russian archaeologists, and the large rich cemeteries which surround them. The most brilliant period of these native cities is shown by the contents of the graves to have been the fourth and third centuries B.C. The population of the cities, according to the objects found in the graves, was a mixture of Greek, Scythian and native elements. Most of the inhabitants must have been merchants.

These cities contributed largely to the formation of constant and regular commercial relations between the shores of the Black Sea and the whole of Central and Northern Russia including the shores of the Baltic. They indicated for all future generations the main commercial highways of Russia, and above all, the great river route from Scandinavia to Constantinople, the future route 'from the Varangers to the Greeks'.

When the Scythian state was destroyed by the joint efforts of the Sarmatians, the osphoran kingdom, the Thracians and the Celts, the place of the Scythians was taken by different Sarmatian tribes. These new formations were by no means stable. Each Sarmatian tribe tended to move westward with the object of reaching the flourishing and civilized Roman provinces. A state of anarchy began to prevail in these lands. The first to exploit this state of anarchy were the Germans. It is well known that in the first century B.C. and the first century A.D. the German tribes showed a tendency to get into touch with the Greco-Roman world both in the west and in the east. They followed the footsteps of the Celts, who in the third and second centuries B.C. had flooded the whole of the Balkan peninsula and had reached even Greece and Asia Minor.

But the German advance was stopped in the west, both on the Rhine and on the Danube, by the Romans. The expeditions of Julius Caesar and of Augustus, and the military efforts of their successors during the first and the second centuries A.D., set up a strong barrier against the advance of the German tribes towards the west and the south. The armed frontiers of the Rhine and the Danube, where Rome concentrated her best military forces, were an insurmountable barrier against the Germans. No wonder if the wave of German tribes was deflected towards the east and the Germans used for their advance to the south the only open and unprotected way, the way which they had known for ages—the great river route 'from the Varangers to the Greeks', the route of the Dnieper.

I have already dealt with this movement. The archaeological data prove with certainty that it began as early as the first century B.C., and became very important in the first and second centuries A.D. We have already seen that, just at this time, German cemeteries and German settlements become common on the Dnieper. One of the most important features which characterize the German graves in Western and Southern Russia is the presence, side by side with certain homemade objects, of large quantities of objects imported from the Greco-Roman world—especially Greco-Roman pottery (such as terra sigillata), Greco-Roman glass-ware, jewellery, &c. A new phenomenon is that the trade of the Greco-Roman world with the Dnieper basin and Russia in general no longer took the form of barter, as in the Greco-Scythian period, but was carried out by means of coined money, Roman silver and copper, the universal currency of the period. Coins of the Bosphoran kings found access even to the Germanized regions of South Russia. Characteristically enough, however, the Sarmatian tribes of South Russia still preserved the ancient Scythian habit of barter, and did not accept Roman and Bosphoran coins, even gold.

It is a pity that there are no full statistics about the finds of Roman coins in South Russia, whether in graves, or in the form of hoards. Observations collected by Russian and foreign scholars, especially the Swedish scholar Arné, show that the trade was liveliest in the second and third centuries A.D., especially in the second, between the reigns of Nerva and of Septimius Severus. Most of the coins belong to the reigns of Antoninus Pius and Marcus Aurelius. The finds are thickest in the region of Kiev, Poltava and Chernigov, that is, in the region where civilized life had attained a high level during the final period of Scythian domination, the fourth and third centuries B.C. But this region was no longer in direct communication with the Bosphoran kingdom, and no longer formed a commercial province of that state. The scarcity of Bosphoran, and the prevalence of Roman coins in the region of the middle Dnieper show that the Bosphoran kingdom was driven from the region of the Dnieper and turned its attention exclusively to bartering with the Sarmatian tribes, while the German population of the Dnieper region entered into direct relations with the Roman provinces of the Danube, and thus came to form, no longer a part of the Greek commercial world, but a kind of annex to the Roman Danube trade. The same conditions prevailed in the region of the upper Dnieper and as far north as the shores of the Baltic Sea. Roman trade was also supreme in the districts which now belong to the Polish state. Thus once again, as in the period before the Greek colonization of the shores of the Black Sea, the west took the leading part in the civilized life of Western and South-Western Russia.

Various Roman objects of the first and second centuries A.D., found in Eastern Russia and Western Siberia, raise the question, whether Eastern

Russia and Western Siberia also belonged to the domain of Roman provincial trade. As far as our knowledge reaches, I am inclined to think that these objects were imported to the region of the Kama and to Siberia not from the region of the Dnieper, but up the Volga, through the medium of the Bosphoran kingdom, which held constant intercourse both with the Volga region and with the steppes of Western Siberia.

This change in the orientation of the commercial relations of Western and South-Western Russia was due to the German occupation of the valleys of the Dnieper and its tributaries. In their own country, the Germans had regular commercial relations with Italy, Gaul, the Alpine and the Danubian Roman provinces. No wonder if, after their occupation of the valley of the Dnieper, they preserved these commercial relations and developed them. It is only natural to suppose that in their expansion towards the south and the east they constantly came into conflict with the Sarmatian tribes which were moving in the opposite direction, towards the west. These constant collisions made it impossible to maintain the old trade relations between the Dnieper and the Bosphoran kingdom, and created conditions which were exceedingly favourable for the merchants of the Roman Danube provinces.

In their gradual occupation of the Dnieper basin, the Germans did not aim at destroying the existing commercial relations and the existing commercial centres. They tried to use these relations for their own profit. No wonder therefore that they do not appear to have destroyed the cities in South Russia. It seems on the contrary that they rather increased the number. The large number of cities mentioned by Ptolemy and located by him on the Dnieper gives the impression that the Germans were more anxious to develop the cities than to do away with them. Further investigation will show if I am right in assuming such a tendency in the Germans of South Russia.

In any case, it is only in the light of this gradual occupation of the Dnieper basin by the German tribes during the early period of the Roman Empire, that we are able to understand the invasion of South Russia by the Goths, and their speedy and successful conquest of the shores of the Black Sea. The Gothic invasion was not the first but the last act of the age-long activity of the Germans in South Russia. If we are right, as I think we are, in assuming the existence of a large German population on the Dnieper in the first and second centuries A.D., we can easily understand that the Germans, some of whom were daring sailors, hankered for the sea-shore, which would give them the opportunity of plundering and holding to ransom the eastern part of the Roman Empire, and of entering into direct commercial relations with the wealthy East. We must not forget that the constant relations of the Germans with Olbia had showed them how much richer and more attractive the Roman East was than the Roman West. It is not to be wondered at, if they used the first opportunity, namely, the internal troubles in the Roman Empire which prevented the Romans from protecting their Greek 'allies' on the shores of the Black Sea, for invading the steppes of South Russia and capturing, first of all, the important harbours of Olbia and Tyras. The capture of Olbia and Tyras was a military necessity, because these cities with their Roman garrisons were the chief obstacle against the Germans seizing and settling down on the shores of the Black Sea. The seizure of Olbia and Tyras did not mean the complete destruction of these cities. Coins and inscriptions show that the cities continued to exist for some scores of years after they were captured by the Goths. But they ceased to be important commercial centres, as the Goths, like the Kievan princes later, preferred to enter into direct relations with the Greek cities on the Thracian Bosphorus and the southern shore of the Black Sea.

We do not know much about the history of the great Gothic state thus established on the shores of the Black Sea, either during its independent existence, or during the supremacy of the Huns. One fact however is characteristic. The Goths did not attempt to destroy the Bosphoran kingdom, and after vanquishing the Sarmatians they preferred to enter into a kind of alliance with them. We know that the Bosphoran kingdom continued to exist, perhaps under the rule of a new dynasty, which was apparently not of German stock but of Sarmatian origin. We know also that the Alans preserved their independence, and continued to exist and to rule on the banks of the Kuban and perhaps of the Don as well. Moreover, the Bosphoran kingdom maintained its commercial relations with the Roman Empire. The rich fourth-century graves already mentioned, were among other objects we notice silver dishes inscribed with the name of the Emperor Constantius, show that the Bosphoran kings received 'presents' (disguised tribute) from the Roman emperors. The Goths probably used Panticapaeum, their vassal, as they used Olbia and Tyras, both as a starting-point for their expeditions against the

Roman Empire, and as a harbour which allowed them to receive goods not only from the Orient through the Sarmatians, but also from the eastern provinces of the Roman Empire. The large quantity of objects of Greek workmanship found both at Panticapaeum and at Chersonesus in graves of the fourth and fifth centuries A.D., and the spread of Christianity in both places at the same epoch, show that the relations between these cities and the Roman Empire were not always hostile. We have every ground for supposing, that Chersonesus never became subject to the Gothic kings, but was kept and fortified by the Roman emperors of the fourth century as the last stronghold of Roman power in the Crimea. An inscription of Valentian published by myself, and certain traditions, half legendary and half historical, which date from the time of Constantine, illustrate the efforts of the Roman Empire to protect Chersonesus from Gothic and Bosphoran attacks. These data show that the period of Gothic domination in Russia was not simply a period of constant Gothic attacks on the Roman Empire by land and sea. We may suppose with great probability that the Goths resumed the threads of the ancient commerce of Russia both with the Orient and with the Greek world. Like their predecessors, the Goths formed an exclusively commercial and military state, and this state lasted for more than two centuries. An important feature of this new formation was that the Gothic state was not ruled by nomads, but by tribes which in their own country were accustomed to the settled life of farmers, warriors and sailors. The Huns who displaced the Goths in South Russia were of course nomads. We know practically nothing of their relations with the Gothic and Sarmatian tribes in South Russia. But the part which the Germans and the Iranians took in the expeditions of the Huns against the Roman Empire, and the fact that they survived until the fall of the Huns, preserving the tribal organization of their state, shows that even during this domination they were vassals of the Huns rather than peoples absorbed by the Mongolian invaders. The Gothic epoch was accordingly a revival of the Scythian and the Sarmatian state in a new shape, a shape which reminds us of the later Slavonic state on the Dnieper and the shores of the Black Sea.

The Germans—warriors and keen sailors—were always attracted by the wealth of the Roman Empire. As soon as they felt that the mighty organism of the Roman Empire, in the critical period of the third century, was beginning to weaken and to break up, they renewed their attacks on the Roman provinces.

The weakest point in the Roman Empire was of course the Danube frontier, a long and difficult frontier without a civilized hinterland. But to overcome the Germans' superstitious fear of the Roman legions, supposed invincible, and to transform scattered attacks into an overwhelming movement, a strong shock from behind was needed. This shock was dealt to the German tribes in Russia by the first Mongolian invaders of Europe, the mighty Huns. Under their pressure a detachment of the German tribes, and of the Iranian tribes with which the Germans lived in a kind of federation, the Visigoths and the Alans, made the first rush into the Roman Empire. The consequence is well known, and I need not repeat the story. Soon after, the Huns themselves under Attila, dragging with them the Ostrogoths and scores of German and Iranian tribes, followed the victorious march of their predecessors.

The outcome of these events was of the utmost importance for Russia. In the fifth and sixth centuries Russia was swept clean of her German, Iranian, and Mongolian rulers and inhabitants. Small fractions of the Alans remained on the Kuban where they still dwell under the name of Ossetes; some tribes of Goths were left behind in the Crimea (the kingdom of Mangup near Chersonesus) and on the Taman peninsula (the Tetraxite Goths near Phanagoria); scattered bands of Huns, after their downfall, came back to the Russian steppes; but not one of these groups played any part in the future destinies of Russia. The place of the Germans was soon occupied by a new European people, the Slavs. They had originally dwelt, as far as our knowledge reaches, on the northern slopes of the Carmathians, towards the Vistula and the Baltic Sea. According to Ptolemy and to Jordanes, they were well known to the Romans, and were divided into three parts—the Wends, the Sclavenes and the Antes. During the domination of the Goths in South Russia they were vanquished by them and formed a part of the Gothic Empire, under a kind of vassalage. But in the sixth century the same Jordanes, a Goth himself who was well acquainted with the condition of north-eastern Europe, knew of their continuous settlements on the Dnieper and of their occupation of the steppes as far as the Black Sea. It is evident therefore that the Slavs repeated the movement of the Germans and replaced them in South Russia. Thus the founded in South Russia a state of the same type as the Germans before them, and naturally inherited from them their towns, their trade relations, and their civilization. This civilization was not, of course, a German one, but the ancient

Greco-Iranian civilization of the Scythians and the Sarmatians, slightly modified. At the very outset of their life in South Russia they were threatened by a great danger. New conquerors of the same stock as the Huns, the Avars, tried to overpower them and to drag them into Western Europe. But the young Slavonic federation was strong enough to repulse this attack and to annihilate the Avars, giving rise to the old Russian saying preserved by our Annals: 'They perished like the Avars'.

The Slavs took firm root on the Dnieper, and spread widely to the north and to the east, occupying all the old highways of commerce. In the north they developed Novgorod, in the east they founded Rostóv, in the south, opposite Panticapaeum, Tmutarakán. The conditions were favourable. Their ancient relations with the Germans secured them the military help of wandering Scandinavian chieftains, who were prepared to serve and to fight for any one, provided that they had good opportunities of enriching themselves. The Germans helped the Slavs to find the ancient way to Constantinople and to protect their commercial fleet on the Dnieper. Southward, the rule of the new masters on the Volga, the Mongolian tribe of the Khazars—the peaceful rule of a trading people—guaranteed them the Oriental market. So they grew strong and rich and developed a lively trade with the German north, the Finnish north-east, the Arabic south-east, and especially the Byzantine south. This was as before the main source of their civilization and their wealth, and it dictated the forms of their political and social life. Their centres were as before the great cities on the Dnieper, and the most important of these cities was of course Kiev, thanks to her wonderful geographical situation in the middle of the Dnieper basin, midway between the Baltic and the Black Sea.

In the light of this historical evolution, the history and structure of Kievan Russia, the Russia of the eighth to the twelfth centuries, assume a new form. The Russia of Kiev was at the same time the last link of an ancient historical chain and the first of a new one. Kievan Russia was the immediate successor of the series of commercial states which had replaced one another in the steppes of South Russia from time immemorial, and at the same time the mother of the subsequent Slavonic Russian states in Western Russia (the Galicia of to-day), on the upper course of the Dnieper (the modern White Russia), and, most important of all, between the upper Volga and the Oka, Great Russia, the *Russia* of modern times.

Kievan Russia, in the first period of her evolution, naturally inherited all the peculiarities of her predecessors. Like them she was an almost purely commercial state; like them she tried to occupy the shores of the Black Sea; and her political and cultural life, like theirs, faced south and east, towards Greece and the Orient, and not west, towards the Western Roman world. It is only natural therefore that the civilization of the Russia of Kiev was a southern civilization, an offspring of classical culture in that Greco-Oriental aspect which was characteristic of Byzantium and the Byzantine Empire. Kiev and Novgorod in Russia were little Constantinoples; so were Trebizond on the southern shore of the Black Sea, the gorgeous Georgian capital, Ani, and the various centres of the Balkan Slavs, especially Sofia in Bulgaria and Belgrade in Serbia. We must not forget that the main centre of political, social, religious and economic life both at Kiev and at Novgorod was the cathedral of S. Sophia, which stood in the same relation to the palace and the person of the Kievan Great Prince (Velíki Knyaz) as the great S. Sophia of Constantinople to the Byzantine emperor and his residences.

But Russia did not receive the whole heritage of the Greco-Oriental civilization. She had not the same opportunities in the East as Italy, France and Spain in the Western classical world. The strivings of the Kievan princes towards the Black Sea and the Caspian Orient were not successful. Svyatosláv, of course, nearly succeeded in destroying and conquering the two strongholds of Oriental civilization in Eastern Russia—the Kaganate of the Khazars on the Volga and the Don, and the kingdom of the Bulgars on the Kama. But his successes were temporary. The Khazars were soon replaced in the steppes of South Russia by a new Mongolian horde, the Pechenêgs: and when the Kievan princes had almost managed to reduce the Pechenêgs to comparative harmlessness, a new and powerful tribe of Mongolians appeared in the South Russian steppes—the Polovtsy or Cumans. The forces of the Kievan princedom were almost entirely absorbed by the constant struggle with these dangerous enemies, who received regular reinforcements from the Orient; and Russia was gradually cut off from the south and the east. She was driven into the Central Russian forests and swamps and into the Carpathian mountains. The final blow to Russia was struck by the hordes of the Tatars, a branch of the mighty Mongolian kingdom in Central Asia. Against such an enemy Russia in her Kievan condition was powerless. The Tatars occupied all the highways of commerce towards the east seized the mouths of the great Russian rivers, drove the Russians from the Dnieper and made them their vassals. Like the Scythians between the eighth and the third centuries B.C., they kept the still important trade with the Western world in their own hands, using as intermediaries the Italian colonies on the Black Sea and in the Crimea, the heirs of the Greek colonies—Kafa (formerly Theodosia), Sudak, Kerch (Panticapaeum) in the Crimea, Akkerman (the ancient Tyras) on the Bug, and the rest. The Russian part in this trade was reduced to furnishing the Tatars with the products of the Russian forests, in the form of tribute. The Russians were forced to retreat to the Carpathians in the west, to the swamps of the upper Dnieper and the Pripet in the north-west, and to the forests of the upper Volga and the Oka in the east.

But in retreating the Russians carried with them the traditions of Kievan Russia and the important achievements in civilized life which had been the result of their constant relations with the Greek and Oriental world during the centuries in which the Kievan state had existed. We must not forget that these centuries enabled the Russians not only to use the blessings of classical civilization, but also to form their own Slavonic classical culture, a culture similar to the Byzantine, but at the same time highly distinctive. The wonderful bloom of art in the Russia whose capital was the city of Vladimir, during the eleventh, twelfth and thirteenth centuries, and in the Galician Russia of the same period, shows how deeply classical civilization had taken root in Russia. The Tatar yoke prevented the Russians from developing this inheritance to the full and from becoming the complete successors of the Byzantine Empire. But this inheritance enabled the Russia of Moscow to escape dissolution in the sea of Eastern nomads, to preserve her nationality, her religion and her state, and later to enter the family of European nations with her own peculiarities and her own national spirit.

In this new period, the development of Russia had no longer its old orientation towards the south and the east. The force of circumstance—the decay of civilized life in the Byzantine Empire, the pressure of the Tatars—made Russia look westward, towards the Baltic; to join Western Europe and its cultural development now became the ultimate goal of Russian effort.

Cut off from the Oriental trading routes; impeded in their movement towards the west by the Germans, the Lithuanians, the Poles, and later the

Swedes; the Russians ceased to be a nation of merchants, and the Russian state became an agricultural state, a state of peasants and landowners. Thus Russia, in a comparatively late period of her existence, set foot on the path which was characteristic of the development of feudal Europe in the early Middle Ages. But here also the peculiar conditions of Russian history made the progress of Russia in this path slow and strange.

History knows no pauses and interruptions in its evolution. Nor are there any in the history of Russia. The Slavonic is one of the epochs in the evolution of Russia as such. But the Slavonic race succeeded in accomplishing one cardinal thing, which neither the Thracians nor the Iranians, neither the Germans nor the Mongolians had been able or willing to perform. For these peoples Russia was an expedient to achieve their main aim—the conquest of Western Europe. For the Slavs, Russia was their final aim and became their country. They bound themselves to the country for ever: and Russia is indebted to them, not only for her name, but also for her peculiar statehood and civilization.

Bibliography

Chapter I. General Bibliography

A. *History of the archaeological discoveries in South Russia.*

M. Rostovtzeff, article on South Russia in the book presently to be published by the Russian Academy, *La Science russe*.

B. *General works on South Russia.*

1. Ebert, *Südrussland im Altertum*, Bonn and Leipsic, 1921 (not accessible to me).

2. Professor N. Kondakov, Count I. Tolstoy, and S. Reinac, *Antiquités de la Russie méridionale*, Paris, 1891 (French translation of the three first volumes of the general work, *Russkiya Drevnosti* (Russian Antiquities))

3. J. Kulakovski, *The past of Taurida*, 2nd ed., Petrograd, 1915 (in Russian).

4. Lappo-Danilevski, Scythian Antiquities; *Transactions of the Russian Archaeological Society in St. Petersburg, Slavonic Section, IV, 1887* (in Russian).

5. Ellis H. Minns, *Scythians and Greeks*, Cambridge, 1913.

6. M. Rostovtzeff, *The Greeks and the Iranians in South Russia*, Petrograd, 1918 (in Russian).

7. E. von Stern, *Die griechische Colonisation am Nordgestade des Schwarzen Meeres im Lichte archäologilscher Forschung, Klio ix, 139 ff.*

8. Id., *Die politische und sociale Struktur der Griechencolonien am Nordufer des Schwarzmeergebietes, Hermes I (1915) 161 ff.*

9. M. Rostovtzeff, *Journal des Savants*, 1920 (general account of the South Russian discoveries and of the learned works on South Russia from 1912 to 1918).

10. M. Rostovtzeff, South Russia in the Prehistoric and Classic Period, *American Historical Review*, xxvi (1921), 203 ff.

C. *Sources*.

(*a*) Literary.

1. E. Bonnell, *Beiträge zur Altertumskunde Russlands*, vols. i, ii, St. Petersburg, 1882, 1897.

2. V. V. Latyshev, *Scythica et Caucasica e veteribus scriptoribus Graecis et Latinis collegit et cum versione Rossica edidit B. Latyshev. Vol. I, Auctores Graeci. Vol. II, Auctores Latini* (published in Transactions of the Russian Archaeological Society of St. Petersburg, vol. xi, 2, and vol. ii of the classical series). A collection of quotations on South Russia from the Byzantine writers: by the same author: in preparation.

3. M. Rostovtzeff, *Studies in the History of Scythia and the Bosphorus*, vol. i, Sources, part 1 (Literary Sources) (in the press; in Russian).

(*b*) Epigraphic.

V. Latyshev, *Inscriptiones antiquae orae septentrionalis Ponti Euxini*, vol. i (1st ed. 1885. 2nd ed. 1917); vol. ii (1890; second edition in the press); vol. iv (addenda) (1901). St. Petersburg, Russian Archaeological Society. [Quoted *I.o.s.P.E.*]

(*c*) Numismatic.

1. P. Burachkov, *General Catalogue of the Coins of the Greek Colonies... within the bounds of what is now Russia*, part 1, Odessa, 1884 (in Russian).

2. A. Berthier-de-La-Garde, *Corrections to P. B.'s General Coin Catalogue*, Moscow, 1907 (in Russian).

3. Minns, l.l., p. 661 ff. (Coin plates) and *passim*.

4. *Moscow Numismatic Society, Numismatic Miscellany*, 1908-1916 (4 volumes).

5. Rostovtzeff, *Studies, &c.*, part ii, Epigraphic and numismatic sources.

(*d*) Archaeological.

1. *Antiquités du Bosphore Cimmérien conservées au Musée impérial de l'Ermitage*, St. Petersburg, 1854 (i-ii, text; iii, plates). Republication of the French text (in abbreviated form with many additions) and the plates by S. Reinach, *Bibliothèque des Monuments figurés*, Paris, 1892 (with copious indices, containing references to the C.R. (see below). Archaeological Commission. [Quoted A.B.C.]

2. *Antiquités de la Scythic d'Hérodote*, i (1866), ii (1873), and Atlas. St. Petersburg, Archaeological Commission. [Quoted A.S.H.]

3. Minns, l.l., chaps. vii-xiii.

4. Rostovtzeff, *Studies*, p. iii, Archaeological Sources.

5. Y. I. Smirnóv, *Argenterie orientale. Recueil d'ancienne vaisselle orientale en argent et or trovée principalement en Russie*, St. Petersburg, 1909.

6. M. Rostovtzeff, *Ancient Decorative Painting in South Russia*, i, text (in Russian), ii, plates (in Russian and French), St. Petersburg, 1913; the same, *Ancient Decorative Wall-painting, Journal of Hellenic Studies*, xxxix (1919).

D. *Periodicals.*

1. *Compte rendu de la Commission [Impériale] Archéologique* (after 1917 without the epithet *Impériale* like the other publications of the [Imperial] Archaeological Commission): 1859-1881, yearly reports (in French and Russian), and supplements by Stephani (in German and Russian), and Atlas; 1882-1888, report (in French and Russian) and Atlas; 1889-, brief reports (in Russian only) with illustrations, no Atlas. Full reports on archaeological excavation from 1898 in *B.C.A.* (see below). [Quoted *C.R.*]

2. *Bulletin de la Commission [Impériale] Archéologique*, 1901- (65 parts in 1918), with special bibliographical supplement. [Quoted *B.C.A.*] A new series of the Bulletin was started in 1921 under the title *Bulletin of the Russian Academy of the History of Material Civilization*. [Quoted *B.A.M.C.*]

3. Materials for the Archaeology of Russia, 1866- (37 parts in 1918). [Quoted M.A.R.]

4. *Transactions of the Historical and Antiquarian Society of Odessa*, vols. i (1844) to xxxii (1915).

5. *Bulletin of the Tauric Record Commission*, i (1882) to liii (1916).

6. *Transactions of the Archaeological Congresses*, vols. i (1869) to xv (1911) [Full list in Minns, l.l., pp. xxv ff.]

7. B. Farmakovski, Reports on archaeological excavations in South Russia, published yearly (last report (for 1913) printed in 1914) in the *Archaeologischer Anzeiger* of the *Jahrbuch des Deutschen Archaeologischen Instituts*, with copious illustrations (quoted as Farmakovski, A.A.).

8. Report (with illustrations) for the years 1916 and 1917, *B.C.A.*, 65 (1918), 157 ff.

CHAPTER II

1. *Painted pottery in South Russia.*

Minns, l.l., 132 ff.; compare Karl Hadaczek, *La Colonie industrielle de Koszylowce de l'époque énéolithique*, Lvov, 1914; M. Hörnes, *Urgeschichte der bildenden Kunst in Europa*, 2nd ed. (1915), 304 ff. and 606 ff.; new finds by Himner near Uman in the Ukraine; E. Majewski, *Bulletin et Mémoires de la Société d'Anthropologie de Paris*, 1913, 226; compare U. B., *L'Anthropologie*, xxvi (1915), 575 (clay model of a house and a dwelling-area on piles, found together with painted pottery). Clay model of a wagon-house found in a grave of the copper period near the Ulski aul (on the Kuban), *B.C.A.* 35, 1 ff.; Farmakovski, *A.A.* 1910, 195, fig. 1. Similar finds of models of houses in neolithic settlements have been recently made in Bulgaria: (1) Kodjadermen barrow near Shumen (B. Filow, *A.A.*, 1915, 218, fig. 1); and (2) barrow near Salmanovo (B. Filow, ibid., 1913, 343 ff., and *Bulletin de la Société archéologique bulgare*, iv (1914), 148 ff.).

2. *Incised pottery of the Kharkov government.*

Gorodtsóv, Bytováya Arkhéológia (Archaeology of Material Civilization), Moscow, 1910; *Transactions of the Archaeological Congress at Kharkov*, xii, 1902, and *Ekaterinoslav* xiii, 1905; *Report of the Historical Museum of Moscow* for 1916.

3. *The origin of iron.*

P. Oxy. x. 1241, v. 3 ff; Belek, *Zeitschrift für Ethnologie*, 1907, 359 and 363; O. Montelius, *Prähistorische Zeitschrift*, v (1913), 28 ff., esp. 328 ff.

4. *The Copper Period in the Kuban district.*

M. Rostovtzeff, *L'âge du cuivre dans le Caucase Septentrional et les civilisations de Soumer et de l'Egypte protodynastique*, Revue archéologique, 1920. Idem, *The Treasure of Asterabad*, Journal of Egyptian Archaeology, 1920.

5. *Pre-Vannic Antiquities in Southern Caucasus.*

Countess P. Uvárov, *The Cemeteries of Northern Caucasus, Materials for the Archaeology of the Caucasus*, viii (Moscow), 1900; A. Ivanovski, *In Transcaucasia*, ibid vi (Moscow), 1911; Farmakovski, *M.A.R.* 34 (1914), 37 (all in Russian); compare the reports on the excavations in supplement Transcaucasia made by A. Rössler and others in C.R. 1895-1905, and *Verhandlungen der Berliner Gesellschaft für Anthropologie*, &c., *Zeitschrift für Ethnologie*, 1895-1905. Previous publications: Chantre, *Recherches anthropologiques dans le Caucase*, i (1885); Fr. Bayern, *Untersuchungen über die ältesten Graber- und Schatzfunde in Kaukasien, Zeitschrift für Ethnologie*, 1885, supplement; J. de Morgan, *Mission scientifique au Caucase*, i, ii (1889); the same, *Mission scientifique en Perse*, iv (1896), 13 ff.; *Recherches au Talysch Persan, Délégation scientifique en Perse, Mémoires*, viii (1905), 251; W. Belck, *Verhandlungen der Berliner Gesellschaft für Anthropologie*, &c., *Zeitschrift fur Ethnologie*, 1893, 64; R. Virchow, *Abhandlungen der Berliner Akademie*, 1895, Phys.-math. Kl, 1 ff.

6. *Religious beliefs of the most ancient population in the Kuban district, and the Amazons.*

M. Rostovtzeff, *Le Culte de la grande de'esse et les Amazones en Russie méridionale, Revue des Etudes Grecques* (jubilee number, 1921).

CHAPTER III

1. *Cimmerians and Scythians in the eighth and seventh centuries.*

(*a*) Oriental tradition.

M. Streck, *Assurbanipal und die letzten assyrischen Könige bis zum Untergange Ninivehs*, Leipzig, 1916 (*Vorderasiatische Bibliothek*), p. ccclxxi, n. 1 (gives a good but incomplete bibliography). In addition to the bibliography given by this writer, see H. Winckler, *The History of Babylonia and Assyria*, London, 1907, 225; Jeremias, *The Old Testament in the Light of the Ancient East*, i (1911), 275; F. Wilke, *Das Skythenproblem im Jeremiabuche* (R. Kittel, *Alttestamentliche Studien*, 13 (Leipzig, 1913), 222); C. H. W. Johns, *Ancient Assyria* (1912), 116 and 136; W. Rogers, *A History of Babylonia and Assyria* (6th ed., 1915), ii. 320, 329, 412 ff.; Thureau-Dangin, *La huitiéme campagne de Sargon*, Paris, 1912, p. x ff.; Olmstead, *Western Asia in the days of Sargon of Assyria* (*Cornell Studies in History and Political Science*, ii), 148.; id., *Western Asia in the reign of Sennacherib*, American Historical Association, Annual Report (1909), Washington, 1911, 94; E. G. Klauber, *American Journal of Semitic Languages*, 28 (1911-12), 101 comp. 247; V. Smolin, *Transactions of Kazan University*, 1914 or 1915 (quoted from memory); S. Feist, *Kultur, Ausbreitung und Herkunft der Indogermanen*, Berlin, 1913, 404 ff.; G. Hüsing, *Völkerschichten in Iran, Mitth. der anthrop. Gesellschaft in Wien*, xlvi (1916) 199 ff; Lehmann-Haupt, Pauly-Wissowa-Kroll, *Real-Encyclopaedie*, ix, s.v. Kimmerier, cp. *Klio*, xvii (1920), 113 ff; H. Vambery, *Primitive Kultur der Turko-tatarischen Volker* (1879), 103 f., 133 (pleads for the Mongolian origin of the Cimmerians), cp. O. Schrader, *Sprachvergleichung und Urgeschichte*, ii (3rd ed.), 528.

(*b*) Vannic Kingdom.

Patkanov, *Journal of the Ministry of Public Instruction*, 1883, December (in Russian); V. Nikolski, *Cuneiform Inscriptions of the Vannic Kings discovered in Russia; Oriental Antiquities* (Moscow), i. 375-453 (in Russian), and various articles in the Transactions of the Russian Archaeological Society, Orienta branch; B. Turáev, *History of the Ancient Orient*, ii (1912), 46 (in Russian); N. Marr, *Bulletin de l'Académie des Sciences de Russie*, 1918 (results of the new excavations in Van during the War; quoted from memory);

Hyvernat, *Du Caucase au Golfe Persique*, Washington, 1892; Prásek, *Geschichte der Meder und Perser*, i. 50 ff.; H. Winckler, *The History of Babylonia and Assyria*, London, 1907, 225 ff.; Lehmann-Haupt, *Armenien einst und jetzt*; Hall, *The Ancient History of the Near East* (1913), 516; S. Feist, *Kultur, Ausbreitung und Herkunft der Indogermanen*, Berlin, 1913, 403. Archaeology: Lehmann-Haupt, *Materialien zur alteren Geschichte Armeniens, Gottinger Abhandlungen*, ix (1907); *Zeitschrift für Assyriologie*, vii. 265; ix. 95; *British Museum: A Guide to the Babylonian and Assyrian Antiquities*, 2nd ed. 1908, p. 106; Perrot and Chipiez ii. 224; Heuzey, *Origines orientales de l'art*, 231; Farmakovski, *The Archaic Period in Russia, M.A.R.* 34 (1914), 45 ff. Hittite inscriptions in Van: Hommel and Sayce, Proceedings of the Society of Biblical Archaeology, 1899 (xx), 238.

(*c*) Greek tradition.

Gutschmid, *Kleine Schriften*, iii. 430; v. 109; Duncker, *Geschichte des Altertums*, i^4. 395, i^5. 463; E. Meyer, *Geschichte des Altertums*, i^1. §§406, 424, 452-3; ii. 1, §286 i, 2^3, §529; compare § 423; Müllenhoff, *Deutsche Altertumskunde*, ii^2. (1906), 162, and iii (*passim*); E. Rohde, *Rheinisches Museum*, 1881, 555; E. Thraemer, *Pergamos*, Leipzig, 1888, 330; U. Höfer, *De Cimmeriis* (programme), Belgrad, 1891; Dittenberger, *Orientis Graeci inscriptiones*, N. 13, compare M. O. Caspari, *Journal of Hellenic Studies*, 1913 (35), 173; W. Leonhard, *Paphlagonia, Reisen und Forschungen* (1915), 298.

(*d*) Greek mythological tradition.

Count I. Tolstoy, *The White Island and the Taurike on the Euxine*, Petrograd, 1913. Compare my review, *B.C.A.* 65 (1918) 177 ff.

(*e*) Ninus and Sesostris.

Gutschmid, *Kleine Schriften*, v. 26 and 90 ff.; Sethe, *Untersuchungen zur Geschichte Aegyptens*, ii; *Zeitschrift für agyptische Sprache*, 41, 34 ff.; Maspéro, *Journal des Savants*, 1901, 594; E. Meyer, *Geschichte des Altertums*, i. 2^3, §281; W. Leonhard, *Hettiter und Amazonen*, 93, 1, compare 97 and Anhang vi. 270.

2. Thracian names in the Bosporus. M. Rostovtzeff, *B.C.A.* 63 (1917), 106.

3. Find of Temir Gora. C.R. 1870-1, p. xx, pl. IV (the carved ivories and the bronze implements of this find are still unpublished).

4. Find in the Taman peninsula. E. Prushevskaya, *B.C.A.* 63 (1917), 31 ff.

5. Find in Bessarabia. E. von Stern, *M.A.R.* 34, 1 ff.

6. Find at Mikhalkovo in Galicia. K. Hadaczek, *Zlote skarby Michalkowskie*, Cracow, 1904; *Oesterreichische Jahreshefte*, vi (1903), 115 ff.; ix (1906), 32 ff.; A Lebedyánskaya, *B.C.A.* 53 (1914), 29 ff.; A. Spitsyn, ibid., 135 ff.; Hörnes, *Urgeschichte der bildenden Kunst*,² 29 and 610. Compare the fibula of Dályi, M. Ebert, *Oesterreichische Jahreshefte*, xi (1908), 260 ff.

7. Massagetians, Minns, 111; Franke, 'Zur Kenntnis der Türkvölker und Skythen Zentralasiens', *Abhandlungen der Berliner Akademie*, 1904, 24 ff.

8. Scythian graves of the sixth to fourth century.

(*a*) Kuban district. Minns, 222 (Kelermes), 223 (Voronezhskaya), 224 (Kostromskaya), 227 (Ulski), cp. G. Borovka, 'The bronze Stag of the Ulski aul', *B.A.M.C.* 1921, 206 (Seven Brothers); Maryinskaya and Elizavetinskaya, N. Veselovski, *C.R.* 1912, 1913-15; *B.C.A.* 65 (1918), 1 ff.; Karagodeuashkh, Minns, 216 ff.

(*b*) Crimea and the Dnieper region. Golden Barrow near Simferopol, Veselovski, C.R. 1890, 4 ff.; Rostovtzeff, *M.A.R.* 37, 40; Tomakovka, *Antiquities of Herodotean Scythia*, pp. 62 ff., pl. XXVI; Rostovtzefi, l.l., 38 ff. Shumeyko barrow, Khanenko, *Les antiquités de la région du Dnieper*, iii, pl. XLV, 461 (on the excavations in this barrow in general, compare the introduction to vol. vi); Melgunov's barrow, Minns, 171 ff.

(*c*) Hungarian group. Minns, 150; Géza Nagy, *A Szkithák*, Budapest, 1909, p. 57; Hampel, *Fuhrer in der Altertumsabteilung des Ungarischen Nationalmuseums*, Budapest, 1911, 65, note 5; Hörnes, *Urg. der bild. Kunst²*, 428.

(*d*) Vettersfelde. Minns, 236; A. Furtwangler, *Kleine Schriften*, i. 469 ff.

(*e*) Caucasus. C.R. 1904, 131, figs. 239-43.

9. Scythian dress, weapons, and implements. Minns, 50 ff.

(*a*) Dress. Sarre and Herzfeld, *Iranische Felsreliefs*, p. 54; P. Stepanov, *History of Russian Dress, I: Scythians*, Petrograd, 1915.

(*b*) Headgear. M. Rostovtzeff and P. Stepanov, 'Greco-Scythian Headgear', *B.C.A.* 63 (1917), 69 ff. G. Borovka, B.A.M.C. 1921, 169 ff. A. H. Smith, *Journal of Hellenic Studies*, 1917, 135.

(*c*) Weapons. Sword. Rostovtzeff, *M.A.R.* 37, 51 ff; Stepanov, l.l. Corslet. Rostovtzeff, ibid., p. 62; A. Hagemann, *Griechische Panzerung, I. Teil: Metallharnisch*, Leipzig and Berlin, Teubner, 1920. Bow, arrows, and bow-case. Bulanda, *Bogen und Pfeil bei den Völkern des Altertums*, Wien, 1913 (ignores the Russian material); P. Reinecke, *Zeitschrift für Ethnologie*, xxviii (1896), 6, 8 ff., 20 ff.; H. Schmidt in R. Pumpelly, *Explorations in Turkestan*, Washington, 1908, vol. i, p. ii, p. 183; A. M. Tallgren, *Collection Tovostine*, 48 ff.; H. Blumner, Γωρυτός, *Berliner philologische Wochenschrift*, 1917, 1121 ff.

(*d*) Mirrors. Farmakovski, *M.A.R.* 34, p. 33; F. Studniczka, *Archäologischer Anzeiger*, 1919, 2 ff.

(*e*) Cauldrons. M. Ebert, *Prahistorische Zeitschrift*, iv (1912), 451; Zoltan v. Takács, 'Chinesische Kunst bei den Hunnen', *Ostasiatische Zeitschrift*, iv (1915), 174 ff.; A. M. Tallgren, *Collection Tovostine*, 46.

(*f*) Horse-trappings. E. Pernice, *Griechisches Pferdegeschirr*, Berlin, 1896 (56, Winckelmanns Programm); R. Zschille and R. Forrer, *Die Pferdetrense in ihrer Formentcklung*, Berlin, 1895 (ignores the South Russian material); Lefebvre des Noettes, *Annales du Service des Antiquités de l'Egypte*, xi (1911-12), 283 (especially Assyrian bridle, pl. II). Oriental horse-trappings (no good study). Perrot et Chipiez, *History of Art in Chaldaea and Assyria*, ii. 357; compare 150, fig. 73. Iranian horse-trappings in North Syria. Woolley, *Liverpool Annals of Archaeology*, vii (1914-16). Very primitive horse-trappings in the animal-style Sumerian (?), Sir Hercules Read, *Man*, 1918, 1, pl. A. Another in the same style, the same, *Man*, 1920. Hittite horse-trappings. E. Meyer, *Reich und Kultur der Chettiter*, 55, fig. 45; *Ausgrabungen in Sendschirli*, iv (1911), p. 334 ff., fig. 245-9; *Carchemish*, pl. B 10, C.

(*g*) Funeral canopies and chariots. Rostovtzeff, *Ancient Decorative Wall-painting in South Russia*, 47 ff. Oriental Standards. H. Prinz, *Altorientalische Symbolik*, 97, compare *Prähistorische Zeitschrift*, iv (1912), 16, and H. Schmidt, ibid. 28.

10. Susa find. De Morgan, *Délégation scientifique en Perse, Mém.* viii. 29 ff.; Oxus find. Dalton, *The Treasure of the Oxus*, London, 1905.

11. Caucasian openwork plaques and other bronze implements. Plaques and trinkets. Rössler, *Zeitschrift für Ethnologie*, 1901, 87, fig. 21 b; 1902, 172, fig. 135 ff.; 1896, 398, pl. VIII; de Morgan, *Mission scientifique au Caucase*, fig. 116; Bayern, *Zeitschrift fur Ethnologie*, 1885, suppl., pl. IX. Swords and other weapons and implements. Rössler, *Zeitschrift fur Ethnologie, Verhandlungen der anthropologischen Gesellschaft*, 1902, 147, fig. 42; ibid., 240, fig. 25, &c.

12. Scythian animal style (compare bibliography to chapter VIII). Minns, 266 ff; Farmakovski, *M.A.R.* 34 (1914), 32; Zoltan von Takács, 'Zur Kunst der hunnischen Völker', *Ostasiatische Zeitschrift*, v (1916), 138 ff.; compare *Arch. Ertes.* xxxv (1915), 65 and 211; and Supka, ibid., chs. iii-v; J. Strzygowski, *Die bildende Kunst des Ostens*, Leipzig, 1916, 27; C. Schuchhardt, *Alteuropa in seiner Kultur und Stilentwicklung*, Strassburg and Berlin, 1919, 325, cp. 332, fig. 101: the same, 'Tierornamentik in Sudrussland', A.A., xxxv (1920), p. 51 ff., cp. H. Schmidt, ibid., p. 42 ff.

13. Contracted figures of animals. *Délégation scientifique en Perse*, xii. 21, N. 1173, fig. 24, to be compared with Scythian monuments, Bobrinskoy, *Smêla*, iii. 20, barrow 346, pl. VI, 1 and 3; Khanenko, *Antiquités de la région du Dnieper*, iii, pl. 45, N. 460; pl. 49, N. 529-31; pl. 57, T; pl. 61, N. 539, 540, and 470. S. Reinach, *Revue archéologique*, xxxvi (1900), 447, fig. 58; and 448, figs. 60, 61.

14. Persian axes. Prototypes. Morgan, *Délégation scientifique en Perse*, vii, 78, pl. XVII, 8 (axe); Harper, *American Journal of Semitic Languages*, xx, 266 ff.; compare Handcock, *Mesopotamian Archaeology*, 250, fig. 40 E (dagger); Handcock, *Mesopotamian Archaeology*, 294, fig. 58 (contracted position of a lion on a Sumerian seal). Hamadan axe in the British Museum. Greenwell, *Archaeologia*, 58 (1902), 9, fig. 11; British Museum, *A Guide to the Antiquities of the Bronze Age* (1904), p. 128, fig. 124. Kinaman axe. Greenwell, *Archaeologia*, 58 (1902), 10, fig. 12. Bactrian axe. Sir Hercules Read, 'A Bactrian Bronze Ceremonial Axe', *Man*, 1914, no. 11, p. 17. Axe of Van. Greenwell, ibid., 8, fig. 10 (compare Handcock, *Mesopotamian Archaeology*, 254, pl. XXVIII).

15. The nationality of the Scythians. Mongolian theory. Minns, 97 (excellent bibliography). Géza Nagy, *A Szkithak*, Budapest, 1909; H. Treidler, 'Die Skythen und ihre Nachbarvolker', *Archiv für Anthropologie* (Wien), 1915, 280; G. Supka, *Oesterreichische Monatsschriften fur den Orient*, xli (1915), 77 ff.

CHAPTER IV

1. The myth of the Argonauts, the Odyssey, and South Russia. O. Maass, *Die Irrfahrten des Odysseus*, Programme, Gutersloh, 1915; Drerup, *Homer²*, 124; P. Friedlander, 'Kritische Untersuchungen zur Geschichte der Heldensage, I: Argonautensage,' *Rheinisches Museum*, 69 (1914), 299; U. von Wilamowitz-Moellendorff, *Die Ilias und Homer*, Berlin, 1916, 362.

2. The Carians in South Russia. W. Leonhard, *Paphlagonia, Reisen und Forschungen*, Berlin, 1915, 323 ff.; O. Maass, l.l., 8; Tomaschek, 'Kritik der alteren Nachrichten'. *Sitzungsberichte der Wiener Akademie*, 1888 (106), 723; Hommel, *Grundriss der Geographic u. Geschichte des alten Orients*, 58 (§30), cp. C. Autran, *Phénicieus*, Paris, 1920.

3. Sinope. W. Leaf, 'The Commerce of Sinope', *Journal of Hellenic Studies*, xxxvi (1916), 1 ff.

4. Greek colonization. E. von Stern, articles quoted above to chapter I (with abundant bibliography, which I do not repeat). P. Klym, *Die milesischen Kolonien im Skythenlande bis zum 3. vorchristlichen Jahrhundert*, Czernowitz, Programme, 1914; E. von Stern, 'Bemerkungen zu Strabons Geographie der Taurischen Chersonesos', Hermes, lii (1917), 1 ff.; J. L. Myres, 'Geography and Greek Colonization', *Proceedings of the Classical Association*, Jan. 1911 (viii), London, 1911, 62; A. Glynn Durham, *The History of Miletus*, London, 1915, 15; A. Gwynn, 'The Character of Greek Colonization', *Journal of Hellenic Studies*, 1918, 94 ff.; F. Bilabel, *Die ionische Kolonisation*, Leipzig, 1920 (*Philologus* Suppl. xiv. 1), esp. pp. 19-28, 60 ff., 197. Greek colonies in Thrace. G. Kazarow, 'Hellenism in Ancient Thrace and Macedonia', *Annual of the University of Sofia*, xiii-xiv (1919) (in Bulgarian).

5. Olbia. Farmakovski, 'The Archaic Period in Russia', *M.A.R.* 34 (1914), 16 ff.: Archaic Olbia.

6. Bosphorus. History: latest treatment, E. von Stern, *Hermes*, l. 179 ff., compare E. Bethe, 'Athen und der peloponnesische Krieg', *Neue Jahrbücher für das Altertum*, xx. 1, 73 ff.

7. *The most ancient coinage of the Bosphoran group of Greek colonies*. The Aeginetan standard of this coinage is explained by the commercial relations of

the Bosphoran colonies, after the fall of Miletus but before the beginning of the Athenian hegemony, with Aegina and the Peloponnese, see Herod. vii, 147; P. Gardner, *A History of Ancient Coinage*, 700-300 B.C., Oxford, 1918. Note that Teos, the metropolis of Phanagoria, had the same Aeginetan standard, and that its chief god was Apollo (the inscription AHOA on the earlier Bosphoran coins). The similarity of type in the archaic coins of Panticapaeum and of Samos is explained by the dominant part played by Samos on the shores of the Propontis in the middle of the sixth century (the time of Polycrates). Gardner, l.l., 192.

8. Bosphoran tyrants. On the tyrannies in general: H. Swoboda, 'Zur Beurteilung der griechischen Tyrannis', Klio, xii (1912), 341; Hampers, in Batemberg and Saglio, *Dictionnaire des Antiquités*, v. 567 (both pay no attention to the Bosphoran tyranny).

9. Cemetery of Panticapaeum. About the *latest excavations*, my article in the *Journal des Savants*, 1920, quoted above. *Analogous cemeteries* are those of Mesambria and Abdera, excavated during the war. Kazarow, *A.A.* 1918, 4 ff., 50 ff.; cp. *Ath. Mitt.* xxxvi (1911), 308 ff., and Amelung, *A.A.*, 1918, 140 ff. *Barrows with chambers*: best analogy in Thrace, see F. W. Hasluck, 'A Tholos Tomb at Kirk Kilisse', *Annual of the British School at Athens*, xvii (1910-11), 76 (pl. XX), cf. xviii; B. Filow, Volume in honour of Shishmanow, Sofia, 1919, 46 (in Bulgarian): other barrows with vaulted chambers in my *Ancient Decorative Painting in South Russia*, passim.

10. Cemetery at Nymphaeum. Minns, 561. Contents of some graves of this cemetery in the Ashmolean; E. A. Gardner, *Journal of Hellenic Studies*, v (1884), 69 (Atlas, pl. XLVII). Graves I, II, and IV certainly belong to the fifth century B.C. (grave IV is dated by red-figured vases). New data on these graves and a new treatment of the whole cemetery will be given in my forthcoming book, *Studies in the History of Scythia and the Bosphorus*, vol. i; ibid., description of the cemeteries of other Greek cities in the Bosphoran state; meanwhile, see Minns, *passim*, cp. my article in the *Journal des Savants*, 1920.

11. Cemeteries of Olbia and the neighbouring Greco-Scythian towns. Farmakovski, *M.A.R.* 34, 16 ff., cf. *Journal des Savants*, 1920; M. Ebert, *Prähistorische Zeitschrift*, iii, 252 and v. 1 ff.; von Stern, *Hermes*, l. 165 ff. Remains of Greco-Scythian towns. Goszkiewicz, 'The "Gorodishche" on the

lower Dnieper', *B.C.A.* 47 (1913), 117; Ebert, *Prähistorische Zeitschrift*, v (1913), 81 ff.

12. *Gold coinage in the Bosphorus.* The precise date of the introduction of gold coinage in the Bosphoran state, and the economic and political reasons for the step, are still conjectural. P. Gardner, *A History of Ancient Coinage*, Oxford, 1918, 293 ff., pointed out that the phenomenon is not peculiar to Bosphorus but common to most of the leading commercial states of Greece: Athens, to his mind, took the lead in the whole movement. Hence the Athenian standard of the Panticapaean gold. I can hardly agree with this opinion. My own view is that the rise of gold coinage in Greece was due to the fall of the Athenian commercial hegemony and the increasing commercial and political influence of Persia. It is possible that Panticapaeum, being independent of Persia, was the first to adopt gold coinage. As its chief market was Athens, Panticapaeum adopted the Athenian standard. Athens followed Panticapaeum, being anxious to keep her lead in the Pontic trade. Cyzicus and Lampsacus and some other cities attempted to oust the Panticapaean coinage by imitating its types. I intend to treat these matters more fully in a special article.

CHAPTER V

1. *The Persians and the Scythians.*
(*a*) Darius's expedition. Minns, 116-17. J. V. Prásek, *Geschichte der Meder und Perser*, ii. 76 and 105; the same, *Dareios*, i (1914) (*Der alte Orient*, 14, 4), 21 ff.; Obst, *Klio*, ix (1909), 413 ff.; Wittneben, *Zeitschrift für Oesterr. Gymnasien*, lxvi (1912), 557 ff.; Lenschau, Bursian's *Jahresberichte d. Klass. Alt.*, 178 (1919), 119 ff.

(*b*) Darius and the Sacians (inscription of Naksh-i-Rustam). Sarre and Herzfeld, *Iranische Felsreliefs* (1910), chaps. II and III, and supplement, p. 251; F. H. Weissbach, *Berichte d. sächsischen Gesellschaft*, 1910 (62), i, and *Abhandlungen der K. Sächsischen Gesellschaft, Phil.-hist. Kl.*, xxix (1911), *Die Keilinschriften am Grabe des Darius Hystaspes*; the same, *Die Keilinschriften der Achämeniden, Vorderasiatische Bibliothek*, Leipzig, 1911. The mention of the over-sea Sacians and the Sacians in the supplement to the inscription of Bisutun (Weissbach, *Die Keilinschriften der Achämeniden*, p. 73, §74) is usually (Herzfeld, 198; Prášek, ii. 93) taken as referring to the expedition of Darius in South Russia, compare Hoffmann-Kutschke, *Recueil des travaux*, 1908, 140.

(*c*) On the ethnographical questions. E. Meyer, *Geschichte des Altertums*, i. 2^3, §578, p. 905 ff.

2. *The Kingdom of the Odrysians.* P. Foucart, 'Les Athéniens dans le Chersonèse de Thrace au IV^{e}s., *Mém. de l'Acad. d. Inscr.*, xxxviii. 1 (1909), 80 ff; J. Kazarow, *Beiträge zur Kulturgeschichte der Thraker*, Sarajevo, 1916; the same, *Hellenism in ancient Thracia and Macedon, Annual of the University of Sofia*, xiii-xiv (1920) (in Bulgarian); Lenschau, (Bursian's) *Jahresb. des Kl. Altert.* 178 (1919), 182 ff.

3. *Scythian objects in Thracian tumuli.* B. Filow, 'Denkmäler der thrakischen Kunst', *Mitteilungen des Deutschen Archäologischen Instituts, Römische Abteilung*, xxxii (1917), 1 ff., compare G. Kazarow, *Beiträge zur Kulturgeschichte der Thraker*, Sarajevo, 1916 (*Zur Kunde der Balkanhalbinsel, II, Quellen u. Forschungen*), 87, 94 ff.

4. The *Celts* in the Balkan peninsula. Minns, 126; Niese in Pauly-Wissowa-Kroll, R.E. vii, 618, compare Brandis, ibid., 522; G. Kazarow, 'Celts in Thracia

and Macedonia', *Transaction of the Bulgarian Academy*, xviii (1919). *Bastarnae*. A. Bauer, 'Die Herkunft der Bastarner', *Sitzungsberichte der Wiener Akademie*, 185, 2, Wien 1918, compare L. Schmidt, *Berliner philologische Wochenschrift*, 1919, 106.

5. On the remains of the fortified cities of the native population in the regions of the Dnieper, the Bug, the Dniester, and the Don (gorodische's), Minns, 147 ff., 175; Spitsyn, 'Scythia and Hallstatt', *Miscellany in honour of Count A. Bobrinskoy* (excavations in the gorodishche of Nemirov in Podolia), St. Petersburg, 1911; the same, *B.C.A.*, 65 (1918), 87 ff.

6. Barrows of the seventh to fourth century on the Middle Dnieper. Archaeological material. Count A. Bobrinskoy, *Barrows and chance Archaeological Finds about the Town of Smêla*, vol. i (1887), ii (1894), iii (1902). Samokvasov, *The graves of the Russian Land*, Moscow, 1908; General Brandenburg, Reports on his own excavations, Petersburg, 1908; B. and V. Khanenko, *Antiquities of the Region of the Dnieper Basin*, vols. i, ii, iii, and vi; Minns, 175. Attempts at classification. V. Chvojka, *The Ancient Dwellers on the Middle Dnieper*, Kiev, 1913; A. Spitsyn, *B.C.A.* 65 (1918), 87 ff., 'The Barrows of the "ploughmen" Scythians.' M. Rostovtzeff, *Studies of the History of Scythia and the Bosphorus*, i, p. iii.

7. Barrows of the fourth to third century B.C. in the Dnieper region.

(*a*) Lower Dnieper. Minns, 152-71 (Lower Dnieper and the Government of Taurida); for the Deev barrow, compare Rostovtzeff, *B.C.A.* 63 (1912), 78. Later excavations: Solokha, N. Veselosvki, C.R. 1912 and 1913-19 (with bibliography); S. Polovtsov, *Revue archéologique*, 1914; Svoronos, 'Explication des trésors de la tombe royale de Solokha', *Journal international d'archéologie numismatique*, xvii (1915), 3 ff. (cf. S. Reinach, *Revue archéologique*, 1916, 310; M. Rostovtzeff, 'Learned Fantasies', *B.C.A.* 65 (1918), 72); Rossbach, *Berliner philologische Wochenschrift*, 1914, 1311. Chernaya Dolina. N. Makarenko, *Hermes* (Russian), 1916, 267. Other barrows excavated after 1911. M. Rostovtzeff, *Journal des Savants*, 1920.

(*b*) Middle Dnieper. Darievka and Ryzhanovka, Minns, 177-80, compare Samokvasov, *Graves of the Russian Land*, 71; Government of Poltava, Minns, 180 ff., compare Samokvasov, l.l.; Novoselki (government of Kiev, district of Lipovets), A. Bydlovski, *Svyatovit*, 1904 (v), 59 ff.; Rostovtzeff, *B.C.A.* 63, 81, 1.

8. Date of this group. E. von Stern, *Hermes*, l. (1915), 192 ff.; cf. *M.A.R.* 34 (1914), 91 and *B.C.A.* 58.

9. Greco-Scythian settlements. Goszkiewicz, *B.C.A.* 47, 117; Ebert, *Prahistorische Zeitschrift*, v. 81.

10. Scythian religion. M. Rostovtzeff, 'The Idea of Royal Power in Scythia and on the Bosphorus', *B.C.A.* 49, and addenda ibid.; the same, 'Iranism and Ionism', *London Historical Congress*, 1913; the same, *Revue des Etudes Grecques*, 1921 (jubilee volume). Thracian engraved ring. B. Filow, *Römische Mitteilungen*, 1917 (xxxii), 4, fig. 1; another almost identical ring found in Adrianople and now in the Louvre, not quoted by Filow, *Le Musée*, iii. 332, fig. 18; Rostovtzeff, *Ancient Decorative Painting in South Russia*, 516, fig. On Herakles as parent of the Scythian tribes. Hes. *Cat.: Oxy. Pap.* xi. 1358, 2, 15-19; Th. Reinach, *Revue des Etudes Grecques*, 1915 (xxix), 120. Enareans. W. R. Halliday, 'A Note on the θήλεια νοῦσος of the Scythians', *Annual of the British School at Athens*, xvii. 95. The sacred oath. Minns, 203, fig. 98 = *A.B.C.* xxxii, 10, and 197, fig. 90 = *A.B.C.* xxxii. 1.

11. The dominant tribe among the Scythians. Th. Reinach, *Revue des Etudes Grecques*, 1916 (xxix), 11.

12. Economic life. 'Σκύθαι ἀροτῆρες and γεωργοί,' Vogel in 'Festschrift für Eduard Hahn', *Studien u. Forschungen zur Menschen- und Völkerkunde, herausgegeben von G. Buschan*, Stuttgart, 1917, cf. H. Philipp, *Berliner philologische Wochenschrift*, 1919, p. 386 ff.

13. Vases with scenes from life in a Scythian camp. M. Rostovtzeff, *M.A.R.* 34 (1914), 79-93.

14. Panticapaean artistic school. M. Rostovtzeff, *B.C.A.* 65, 72 ff. Compare e.g. the scenes on the silver vases from Solokha (pl. XX, 1, 2) with the monuments analysed by P. Perdrizet, 'Venatio Alexandri' *Journ. of Hell. St.* xix (1899), p. 273 ff., pl. XI and Winter, *Der Alexandersarkophag von Sidon*, 1912.

CHAPTER VI

1. Sarmatians and Sauromatians. My article in *Revue des Etudes Grecques*, 32 (1921), p. 470.

2. Sarmatians and Alans. Müllenhoff, *Deutsche Altertumskunde*, iii, *passim*, chap. 120 ff.; Minns, 117 ff.; W. Tomaschek, art. Alani in Pauly-Wissowa, *R.E.*; J. Kulakovski, *The Alans according to the Testimonies of Classical and Byzantine Writers*, Kiev, 1899. E. Taubler, 'Zur Geschichte der Alanen', *Klio*, ix (1909), 14 ff.; M. Rostovtzeff, *History of Decorative Painting in South Russia*, 340 ff. Their dress and weapons. Rostovtzeff, ibid. 326 ff.; ibid., the extant ancient monuments representing Sarmatians: add to this list a figure of a Sarmatian horseman—a perfect counterpart of the Sarmato-Bosphoran horsemen in the Panticapaean painted tombs (pl. XXIX)—carved on a rock on the banks of the river Yenissei in Siberia: often published, e.g. *Inscriptions de l'Yenissei*, Helsingfors, 1889. cp. B. Laufer, *Chinese Clay Figures*, i, Chicago, 1914, 222, fig. 35. The Yenissei carvings testify to the lasting occupation of a large part of Western and Central Siberia by the Sarmatian tribes. Sarmato-Roman soldiers wearing Sarmatian arms (note especially the conical helmet) are often represented on late Roman and early Byzantine historical reliefs. Besides the arch of Galerius (A.D. 297: lately discussed by O. Wulff, *Altchristliche u. Byzantinische Kunst*, i (1914), p. 160 ff., compare E. Hébrard, *Bull. de Corr. Hell.*, xliv (1920), 5 ff., on the new excavations conducted during the war), I would mention a wooden capital from Alexandria, of the fifth to sixth century A.D., which represents a besieged city (O. Wulff, Kon. Mus. Berlin, *Beschr. der Bildwerke der christl. Epoche*, iii, *Altchristliche etc. Bildwerke*, i (1909), no. 243, p. 80 ff., pl. VI), and the bronze plaque from the throne (?) of the Lombard King Agilulf (A.D. 590-616) found at Val di Nievole in Tuscany (O. Rossbach, *Neue Jahrb. f. kl. Altertum*, xxxi (1913), 269 ff.).

3. Scythians in the Dobrudzha. J. Weiss, 'Die Dobrudscha im Altertum' (*Zur Kunde der Balkanhalbinsel, II, Quellen und Forschungen*, 12). Coins of Scythian kings of the Dobrudzha kingdom. J. Weiss, l.l., cf. M. Soutzo in the *Transactions of the Rumanian Academy*, 1916, and A. Orêshnikov in *Moscow Numismatic Miscellany*, iii (1916).

4. The kingdom of Skiluros in the Crimea. Minns, 119; Stern, *Hermes*, l., 206.

5. Excavations in the region of Orenburg. M. Rostovtzeff, *M.A.R.* 37.

6. Excavations near Tanais. Minns, 567. Sarmatians near Tanais, Diod. ii, 43.

7. Excavations near Stavropol (Kazinskoe farm). Pridik, *M.A.R.* 34, 107 ff.

8. Excavations of Veselovski in the Kuban region. N. Veselovski, 'Barrows of the Kuban district in the time of Roman dominion in the Northern Caucasus', *Bulletin of the XIIth Archaeological Congress*, Kharkov, 1902; Minns, 232, note 4. The last important find on the Kuban was made accidentally in 1911 and acquired by the Archaeological Commission. It belongs to the group of the earlier Sarmatian graves (second to first century B.C.—first century A.D.) and contains many interesting objects, e.g. two gold mountings of glass or horn rhyta, one richly adorned with coloured stones and transparent glass, the other with embossed figures in the style of the silver phalarae mentioned below. Published by Farmakovski, *A.A.*, 1912, 323 ff. Finds in Akhtanizovka and Siverskaya. Spitsyn, *B.C.A.* 29, 19 ff. Artyukhov's farm and Anapa. Minns, 430 ff.; G.R., 1882-3. Buerova Mogila *C.R.* 1870-1871, ix ff.; 1882-1888, lxxxii; *M.A.R.*, 37, 43. Many finds of the same type have been made in Central Caucasus, especially in the cemeteries of Kambulta, Kamunta, Katcha, &c., see Tolstoy and Kondakov, *Russian Antiquities*, 463 ff. These finds of the Sarmatian epoch must not be confounded, as in the book of Tolstoy and Kondakov, with the prehistoric grades of the Kuban and with prehistoric burials in the cemeteries enumerated above. The Caucasus finds in general need careful revision and investigation. A well dated Caucasian cemetery (1st to 2nd century A.D.) showing strong Sarmatian influence is that of Bori in the province of Kutais, recently published by E. Pridik in *M.A.R.*, 34.

9. Novocherkassk. Tolstoy and Kondakov, *Antiquités de la Russie méridionale*, 488 ff.; Ch. de Linas, *Origines de l'orfévrerie cloisonnée*, vol. ii; A. Odobesco, *Le trésor de Petrossa, passim*; Minns, 235. Other finds on the Don. Migulinskaya, *B.C.A.* 63, 106; Chulek, Tolstoy and Kondakov, *Ant.*, 496 ff.

10. Silver phalarae from South Russia. Spitsyn, *B.C.A.* 29, 19 ff.; A. Odobesco, *Le trésor de Petrossa*, i, p. 293, fig. 116, cf. p. 513, fig. 217. The same technique, style and the same selection of figures on certain gold-mountings

of glass, wood, or horn rhyta are found on the Kuban and the Don. Many such are forged, but some are certainly genuine, e.g. *A.A.* 1912, p. 326, fig. 4, which is a good representative of the whole class. The phalara from Vozdvizhenskaya, *C.R.* 1899, 43, fig. 70, cf. 1896, 58, fig. 284. The cauldron of Gundestrup, the Raermond phalara, and the plaques of Pontus (?). S. Reinach, *Revue celtique*, xxv (1904), 211; *Cultess, Mythes et Religions*, i. 282; F. Drexel, 'Ueber den Silberkessel von Gundestrup', *Jahrbuch des Deutschen Archäologischen Instituts*, xxx (1915), 1 ff. Gilt silver phalarae, with floral patterns, inset with transparent glass, found in horse-graves on the Vasyurinskaya Gora in the Taman peninsula. Rostovtzeff, *History of Decorative Painting in South Russia*, p. 41, n. 2, and p. 510.

11. Silver phalarae of the South Russian type in Bulgaria, *Bulletin de la Société archéologique bulgare*, vii (1919-1920), p. 147 ff., figs. 106 and 107.

12. Tsvêtna, *C.R.* 1896, 89 and 216.

13. Contzesti. The important find of Contzesti (see *A.B.C.*, Fr. ed., p. 91, data, gathered by Odobesco, about the grave where the objects were found), which contained two Silver vases (*A.B.C.* pl. XXXIX-XLII) and three sticks, covered with silver, in the form of thyrsi (*A.B.C.* xxvii. 1, 2, erroneously attributed to Kul-Oba, but belonging to the find of Contzesti, as is shown by documents preserved in the Hemitage), which probably formed the supports of a funerary canopy, certainly belongs to the Sarmatian epoch, cf. the rhyton of Poroina (Odobesco, *Le trésor de Petrossa*, i, p. 498, fig. 205) and the rhyton of Kerch (*A.B.C.* xxxvi. 1, 2, cp. *Winter, Oesterr. Jahreshefte* v (1902), 112 ff.), also the find of Petroasa. On the silver amphora of Contzesti, Drexel, *Jahrbuch des Deutschen Archaologischen Instituts*, xxx (1915), 202. All these monuments present the same technique as the silver phalarae mentioned above. It is a pity that the crown of Contzesti, of gold inset with precious-stones, has disappeared.

14. Siberia. N. C. Witsen, *Noord en Oost Tartarye*, 1785 (3rd ed.); W. Radloff, *M.A.R.* 3, 5, 15, 27. Tolstoy and Kondakov, *Antiquités*, 379 ff.; Ch. de Linas, *Origines de l'orfévrene cloisonnée*, vol. 11; Minns, 271 ff. The whole find ought to be republished in good reproductions, together with Witsen's drawings, and with the documents about the discovery, and the eighteenth-century drawings, preserved in the archives of the Russian Academy of Science.

15. Characteristic objects found in the graves of Kuban.

(*a*) Glass vases imitating metal vases. Zubov's farm, *B.C.A.* i. 96, fig. 9 (first barrow); 101, fig. 24 (second barrow); Akhtanizovka, *C.R.*, 1900, 107, fig. 208; Siverskaya, Spitsyn, *B.C.A.* 29, 19 ff.; Vozdvizhenskaya, *C.R.*, 1899, 45, fig. 73; Yaroslavskaya, *C.R.*, 1896, 56, fig. 218; Tifiisskaya, *C.R.*, 1902, 66, fig. 135; Armavir, *C.R.*, 1902, 87, fig. 194. This group of vases, some of which are adorned with gold mountings inset with precious stones (e.g. the vases of Siverskaya; the rhyton from the Kuban, *A.A.* 1912, 323 ff., figs. 1, 2; another, ibid., p. 325, fig. 3; the rhyton from the Besleneevskaya stanitsa; Minns, p. 58, fig. 11, &c.), is indeed unique. It is the first attempt of the Greeks to replace metal, stone and clay vases by glass vases, the glass used being not coloured but transparent, like crystal, though slightly opaque. The whole class has never been studied seriously, as regards either technique or style. As far as I have studied the vases myself I suppose that they were either cast in moulds and afterwards polished, or hewn out of solid blocks of cast glass. The latter technique prevailed in China after glass began to be manufactured there in the fifth century A.D. (see B. Laufer, *The Beginnings of Porcelain in China*, Chicago, 1917, p. 140 ff.). The models used by the Chinese were undoubtedly vases of the kind described above, which were manufactured, probably in Alexandria, for the special purpose of export to the East—South Russia, China, India. It seems that the Oriental peoples were very fond of such vases, especially if set in gold mountings. One of the earliest monuments of this kind found in the Far East is the large vase of opaque glass, adorned with medallions engraved with the head of Athena, now in the Royal Ontario Museum at Toronto (second century B.C.?). In the West these vases were not popular and were soon replaced by blown glass and various kinds of coloured glass. See Kisa, *Das Glas im Altertume* (1908), ii, p. 378; Morin-Jean, Daremberg et Saglio, Dict. v, 934-949.

(*b*) Clay vases in the form of animals and human heads. *C.R.*, 1902, 73, fig. 157; 67, fig. 136; 72, fig. 152 (all from Tiflisskaya stanitsa); Ladozhskaya, *C.R.*, 1902, 87, fig. 162, cf. Ust-Labinskaya, *C.R.*, 1902, 81, fig. 174. On this group of late Hellenistic and early Roman vases, see Farmakovski in *Miscellany in honour of Countess P. Uvarov*, Moscow, 1916, 311 ff. (in Russian).

(*c*) Brooches. Artyukhov's farm, *C.R.*, 1880, Atlas, pl. II, 3. Akhtanizovka, *C.R.*, 1900, 107, fig. 211. Titorovskaya, *A.B.C.* xxiv. 10. Zubov's farm, *B.C.A.*

1, pl. II and fig. 1. Vozdvizhenskaya, *C.R.*, 1899, 44, fig. 68. Geymanov's settlement, *C.R.*, 1900, 44, fig. 103. Ekaterinodar, *C.R.*, 1899, 131, fig. 258. Usahélo near Kutais (Caucasus), *M.A.R.* 34, p. 109, pl. I, 1, 2. All ornamented with geometric patterns in filigree and embossed work. Brooches ornamented with figures of animals inset with coloured stones. Kurdzhips, *C.R.*, 1896, 64, figs. 305 and 306; 1895, 62, fig. 296; 152, figs. 501 a and 502. Zubov's farm, *B.C.A.* i. 101, fig. 20. Tiflisskaya, *C.R.*, 1902, 67, fig. 139. Ladozhskaya, ibid. 77, fig. 161. Ibid. 78, fig. 164. Ust-Labinskaya, *C.R.*, 1902, 82, fig 177 (two griffins); cf. Kondakov and Tolstoy, *Antiquités,* 486, fig. 440, and the Siberian plaque, Odobesco, *Le trésor de Petrossa*, 511 fig. 215. The earliest brooches of this kind were found in graves of the third to first century B.C.—at Kurdzhips, Akhtanizovka and Artyukhov's farm. The type is therefore a creation of the Hellenistic epoch.

(*d*) Tendril fibulae. Tiflisskaya, *C.R.*, 1900, 103, fig. 186. Timoshevskaya, *C.R.*, 1894, 38, fig. 41. Anapa, *C.R.*, 1894, 85. Vodyanoe (government of Taurida), *C.R.*, 1902, 133. In form of animals and geometric figures. Ust-Labinskaya, *C.R.*, 1899, 17, fig. 87; 1902, 81, fig. 175, &c. Kurdzhips, *C.R.*, 1896, 155, fig. 513, cf. Martin, *Kongelige Vitterhets Historisk och Antiquarisk Akademiens Mådnadsblad*, 1894, Bikang (*Fibulor och soljor från Kertch*). On the type of fibula for which the Germans use the term 'Fibula mit umgeschlagenem Fusse' and which was generally used by the Goths, see Ebert's articles quoted in note 15. I lay stress on the fact that many of the tendril fibulae found on the Kuban, some of which belong to the first century A.D., present all the peculiarities of the fibula 'mit umgeschlagenem Fusse'.

(*e*) Cauldrons (Asiatic) with family devices. *C.R.*, 1899, fig. 96, cf. Vozdvizhenskaya, ibid. 43, figs. 77 and 78; Zubov's farm, *B.C.A.* 1, fig. 7; Ust-Labinskaya, *C.R.*, 1902, 83, fig. 183.

(*f*) Gold bottles inset with stones. Ust-Labinskaya, *C.R.*, 1902, 83, fig. 184; Olbia, *C.R.*, 1868, Atlas, pl. I, 10; and *A.A.* xxix (1914), p. 256, fig. 79.

(*g*) Openwork. Hellenistic and early Roman period: Besleneevskaya stanitsa, Minns, p. 58, fig. 11 (mounting of a rhyton); Kuban region, *A.A.*, 1912, p. 325, fig. 3 (the same); Bori (Caucasus), *M.A.R.* 34, p. 96, 1, 2, pl. I, 8, 9; cp. p. 98, 14, pl. I, 6; Novocherkassk, Minns, p. 234, fig. 139 (torc), compare Akhtanizovka, Minns, p. 215, fig. 118 and the figures on the Bulgarian phalarae quoted above no. 11; to a later period belongs the vase of violet glass in a silver openwork mounting found in the Caucasus, *C.R.*, 1872, 144, Atlas, pl. II, 1-3; Kisa, *Das Glas*, figs. 208 and 208 *a* (pp. 430, 431) and p. 602 ff, where other examples of the same kind are given from Northern Europe. Openwork belt-plaques of the early Roman Empire. Kazanskaya stanitsa, *C.R.*, 1901, 76, fig. 153.

(*h*) Gold garment plaques. See p. 131 fig. 17, with indication of proveniences. Besides the plaques found in datable graves, large sets of identical plaques, all bought in South Russia, mostly at Kerch, are preserved in various museums; the Louvre (a set bought in 1889, Inv. MNC 1120 and another bought in 1920 with the Messaksudi collection); the Metropolitan Museum at New York (some hundreds of plaques bought at Kerch).

(*i*) Mirrors. *M.A.R.* 37, 72; Zubov's farm, *B.C.A.* 1, 102, fig. 25; Armavir, *C.R.*, 1903, 63, fig. 102.

(*j*) Swords of the type used in Kerch. Novokorsunskaya stanitsa, *C.R.*, 1902, 135, figs. 240 a and 240 b; *M.A.R.* 37, 51.

16. Archaeological evidence for the Dnieper region in the Roman period. Reinecke, *Mainzer Zeitschrift*, 1906 (i), 42 ff.; Ebert, *Prahistorische Zeitschrift*, v (1913), 80; the same, *Baltische Studien zur Archaologie und Geschichte*, Berlin, 1914, 85; T. Arné, *Oldtiden*, 1918, 207 ff. *Det Stora Svitgod*, Stockholm, 1917, p. 7 ff; Rostovtzeff, *Studies*, p. iii.

CHAPTER VII

1. History of the Bosphorus in the first century B.C. M. Rostovtzeff, 'Caesar and the South of Russia', *Journal of Roman Studies*, 1917, 27 ff.; 'Queen Dynamis of Bosphorus', *Journal of Hellenic Studies*, xxxix (1919), 88.

2. History of the Bosphorus during the Roman Empire. My articles quoted by Stern, *Hermes*, l., 209, note 1; cf. 'Pontus, Bithynia, and the Bosphorus', *Annual of the British School at Athens*, xxii. Military occupation of Olbia by the Romans, *B.C.A.* 58, 1 ff. Military occupation of Armenia, *B.C.A.* 32, 1 ff., and *Christian Orient* (in Russian), iii.

3. Political, social, and economic conditions in the Bosphorus during the first to third centuries A.D. Minns, 612 ff. Stern, *Hermes*, l. (1915), 211 ff. (he quotes all my articles on this subject). Cf. K. J. Neumann, 'Romische Klientelstaaten', *Historische Zeitschrift*, 1917, 1 ff. On the titles Φιλόκαισαρ and Φιλορώμαιος, R. Munsterberg, *Jahreshefte des Oesterreichischen Institutes*, xviii (1913), Beiblatt, 318.

4. On the religious conditions see my articles: 'The Idea of Kingly Power in Scythia and on the Bosphorus', *B.C.A.* 49; 'Iranism and Ionism', Historical Congress, London, 1913; and 'Ancient Decorative Painting in South Russia', *passim*, especially the chapter on the late Panticapaean painted tombs; compare my article on the Great Goddess *in Rev. d. Ét. Gr.*, 1921. On the names of the Great Goddess and her consort—Astara and Sanerges—see the note of Hiller von Gaertringen and E. von Stern to Dittenberger, *Sylloge^3*, no. 216. Von Stern is inclined to compare these names rather with the Thracian names Ἄσται, Σάνη, Ἐργῖνος than with the Semitic Astarte and the Hittite (?) Sandas. I am not sure that the name Sandas for the God of Tarsus is not also of Thracian origin. The fantastic clay figurines which are regularly found in Panticapaean graves of the first and second century A.D. (see e.g. *A.A.*, 1912, 345, fig. 29; 1913, 193 ff., figs. 32, 33; Minns, pp. 369, 370, fig. 268) are puzzling. They are certainly not toys: their religious significance is beyond doubt. The best analogy is furnished by Chinese clay figures of the Han dynasty (B. Laufer, *Art and Archaeology*, vi (1917), p. 300), which also have movable limbs. Their apotropaeic character is indicated by their being ithyphallic and playing musical instruments or clashing their swords and

shields. Analogous figures are common in the paintings of later Panticapaean graves, mostly of the second and third centuries A.D.

5. Sarmatian system of writing. Škorpil, *B.C.A.* 37, 23 ff.; Minns, pp. 316-318. Similar signs on the tiaras of Sassanian kings (coins and engraved stones). On the Hittite 'hieroglyphs', A. E. Cowley, *The Hittites*, London, 1920. Note that the same signs appear both at Panticapaeum in the second to third century A.D. and on the Kuban (cauldrons—ch. vi, no. 15 (e); gold bottles—ibid., no. 15 (f)); compare the mark on the rump of the horse of the Sarmatian horseman on the Yenissei (ch. vi, no. 2).

6. Relations between Panticapaeum and the cities on the southern shore of the Black Sea. I have collected the evidence in my articles on Roman Olbia. New evidence is furnished by two inscriptions: one, from Sinope, republished by Th. Reinach, *Rev. arch.*, 1916, p. 345, no. 7, is the funeral inscription of Julius Callinicus a ναύκληρος, compare Jos. P.E. iv. 72, from Chersonesus mentioning a certain Γ. Κάιος Εὐτυχιανὸς ναύκλαρος Σινωπεύς (even if Eutychianus assumed the predicate Ναύκλαρος as a second cognomen it is sufficient evidence for his profession); the second is the inscription of Zela (Cumont, *Stud. Pontica*, iii (1910), 246, no. 273, compare Th. Reinach, *Rev. arch.*, 1920, p. 185 ff.); the deceased woman Chelidon is a Maeotian and her husband bore the name of Πόντος, common in the form Ποντικός, &c., in the Bosphorus.

7. The polychrome style in Panticapaeum. On the sarcophagi with incrustations: Rostovtzeff, *Ancient Decorative Painting in South Russia*, p. 213. The group of graves belonging to the family of Rhescuporis II. Minns, p. 434; Škorpil, *B.C.A.* 37, pp. 23 ff. The grave of 1910 was discovered in the same region as the first three: the diadem inset with garnets, Farmakovski, *Archaologischer Anzeiger*, 1911, 198, and fig. 9 on p. 202. A better reproduction: Rostovtzeff, *Ancient Decorative Painting in South Russia*, p. 575, fig. 97; cf. p. 319.

CHAPTER VIII

1. Polychrome style in jewellery. Minns, p. 282, no. 2; E. von Stern, *Sitzungsberichte der Prussia*, xxi (1900), 243 ff., pl. XXIV; idem, *Hermes*, l. (1915), 213; Reinecke, *Mainzer Zeitschrift*, i (1906), 47, no. 30; S. Reinach, *Revue archéologique*, 1900 (xxxvi),441 ff.; idem, ibid., 1905, 309 ff; M. Ebert, 'Die Wolfsheimer Platte und die Goldschale des Khosrau', *Baltische Studien zur Archaeologic und Geschichte*, Berlin, 1914, 57 ff. A. Götze, 'Gothische Schnallen' (*Germanische Funde aus der Völkerwanderungszezt*), Berlin, *s. d*.; idem, Mannus, I (1909), 122 ff.; idem, *Kaiserliche Museen zu Berlin, Frühgermanische Kunst, Sonderausstellung ostgothischer Altertumer der Völkerwanderungszeit aus Südrussland*, Berlin, 1915 (2. Aufl.); E. Brenner, *Der Stand der Forschung über die Kultur der Merowingerzeit*, 252 ff.; 'Die Sudrussisch-donaulandische Germanenkultur', *Kaiserliches Archäologisches Institut*: VII. *Bericht der romisch-germanischen Kommission*, Frankfurt a. M., 1915; R. Zahn, *Amtliche Berichte aus den koniglichen Museen*, xxxviii (1916), no. 1, 1 ff.; A. Rosenberg, *Monatshefte für Kunstwissenschaft*, ix (1916); J. Strzygowski, *Altai, Iran und Völkerwanderun*, Leipzig, 1917, 274 ff.; E. Mâle, *Études sur l'art allemand, Revue de Paris*, 1917, cf. E. Mâle, *Studien uber die deutsche Kunst, herausgegeben mit Entgegnungen von...* A. Götze... Géza Supka... Leipzig, 1917; G. Kossinna, *Altgermanische Kulturhohe*, Jena, 1919.

2. 'Gothic' find of 1904 in Ketch, and later finds in South Russia. Minns, p. 386, no. 1, 2; Brenner, l.l.

3. The treasure of Petroasa. A. Odobesco, *Le trésor de Petrossa*, t. i, Paris, 1889-1900; t. ii, 1896; t. iii, 1900; Géza Supka, *Arch. Ertesitö*, 1914. 29; Dionisie Olinescu, *Gothisch-Skythische Goldschmiedekunst in Dacien u. Pannonien, Jahrbuch des Bukowina Landes-Museums*, 1912, p. 55 ff.

4. Siebenbrunnen graves. W. Kubitschek, 'K.-K. Zentral-Kommission für Kunst und Historische Denkmaler', *Jahrbuch fur Altertumswissenschaft*, v (1911), 32 ff.; Brenner, l.l.

5. Finds in Africa. Find of Carthage (Koudiat Zateur, unpublished). Delattre, *Compte rendu de l'Académie des Inscriptions*, 1916, 14 ff.; Merlin, *Bulletin archéologique da Compté*, 1916, p. ccxiii; finds of Thuburbo Majus (unpublished): the first, *Compte rendu de l'Académie des Inscriptions*, 1912,

pp. 358 ff.; the second (of 1920), still unmentioned; cf. other finds, *Bull. arch. du Com.*, 1895, pl. XV-XVII; Doublet and Gauckler, *Mus. de Constantine*, p. 54; *Bulletin archéologique du Comité*, 1902, p. 444; Besnier and Blanchet, *Collection Farges*, pp. 66 ff.; de Baye, *Bulletin des Antiquaires de France*, 1914, 212 ff. These references all kindly supplied by A. Merlin.

6. Find of Szilagy-Somlyó. F. von Pulszky, *Die Goldfunde von S.S.*, Budapest, 1890; Baron de Baye, *Le trésor de S.S.*, Paris, 1892; Hampel, *Altertumer des frühen Mittelalters in Ungarn*, ii, 15 ff.; iii, pl., 14 ff.; A. Riegl, *Die spatrömische Kunstindustrie*; Strzygowski, *Altai und Iran*, 47 ff.

7. Merovingian brooches. *France*, H. Hubert, Fibules de Baslieux, *Rev. arch.* xxxiv (1899), 363 ff.; Boulanger, *Le cimetière franco-mérovingien et carolingien de Marchélepot*, Paris, 1909. An important collection of such fibulae, mostly of French origin, formed by J. P. Morgan, is now in the Metropolitan Museum at New York. *Italy*, Castel Trosino: *Monumenti antichi d. Acc dei Lincei*, xii (1902), 145 ff. Lingotto: Rizzo, *Not. d. Scavi*, 1910, 194, fig. 1. Senise: *Not. d. Sc.*, 1916, 329, fig. 1. In general: Venturi, *Storia dell'Arte Italiana*, iii, 44 ff.; Orsi, *Atti e Memorie della R. Deputazione di Storia per la provincia di Romagna*, iii, vol. v, p. 332 ff. It is noteworthy that the scabbards of the swords and daggers found in Italy (sixth to seventh century A.D.) (one in the Metropolitan Museum) show in their lateral prominence great similarity to the Scythian scabbards. *Germany*, Bondorf in Baden (Museum of Carlsruhe), Lindenschmidt, *Alt. unserer heidn. Vorzeit*, iii, Heft ix, pl. 6. *England, Kent*, G. Baldwin Brown, *The Arts in Early England*, iv (London, 1915), chap. x, pp. 508 ff. 'Inlaid jewellery', especially pl. CXLV, CXLVI, CXLVII; E. Thurlow Leeds, *The Archaeology of the Anglo-Saxon Settlements*, Oxford, 1913, pp. 99 ff.

8. The Syrian and Celtic polychrome styles. I attribute the revival of the polychrome tendency in the Hellenistic world in general to the influence of Persia through Syria and in a minor degree to the revival of the polychrome style in Egypt, where it never completely died out. See the numerous mentions of λιθοκόλλητα in both the epigraphic and the literary sources of the Hellenistic period, e.g. the gift of Seleucus I to Apollo of Didyma, Dittenberger, *Or. gr. inscr.* 214, 47: ψυκτὴρ βαρβαρικὸς λιθόκολλος, cp. Theophr. *Charact.* 23; Parmenion Athen. 11, p. 781 e, cf. p. 784 a; Theopomp. *Hist.* 125 (vases); Callix. Athen. 5, p. 200 b (chiton); Plut. *Alex.*

32 (περιτραχήλιον), &c. Another expression constantly used to designate jewels and other objects adorned with gems is διάλιθος, see e.g. Ditt. Syll.² 5, 86, 63 (Athens); 588, 4, 184, 198 (Delos), cp. Callix. apud Athen. 5, p. 197 ff. (*passim*); Men. iv, 219; Aristoph., fr. 330 (Blaydes); Ael. *N.A.* viii. 4 (p. 203, 24); fr. 272, 20; Strabo xv, p. 709, &c. Note that almost all these authorities mention Persian, Syrian, Egyptian, Indian jewels and plate. A good archaeological instance is the recent find of silver plate and gold jewels in Thessaly, Arvanitopullos, *Ath. Mitt.* 1912, p. 73 ff., pl. VI. The date (second century B.C.) is given by silver vases of Neo-Attic style. This revival of the feeling for polychromy in the Hellenistic world probably influenced (through Massilia) the ancient Celtic metal industry (enamel never ceased to be used in Persia and Egypt, and had a revival in Egypt under the Ptolemies, instance—the Meroe find), which was always fond of bright colours. It gave rise just at that time (third to second century B.C.) to the famous Celtic enamels of Gaul, Germany, and especially Britain (see *British Museum Guide, Early Iron Age*, London, 1905, 87 ff.; S. Reinach, *Rev. arch.* 1905 (ii), 309 ff.; Kisa, *Das Glas*, i, 151 ff. On La Tène art in general, Reinecke, *Mainzer Festschrift*, 1902, 53 ff.). To these early influences Europe owed the powerful movement towards polychromy in early and late Roman times, and this movement in its turn prepared the ground for the triumphal march of Sarmato-Gothic jewellery. It is worth noting that Hellenistic polychrome jewels of the Syrian kind found their way to South Russia, where they mingled with Sarmatian jewellery as early as the second century B.C. (Artyukhov's barrow). The Celtic enamels of the second and third century A.D. (the workshop of Antheus) were also brought to South Russia, probably by Roman soldiers (scores of them have been found at Ai-Todor, Chersonesus, Kerch, &c.). But they are easily distinguishable from the products of Sarmatian art.

9. The part played by the Alans in the Gothic invasion of Europe. In most of the works on the period of migrations, the part played by the Sarmatians and especially by the Alans in the conquest of Western Europe is almost ignored. But we must not forget that the Alans long resided in Gaul (L. Schmidt, *Allgemeine Geschichte der germanischen Völker*, 1909, p. 41), near Orleans, that they and other Sarmatian tribes never disappeared from the Danube; that they invaded Italy, and that they came with the Vandals to Spain

and conquered Africa ('rex Alanorum et Vandalorum' is the title of the rulers of Africa).

10. Animal style in the earliest period. The articles quoted above to chapter III, and the bibliography given in those articles.

11. The fantastic animals. The history of these creatures of Sumerian fancy is not yet written. H. Prinz (see E. Meyer in the preface to H. Prinz, *Altorientalische Symbolik*, Berlin, 1915, p. vi) proposes to give a full catalogue of them as far as oriental art is concerned. Meanwhile see his article 'Greif' in Pauly-Wissowa-Kroll, *R.E.* On the dragon, see Sarzec-Heuzey, *Découvertes en Chaldée*, p. 234 (on pl. XLIV, 2); Heuzey, *Rev. d'Assyriologie*, vi, 95 ff.; the same, *Les origines orientales de l'art* (1915), 345 ff.

12. The Assyro-Persian sword-hilts. Perrot et Chipiez, *Hist. de l'art*, ii, 532, fig. 246 (Louvre); Woolley, *Liverpool Annals of Archaeology*, 1914-1916 (vii), pl. XXIII, 1, 2 (Ashmolean Museum).

13. Scythian animal style. Minns, 261, and addenda to p. 226. Rostovtzeff, *Journal of the Russian Ministry of Public Instruction* (in Russian), 1913, November, p. 184; B. Farmakovski, 'Archaic Period in Russia', *M.A.R.* 34, pp. 29 ff.; S. Reinach, 'Galop Volant', *Revue archéologique*, 1901; A. M. Tallgren, *Collection Tovostine*, Helsingfors, 1917, 66 ff.

14. The horse-trappings reproduced on figs. 21 and 22 belong to the following finds: (1) Kuban (sixth century B.C.)—fig. 21 B; (2) The 'Seven Brothers' barrow on the Kuban (fifth to fourth century B.C.)—fig. 21, C, F, G; fig. 22, A, B, E; Nymphaeum (Ashmolean Museum) (fifth century B.C.)—fig. 22, C; Elsavetinskaya stanitsa (fourth century B.C.)—fig. 21, D, H; fig. 22, D, F, G, H, I; Dnieper region (fourth to third century B.C.)—fig. 21, E.

15. Siberian animal style (Minussinsk). A. M. Tallgren, *Collection Tovostine des antiquités préhistoriques de Minoussinsk conservées chez le* Dr. *K. Hedman à Vasa; Chapitres d'archéologie sibérierme, Helsingfors*, 1917 (with full bibliography); idem, *Trouvailles isolèes siberiennes préhistoriques au Musée National de Finlande*, Helsinki, 1919.

16. The animal style in China. The bibliography and the monuments will be found in my forthcoming article: 'South Russia and China' in *L'Art Russe*, vol. i, Paris, 1922. Meanwhile a short selection. Chu period. The best repertory of monuments in Munsterberg, *Chinesische Kunstgeschichte*, i (1910); ii (1912). Cf. Gieseler, 'Le mythe du dragon en Chine', *Rev. arch.*,

1917, p. 127 ff., figs. 6 and 7 (replica of Mrs. Meyer's vase). Han dynasty. The standard works on the civilization and art of this period are those of E. Chavannes and B. Laufer. E. Chavannes, *La sculpture sur pierre en Chine*, Paris, 1893; Mission archéologique dans la Chine septentrionale i, 1, *La sculpture à l'epoque des Han*, Paris, 1913. B. Laufer, *Chinese Pottery of the Han dynasty*, Leyden, 1909; *Beginnings of Porcelain in China*, Chicago, 1919; *Jade, a study in Chinese Archaeology and Religion*, Chicago, 1912; *Chinese Clay figures*, i, Prolegomena to the history of Defensive Armour, Chicago, 1914; *Sino-Iranica*, Chicago, 1919 (all, except the first, publications of the Field Museum of Natural History in Chicago, Anthropological Series).

17. Supposed influence of China on South Russia. Reinecke, *Zeitschrift für Ethnologie*, xxviii (1896), 1 ff. and xxix (1892), 141 ff.; Münsterberg, l.l., i, 36 ff.; Minns, 280.

18. The 'Siberian' plaques in China. Minns, 280; Sir Hercules Read, *Man*, 1917, 1 ff., pl. A; *Bulletin of the Metropolitan Museum of Art*, June 1918, 135 ff.

19. Scythian influence on Central and Eastern Russia. A. M. Tallgren, *Die Kupfer-und Bronzezeit in Nord- und Ostrussland: I. Die Kupfer- und Bronzezeit in Nordwestrussland. Die ältere Metallzeit in Ostrussland*, Helsingfors, 1911; *II. L'époque dite d'Ananino dans la Russie orientale*, Helsingfors, 1919 (with full bibliography), cf. idem, *Collection Zaoussailov au Musée historique de Finlande à Helsingfors*, Helsingfors, 1918.

20. Animal style in the Perm district. Hj. Appelgren-Kivalo, 'Die Grundzüge des skythisch-permischen Ornamentstiles', *Suomen Muinaismuistoyhdistyksen Aikakanskirja* (Journal of the Finnish Archaeological Society), xxvi (1912); idem, 'The Main Features of the Scytho-Permian Ornamental Style' (in Russian), *Proceedings of the Fifteenth Archaeological Congress at Novgorod*, 1914, vol. i; A. Spitsyn, 'Antiquities of the *Chud folk* on the Kama in the Teploúkhov Collection', *M.A.R.* 26, St. Petersburg, 1902 (in Russian).

21. North German animal style. B. Salin, *Die altgermanische Thierornamentik*, Stockholm, 1904; Appelgren-Kivalo, 'Om den s. k. Karolingiska stilens ursprung' (On the Origin of the so-called Carolingian Style), *Opuscula archaeologica O. Montelia dicata*, 1913; Brøgger, *Oseberg-skibet*, Cristiania (vol. i, 1918; vol. iii, 1920).

CHAPTER IX

The current view which denies the existence of any link connecting the history of Slavonic and the history of pre-Slavonic Russia or rather the possibility of finding such links is expressed in the leading works on Russian history, e.g. V. O. Kluchevski, *A History of Russia* (transl. by C. J. Hogarth), vol. i (London and New York, 1911); S. Platonov, *Lectures on Russian History*, Petrograd, 1917 (the latest edition accessible to me), &c. D. Bagalei's point of view, in his *History of Russia*, Charkov, 1912, is different: but his treatment of the two periods is apposition not connexion. The same must be said of the works of Hrushevski on the history of the Ukraine (M. Huševsky, *Geschichte des Ukrainischen Volkes*, i, Leipsic, 1906, cp. *Abrégé de l'histoire de l'Ukraine*, Paris, 1920). The only scholars who have felt (rather than proved) this connexion are the archaeologists, e.g. Zabêlin (*History of Russian Life*) and Kondakov. Compare my forthcoming article, 'Les origines de la Russie Kievienne', *Revue des Etudes Slaves*, 1922. For the archaeological data on which my summary is based, see the preceding chapters. For the Germans on the Dnieper, see the works of Arné quoted on ch. vi, no. 16.

www.ingramcontent.com/pod-product-compliance
Lightning Source LLC
Chambersburg PA
CBHW020417010526
44118CB00010B/288